DEBORAH YARSIKE

Russian Literature
Since the Revolution

Russian Literature Since the Revolution

REVISED AND ENLARGED EDITION

Edward J. Brown

Harvard University Press
Cambridge, Massachusetts, and London, England
1982

Library of Congress Cataloging in Publication Data

Brown, Edward James.
    Russian literature since the Revolution.

    Bibliography: p.
    Includes index.
    1. Russian literature—20th century—History and
criticism.   I. Title.
PG3022.B7 1982   891.7'09'004   82-6064
ISBN 0-674-78203-8   AACR2
ISBN 0-674-78204-6 (pbk.)

Contents

**Russian Literature
Since the Revolution**

Introduction: Literature and the Political Problem

To link politics and literature when we speak of contemporary Russia is natural. All forms of literature are quite frankly and directly used by the Soviet government for political purposes; the possibility of a work of art without political commitment or social involvement is not officially admitted. One cannot imagine a Soviet writer producing, for instance, the novel *Lolita*, which was the work of a Russian writer of the emigration; but if in some strange way such a novel should have come to light inside Russia, it would have been an intensely political document, a defiance of ideological requirement in the name of love, yes, even of perverted love; it would almost certainly have been intended as a ringing statement in favor of civilized literary pornography against the stifling puritanical demands of official critics. It would have become a political *cause célèbre*. And Pasternak's *Doctor Zhivago*, a novel about a "thinker, poet, and philosophical seeker," a nonpolitical novel, indeed an antipolitical novel, a novel by a poet in a poet's language, became, in the paradoxical nature of things, one of the most courageous political documents of the modern period. No piece of literature produced in the Soviet Union can escape involvement with politics.

The most pervasive and characteristic concern of Russian literature since the Revolution has been the paramount political problem: the fate of the individual human being in a mass society. This theme is a familiar one in the West; it is perhaps the main preoccupation of twentieth-century literature as a whole; it is our own theme. There should be no occasion for surprise if Soviet writers too, in those intervals when they have been to some extent free of official tutelage, concern themselves with the individual, with the problem of freedom and responsibility, with the relationship of each separate unit of humanity to the sum total—call it the collective, the broad masses, the organization, the society, or the group. This is what Russian writers, whether Party or non-Party, pro- or antiregime, are concerned with. The theme is recurrent and inescapable; it appears in the earliest things written on the day after the Revolution; it is the basic concern of *Doctor Zhivago* and of some of the most recent and controversial Soviet writing.

The present study is not offered as a complete and detailed history of Russian literature since the Revolution; nor is it concerned with the relationship of literature to the Soviet dictatorship. It is, rather, a search for the theme of the individual human being as developed by the finest writers of the period in their major work. It will soon become evident that Russian literature in the modern period offers a rich variety of literary situations the underlying theme of which is the tragic one of the individual person who resists the implacable pull of the "swarm life," or, as a Soviet critic might express it, "who is out of tune with history."

As we trace this theme through more than half a century of literary history it is possible to see meaningful patterns of development in what might otherwise seem an accidental miscellany of historical facts; and we may even be able to construct a working hypothesis to explain the behavior of Soviet writers and perhaps give some basis for a tentative forecast of future events. To give one example: During the decade of the twenties there were in the Soviet Union a wide variety of literary schools, each with its own theory of literature. One faction emphasized the primary importance of intuition in the literary process; another held that the writer is psychologically conditioned by his class environment and cannot produce artistic images on demand; a third group favored factual reporting exclusively, free of ideology or invention; a fourth abjured purpose and ideology in favor of the free play of the imagination; a fifth held that literature is a craft, the tricks and devices of which can be learned by anyone, regardless of class origin or political orientation; and there were still other variations on these main ideas, of which no detailed and adequate treatment now exists. It would not be very helpful simply to list the various literary schools and painstakingly describe the tenets of each. The *meaning* of the great literary debate does not appear at all until it is shown that each group in its own way is seeking to escape the crudely utilitarian demands of the state, whose "theory of literature" threatened the existence of them all. For one of the tenets held in common by almost all the working writers of the twenties was that literature is the product of individual and free responses to the data of experience. Because such responses are autonomous and unpredictable, the state, looking upon writers with justified apprehension, sought to direct their work into useful and "good" channels. Russian writers during the Soviet period have often resisted, or nullified, or evaded this crude guidance. Alongside official writing, which celebrates in pious numbers the new life, the new man, and the socialist future, there has always been another literature sounding a discordant note and calling in question the values of the totalitarian state. Beginning in the 1960s, many representatives of that literature withdrew into clandestine publishing (*samizdat*), or went into exile. The two kinds of Russian literature, taken together, are a vital commentary on the dilemma which faces the writer who must live in a society and yet be to some extent free of it.

This book is intended to throw light on the nature of the dilemma and to examine the behavior of sensitive human beings who have faced it in its sharpest and most terrible form. We shall see how Russian writers have dealt with the basic political problem, and in what ways they have solved, ignored, or evaded it. We shall examine the kind of human situation those writers were drawn to portray, and we shall see how the exigencies of time and the state formed and shaped their writing. We shall learn that, in the process, many of them made fascinating discoveries in the area of form and style.

Chapter 1 presents a concise account of Russian literary history from 1917 to the present. It will provide the reader with the necessary framework for an understanding of the authors and works that will be discussed in detail throughout the book.

A word should be said about the formidable problems of selection and emphasis involved in planning a book dealing with a literature of the twentieth century many of whose authors are still alive and writing and still developing their careers. The difficulty is compounded by the role of the Soviet government throughout the period as publisher, tutor, and censor of literature. Crude state intervention has skewed the development of Russian literature, often elevating nonentities and inhibiting men of genius, with the result that conformist writers such as Gladkov have acquired importance as spokesmen of a state-sponsored literary codex, while genuine poets have been persecuted or driven into exile. A book on Russian literature in the twentieth century cannot fail to deal in some measure with the effect on the production of literature of unusual and unhealthy official forces.

Complete coverage of the period is possible only for reference works such as Wolfgang Kasack's meticulous and excellent *Lexikon der russischen Literatur ab 1917* (Stuttgart, 1976). In the present book I offer a selection of those writers whose works illustrate most vividly its overarching theme: the individual person in his confrontation with social reality and social demand. Any such selection involves some omissions, and many of those omitted may arguably be more important than some of those included. But time is a cruel judge of literary opinions, standards, and selections, and no doubt at some point it will be discovered that not-fully-flowered genius was never noted here or that celebrated mediocrity was not exposed. Readers in the twenty-first century (if it comes) may think it exceedingly odd that Gladkov was mentioned at all. I have a recurrent nightmare set in the future: a reader at Stanford or Harvard in the year 2082 takes this book off the shelf and cannot even find *in the index* the name of the writer then acknowledged as the greatest figure of the Russian *fin de siècle*. To any such reader I offer my sincere regret at having failed to see what is so obvious to him.

Another word should be said on the presentation of titles. English titles only are given if those titles are a direct translation from the Russian; otherwise the transliterated Russian title in parentheses follows the English title.

The so-called popular transliteration system is used throughout.

1 Since 1917: A Brief History

Soviet Literature

Because the term "Soviet literature" has no exact meaning and is charged with political connotation, it will be used sparingly in this book. In the Soviet Union the term is taken to mean all the literature produced since the Revolution, including that written in the languages of the Union republics. Excluded from the category of truly Soviet, however, are those writers whose work is alien to Soviet ideology, though their work may have been written and even published in the Soviet Union. Solzhenitsyn is a case in point. Outside the Soviet Union little or no attention is paid to literature in languages other than Russian, and therefore the term Soviet loses much of its meaning. Non-Soviet critics, moreover, are reluctant to place under the rubric Soviet those writers whom the Soviets claim but who seem to be more closely bound to Western democratic habits and attitudes—Blok and Pasternak, for instance. We shall be concerned here not so much with the didactic and Party-oriented literature, which the term Soviet suggests to the Western mind, but primarily with that Russian literature, wherever written or published, which has managed to preserve and build upon the great heritage of the nineteenth and early twentieth centuries.

The term Soviet suggests a break at the year 1917 in the continuing tradition of Russian literature. The break in continuity was neither abrupt nor complete, but it was real. The Bolshevik Revolution brought about radical changes in the literary world, and while the transformation of the Russian writer was painful and slow, the new regime made an effort from the start to change the writer's attitude toward his work. The literature created during the nineteenth century by highly individualistic intellectuals, who were independent and often rebellious against authority, was gradually to be replaced by "Soviet literature," produced by Soviet intellectuals, who, finding inspiration and purpose in the collective, would be firmly tied to the aims of the state. In this historical sense the term Soviet as applied to certain literary phenomena has real meaning. But the regime has had only indifferent success in educating a new kind of writer, and the results of complex interaction between old tradition and new ideas were not always the expected and predicted ones.

Persistence of the Past

The modernist revolution in Russian art and literature took place before the political revolution of 1917. The painters Malevich, Kandinsky, and Chagall, the composer Stravinsky, and the poets Mayakovsky, Khlebnikov, Akhmatova, Mandelshtam, and others all began their careers between 1908 and 1913. The period immediately before 1917 was one of bold experimentation in all the arts, of new discoveries and new directions. There was a Symbolist revolution between 1890 and 1910, primarily in the analysis and making of poetry. There was a Cubo-Futurist revolution from 1910 to 1917 in both painting and poetry; Mayakovsky was its principal figure. There was a revolution in painting, architecture, and sculpture involving artists later famous in the West but largely ignored in the Soviet Union. In literary criticism a Formalist revolution, closely related the probing for new forms in all the arts, radically altered the study and interpretation of literature.

During the early years of the Soviet period many of the artists and writers active in Russian modernism remained in the Soviet Union and attempted, with only indifferent success, to put their revolutionary ideas at the service of the new state. As a result, during the first years of the Soviet period, and especially after the liberalization signalized by Lenin's New Economic Policy (NEP), which was introduced in 1921, the Russian literary world might have appeared basically unchanged to a casual observer. It is true that very many of the leading writers had emigrated, but the majority had not; and Russian literature during the twenties presented a motley spectacle in which prerevolutionary literary figures and styles still dominated the scene, often disguised in proletarian garb. The literary manner of the Symbolists Bely and Remizov was imitated, perhaps unconsciously, by the young proletarian novelist Libedinsky. Proletarian poets celebrated the cosmic sweep of their revolution in poetic rhythms that suggest the work of Symbolist aesthetes. The most important figures in the prewar Symbolist movement, Alexander Blok and Valery Bryusov, lectured on the techniques of poetic composition in literary studios set up by the Proletarian Cultural and Educational Organization in 1918. The Russian Futurists, a brashly iconoclastic group before the Revolution, placed their exuberant nihilism at the service of the revolutionary government. When the novel was revived as a form in the middle twenties, its principal artificers consciously followed the paths laid down in the late nineteenth century by Gorky and the realistic school, or, departing from realism and social content, experimented with the medium in the manner of the prewar moderns.

The persistence of the past was even more striking in the area of literary habits and attitudes. A conscious effort was made to preserve the independence and individualism of the writer and artist—to maintain, in other words, the literary profession as an activity independent of state control. The Soviet government, in the person of its Commissar for Education, Lunacharsky, discouraged the eager efforts of the Futurists and of proletarian literary groups to set up a kind of art dictatorship. As Russia recovered from war and revolution, a degree of private enterprise was readmitted in the literary field as well as in other areas of life. Cooperative and even private publishing houses were organized to satisfy a growing and heterodox demand for literature. Tales of revolutionary heroism appeared in the bookstores alongside works on religion, essays on Kantian philosophy, and translations of the novels of Edgar Wallace and Fannie Hurst. Russian writers maintained lively contacts with the European literary world, contacts which were not only cultural but commercial. Many works published during the middle twenties bear a double imprint, such as "Berlin-Petrograd," indicating that the work was published under contract to a Western publisher. Travel to Western Europe by Russian writers was frequent and to a degree informal. Ehrenburg lived alternately in Paris and Moscow, and Babel had lively and prolonged intercourse with French intellectual circles. Pilnyak made frequent journeys to the West, and Zamyatin's novel *We* was originally published, under contract, in English translation. The policy of forbearance in the literary field, effected in practice since 1921, was solemnly affirmed after a violent debate within the Party. In July 1925, a resolution of the Central Committee was published, entitled "On the Policy of the Party in the Field of Belles-Lettres," which announced the liberal doctrine in severely dogmatic terms.

As a result of that liberal policy, from 1921 to 1932 a body of literature arose in Russia which is thoroughly congenial to the taste of Western intellectuals. The astonishing variety and high quality of that literature are not generally realized. It is true that much of it reads like the testament of a few men who have survived a general disaster and are still severely shaken and suffering from emotional displacement. In their best works they treat problems that agitate Western human beings in the twentieth century, particularly the problem of sudden and catastrophic social change. In form and style the literature of the twenties is sometimes traditionally realistic but more often given to highly sophisticated formal device. Many writers were consciously concerned with the forms of art. Olesha's work, for instance, is a study in the defamiliarization both of language and of objects in space. Literary criticism, far from being confined to the repetition of sociological formulas, was daring and original. Indeed surface appearances suggest a literary evolution in Russia along paths analogous to those traveled by other European literatures.

Fellow Travelers

Perhaps the most striking example offered by the Russian intelligentsia of their persistent attachment to individualistic attitudes was the group which called itself the Serapion Brotherhood, whose one tenet was that the group as such held no tenets in common, but that each member might have views on politics and literature that differed somewhat from those of all other members. Literature, they felt, should be created by individuals free of ideological control. Each member of the Brotherhood had his own ideology and figuratively lived in his own cottage, which he "painted according to his own taste."

The Serapion Brotherhood was named for a character in one of E. T. A. Hoffmann's tales, who believed that his personal poetic intuition provided a true vision of reality. The Brotherhood included some of the leading figures in Russian literature of the twenties, many of whom are still regarded highly in the Soviet Union. They were all in their early twenties when they published, in 1921, manifestoes and platforms which were ironic parodies of the ringing literary pronouncements delivered in all seriousness by other literary groups. Perhaps the most prominent and influential of the Serapions was Eugene Zamyatin, whose novel *We* (1920) anticipated both Huxley's *Brave New World* and Orwell's *1984*. Michael Zoshchenko was an eccentric genius who wrote short sketches in which the characters are grotesque human fauna who speak an invented language; their creator describes and comments upon them with a whimsy born of despair. Boris Pilnyak wrote a number of stories and novels which present, using the most modern devices of form and symbol, vexed scenes from the period of the Civil War.

Konstantin Fedin, in *Cities and Years* and other works, deals with the problem of the intellectual at odds with himself and with his time. Venyamin Kaverin in *Artist Unknown* (1931) develops the theme of the artist's need for freedom. Many writers not formally connected with the Serapions were close to them in outlook. Leonid Leonov's *The Thief* (1927), a novel of sophisticated and complex structure, explores the psychology of a disillusioned revolutionary. Yury Olesha's *Envy* (1927) presents in expressionistic style the conflict between a fanciful poet and a Babbitt of the new order. Isaac Babel's highly subjective apperception of the Civil War, *Red Cavalry* (1926), transmutes scenes of blood and violence into exotic ornamental prose. Valentin Katayev's *The Embezzlers* (1927), relating the travels through Russia of a pair of absconding and inebriate officials, is an experiment in the representation of reality as refracted through an alcoholic haze.

The writers whose major work I have mentioned briefly, those who came to be known as fellow travelers (a name supplied for them by Trotsky), seem to have been the direct heirs of the nineteenth-century literary tradition, and their work deals precisely with the problem of the intellectual confronted with a new and alien world. The list I have given is only a partial one; other writers of a similar cast of mind and other works of those I have mentioned will be analyzed later. Although their work as a whole is concerned with the aftermath of revolution and civil war, they were interested in many other things. Human sexual behavior in particular concerned them, and they presented scenes of love as well as of violence with frank interest.

Proletarians

Alongside the so-called fellow travelers were the variegated groups which considered themselves proletarian. They claimed to orient their work toward the masses and to eschew both individualism and effete modernism. They did not form a cohesive whole but were broken into many factions. The poets of the Smithy and the Cosmos, two organizations of proletarian writers, composed stirring hymns to the iron-willed proletarian collective, wherein no individual hero can be discerned. Alexander Serafimovich, a realist of the Gorky school, wrote a novel called *The Iron Flood* (1924), in which the focus of narrative attention is the mass movement of an army, its wives and children, and all its provisions and possessions. Dmitry Furmanov gained fame with his novel *Chapayev* (1923), which he claimed was not a novel at all but a sober record of peasant guerrilla operations under a leader whose role it was, simply, to direct the heroic mass.

Yet the collective hero did not always meet with favor among the proletarian writers, and even they tended to abandon sober realism in favor of stylized narrative or verbal ornament. We have already seen that the proletarian poets were in debt to the Symbolists. Serafimovich at times describes the relentless march of his iron men in prose that bears more than a suggestion of Bely, and Furmanov's purely factual manner of narration is in itself a kind of literary device, employed characteristically by certain Futurist prose writers. But the rock on which proletarian unity broke was the stubborn problem of how the individual human being should be portrayed in relation to the masses.

The earliest novel written in the proletarian milieu was Yury Libedinsky's *A Week* (1922), which sketches in sharp and cruel detail a peasant revolt against Communist rule. The reader experiences the violence directed at them from the viewpoint of the individual Communists themselves, each of whom is shaken inwardly. The masses exist in Libedinsky's story only as a hostile element in which the individual Communists find themselves immersed and which threatens them with destruction. The focus on individual psychology in this novel, and the absence of a healthy and heroic collective, was regarded at the time of its publication and is still officially regarded as a fault. Yet the proletarians continued to explore the complex experiences of the separate human beings who made up the masses. Alexander Fadeyev's *The Nineteen* (1927) examines the varieties of individual reaction to strain in a small band of Communist guerrillas operating in the Far East. Sergey Semyonov's *Natalya Tarpova* (1927) analyzes the inner struggle of a supposedly dedicated Communist woman who falls in love with a bourgeois. Vladimir Bakhmetev's *Crime of Martyn Baimakov* (1928) is a clinical dissection of the self-doubt and guilt felt by a young man who, like Conrad's Lord Jim, fails of courage in a crisis.

Much of the work of the proletarian novelists of the twenties was concerned with psychological realism, and the problems involved in remaking the world are reflected through the prism of the individual mind. The official "Creative Platform" of the Association of Proletarian Writers urged upon its members the necessity to "show forth the complex human psyche, with all its contradictions, elements of the past and seeds of the future, both conscious and subconscious." And proletarian writers, in their exploration of the inner recesses of individual minds, found doubt, struggle, and perplexity. The romantic revolutionary poetry of the Smithy and the Cosmos and the prose of Serafimovich fell into disfavor even with proletarian writers. The work of Mikhail Sholokhov represents the best product of the proletarian milieu. In his *The Silent Don* (1928–1940), no doubt the most famous of Soviet novels, Sholokhov constructed a complex and realistic panorama of the revolutionary period with its clash of ideologies and parties; but his hero, Gregor Melekhov, is an individualist who belongs to no party. From the viewpoint of official criticism, that was Gregor's tragedy: he was "divorced from the masses."

The Stalinists

The great majority of Russian writers of the twenties—proletarians, fellow travelers, and others—were concerned with exploring the strain and conflict experienced by individual human beings in adjusting to the demands of the "collective," or, in Tolstoy's phrase, the "swarm life." The literary world itself mirrored this persistent individualism in the multiplicity of distinct and separate literary groups which proliferated. There is as yet no adequate study of this peculiarly Russian phenomenon. There is not even a catalog of the literary organizations and literary groups, and the fractions and caucuses within the literary groups and ephemeral clusters which variegated the literary scene, consuming vast quantities of precious paper with their creative effort and their bitter and prolonged polemics. The groups increased and multiplied as the result of a conscious policy of the Communist Party under the guidance of Nikolai Bukharin, a powerful political figure of the twenties. He maintained that in the literary field there should be no attempt to hold everyone in a rigid mold, but that "anarchic competition" should be encouraged and no artificial restraints should be placed upon the competing individuals and groups. There were, of course, some limits: any group openly announcing anti-Communist views would certainly have suffered; but there were none of those above ground.

I have already mentioned the Smithy, where poems of iron were heated with the ardor of the Revolution, though they were shaped with the tools of the Symbolists, and the Cosmos, whose writers cultivated a mystique of interplanetary revolution, a mixture of science-fantasy and pseudoreligious elation. Both of these groups issued from the Proletcult, or Proletarian Cultural and Educational Organization, whose *raison d'être* was the creation of a new proletarian literature through the intensive training in "litstudios" of new working-class writing cadres. The Futurists, who had been horrifying the bourgeois since the 1912 publication of their brash "Slap in the Face to Public Taste," had earlier split into Ego-Futurists and Cubo-Futurists. Under the leadership of Mayakovsky, the Cubo-Futurists formed the Left Front of Art, in whose magazine *Lef* the Futurist poets themselves and their avant-garde allies published some of the most original literary work of the period. The Constructivists were a small group, for the most part poets, related to the Futurists though at odds with them, who stressed in their poetry the conscious planning of literary work and the loading of the literary vocabulary with the latest scientific and technical connotations. Among the groups of poets, the Imagists and Acmeists, in their brief period, also left a distinct mark on the Soviet literary world; Sergey Yesenin and Anna Akhmatova, both poets of subjective experience, have always been popular in spite of official frowns.

The group called Pereval (The Divide), which I shall later treat at length, was composed for the most part of young Communists who had rejected the proletarian stereotypes and who portrayed the contemporary scene in city and village in stories of a harsh but sympathetic realism. The Russian Association of Proletarian Writers (RAPP), which presumed to speak for the Party in literary affairs, was itself split into several factions engaged in lethal politico-literary dispute.

The season, as we now know, was a brief Indian summer in which flourished values that belonged, essentially, to an earlier culture. The new men who grew into authority under Stalin found that in the area of literature there was neither discipline nor purpose. They regarded with contempt writing that seemed to them "difficult" or "decadent." They evidenced a visceral suspicion of the endless and many-faceted polemic over literary themes and literary styles and over literary theory which divided even Communist writers from one another. When the First Five-Year Plan was adopted in 1928 all forces were mobilized behind it, and there is ample documentary evidence to show that no exception was made for the forces of literature. Ultimately there was to be no escape for the writer from social tasks. Party newspapers, beginning in 1929, carried editorials calling for a "consolidation of forces" in literature and for the application of literary talent to celebrating the achievements, real or projected, of the Plan. *Pravda* and other papers published a series of ignorant, oppressive attacks on the errors of specific groups, and the groups, sensitive to the new situation, recanted or modified their views. Gradually the amount of variety on the literary front was greatly reduced. After 1929, when Bukharin fell from power (Trotsky was already in exile), a new kind of organization man intruded himself on Russian intellectual life.

What manner of men were the Stalinists who dealt so rudely with the limited intellectual freedom that existed in the twenties? What motives drove them? The chief among them was Lazar Kaganovich, a member of the Politburo and an intimate of Stalin, who believed that literary men should match the achievements of labor by producing works of literature describing and celebrating great industrial projects. The poet Alexey Surkov was a passionate hater of every deviation from a politi-

cal line that seemed to him true and straight, and his interest in literature was strictly secondary. Pavel Yudin was a Marxist philosopher
who abjured all doubt or discussion as to the correctness of philosophical views that he found in the works of Lenin and Stalin, and who bur-
rowed in the writings of his opponents only to find there passages
which, quoted out of context, betrayed the presence or the influence of
heresy. In the writings of many literary critics he found evidence of
Kantian, Jungian, Bergsonian, Freudian, and, of course, Trotskyite in-
filtration, and all of this seemed to him the work of hostile forces. L.
Mekhlis, secretary of the editorial board of *Pravda* in 1931 and a potent
Stalinist, honored many times for his labors in peace and his heroism in
war, believed that the failure of literature to reflect adequately the great
issues of the day was due either to lack of planning in the literary organizations or to the excessive interest in writers in individual psychology. These men were among the leaders in the movement for a "consolidation of forces" in literature which ultimately led, in 1932, to the
liquidation by Party directive of all autonomous literary organizations
and the enforced membership of all Russian writers in a Union of Soviet Writers under the direct auspices of the Party. With the First Congress of Soviet Writers in 1934 the Union of Writers became a fact and
the Stalinist period was launched. According to the constitution of that
Union all of its members must "accept the program of the Communist
Party . . . and strive to participate in socialist construction."

The state under Stalin used writers as its instruments of education
and propaganda. Many of those whose reputations had been made in
the twenties or earlier conformed to the new demands and produced
educational fiction on topical themes. Leonov described the building of
a paper plant in the far north; Sholokhov turned out a novel on the collectivization of agriculture; Katayev devoted his considerable talents to
the production of a novel about the building of a steel plant at Magnitogorsk; Zoshchenko, always an artist of paradox, wrote of a criminal's
rehabilitation in the work camps of the security police; Pilnyak took for
his topic the creation of a great dam and hydroelectric station, as did
Marietta Shaginyan, who urged upon her comrades the poetic power of
just such themes: "The poet Blok called upon all of us to 'hear the
music of the Revolution.' The real music is only beginning now: listen
to it, comrades! Because the real music of the Revolution is socialist
construction!"

During the period of Stalin a number of works were written explicitly to inspire Communist ideals in the young. These works, which do
not recommend themselves to the sophisticated literary taste, have circulated in the Soviet Union in millions of copies and are widely and

approvingly read by young people wherever the Soviet system reaches. Nikolai Ostrovsky's *The Making of a Hero* (1934) is the story of a poor boy who joins the underground and, overcoming obstacles of poverty, crippling wounds, and poor education, realizes his ambition to carry on the fight as a writer. Anton Makarenko's *A Teacher's Epic* (1934) describes the education of homeless and ragged delinquents in a colony for wayward boys. Boris Polevoy's *The Story of a Real Man* (1946) relates the saga of a Soviet aviator who is shot down by the Germans and though crippled by the loss of both feet, insists on returning, equipped with artificial limbs, to active air duty. Works such as these, regarded with disdain by the literary critic, seem to have had an effect wherever they are read by young and unformed minds.

A number of new writers now emerged who had been formed in the Soviet schools and whose work was patterned to fit the requirements of the day. Among these were Konstantin Simonov (b. 1915), whose later war novel *Days and Nights* (1944) described the Battle of Stalingrad; Yury Krymov (1908–1941), the author of *Tanker Derbent* (1938), a skillfully contrived study of socialist competition in the transportation industry; N. Y. Virta (b. 1906), a novelist and dramatist who devised the theory of "conflictless" drama; and S. P. Babayevsky (b. 1909), whose postwar *Cavalier of the Gold Star* (1947) tells of the developing sense of collective property on the land but lacks verisimilitude.

Two writers of the older generation, A. N. Tolstoy and Ilya Ehrenburg, who had emigrated and lived abroad for many years, returned and remained in Russia, becoming brilliantly successful practitioners of the new literary code, and—it can be said without exaggeration—apologists for Stalin's regime. After his return Tolstoy completed his long novel *Road to Calvary* (1920–1941), which deals explicitly with the problem of the intellectual and the Revolution; and in 1937 he published a novel, *Bread*, which Soviet authorities now insist falsified history in order to enhance the figure of Stalin as the defender of Tsaritsin in 1918. His *Peter the First* (1929–1945), on the other hand, is a masterful exercise in the genre of historical fiction.

Ilya Ehrenburg's *The Extraordinary Adventures of Julio Jurenito and His Disciples* (1922), in spite of its modernistic style and its flavor of Montparnasse, contains the germ of that cynical nihilism toward the values of Western bourgeois society which he himself has expressed in his career as a Soviet writer. Yet he too has faced the problem of the sensitive intellectual's alienation from the new world of massed Petyas and Anyas, and his *Out of Chaos* (1933) explores the inner tribulations of such a one. Ehrenburg, moreover, was before his death associated with the movement for liberalization in literature which followed the death of Stalin.

Socialist Realism

The official, obligatory style of Soviet literature under Stalin was "socialist realism." Much intellectual effort has been spent in a quest for the meaning of this term, the genesis of which is a concrete study in the operation of the Stalinist mentality. In the first place, realism in art had in the discussions of the late twenties been equated with materialism in philosophy, and thus received official sanction as correct for Marxist writers. But what kind of realism should be cultivated remained a problem. Psychological realism seemed to lead into the bypath of individual psychology. Objective realism sometimes revealed negative and repellent aspects of Soviet life which were not regarded as typical. Critical realism exposed the faults of society but affirmed nothing. Realism's cousin, naturalism, paid attention to biological rather than social factors in human development. The "dialectical materialist method" in realism, supported by RAPP, was both vague and doctrinaire. It was discovered in 1932—no one knows by whom, but the inspiration was attributed to Stalin—that "realism" might be qualified by the term "socialist." And since the term socialist had a generally positive connotation but dubious meaning as applied to literature, the meaning of "socialist realism" could be worked out in practice and by directive, and would be, in the end, whatever the going authority said it was. The authoritarian imposition of this meaningless term on the consciousness of Soviet writers led to monotonous uniformity in the content and form of Russian literature during the Stalin period. Very few writers escaped its noxious effect. The confirmed and incorrigible individualists, the "heretics and dreamers," either fell silent or emigrated, and the production of literature tended to become an organized and disciplined effort whose social purposes far transcended the individual human being. The literary product of those years, even when technically competent, lacked individuality and creativity. The deterioration increased sharply after 1946, when Andrey Zhdanov, a political leader close to Stalin, became the Party spokesman in literature. He and his lieutenants expressed the demand for tendentious works in crude, direct terms, and the abuse of deviant writers reached incredible extremes of harshness.

Literature under Stalin presented a striking contrast to literature in the West, as also to the innovative form and content of Russian modernism. Modernist departures from verisimilitude have usually been regarded by official Soviet critics as dehumanization and evidence of bourgeois decadence. The frequent notes of individualism and pessimism in contemporary Western writing and its concern with sex, perversion, violence, and absurdity are treated as an index of the decline of a civilization—as indeed they may be. A classic in the Soviet Marxist theory that literature must reflect social reality was Lenin's article on

Tolstoy, with the evocative title "Leo Tolstoy as a Mirror of the Russian Revolution" (1910), the authority of which was unquestioned in the period of socialist realism. Writers under Stalin and Zhdanov were obliged to adopt procedures different from those that appeared dominant in the West, to "reflect reality in its revolutionary development," to operate only with universally intelligible language and literary forms, to present positive heroes, and to sound bright, optimistic notes. If we assume for the moment that Lenin and the Soviet theoreticians are right and that literature is a kind of social barometer—though, of course, the matter is infinitely more complicated—then it would seem that they are only a little more sophisticated than the savage who smashed the barometer when it indicated rain; they preserved the barometer but tried to fix the instrument so that it would always point to fair weather. The outcome, as Sinyavsky pointed out in his essay "On Socialist Realism," was predictable: their literature never worked as literature and gave them false information about the social weather. There is evidence also that socialist realism never worked as an educational instrument.

The regimentation of literature affected all writers to some extent, but there were some who, because of the nature of their work, remained relatively free of pressure. Mikhail Prishvin (1873–1954), whose earliest work long antedated the Revolution, is perhaps not fully appreciated even in the Soviet Union for the variety, interest, and power of his work, and he is little known elsewhere. His works are full of knowing observations of wood, field, and stream, and they contain, along with the lore of nature, poetic and philosophic reflections at times reminiscent of Thoreau. His treatment of nature is never divorced from human activities, and he records ethnographic as well as natural information. Another writer of the older generation who continued in his own characteristic vein was A. S. Grin (Grinevski, 1880–1932), a writer of fantastic tales. Long passed over by the authorities because of his romanticism, he has in recent years been accorded a growing respect for his mastery of language and storytelling art. K. G. Paustovsky (1892–1968), a writer with a variety of thematic and stylistic turns, is a lover of nature and a recorder of the transformation of nature being wrought in modern times. Each of his works, he has said, is a journey to some area of the Soviet Union.

The Thaw

Uniformity of purpose and method, or at least the appearance of such uniformity, was ruthlessly enforced throughout the era of Stalin, as is now well known. However, the thirst for variety and individuality continued to exist under the bland surface. This became clear when, after Stalin's death in 1953, the mild relaxation of controls known as the literary thaw occasioned an eruption of articles and books revealing the existence and asserting the rights of individual human beings with their own unique and particular feelings, thoughts, and responsibilities. Among the works which appeared were Dudintsev's *Not by Bread Alone* (1956), wherein the hero is an individual who, for the sake of an idea, separates himself from the Soviet "collective" and elects to travel a "lonely, austere path." The fact that his "original idea" is a new method for the centrifugal casting of large-diameter iron drainpipes is only a detail.

Additional evidence of the persistence of life behind the monumental façade of socialist realist literature is the continued popularity of poets such as Anna Akhmatova and Boris Pasternak. Akhmatova's highly personal lyrics had been republished in a new edition in 1940; she herself finally reappeared at the Soviet Writers' Congress in 1954. Pasternak's deepest responses to life are out of tune with the society in which he lived. No new editions of his poetry appeared for many years; yet his work was well known to readers of poetry, and works which had never been published were passed from hand to hand, copied and recopied, and widely circulated. A new edition of his poems appeared in 1965, five years after his death, with an introduction by Andrey Sinyavsky. His poetry expresses particular, personal emotion in a strikingly original idiom. His novel, *Doctor Zhivago* (1956), written in the Soviet Union over a period of about twenty years, is a sensitive judgment on those years. It is the judgment of a poet and philosopher whose vision of the world was singular and arbitrary to the point of strangeness; and of one who, moreover, did not allow his thought, or the poetic idiom in which that thought took shape, ever to become engaged with the vulgar practices of the state.

Eugene Zamyatin, author of the brilliant anti-utopia *We*, was commissioned in 1919 to write a kind of manifesto for a newspaper to be published by a group of Petrograd intellectuals who were trying to find their place in the new world. The newspaper was to be called *Tomorrow* and, though only a single issue appeared, it exuded hope and confidence in that "tomorrow."

> Yesterday [wrote Zamyatin] there was a czar and there were slaves; today there is no czar, but there are still slaves; tomorrow there will be only czars. We are marching in the name of tomorrow's free man, the czar. We have lived through the epoch of the suppression of the masses; we are now living through the epoch of

the suppression of the individual in the name of the masses; but *tomorrow* will bring the liberation of the individual in the name of humanity.

The Sixties and Seventies

Everyone asks what tomorrow will bring to Russian literature. There is good reason to hope for a revival in it of a high degree of individualistic expression, and there are facts which point to such a development. In the sixties and seventies the Soviet journals continued to feature good and useful materials produced by disciplined writers with social ends in mind. But frequently a new note was heard. Valentin Katayev's *The Holy Well* (1966) was a symbolic fantasy, and in a series of works this venerable and established Soviet writer with irreproachable credentials boldly experimented with the time dimension in his search for the memory of his own youth, and in his effort to evoke the Russian past. A number of young writers managed to publish excellent work, though for the most part they ignored social themes. The literature of *samizdat* provides evidence that taboo themes, from sex and vodka to satirical treatment of the security police, would surely surface should censorship and restraints be lifted. And Russian exile literature has at all periods offered works of astonishing originality and power, from Nabokov and Khodasevich in the early period to Sinyavsky, Solzhenitsyn, and many others in the so-called third wave of the 1970s. I will examine these fascinating developments in the final chapters.

2 Mayakovsky and the Left Front of Art

The Suicide Note

No other poet of the twentieth century has been accorded as much honor in Russia as Vladimir Mayakovsky. He is the object of a kind of collective worship actively supported by the Soviet state. His apartment in a quiet Moscow side street (Mayakovsky Lane) housed for many years a museum dedicated to the life and works of the poet, until in the early seventies it was moved to larger quarters in a downtown building where he once had an office. The former "Triumphal Square" in Moscow has been renamed Mayakovsky Square, and the "Metro" station bearing his name, finished in baroque ornament of rust-proof steel, features the fine head of the poet in giant dimensions. On the square itself he stands solidly on a block of granite, a bronze statue, shoulders back and coat open, afraid of nothing.

Yet the poet's biography did not yield easily to mythographic treatment. He shot himself in 1930, a deed which so shocked his young literary admirers that some of them refused to believe it. One reported that when he received a telegram in the provinces informing him simply, "Mayakovsky has killed himself," dated April 14, 1930, he thought it an April fool joke, and explained the date as April *first*, Old Style.[1] But it was a fact that Mayakovsky had taken his own life in Moscow, leaving the following note:

To All of You:
   Don't blame anyone for my death, and please don't gossip about it. The deceased hated gossip.
   Mama, sisters, comrades, forgive me. This is not a good method

(I don't recommend it to others), but for me there's no other way out.

Lily, love me.

Comrade Government, my family consists of Lily Brik, mama, my sisters, and Veronica Polonsky.

If you can provide a decent life for them, thank you.

The verses I have begun give to the Briks. They'll understand them.

As they say, "The incident is closed."

> Love boat
> > Smashed on convention.
> I don't owe life a thing
> > And there's no point
> In counting over
> > Mutual hurts,
> > > harms,
> > > > and slights.

Best of Luck!

Vladimir Mayakovsky

4/12/30

Comrades of the Proletarian Literary Organization, don't think me a coward.

Really, it couldn't be helped.

Greetings!

Tell Yermilov it's too bad he removed the slogan; we should have had it out.

V. M.

In the desk drawer I have 2000 rubles. Use them to pay my taxes. The rest can be gotten from the State Publishing House.[2]

No doubt we should honor the wish of the deceased not to gossip about his deed. I shall not, therefore, speculate about the story that he played Russian roulette and lost, a story soberly reported as fact (and supported by Ilya Ehrenburg in his memoirs[3]), although, the shot having been fired in private, there could be no evidence to confirm it. A few footnotes to this last letter may serve as an illuminating introduction to Mayakovsky.

It is a model suicide note. There is not a scintilla of self-pity or self-accusation in it; neither is there any suggestion that others—the world, the government, his friends or enemies—bear any share of blame. Neither is life to blame, since the suicide, having paid his own debts, refuses to count over any that may be owed to him. Lily Brik, the wife of Osip Brik, his colleague in the Left Front of Art, may have served as the motivation for the mock-sentimental lines about a "Love

Boat/Smashed on convention." He had loved her for most of his life. She is included in his "family," and he seems quietly confident that his "Comrade Government" will take care of her and the others. There is no anger, even at the literary bureaucrats who called themselves proletarian writers and with whom Mayakovsky during the last years of his life had carried on a violent polemic. The "slogan" referred to was one of many agitational verses with which the auditorium was decorated during the performance of his play *The Bath* (1930), an attack on the bureaucrats and other petty forms of life which we shall examine later. This slogan, which the proletarian literary leadership insisted upon having removed, was a personal attack on one of those leaders, V. Yermilov:

> It isn't easy to clean out
>   the bureaucratic swarm.
> There aren't enough baths
>   nor is there soap enough
> And these bureaucrats
>   Are given aid and comfort by critics
>   Like Yermilov.

The reference to his proletarian comrades recalls his entrance into RAPP, the proletarian literary organization, just two months before his suicide. He held out until then before joining the disciplined writers' collective which had the Party's support. And when he did join under pressure, the leaders received him coldly as befitted a candidate whose tongue and pen had so often lashed them. The busy writers of RAPP, concerned as they were with discipline, planning, and organization, always regarded Mayakovsky as a dubious ally. He had come to them from literary bohemia, and had to, they said, overcome the petit-bourgeois individualist inside himself. The capitulation to RAPP which the Party exacted from Mayakovsky was no doubt the single event that made his suicide, in one form or another, inevitable. "It couldn't be helped, comrades," he told them in his letter.

The lines "Love boat/Smashed on convention" have been translated and interpreted in many ways. The word *byt*, which I have translated as "convention," has sometimes been rendered as "mores," or the "grind of everyday life." It is a word Mayakovsky often used in his poetry, referring to the alien element of encrusted habit and custom in which human beings live. *Byt*, which means ingrained habit, social custom, hallowed prejudice, routine and regularity, the established pattern of life, was his personal enemy. The life he lived and the poetry he wrote were an effort to overcome for himself the social routine that channels and controls the lives of most men. When, as a boy of fifteen, he joined the Social-Democrats, Bolshevik faction, and carried on propaganda among bakers and printers, he was asserting, much more than any political doctrine, his own self, Vladimir Mayakovsky. His understanding of Marx was elementary, but the ideas of Marx threatened the rigidities of Russian life, and he, Mayakovsky, found the propagation of those ideas a perfect method of self-expression on a grand scale. Marx was one weapon against *byt*, and others were soon found.

While a student of painting he met the artist David Burlyuk, who managed to stand out from his background by his arrogant manner and foppish dress. It was Burlyuk who discovered that Mayakovsky was a poet and encouraged him, and Mayakovsky avers that Russian Futurism was born one night in Moscow when they both left a Rachmaninoff concert in boredom and disgust. The quotation is from his autobiography, *I Myself*:

> *A Most Memorable Night.* Conversation. From Rachmaninoff boredom to school boredom, from school boredom to whole range of classical boredom. David had the anger of a master who had outpaced his contemporaries, I, the fervor of a Socialist aware of the inevitable doom of the old. Russian Futurism was born.[4]

The Futurist movement was for Mayakovsky an effort to create for himself a self that was really his own. The notion that the poet "creates himself" is embedded in Mayakovsky's life as well as his writing. He created a physical image of himself which the eye of even the tired observer could not fail to see. In his travels around Russia in the company of other Futurists he wore a yellow blouse with black stripes, a frock coat, and a top hat. Too poor for dandyism, he managed to create new sartorial concepts out of old and obvious materials:

> *The Yellow Blouse.* Never had a suit. Had two blouses—hideous-looking affairs. A tried method was to use a tie for decoration. No money. Took a piece of yellow ribbon from my sister. Tied it round my neck. Furor. So the most conspicuous and beautiful thing about a man was his tie. Evidently if you increased the size of the tie, you increased the furor. As there is a limit to the size of a tie, I had resort to cunning. I made a tie-shirt and shirt-tie. Impression—irresistible.[5]

His poetry was a struggle against literary *byt*. The poet's word in conventional style and setting might not be heard, just as the poet himself in bourgeois dress might not be seen. Therefore the poet must *shout* his lines. His rhythm is the rhythm of shouted remarks. Each line is short, heavily accented, self-sustaining, written "at the top of his voice." His metaphors are deliberately offensive to the conventional taste, his diction is peppered with vulgar vernacular, his rhymes are a clownish play with language and thought. Yet the total effect is one of singular beauty. Tender human feelings are expressed somehow by the phrase "sobs that leap out like prostitutes," and by "the poet's soul, deposited on the spears of houses, shred by shred." Mayakovsky's poetry is a conquest of literary convention.

The precise allusion of the lines "Love boat/Smashed on convention" is still the subject of speculation, as well as of the gossip that Mayakovsky disliked; but there can be no doubt about the general import of the line. The poet's own life was, at the time he wrote, caught in the web of new conventions and tangled by routine. Marxian ideas, once a weapon against rigidity, had been reduced to fixed formulas. Mayakovsky had discarded the mock haberdashery of Futurism for conventional jackets and properly invisible ties. He had become one of the members of the vast organization of proletarian writers, on a comradely footing with various Sutyrins and Yermilovs. He had his picture taken with literary hacks: Fadeyev, Surkov, and Stavsky. He was an honored employee of the state. He drew propaganda posters—three thousand of them, he said. He produced hundreds of advertisements for Soviet retail trading organizations, such as:

> Where can you buy and eat for your money
> The best and the tastiest macaroni?
> Where? Only in the Moscow Food Stores.[6]

He considered the above, apparently without irony, to be "poetry of the highest caliber." During the last full year of his life, 1929, in addition to producing a great mass of agitational verse, he made speeches and reports almost daily in widely separated parts of the country, took part in rallies and meetings, and at the same time arranged for the presentation of his two last plays, *The Bedbug* and *The Bath*. The "love boat" of his poetry, one might conclude, had indeed been smashed.

Vladimir Mayakovsky, A Tragedy

Some sixteen years earlier, in the Luna Park theater in St. Petersburg in December 1913, Mayakovsky had presented his verse "tragedy," *Vladimir Mayakovsky*. He played the principal part himself, and he was also the director and producer of the spectacle. The presentation was a *succès de scandale*. The audience was mocking and derisive; the reviews were for the most part contemptuous. It was another Futurist Golgotha in which the *outré* poet and irreverent innovator offered himself as a willing victim to the established literary priesthood. And they crucified him.

But there was also an appreciative audience. Not only his Futurist comrades but others who were present found the spectacle moving and were reduced to tears. The conception was simple enough. The central character was the "Poet," who, in his own person, stood on a pedestal against a backdrop which represented "a city with its spider web of streets." With him was his feminine companion—over six feet tall and broad in the shoulders—who had no lines and no business, except to stand at his side. She is perhaps an ironic counterpart to Blok's "unknown lady." The Poet on his eminence received in turn the characters in the play: "an old man with dry black cats; a man missing an eye and a leg; a man without an ear and a man without a head; a man with a long face; a man with two cardboard kisses; an average young man; three women, one with an ordinary tear, another with a little tear, a third with a huge tear; together with reporters, boys, girls, etc."

The play is about people who live in the city and who are enslaved to objects, to things which have no mind or heart as far as one can tell, though "they may have ears where people have eyes" or vice versa. These people are crippled, wounded, and afraid, and they bring to the Poet their suffering, their fright, and their tears. The Poet discusses these matters with them. The man with three dry old cats counsels rubbing such animals, for the sparks that these living creatures give out may run trains and light cities. God, he says, must be abandoned with all his talk of vengeance upon human beings, whose poor little souls wear only worn-out sighs. The earless man tells of cripples in the city where legends of agony grow, where the chimney pots dance the "matchish," where the side streets have their sleeves rolled up for a fight, where melancholy grows like a tear on the mug of a crying dog. The Poet then discusses "god" and avers he never found a soul to insert in the wound of his lips. (Except once he thought he'd found one. It wore a blue dressing gown, and said, "Come in and sit down. I've been waiting for you. Won't you have a cup of tea?") The "Average Young Man," on hearing all of this, is horrified at the very thought of destroying the accumulated culture of the ages. Things are really not so bad, for he himself has invented a machine to cut up chops automatically, and a friend is working on a trap for bedbugs. Moreover, he has a wife, who will soon have a son and a daughter. It's terrible to talk like this, he says. They should let things be as they are and should be, for he has a sister, too, named Sonya. "But," says the Poet, "if you had been hungry as I have been, you would devour the distant skies as the sooty mugs of factories devour them." The man with the long face says, "If you had loved as I have loved you would murder love." The man without an eye and a leg announces that "on the streets, where the faces, like a burden, are all exactly the same, old-lady-time has given birth to a huge mouth-twisted rebellion! Before the mugs of crawling years, old residents of the earth have grown mute, and anger has blown up rivers on the foreheads of cities—thousand-mile-long veins. Slowly, in horror, the straight arrows of hair are raised up on the bald crown of time. And suddenly all things have shed the ragged habiliments of their worn-out names." The things themselves have rebelled, and the Poet must find new names for them. The whole first act is an allegory of revolution, where even objects reject their established definitions.

In the second act Mayakovsky appeared again as the Poet in a toga and wearing a laurel wreath. The setting is a postrevolutionary metropolis, and the pregnant stage direction for the scene is "boring and sad" (*skuchno*). The crowd is ready to worship him, and comes bearing gifts. A woman brings him a tear. A second, whose son has died, brings him another tear, which would serve, she says, as a nice silver ball for his shoe buckle. There is a man with two kisses, who tells how, in women's boudoirs, "factories without smoke or smoke stacks," millions of little kisses are manufactured. The Poet gathered up all the tears in his suitcase and announced that he must abandon the laurel wreath, his happiness, and his throne, in order to carry off these tears to the farthest north, there where "in the vise of endless melancholy, with the fingers of waves, eternally, cruel ocean tears its breast. I will reach my goal, tired out, and in my last delirium will cast your tears to the dark god of storms, at the very source of beastly faiths."

Perhaps this summary gives some notion, however, inadequate, of the Futurist poet and political revolutionary, Mayakovsky. He is a poet of the city, who gathers up in grotesque images the human pain that he found in the city, and who has taken that pain upon himself as a burden of suffering.[7] It may be that this image of himself is merely a poetic persona, but it seems more likely that Mayakovsky, a man who had suffered imprisonment and persecution, felt this role as peculiarly his own. Ensconced in the tough chain mail of Futurist sound and symbol, his tender soul, hypersensitive to pain in both people and animals, can hardly endure the city-monster of his own times.

The Cloud

"A Cloud in Pants" (1915), a poem about love, revolution, and God, expresses, like the tragedy, the vaulting egoism of a Mayakovsky who felt in himself the stir of genius, and who had, as Pasternak put it, made this genius of his a "prescribed theme for all time."

Mayakovsky once explained in a speech to a group of young Communists how the poem happened to get its title. The explanation is ironic and apocryphal, but it is characteristic:

> "A Cloud in Pants" was first called "The Thirteenth Apostle."
> When I presented my work to the censor, I was asked, "What's the matter, do you want to go to jail?" I said, no, I didn't look with favor upon the idea. Then they cut out six whole pages, together with the title. That's how the problem of a title came up. They wanted to know how I could combine lyricism with coarseness, and I said, all right, if you like I'll be a madman, if you like I'll be most tender, not a man, but a cloud in pants.—Hardly anybody bought it, because the customers for verse in those days were mostly well-brought-up gentle ladies, and they couldn't buy it because of the title.[8]

Mayakovsky in these brief but inspired remarks to the assembled young Communists provides the key to his own personality and to his poetry. Harsh though they might be, and jangled out of tune, his lines could express the most tender love, the gentlest pity, the purest sympathy. Part I of "A Cloud" is an account of the pain caused by frustration in love. It is a long and raucous plaint in which the poet draws upon the linguistic reserves of the city streets and the unbridled imagery that was his alone in handling the theme of unrequited male love: the enormous pain experienced by a huge, sinewy clod, whose coarse bulk cries out for the soft and feminine. The heart on fire with love gives off a smell like roasted meat; a wild call brings the firemen to put out the fire:

> Don't wear boots!
> Tell the firemen:
> You climb a burning heart with caresses.
> I'll take care of it!
> I'll pour barrels of tears from my eyes.
> I'll brace myself against my ribs.
> I'll jump out! Out! Out!
> Collapsed!
> But you can't jump out of your heart!

Part II suddenly drops love for the themes of poetry and social revolution. The poet announces confidently his program of creative destruction:

> Praise me,
> I'm more than a match for the mighty.
> To everything that's been done
> I give the mark *"nihil."*

This section contains what is no doubt the best statement of Mayakovsky's poetic program: the source and inspiration of his poetry is the city street with its crippled beggars, its consumptives, its weird cacophony:

> What do I care
> if neither Homer nor Ovid
> thought of characters like us,
> sooty and pock marked.
> I know
> the sun would dim, seeing
> the gold mines in our souls!

He foresees the coming of revolution in "the year 1916," and he, like John the Baptist, is the forerunner:

> I am wherever pain is—anywhere;
> on each drop of the tear stream
> I have crucified myself.
> Nothing must be forgiven any more!
> I've burnt out of souls the place where gentleness grew.
> It was harder than taking
> a thousand thousand Bastilles!

> And when,
> his advent
> with riot proclaiming,
> you come out to meet your savior—
> for you I
> will tear out my soul;
> I'll stamp on it and trample it
> till it spread out!—
> and I'll give it to you—a bloody banner.

The revolutionary note upon which Part II ends prepares a transition to Part III, in which the love lyric has been resolutely abandoned, the poet's song has been brought down into the streets, and he calls upon the streets to rebel against the old world. The rebellion takes place in such lines as "Come on! Let's paint Mondays and Tuesdays red with blood and make holidays out of them." The poetic outcome of the revolution is no triumph, but rather an abrupt transition, after betrayal by a sky like Judas and a night "like the traitor Azev," to defeat and huddled despair. Part III ends on a new note of gently thoughtful melancholy, which introduces again the love theme:

> I, who sang the machine and England,
> maybe I am just
> the thirteenth apostle
> in the usual gospel.

And whenever my voice
shouts bawdily—
then, from hour to hour,
all day long
maybe Jesus Christ is sniffing
the forget-me-nots of my soul.

Part IV returns again to the theme of love, a tragic love, the love that might save a man but cannot be consummated. In the name of this unrealizable love the poem closes with a mock-blasphemous attack on heaven and on God, who hears nothing, and does not answer:

The universe is asleep,
its huge ear
star-infested
rests on a paw.

Roman Jakobson, one of the most perceptive students of Mayakovsky, has pointed out that there is a regular alternation in his work between lyric themes and social or political themes—the theme of love alternating with the theme of revolution. "A Cloud in Pants," in its alternation of lyrical and political motifs, is thus a kind of microcosm of Mayakovsky's poetry and a guide to his life.

"The Backbone Flute"

Beauty in poems by Mayakovsky eludes translation and deceives the conventional taste. Thus Mayakovsky's wonderful song about love, which is dedicated to Lily Brik but probably meant for all women, has passed unnoticed outside of Russia. "The Backbone Flute" (1915) is a male lyric on the theme of love's madness and pain. The poetic figures which carry the burden of desire neither chasten nor sublimate, but present the poet's love in terms of delirium. The "her" to whom the verses are offered is a thing of hellish fantasy, invented by some heavenly Hoffmann; his thoughts are simply clots of blood issuing from the skull; he will dive down and brain himself on the pavement of Nevsky Bouvelard; God brought her up out of the hot depths of hell and gave her a human husband, and human music to set on her piano, but if one should make the sign of the cross above the quilt that covers her there would be at once a smell of scorched wool and sulphurous fumes. Even in drunken battle the words of love are not obsolete. The German speaks of Goethe's Gretchen; the Frenchman dies with a smile, remembering Traviata; but the source of his hell is no conventional literary type: she is a redhead with a painted face. When the centuries have whitened beards only she will be left—and he, rushing after her from city to city; in London fogs he will imprint on her lips the fiery kiss of street lamps; in Paris, when she wanders onto a bridge and looks down, it's him she will see pouring himself out Seine-wise and calling to her; when she rides out on the bridle path in Sokolniki Park, he will rise over the trees, naked and expectant, a moon to torment her. But the lady's virtue is cold as monastery rock; the husband asserts his rights, and oh, that night! He tightened despair about his throat, and at his howls and laughs the smug mug of his room twisted out of shape with fright. He surrendered her; and King Albert of Belgium, all his towns surrendered, was a happy-birthday-boy by comparison.

This pale paraphrase may give some notion of how Mayakovsky consciously employed near-psychopathic imagery to convey the intense force of sexual passion. Such poems do reflect Mayakovsky's own nature and his emotional experience in love, though it must be remembered that in them he is also a conscious poetic craftsman experimenting with the linguistic means for the expression of violent emotions. The complete results of his experiment we can know only if we read Russian. That experiment involved the invention of new words, and of new morphemes or endings for already existing words; renovation of the verbal repertory by way of new accents; the use of rhymes, sometimes conventionally correct, sometimes outrageous: for instance, the writer E. T. A. Hoffmann entered "The Backbone Flute" only because the name in rapid colloquial delivery fortuitously, and humorously, rhymes with an unusual Russian verb in which the root vowel has disappeared. Thus the reader's legitimate amusement at a funny rhyme is mingled with subconscious awareness of linguistic processes. There are also occasional clichés suggesting the conventional love lyric, and realistic bits of dialogue. The meter is accentual, each line made up of three or four heavily accented phrase segments.

One must be wary, in the case of a literary craftsman like Mayakovsky, of searching his work for a guide to his biography. Yet there is clear evidence that Mayakovsky himself experienced the kind of irrational attack of wild emotion that his best poetry describes. Kamensky, one of his biographers, records that in Odessa once Mayakovsky fell in love with a beautiful young girl, that he "roared and stormed" and could not "cope with the great feeling." Professor Jakobson recounts how the poet acted out in a series of telegrams from Moscow to a young Russian girl in Paris a whole poem on love. His close friends have left the record of a number of incidents in which he displayed either manic elation or sudden weeping despair. Lily Brik relates that at the first reading of "The Backbone Flute" in 1915, "Volodya, upset at seeing a small group of friends instead of a packed auditorium, broke down and wept, refused to read, and went off into another room." Only with difficulty was he calmed down and persuaded to return to the assembled and expectant guests and resume his reading. His chauffeur reported that a few days before his suicide, when he was returning from a rehearsal of his play *The Bath*, Mayakovsky wept:

> On the day of the opening Mayakovsky was in the theater in the afternoon. And when we were returning home I noticed that something was wrong. I heard him crying and sobbing, and one could tell he was having some deep trouble. We drove past Passion Place. Vladimir was silent. I tried to question him: "Vladimir Vladimirovich, it seems you've had some trouble?" He sighed. "It's nothing," he said, but in a few seconds he added, "Don't come to the theater tonight, there won't be any performance."[9]

Ilya Ehrenburg in his reminiscences emphasizes Mayakovsky's preternatural sensitivity and insists that though he called himself an ox and claimed to have a pachyderm's hide Mayakovsky "did not even have ordinary human skin."

It is fair to say, then, that Mayakovsky's poetry reflects a highly emotional and undisciplined human personality. His emotions are experienced and expressed in a personal and individual style. The ego of the poet is implicit in every line and explicit in every other. He himself is the hero of his *Tragedy*; the stages in his own life are the matter of his poem "Man"; a number of the lyric poems either have the first person singular pronoun in the title or the name of the poet himself. He is totally concerned with and writes only about "I myself," the title of his autobiography. Therefore it is not surprising that in the last decade of his life, after he had helped the Bolsheviks to destroy the old society, the old culture, and the old poetry, he should have experienced some pain, bedded on eiderdown though he was, on the procrustean couch of a collective society. His suffering, outsized and hyperbolic like his poetry, reached a point at last where a bullet seemed a possible anodyne. The tragedy was not his alone, and his shot at himself expressed the anguish of others like him.

The Commune and the Left Front

But first he tried to organize and discipline himself. That is the real meaning of the Left Front of Art, of which he was the inspiration and the leader, and of his earlier activities as editor of *Art of the Commune* and, for a brief time, arbiter of the new literary taste.

The one literary group whose members as a whole welcomed and supported the Bolshevik Revolution was the Moscow Futurists; they proclaimed their readiness to celebrate it in raucous numbers. The result of this was an adventitious and short-lived alliance between Futurism and Bolshevism. The Futurists, who were installed as editors of the official journal of the Commissariat of Education, *Art of the Commune*, became the semiofficial leaders of artistic and literary life. In flamboyant pronouncements the Futurists claimed to be the original revolutionaries in art and to speak in such matters for the proletarian state. Their intransigent nihilism and their policy of a "clean sweep" for the old order of things were *at the moment* in line with official policy. The idea of radical, absolute solutions permeated the air, and the Futurists, from their eminence as friends of the new regime, spoke of a "proletarian dictatorship" in the arts. Mayakovsky's statements of the official program, whether couched in prose or poetry, betray the strident emotional extremism that characterized both himself and the times. The poem entitled "It's Too Early to Rejoice" (1917) calls for an attack on "Pushkin, and other classic generals," and the position of the publication *Art of the Commune* was that the art of the past was of no use to the factories, the streets, and the working-class quarters of the city, and therefore should be eliminated.

Mayakovsky and his Futurist allies soon found themselves not only out of step with the proletarians, whose taste in literature, if it existed at all, tended to favor the classics and to reject the sophisticated linguistic contortions of the Futurists, but also sharply at odds with the leaders of the Party-State. It is well known that Lenin regarded Mayakovsky's work with frank distaste: "Pushkin I understand and enjoy," he said, "Nekrasov I acknowledge, but Mayakovsky—excuse me. I can't understand him." The concern of Lenin and other Party leaders for preserving what they called the "cultural heritage" led them to stern disapproval of the Futurist attack on the art of the past.

The most important factor in their low estimate of Mayakovsky was the "difficulty" of his poems, and however radical the Futurists claimed to be, their message was lost not only on Lenin but on proletarian readers who knew nothing about the old culture of the nineteenth century or the Futurist rebellion against that culture. As Trotsky put it: "The Futurist break with the past is, after all, a tempest in the closed-in world of the intelligentsia which grew up on Pushkin, Fet, Tyutchev, Bryusov, Balmont, and Blok . . . The Futurists have done well to push away from them. But it is not necessary to make a universal law of development out of the act of pushing away."

Mayakovsky's two most important works of the immediate revolutionary period were the long poem called "150,000,000," and the verse drama *Mystery Bouffe*. In them he makes a conscious effort to remove his "self" into the background in favor of the masses.

The verse play *Mystery Bouffe*, a modern variant of the medieval mystery, with added ingredients of farce and blasphemy ("bouffe") was presented in its first version in 1918 on the anniversary of the October Revolution under the directorship of Meyerhold. It was difficult to find actors willing to perform in it. An advertisement in the Petrograd papers announced preparations for the staging of the play and called upon actors wishing to take part in it to present themselves in a certain place at a certain hour. The advertisement rang with revolutionary fervor:

> Comrade Actors! You are under obligation to celebrate the great anniversary of the Revolution with a revolutionary production. You must present the play *Mystery Bouffe*, a heroic, epic, and satiric portrait of our era, written by Vladimir Mayakovsky . . . To work, everyone! Time is precious![10]

The plot, if sensational, was very simple. After the earth has been destroyed by a flood there remain aboard an ark, seeking refuge at the North Pole, "seven pairs of Clean" and "seven pairs of Unclean." The "Clean" are various bourgeois types, such as Lloyd George, Clemenceau, and a Russian speculator; the "Unclean" are proletarians: a miner, a carpenter, a laundress, and so forth. The Unclean are deceived by the Clean, whom they throw overboard. The settings where the action takes place are various: the Universe, the ark, hell, heaven, the cloud country, the Promised Land. The Unclean, after overthrowing the Clean, visit hell, where they deposit the latter; then they go to a traditional heaven which they leave in disgust; and finally they return to earth and the Promised Land of the Communist Paradise.

The play is a kind of working model of the flamboyant revolutionary literature of the moment, and it succeeds in conveying the spirit of that moment, as Mayakovsky felt it. It contains the elation of victory that the Bolsheviks and their close sympathizers felt on the day after the Revolution, and it contains also an ingredient of revolutionary ethos common to the writings of Gorky and Lenin: contempt and black hatred for the "clean" world. It has a sense of the future and of historical movement. Mayakovsky speaks in it of the storming of the planets by "airships of the commune, fifty years hence"; and the "Very Ordinary Young Man" in the play speaks of a time when the "sun will perform such tricks that pineapples will yield six crops a year from pickle shoots." The play is blasphemous: Jehovah himself—the old institutionalized religion—is conquered by the Unclean, who, Prometheus-like, steal his lightnings from him and use them for electrification. It is frankly topical and ephemeral, and it includes not only persons but phrases and ideas that were alive to the spectators of 1918 but which have only a historical interest today. Mayakovsky, in his introductory remarks to the second variant, produced in 1921, advises his posterity to introduce new topical material for each future performance—material significant for *their times.* Thus the individual ego of the author seeks to screen itself behind the mass, the Party program, and political matters of the passing moment.

The poem "150,000,000" was written in 1919 and published, after long epistolary haggling with the State Publishing House, in April 1920. In his autobiography, *I Myself,* Mayakovsky wrote for the year 1919: "My head full of 150,000,000. Started agitational work in ROSTA [State Telegraph Agency]." The juxtaposition is not accidental. "150,-000,000" is frankly propagandist, just as were the cartoons and posters which he produced for ROSTA. And both varieties of propaganda were, in the poet's intention, anonymous. He goes on to say about the poem: "Finished 150,000,000. Published it without my name. I wanted anyone at all to add to it and improve it." But the device did not work, since the hand of Mayakovsky was clearly visible: "But no one did add to it and anyway everyone knew who wrote it. What's the difference. Publish it now under my name."

Not only was the "mass"—150,000,000 Ivans (the 1919 population of the USSR)—the hero of this poem, but the opening lines announce that the "mass" is also its author:

> 150,000,000 is the name of the creator of this poem.
> Its rhythms—bullets,
> its rhymes—fires from building to building.
> 150,000,000 speak with my lips . . .
> Who can tell the name
> of the earth's creator—surely a genius?
> And so
> of this
> my
> poem
> no one is the author.

However, just as the poetic concepts, the characters, the rhythms and profoundly self-conscious rhyming devices employed in *Mystery Bouffe* clearly revealed the hand of the author, so in "150,000,000" the exclusive personal authorship of an intensely original individual, Mayakovsky, was immediately obvious. Considered as a literary production the poem is a sophisticated parody on the ancient folk epic, the *bylina,* a literary form developed among the more primitive peoples of the Russian empire for hundreds of years and handed down from generation to generation by word of mouth. The *bylina*, whose hyperbolized heroic figures and primitive verse system Mayakovsky imitates, was indeed an impersonal creation of the Russian mass; but the poem "150,000,000" is the work of a particular craftsman. There are two figures of heroic proportions in the poem: Wilson, the defender of world capitalism, and Ivan, a thoroughly Russian champion of the downtrodden. Wilson is located in Chicago, a city which stands on a single screw and is completely "electro-dynamo-mechanized." Even when a Chicagoan lifts his brow the work is done by electric power. Wilson has pistols with four cocks and a saber bent into seventy sharp blades. Ivan has only "a hand and another hand, and that one stuck in his belt." But, as in the Russian folk epic Ilya of Murom vanquishes the frightening enemy without serious difficulty, so here there is never any doubt that Wilson, "whose drawers are not drawers but a sonnet," who eats and grows fat "adding one floor after another to his belly," will succumb to the Paul Bunyan-like "Ivan." Wilson is of course no real figure but a literary symbol of evil power modeled on the Tartar enemies with whom the Russian folk heroes in the *bylina* regularly do battle. The faraway mysterious capital from which those enemies usually issued forth has become a certain "Chicago," and their devilish magic is nothing but "mechanization." Viewed as a literary production the poem is a triumph of sophistication and verbal skill; read as political commentary or propaganda it is nothing at all.

Party leaders reacted to both these works with a kind of obtuse, instinctive hostility. Lenin wrote in a note to Lunacharsky: "Aren't you ashamed of yourself for voting to publish '150,000,000' in 5000 copies? Nonsense, stupidity, double-dyed stupidity and pretentiousness! In my opinion only about one in ten such things should be published, and in editions of not more than 1500 copies—for libraries and eccentrics."[11] Trotsky, though somewhat more perceptive than Lenin, still could find no good use for Mayakovsky's agitational pieces: "How out of place and how frivolous do these primitive ballads and fairy tales sound when hurriedly adapted to Chicago mechanics and to the class struggle!"[12] In short, Mayakovsky's brave beginning as a propagandist of the new regime ended in failure. The futurist ego of the poet, his ever restive imagination, his instinctive iconoclasm of imagery and diction, seemed to Lenin a kind of literary "hooliganism." Such people could not be trusted. *"Mystery Bouffe,"* wrote Mayakovsky in his autobiography, "was produced three times, them lambasted. Replaced by various Macbeths."

There were other, shorter, and perhaps more successful things written in the first days of the Revolution, and Mayakovsky as an agitator and declaimer of verse was much in demand at meetings and rallies in spite of the cool reserve of the Party leaders toward his work. Physical contact with the mass Mayakovsky had established in his art work and through his speeches, yet something was missing. Proletarians and Party bureaucrats repeated the easy and obvious charge that he was "too much of an individualist," and he attempted to deal with this charge in a poem, "The Fifth International," which he never finished:

> The Proletcultists never speak
> of "I" or of the personality.
> They consider
> the pronoun "I"
> a kind of rascality.
> But in my opinion
> if you write petty stuff, you
> will never crawl out of your lyrical slough
> even if you substitute We for I.

Excessive individualism, unintelligibility, rowdy disrespect for fine literature, such were the shortcomings of Mayakovsky; and they threatened him with isolation from the working-class audience. Aware of this danger, he modified his literary style, did violence to his own talent, "stepped," as he himself put it, "upon the throat of his own song." At a reading of his poems in 1930 he revealed clearly the mechanics of his evolution: "One of the main difficulties in communicating with the 'workers' auditorium,'" he said, was the low standard of culture of these workers and the difficulty of communicating with them. His own things had been criticized as incomprehensible, "so the question of a clear meaning for everybody rose before me, and I started to write more for the masses."

To institutionalize and rationalize the new departure forced by circumstance, Mayakovsky and his Futurist friends organized in 1923 the Left Front of Art (Lef) and began publishing the magazine *Lef*. Mayakovsky recorded and briefly characterized these events in his autobiography:

> We organize "Lef." "Lef" may be defined as the encompassing of the great social theme by all the instruments of Futurism. This definition, of course, does not exhaust the question. Anyone interested should look at the issues of *Lef*. We closed ranks firmly: Brik, Kushner, Aseyev, Arvatov, Tretyakov, Rodchenko, Lavinsky . . . One of the slogans, and one of the great achievements of *Lef*, was the de-aestheticizing of the productive arts, constructivism. Poetic supplement to the magazine: agitational pieces, and also commercial agitation: advertisements.[13]

The persons mentioned were all active figures in the Futurist movement of the Lef period. Osip Brik was Mayakovsky's publisher, his friend, and the husband of Lily; Boris Kushner was a critic and a specialist in the literary "sketch"; N. N. Aseyev was a poet, follower of Mayakovsky; Sergey Tretyakov was a playwright, poet, and movie scenarist whose most famous work is the anti-imperialist propaganda play *Roar China!* (1926); Rodchenko was an artist and the author of travel sketches. Others prominent as contributors in the journal *Lef* were Victor Shklovsky, a provocative and original critic and one of the early Formalists, Boris Eichenbaum and Boris Tomashevsky, literary scholars and critics whose works on Pushkin and Tolstoy, respectively, are solid monuments of scholarship. Futurist poets of a "dadaist" complexion, Kruchonykh for instance, occasionally contributed their suggestive verbal play. The early stories of Isaac Babel and Valentin Katayev appeared in *Lef* and *New Lef*.

Missing from the list given by Mayakovsky when he wrote those lines in 1928 is one very important name: N. F. Chuzhak-Nasimovich, the most dogmatic and articulate theoretician of Futurism in the period of Lef, and an editor of the magazines *Lef* and *New Lef*. His ascendancy is both symptomatic and illuminating. Chuzhak was a Bolshevik journalist to whom journalism seemed the highest order of creative activity under the new order of things, and his notions as to the function of literature in building life rather than "palely reflecting" it dominated the theoretical section of the magazine. The platform for *Lef*, developed in part under his guidance, made the following points:

> It is our purpose:
> 1) To aid in the discovery of a Communist path for all varieties of art.
> 2) To re-examine the theory and practice of so-called "left" art, freeing it from individualistic distortions and developing its valuable Communist aspects.
> 3) To struggle with decadence and aesthetic mysticism, as well as with self-contained formalism, indifferent naturalism, and for the affirmation of tendentious realism, based on the use of the technical devices developed in all the revolutionary schools of art.[14]

Like so much of the manifesto literature of the twenties this document sounds to the modern reader something like a formal prayer addressed to a God whose character and attributes have been forgotten. Yet these formulas can be translated into simple prose. Most important is the promise to "re-examine" the position taken in the recent past by the Futurists and condemned by the Party. "Individualistic distortion" refers to Mayakovsky's besetting sin of which he must purge himself. "Decadence" echoes a phrase by Lenin in his public letter on the Proletcult, in which he linked Futurists with "decadents of every stripe." To struggle against "self-contained formalism" means simply to dissociate oneself from critics such as Shklovsky and others of the Formalist school who studied literature as form and device rather than as social evidence. Note, however, that the qualification "self-contained" leaves the way open for any of these people to purge themselves of sin without giving up their basic heresy. The "affirmation of tendentious realism" is a retreat into the past and implies a condemnation of the epic and heroic style of both *Mystery Bouffe* and "150,000,000."

The Formalists and linguistic specialists who had been close to the Futurist movement from the start continued to have a prominent place in *Lef*. A natural affinity existed between those poets who were, like Mayakovsky and Khlebnikov, laboratories of linguistic experiment themselves and scholarly specialists in the study of language. The lively interest of Mayakovsky and Roman Jakobson in each other's work may be explained in this way. Articles in *Lef* were heavily weighted in the direction of the *formal* or *linguistic* study of literature; evidence that the Formalists were no longer self-contained but were now in contact with reality was provided by the lead article in one of the first numbers of *Lef*: "Lenin's Language." Formalist investigation published in *Lef* emphasized the study of specific characteristics of language as used in literature.

The magazine *Lef* was not well received, and its circulation remained small, partly, according to Mayakovsky, because of sabotage by the State Publishing House. It stopped publication in 1925 after only seven numbers, was revived as *New Lef* in 1927, and finally disappeared at the end of 1928. During the final year of *Lef* its small body of theoreticians developed in radical form the notion of the literary man as a craftsman and of literature as a craft not basically different from other socially useful occupations. The highest form of literary activity in this paradoxical theory, and the most useful "in the epoch of socialism," was factual reporting: the writing of sketches, biographies, diaries, travel notes, and the like. The concern of the writer should be with *facts*, rather than with his own invention or fantasy. The fixation of objective fact was to be required of him, rather than the creation of artistic wholes, which tend to "destroy or disfigure the *fact*" in accordance with a subjective purpose. The activity of the craftsman-writer, moreover, should be determined by the *demand* of his client, who is, "in the epoch of socialism," the proletarian state. Since literary production is by its nature no different from other kinds of production, the writer, whatever his class origin or orientation, is simply a producer working for a client. Implicit in this theory is the tenet that the writer's ideology is not of crucial importance. Though their theories have the ring of dogma and the limits they suggest for the new "Literature of Fact" seem straitened and confining, yet it is clear that the ideas they developed would, if accepted, have had the effect of liberating the writer from the much more confining demand that he *interpret* reality in the light of dialectical materialism. To fix the writer firmly on the ground of *fact* meant to free him from the obligation to produce ideologically tendentious "artistic literature." The Soviet opponents of *Lef* did not "expose" them in this, but they left no doubt that the factual emphasis of the Left Front of Art would deprive the state of a useful propaganda weapon.

A glaring anomaly in the first number of *Lef* was the featured publication there of Mayakovsky's long poem "About That" (1923), a work which revives the subject of love and once more describes the frantic suffering of a lover rejected by (who else?) Lily Brik. Mayakovsky's old enemy, *byt*, torments that lover, who suffers contumely, contempt, and even death at the hands of philistines. There was "no way out" for him except to die—and then to be resurrected in the thirtieth century, a time when the golden age is in full flower, and private, possessive *eros* has been transformed into selfless, universal *agape*. Chuzhak and others on the editorial board angrily protested the publication of this beautiful poem.

The alliance between Formalist critics and Futurists continued in *New Lef*. Shklovsky published there a number of stimulating and highly original studies, among them his "Tolstoy's *War and Peace*, a Formal Sociological Study," and a penetrating analysis of Pushkin's *The Captain's Daughter*; Osip Brik's "The Rout of Fadeyev," a shrewd attack on the proletarian writers as poor epigones of nineteenth-century realism, appeared in 1928; Mayakovsky's irreverent letter in verse to Gorky was published in the first number; Boris Kushner's travel sketches of Western Europe, one of the finest things in the sketch genre, were published in an early number of *New Lef*. In general, the material published was interesting and original, even when its purpose was agitational. In an article entitled "For Innovation," Osip Brik wrote that since Soviet literature ought to have something new to contribute to world literature, the experimenters should not be hampered in their laboratory work by the requirement that the work be intelligible to millions of new readers: "It is a mistake," he said, "to demand that every cultural work be multiplied and distributed in the hundreds of thousands."

New Lef was published in a small edition of between 2000 and 3000 for each number. It received no warm reception either in the government offices or among the reading mass. Even its agitational and propaganda emphasis was suspect, since those functions were carried out in its pages by iconoclastic literary critics such as Victor Shklovsky and Futurist artists indifferent to conventional standards of taste. As a result of pressures which have never been wholly explained, Mayakovsky resigned from the editorship of *New Lef* in July 1928, after No. 7 of the magazine had been issued.[15] He explained later that "tiny literary fractionlets had outlived themselves, and instead of organizing groups literary men should transfer their activities to mass organizations carrying on agitational work: newspapers, 'agitprops,' commissions, etc. . . ." In 1929 Mayakovsky and those comrades who had together with him abandoned *Lef* formed a new organization which they called Ref, the Revolutionary Front of Art. At a public meeting in October of that year he explained that the new organization was needed to carry on the struggle with "apolitical tendencies." From this must follow rejection of the theory of the "bare fact" and the demand for tendentiousness and ideas in art.

The Bedbug and *The Bath*

The plays written by Mayakovsky in 1928 and 1929 constitute a two-part dramatic satire directed against old enemies of his, whom we have already met under the generic name *byt,* and who appear now in the form of *bourgeoisis vulgaris,* a species closely allied with *bedbugus normalis,* and "the Soviet bureaucrat." Both plays are satiric utopias in the sense that they purport to foresee a future in which the world will be purified of such specimens. *The Bedbug* is a two-part drama in which the action of the first part takes place in the year 1928 and of the second part fifty years later in a well-ordered Communist state of the future. The principal character is one Prisypkin, a successful Soviet "promoted worker," for whom proletarian blood, callused palms, and the trade-union card have become symbols of privilege and power. As the play opens he has jilted his working-class girl friend for a beauty shop operator and manicurist, Elzevira Renaissance, and is shopping in a huge department store in preparation for the wedding. Various salesmen are promoting their wares—buttons, dolls, whetstones, lampshades, glue, perfumes, fur-lined brassieres and the like—in jingles reminiscent of Mayakovsky's own commercial poetry. Prisypkin, with bourgeois persistence, acquires a variety of such wares, announcing that his house must be filled with such things "like a horn of plenty." The scene shifts to the wedding party, where the drunken guests set fire to the house, destroying all the inmates. Fifty years later the bridegroom Prisypkin together with a companion, a bedbug, are found, by workmen excavating for a new structure, perfectly preserved in a block of ice and are brought to life again by scientists of the "Bureau for the Resurrection of the Dead."

Prisypkin's resurrection, while a scientific success, is not an unmixed blessing to the inhabitants of the future, for the man is found to contain the petit-bourgeois infection of love, along with a fondness for strong drink and sentimental songs. He infects others with that ancient disease called love, "a state in which a person's sexual energy, instead of being rationally distributed over the whole of his life, was compressed into a single week and concentrated in one hectic process. This made him commit the most absurd and impossible acts."

The authorities in the State of the future place Prisypkin, the revived bourgeois, in a cage and display him for the education and edification of the citizens. Those men of utopia have forgotten a way of life that called for the use of poison (vodka), the disorderly consumption of tobacco in the form of cigarettes, the use of foul language, the strumming of guitars, and idle talk about one's "heart strings." But when the director of the zoo where Prisypkin is kept lets him out to see the spectators and to address a few words to them in order to prove that he has mastered human speech, Prisypkin, suddenly looking out at the theater audience, is overjoyed at seeing people like himself and addresses them directly:

> Citizens! Brothers! My own people! Darlings! How did you get here? So many of you! When were you unfrozen? Why am I alone in the cage? Darlings, friends, come and join me! Why should I alone suffer? Citizens!

This speech has been interpreted as a veiled attack on the Soviet police state, but it is probably not that. Prisypkin's apostrophe to the Soviet audience of 1928 is reminiscent of a very similar scene in Gogol's *Inspector General*, when the dishonest and foolish mayor turns to the audience to ask them whether they aren't laughing at themselves rather than at him. You all have a bit of Prisypkin in you, Mayakovsky is saying in this scene, you are all attached to vulgar bourgeois values. Like Prisypkin you smoke, drink, and use intemperate language. Like him you want your houses to be "horns of plenty," chocked with buttons, brassieres, and bathos, and like him you have debased the humanitarian ideas of the Revolution to the pursuit of comfort and power. Worst of all, you still preserve the infections of individualism and sexual love.

Mayakovsky's satire in *The Bedbug* is directed at himself as well as at his contemporaries. We have already noted that the ditties recited by department store salesmen in the first scene are a parody of his own verse written for the Moscow Food Stores. Mayakovsky's most accomplished work is a poetic expression of that "disease of the brain" known as sexual love. It has been pointed out that Mayakovsky, in satirizing Prisypkin's yearning for "roses" and "visions," may be lecturing himself: "Only books on horticulture have anything about roses, and visions are mentioned only in the medical books, in the section on dreaming."[16] And the ugly caricature of a bourgeoisified proletarian Prisypkin in search of conventional marital bliss may be that alter ego of the poet himself, with whom he disputed in the poem "About That":

> Have you greased your way
>   into that caste of theirs?
> Will you kiss?
>   Feed yourself?
>   Grow fat?
> Do you intend
>   Yourself
> To dig yourself into their way of life
> And practice that family happiness of theirs?

The Bedbug is, therefore, a complex satiric system. The Soviet philistine symbolized by Prisypkin is the normal Soviet man of the late twenties who has deserted the trenches of revolution for the sake of middle-class happiness. He is also Mayakovsky himself, the unreconstructed poet of his own all-important self, who has not quite succeeded in choking off the love lyric. With his barbarous ways, Prisypkin seems no better than an animal to the citizens of the rationalized world of the future; but that world itself is presented in satiric images by the Mayakovsky who is himself part Prisypkin: the worldwide mechanical voting apparatus, the organized mass dances which are the only kind that survived, the comical search among old books for something on love, and the steel, concrete, and glass backdrop against which the man of the future lives are hardly offered as a happy prospect. Mayakovsky ridicules the philistine individualism of Prisypkin, but he does not seem to believe either in the hardening mass organization that crushes him.

The Bath, produced in 1930, is similar in theme to *The Bedbug*, though it is more simply and pointedly directed against the Stalinist bureaucracy which was taking form at the time. It portrays in one Pobedonosikov the new Communist officials who were moving into positions of power in the government and Party apparatus, to replace the revolutionaries of the Civil War period. They are a narrow-minded and conformist generation, sycophants, opportunists, and timeservers, people of vulgar ambition and vulgar tastes, philistines mouthing Marxist phrases but interested only in power and the exercise of power. It is understandable that neither *The Bedbug* nor *The Bath* was well received by the literary bureaucrats, and one of these, Yury Libedinsky, a leader of RAPP when the play was produced, wrote in his memoirs that at that time the secretariat of his organization thought Mayakovsky was exaggerating the amount of bureaucratism in the Party apparatus. He later found, he says, that Mayakovsky was right and that he and his comrades were wrong.

Mayakovsky as a Monument

The Vladimir Mayakovsky that I have presented here—and I have tried to be objective—has hardly anything in common with the heroic statue that stands on a pedestal in Moscow's Mayakovsky Square. Is something missing from my account? Would a Soviet critic object that something vital has been left out? Would he say that we have studied only the bohemian intellectual "who was never really a Futurist," to the neglect of the Bolshevik political agitator? Would he present a long list of poems not mentioned in this brief survey and accuse me of a certain bias in selection?

Indeed he would, and perhaps we should look at that other side of Mayakovsky. If Mayakovsky had written only such poems as "Lenin," "Very Good!" and "At the Top of My Voice," would his image for us be quite different, and more like that created by his Soviet biographers and critics, who, on their side, tend to neglect the love lyric?

We must remember that Mayakovsky even when performing the function of a partisan-poet remained that peculiar and original phenomenon, Mayakovsky, and was always more poet than partisan. The nineteenth-century civic poet Nekrasov wrote: "A poet I may be, but a citizen I must be." Mayakovsky would have reversed that dictum: he was perfectly capable of being a citizen, even a propagandist, but could never escape the necessity of being a poet. The best illustration of this is a famous passage from the poem "Home!" where Mayakovsky attempts to describe his function as a poet. To make the point, the Russian text is here translated and transliterated:

Along with reports on pig iron and *steel*	S chugunom chtob i s vydelkoi *stali*
I want a report on verse production on behalf of the Politburo	o rabote stikhov, ot Politburo
	chtoby delal
From *Stalin*.	doklady *Stalin*

No doubt these lines written long before Stalin had reached his eminence had much to do with forming the latter's opinion of Mayakovsky as the "best and most talented poet of our Soviet epoch," but the lines do not contain the flattery he saw in them. The name *Stalin* (man of steel) was chosen, not from political but from poetic considerations: it furnishes both a pun and a rhyme for the word *stali* (steel). At the same time the choice of the particular person heightens the irony of the line and the humor of the pun, since the prosaic Stalin was the least suitable member of the Politburo to give a report on poetry.

The poem "Lenin," written on the occasion of Lenin's death, is a skillful piece of rhetoric which gives in a rhymed and readable capsule a summary of world history from the Marxist viewpoint and treats the figure of Lenin as a kind of predestined savior who appeared according to history's law at the moment of capitalism's decline and violent fall. Voronsky complained that the Lenin of the poem is a schematic and unreal figure in which no one can believe, yet here it would seem that a normally sensitive critic has missed the poetic point. Mayakovsky was not interested in the real Lenin, in his personal psychology or the nature of his peculiar political genius. Libedinsky reported that Mayakovsky flatly rejected any demand that he portray "individual psychology," and thus Voronsky's strictures on the poem are beside the point, though his remarks convey the spirit of the thing better than anything else that has been written about it: "Mayakovsky's Lenin is a figure of stone, frozen into an emblem. He doesn't walk, he marches; he doesn't act, he performs." Precisely so. The Lenin in Mayakovsky's poem is a myth. He is the messiah foretold in the scriptures of Marxist prophecy, and the story of his great deeds, like the chronicle of the Christian Savior, begins with the creation of the world. To criticize "Vladimir Ilych Lenin" as a serious biographical study is to be wide of the mark.

"At the Top of My Voice" is Mayakovsky's last important poem. It is a colloquy "at the top of his voice" with his comrades of the Communist future, who, he assures himself, will understand him and his verse, which "will break through into their lives like an aqueduct in our day, built by Roman slaves." The stirring imagery and wordplay of this poem remind us of the young Mayakovsky whose fire again flares up in them. But the verses we know under the title "At the Top of My Voice" are not the poem he was actually writing, but only an introduction to it. And they are not even the whole introduction but only the first part of it. "At the Top of My Voice" is a civic poem, boldly declaring Communist beliefs and presenting the poet as an agitator and a rabble rouser. There was to be a second introduction, and the few fragments found in his papers after his death reveal that the speaker of the second introduction was to have been a lyric Dr. Jekyll to the civic Mr. Hyde of the first, as soft and tender, indeed, as a cloud in pants:

> It's after one.
>   You must have gone to bed.
> The Milky Way runs like a silvery river through the night.
> I'm in no hurry
>   and with lightning telegrams
> There's no need to wake and worry you.
> As they say
>   the incident is closed
> The Love boat
>   has smashed against convention
> Now you and I are through
>   No need then
> To count over mutual pains, harms, and hurts.
> Just see how quiet the world is!
> Night has laid a heavy tax of stars upon the sky
> In hours like these you get up and you speak
> To the ages, to history, and to the universe.

Such was to have been the mood and style of the lyrical introduction. Six lines of this fragment Mayakovsky introduced into his suicide note, with the change of "you" to "life."

About the poem itself for which the double introduction was written nothing is known except that it was to have been about "The First Five-Year Plan." This final performance of Mayakovsky contains a symbolic commentary on his life. There is no easy answer to the question asked by normal people: who and what was he? Was he a convinced poet of the Revolution, or was he playing a part? Was he all wounded tenderness and sensitive to the slightest hurt or was that, too, a pose? What was the real poem to which his thirty-seven years provided only a double introduction? Perhaps there is no answer to a question such as this. Pasternak, who hated the Mayakovsky monument and was deaf to his revolutionary poetry, has provided a cryptic answer in his remark that "Mayakovsky, disdaining to play a part in life, played at life itself."

Poets of Different Camps

Mayakovsky's tragic fate as a poet in the service of the Revolution takes on special, poignant overtones when he is considered in the company of poets who were his contemporaries but not necessarily his comrades and friends. For it is well to remember that his civic poetry of the twenties was not widely favored by other great poets of the day, most of whom were deaf to his agitational verse, if indeed they were not repelled by it. Alexander Blok, who died in 1921, was a special case.

The Symbolist Blok was a favorite of Mayakovsky, who spoke and wrote about him with warm respect. Soon after the Revolution Blok, one of the last legatees of nineteenth-century Russian intellectual culture and one who had experienced in his own person the savage liquidation of that culture then in process, secluded himself for a few days to write a magnificent account in verse of what was happening at the moment on the streets of Petrograd. In his poem *The Twelve* (1918), he included some eloquent poetic speculation on the meaning of the Revolution in the relentless spiral of human history. His performance in that poem reflects the poet's personal defeat and the heavy loss he and his class had suffered, but it carries at the same time his conviction that the horror he celebrates is necessary and even "good." Mayakovsky in his brief obituary "Alexander Blok Is Dead" wrote of a meeting with the poet: "I remember during the first days after the Revolution I was walking past a thin, bent figure looking like a soldier and warming himself at a bonfire set out in front of the Winter Palace. Somebody called to me. It was Blok. And I asked him 'How do you like this?' 'It's good' Blok said, then he added: 'On my estate in the country they burned my library.' 'It's good,' and 'They burned my library,' were the two contrasting apprehensions of the Revolution linked fantastically in his poem *The Twelve.* Some found in this poem a satire on the Revolution, others a celebration."

Ambivalence pervades that poem, and contrast is its structural principle. The line "Black is the night—White is the snow" opens a poem which features alternately revolutionary marching songs, slogans, factory songs, the orthodox liturgy for the dead, colloquial vulgarity, popular sentimental songs. It has been called a polyphonic poem, in the sense that nearly every voice in it is distinct from every other, and all are distinct from the author himself. His own voice occurs only in occasional asides and, of course, in the final solemnly triumphant lines which tell us of the apparition of Jesus Christ ascendant in the end. The poem exemplifies the linguistic revolution that was taking place in the streets and that would penetrate literature: the clash of low dialect with the finely developed standard language, the language of literature and of poetry that Blok himself had done so much to fashion. Mayakovsky too, with his use of raucous street rhythms, had been an early reflection of this process.

Blok's *The Twleve* is a Symbolist poem, but it bears the mark of Mayakovsky in language and imagery. It expresses also the shock of horror experienced both by the opponents and by the propagators of revolution when they looked into its face. That shock would become a regular component of Russian literature during the Soviet period, as witness the work of Babel, Pilnyak, Ivanov, Solzhenitsyn, Platonov, Aleshkovsky, Zinoviev, and many others. Mayakovsky was one of the first, after Blok, to experience that shock of surprise and dismay when he dealt with the most persistent enemy of originality in art and literature: the Soviet philistine.

Anna Akhmatova (1899–1966), one of the major poets of the century, offers a contrast both to the Symbolist Blok and to the Futurist Mayakovsky. Her verses when they first appeared in 1912 (the year also of Mayakovsky's first publication) took deliberate issue with Symbolist poetics, rejecting its mystical vocabulary in favor of reconstituting in poetry the body and texture of real things, their concrete olfactory, visual, and auditory existence. She was a contrast to Mayakovsky in both the private locale of her poems and the register of her voice. As Korney Chukovsky put it: "It would be hard to imagine two human beings less alike than Akhmatova and Mayakovsky. Akhmatova is shrouded in silence, in whispered, almost inaudible words. Mayakovsky shouts like a thousand-throated public square."

Her attitude toward the Revolution was unfriendly, and for long periods nothing of hers appeared in print, yet she remained her whole life in Russia. When, in 1946, there was the beginning of a revival of interest in her work, she was viciously attacked by Stalin's cultural specialist Zhdanov (see chapter 9). She suffered the execution of her husband, the poet Gumilyov, and the arrest and imprisonment of her son, events in her life commemorated in a long and sorrowing lament, the poem "Requiem" (1963). Her best poem of the last period, "Poem without a Hero" (1961) is devoted to the events and the people in her life, and the history of her time. The last two have never been published in the Soviet Union.

Mayakovsky's principal rival during the twenties was Sergey Yesenin (1895–1925). Yesenin's specialty was village scenes and village memories; his poems are melodious and highly singable, and many of them have been set to music. The harsh urban accent that marks Mayakovsky is foreign to Yesenin. The city in his work is an infernal place, and industrial progress only awakens nostalgia for the old Russian village. He is, in fact, an early progenitor of the village writers of the sixties and seventies (see chapter 14). Mayakovsky, during Yesenin's life and even after his suicide, berated him as backward and decadent. In fact Yesenin's suicide was the occasion for a long poem that pronounced an anathema on "yeseninist" attitudes that were widespread at the time.

Two major poets roughly contemporary with Mayakovsky, Osip

Mandelshtam (1891–1938) and Nikolai Zabolotsky (1903–1958), were removed as far as possible from Mayakovsky's poetics and his politics. Mandelshtam is one of the outstanding lyric poets of modern times and a major figure in the pre-Soviet period of Russian literature. His work has attracted and taxed the ingenuity of the most acute literary critics and theorists. He is himself a major literary critic, and his prose essays on many literary topics fill a large volume. Mirsky maintained that Mandelshtam's essays written before the Revolution contained "perhaps the most remarkable, unprejudiced, and independent things that have ever been said on modern Russian civilization and the art of poetry."

Mandelshtam was a contrast not only to Mayakovsky but to most other contemporaries in that he was magnificently erudite, deeply conscious not only of the Russian past but of the long human enterprise in the invention and building of culture. In some of his most moving poems he links his own work as a poetic craftsman to that of the architects who constructed Notre Dame and Saint Sophia and associates himself enthusiastically with the medieval builders who fashioned lacy gothic patterns out of heavy stone. His work as a poet involved the making of verbal structures that take fully into account all the hidden weights and stresses in words themselves. The pursuit of his meaning is a surprisingly rich and rewarding process. His work does not yield easily to translation.

After 1933 Mandelshtam was practically banished from Soviet literature, and he died in 1938 in a transit prison camp in Vladivostok. He was "rehabilitated" in 1956, and in the sixties and seventies modest selections from his works were published in the Soviet Union. His complete collected works were published only in the United States under the editorship of Gleb Struve and Boris Filippov from 1955 to 1972.

The career of Mandelshtam in Russian literature gave rise to two volumes of memoirs by his widow, Nadezhda Mandelshtam, *Hope against Hope* (*Vospominaniya*, 1970), and *Hope Abandoned* (*Vtoraya kniga*, 1972). Based on her life with Mandelshtam and their experience in the literary and political worlds for the sixteen years they were together, those volumes are not only a literary and historical source of surpassing value, they are also a work of art. In them she succeeds in creating an aesthetic structure out of the facts of her own life, out of the genius and destiny of a great poet, her husband, and the very large array of characters they knew. There is great power in her writing, and a vital fund of insight that endows even despicable men and women with human verisimilitude.

Nikolai Zabolotsky is a poet who stands apart from his contemporaries in many ways. Perhaps a key to understanding him is that very early he wrote verse and prose for children, and that he was associated with the Russian "Absurdists" of the twenties and thirties, who called themselves "Oberiu," a coinage formed from the Russian words for Association for Real Art; he was one of the authors of their 1928 manifesto. He was probably influenced by the early Futurists' experimentation with poetic language. His first book of verse, *Scrolls (Stolbtsy,* 1929), presents weird, nightmarish views of Leningrad in the twenties, featuring items of everyday life in a surreal displacement, reducing the mighty city depicted in Gogol and Dostoevsky to a grotesque. His literary style left him open to the suspicion of being at best antirealist and at worst antihuman. He was stupidly and violently attacked for *Scrolls*, as also for the long poem "Triumph of Agriculture" (1933) written at the height of the collectivization program. The ironic structure of a poem which speaks of death and the soul, in which animals converse about their sufferings and the dead participate in debates on the after life, a poem featuring both parody and the grotesque, was interpreted by the ignorant as a lampoon on the collectivization program. The stamp of suspicion plainly on him, Zabolotsky was arrested in 1938, brutally interrogated, and sentenced to five years at hard labor. His own account of his arrest, maltreatment, and imprisonment, published only many years after his death in the *Times Literary Supplement* (October 9, 1981), is important evidence on one aspect of literary life during the Great Purge. After his release Zabolotsky abandoned the style of his early poems in favor of a quieter, more lucid style, and a contemplative, philosophical treatment of nature. His work, both early and late, is among the freshest and most original Russian poetry of the twentieth century.

Marina Tsvetaeva (1892–1941) also belongs to prerevolutionary poetry and to exile literature. Since she held herself aloof from the literary schools of the day, she fits no easy classification. She was married to an officer in the White Army and emigrated to Prague and then to Paris in 1925. Nor did she fit into the Parisian *émigré* ambience, though some recognized her superb gift as a poet. Her judgments and her poetic preferences seemed to the *émigrés* paradoxical if not eccentric. Her two "favorite contemporaries" were Mayakovsky and Pasternak, a vociferous ironic poet and an experimental lyricist. On the occasion of Mayakovsky's death she wrote a cycle of seven poems celebrating a poet whose genius stood above politics and propaganda, and in a superb essay, "Epic and Lyric in Contemporary Russia" (1932), she linked Mayakovsky and Pasternak as the great poetic spokesmen of the age: "If I place Pasternak and Mayakovsky side by side . . . I do so in order to show forth doubly something which with God's grace might happen once in half a century but here is manifested by nature twice in half a decade: the full, absolute, perfect miracle of a poet."

Tsvetaeva's own lyrics combine certain features of Pasternak and Mayakovsky. Her syntax is often like Pasternak's in its colloquial ellipsis and frequent omission of verbs, and her diction is sometimes reminiscent of Mayakovsky in her use of harshly vulgar colloquial expressions. She produced in colloquial language poetic statements of shattering emotional experience, as well as elevated and eloquent treatment of mythological or fairy-tale subjects. Her poetic genius was kaleidoscopic, impossible to fix or classify.

She returned in 1939 to Russia, where the literary establishment's attitude toward her ranged from indifference to odious hostility. She committed suicide in 1941, an event foreshadowed even in her earliest verse, which speaks of early death as a crowning happiness.[17]

Velimir Khlebnikov (1885–1922) was one of the most important figures in the prewar Futurist movement, and though his contribution to Russian literature "since the Revolution" was modest, his earlier work of discovery in the possibilities of poetic language was important to many modern poets, including Mayakovsky, who spoke of him as "that discoverer of new continents that we now cultivate and populate." Yet the revolutionary regime had little understanding or use for him, and he died without honor.

Mayakovsky's other great contemporary was Pasternak, with whom I shall deal in a later chapter. The tragic destiny in revolutionary Russia of many poets—and we could expand the list—some of whom were Mayakovsky's peers and who shared with him the same poetic space, sheds somber light on his own ambivalent feelings about the reality of the "revolution" whose spokesman he had become.

3   Prophets of a Brave
New World

The Machine and England

Mayakovsky, whom Stalin proclaimed "the best and most talented poet of our Soviet epoch," and Eugene Zamyatin, who left the Soviet Union under a cloud in 1931, are both concerned with the problem of how separate items of humanity are to be related to the inescapable mass. Both devise literary images of the Communist future, and both deal with the effect on human beings of, in Mayakovsky's phrase, "the machine and England." Both study love and investigate sex, speculating on the modifications that may one day occur in these areas of individual experience as subjective feeling gives way to the rational organization of life. Each is an innovator in his own literary medium, Mayakovsky as a poet, and Zamyatin as a novelist, short-story writer, and critic. Zamyatin is, like Mayakovsky, a declared enemy of fixed philistine values in literature and in life. Zamyatin's hatred for the established and secure was no less than Mayakovsky's, and his contempt for the servants of *byt*, an enemy which he knew under the term "entropy," was equal to Mayakovsky's.

Zamyatin is a self-conscious mirror of a world in violent process, and therefore his prose tends to the grotesque in both form and content. His art, to use his own phrase, portrays the world as it might be seen in a storm from the mast of a ship listing at a forty-five-degree angle "when the green jaws of the sea are gaping, and the ship itself is cracking." At such times it is impossible to present land- and seascapes of settled Euclidean dimensions.

Zamyatin's writings—his novels and stories as well as his essays—
are a systematic defense of heresy as a way of life. Perhaps the best
statement of his "philosophy" is from an essay entitled "On Literature,
Revolution, and Entropy":

> If you were to ask the straight question "What is revolution?"
> you would get many answers.
>
> Some would answer à la Louis XIV: "The revolution, *c'est moi*";
> some would answer according to the calendar, giving the month
> and year; some would answer by spelling out the word. But if we
> proceed from spelling to speaking, then we must say the following:
>
> Two dead, dark stars collide with an unheard but deafening
> thunder, and they give fiery birth to a new star: that is what is
> meant by revolution. A molecule tears free of its orbit and, invad-
> ing a neighboring atomic universe, gives birth to a new chemical
> element: that is what is meant by revolution. Lobachevsky [a pio-
> neer in non-Euclidean geometry] with a single book burns out the
> walls of the thousand-year-old Euclidian world: and that is what is
> meant by revolution.

Zamyatin, who was educated as an engineer, was sent to England
during the First World War by the Russian government, where he took
part in the construction of the ship *Alexander Nevsky*, an icebreaker intended for use in the Arctic Ocean. At the same time he gathered materials for his first novel, *Islanders*, partly written in England during his
stay there and published in Petrograd in 1918.

This short novel is a satirical treatment of British middle-class respectability, as Zamyatin, not without the help of Shaw and Wells, was
able to perceive that phenomenon. His experience of England was neither wide nor prolonged, and the novel is rather a piece of literary autobiography than an objective commentary on that experience. The work
does reveal the main concerns of Zamyatin both as a thinker and as a
literary stylist, and it must be regarded as a kind of preliminary sketch
for the later novel on which his renown is based: *We*. The British middle class, both the source and the product of industrial civilization, repelled him by the rigid demands of its code of respectability. Under
such a regime the individual human personality, held firm in the forms
of convention, must either atrophy or rebel. In *Islanders*, the chief bearer
of ideas and attitudes repugnant to Zamyatin is a certain Vicar Dooley,
the author of a work called *The Testament of Compulsory Salvation*. In
order to achieve both holiness and happiness, Vicar Dooley had
worked out a rational schedule for all necessary human activities. According to this schedule, which is displayed in Mr. Dooley's library,
certain hours were set aside for taking food, certain days for repentance

(three per week), and certain others for charitable activities, and a portion of each day was reserved for walking in the fresh air. There was at the end of the list a final item which concerned Mrs. Dooley and where the modest notation was made: "Saturday of every third week." Mrs. Dooley, should she invite caresses at times set aside for other things, heard the following gentle remonstrance: "My dear, this may seem a very slight deviation from the rules, but you must remember what I say in Chapter II of my Testament: our lives should move like graceful and well-made machines, and with mechanical certainty proceed to the desired goal."

For Vicar Dooley the "desired goal" is salvation and the promised bliss. He believes, moreover, that his strict moral regimen should be enforced throughout England, and it is his intention to have Parliament adopt a bill making it obligatory upon all. And why not? Shouldn't everyone be compelled to save his soul? "Far better that we should be slaves of the Lord than free sons of Satan." In Dooley, Zamyatin has created a grotesque caricature of bourgeois respectability braced by religious dogma but having ultimate recourse to the police.

The main character, Campbell, whose life has up to the time we meet him held strictly to the rails of propriety, and who is repeatedly compared to a machine, suddenly and unaccountably loses control when he meets a music hall entertainer by the name of Didi. But he has been so well trained by his mother, Lady Campbell (who thinks the faces of cultivated people should all be alike, in fact, a cultivated person "should not really have a face"), that even this "deplorable and unconventional" liaison he seeks to make regular, respectable, and decent. He would marry the girl. They must have a house in the suburbs with furniture in it, and he will buy her an electric iron. The house, the furniture, and the electric iron must be acquired before the marriage in order to give it a frame of respectability.

The representatives of British respectability are contrasted, following a literary convention that Zamyatin's Russian readers may not have been aware of, with a carefree Irishman named O'Kelley, who is disorganized, funny, and immoral, and who practices nonconformity as a matter of principle. "Have you heard?" he says to Didi. "A bill has been brought into Parliament to force all Britons to have noses of the same length. And why not? This difference in nose length is the only remaining one, and it must be done away with. Then they will all be as alike as buttons, or as Ford cars."

Zamyatin in *Islanders* not only provides a preview of the main themes of *We* but practices the literary devices that he would later use in that novel to such good effect. Characters are identified by the device of the repeated metaphor: Campbell is regularly a "lumbering truck," then "a truck out of control." Or they are metonymically associated with objects that typify them for the reader: for instance Mrs. Dooley's "basic organ" is her pince-nez. Vivid, impressionistic pictures are provided by a few simple line strokes: the "two brows of a face raised to form a triangle." The narration moves in a brisk staccato, with swift ellipses and insistent repetition of key visual images. The eye of Zamyatin's camera moves abruptly from one scene to another. Zamyatin is a mannered literary artist whose style belongs to the school of Remizov and Bely, and to that style Zamyatin has given the fillip of his own preoccupation with modern mathematics, which no doubt made congenial to him the systematic distortion of those visual images based on the old-fashioned geometry. The effect of his imagery in *Islanders* is to render fantastic the prosaic characters and scenes of contemporary London, and that same style in the later novel *We* is a perfect instrument for the creation of a genuinely fantastic world.

Islanders is an important event in Russian literary history, for the novel places in clear focus the real nature of Zamyatin's rebellion against the machine and mechanized civilization. The novel *Islanders* was obviously not inspired by an apocalyptic vision of a future society governed by the proletarian mass; rather it describes an industrial society of the present dominated by a smug and conformist middle class. The author of that mass regimentation which Zamyatin in *We* foresaw as the future lot of mankind was not backward Russia but the industrialized West, and the Table of Hours imposed on the people of the twenty-ninth century by the benevolent dictator in *We* is nothing else but Vicar Dooley's rules and schedules. Zamyatin's rebellion, then, is not against any particular version of the modern mass society. It is not directed at socialism or Communism as such but rather at forms of the regimentation which has resulted from the growth of a huge and complex industrial civilization. The burden of rebellion against the rational gods of Ford, F. W. Taylor, and Vicar Dooley is carried in *Islanders* by the disorganized Irishman, O'Kelley, the demimondaine Didi, and Campbell himself, in whom the irrational forces at last break free of confinement. In *Islanders* Zamyatin rejects "the machine and England," and presents as their antagonists a few unpunctual and happy-go-lucky individualists, themselves conventional bohemians. And the reader is certain that they will be crushed by the Lady Campbells and the Vicar Dooleys. Zamyatin's problem is similar to that of Mayakovsky in his last two plays and in his life as a whole, but the solution suggested by Zamyatin is, as we shall see, the reverse of Mayakovsky's.

The political environment of Eugene Zamyatin, the Russia of

1918–1919, was one in which the mass had triumphed—at least according to the official version—and where collective interests transcended the individual. There were self-styled proletarian poets and writers who proclaimed in sonorous verse that there could be no more individual heroes: the great laboring mass of humanity is now the hero, they said, in history, and must be the hero in our literary works. "The collective 'We' has driven out the personal 'I'," shouted the youthful Bezymensky, and among the proletarian poets and novelists there developed a mystic belief in the collective as an entity in which the individual finds happiness by losing himself, like a Buddhist saint in nirvana. The regimented paradise was a frequent theme of the poet and novelist Gastev, a member of the Smithy group of proletarian poets, whose eloquence on this subject had a cosmic swing. He wrote:

> The mechanization, not only of gestures, not only of production methods, but of everyday thinking, coupled with extreme rationality, normalizes in a striking degree the psychology of the proletariat ... It is this that lends proletarian psychology such surprising anonymity, which permits the qualification of separate proletarian units as A, B, C, or as 325,075, or as O, and the like. In this normalization of psychology and its dynamism is the key to the prodigious elementariness of proletarian thinking ... In this psychology, from one end of the world to the other, flow potent massive streams, making for one world head in place of millions of heads. This tendency will next imperceptibly render individual thinking impossible, and thought will become the objective psychic process of a whole class, with systems of psychological switches and locks.

Proletarian poets of the Smithy group not only proclaimed the total regimentation of this world as a consummation devoutly to be wished, but celebrated in their verse the spread of such a system to other worlds as yet unknown that are scattered through the cosmos. This quasi-religious tendency came to be known as "planetarity." Its sources were to be found both in literature and in science. The science-fiction fantasies of H. G. Wells and his imitators had a pronounced influence in Russia. A more immediate and more Russian influence were the works of the scientist Tsiolkovsky, who had written popular works on such topics as rocket propulsion, intercontinental missiles, and interplanetary travel, and whose lectures at the literary studios of the Proletcult undoubtedly influenced young proletarian poets. Another probable source of proletarian "planetarity" were the Symbolists who taught "verse-making" to these poets. Perhaps the striving for a quite literal "communion with other worlds" through science, in proletarian poetry of the early period, is only a rationalist version of the metaphysical-religious search of the early Symbolists.

At the very moment when the mass man was being celebrated in prose and verse Zamyatin wrote the novel ironically entitled *We*, certainly the most humorous and probably the most perceptive of the twentieth-century negative utopias. Written in Russia in 1919 and 1920 and published in English in 1924 but never published in Russia, *We* belongs to the family of modern novels which forecast for us in the future a dehumanized, machine-made world, a dull world organized for the greatest good of the greatest number, aimed at building paradise on earth. Huxley's *Brave New World*, published in 1932, echoes many of Zamyatin's themes, and George Orwell's *1984* owes a fully acknowledged debt to Zamyatin but differs from *We* in some important particulars. Compared with either work Zamyatin's novel turns out to be superior in its quality of ironic humor. Zamyatin himself described *We* as his "most jocular" work, and it is best read not as a dire prophecy of modern Fascism or Communism, but as a very funny commentary on the vagaries of reason. It resembles not so much Samuel Butler as Anatole France, who was a favorite of Zamyatin and whose spirit communicated itself to him. Zamyatin might have said of *We* what France said of his own work: "The irony which I acknowledge is not cruel, it does not make fun of love nor of beauty; but it teaches us to laugh at those who are mean and stupid, and without this laughter we might allow ourselves the weakness of hating them."

The story of *We* is based on the diaries of one of the leading mathematicians in a state of the twenty-ninth century. We see the precisely regimented world of that day through his eyes. At first, as a loyal mathematician and as builder of the space ship *Integral*, which is to carry the message of reason to distant worlds, the author of the diaries moves with perfect contentment as an obedient wheel in the social mechanism. But reason breaks down when he finds that not everything in the world is reducible to logarithmic systems. And that is the theme of the novel.

In *We* human beings of the twenty-ninth century are citizens of a city-state known as the Only State. The civilization of that day represents the final triumph of the *city*, the last step in civilization. In the course of a two hundred years' war which the people of the twenty-ninth century have only read about in their history books, the city had finally been victorious over the country. This terribly destructive war isolated one city from another and destroyed existing civilization. Only two-tenths of one percent of the world's population survived the holocaust. After the invention of an artificial petroleum food had made the city independent of the country, the city dwellers cut themselves off from nature. Almost all surviving human beings were walled up in the city and sealed off from the country by a wall of glass. Inside the Glass

Wall all life is rationally organized, and the benevolent state controls everything. There can be no accidents, no surprises: nothing unexpected ever happens, in fact nothing just happens, everything enters into the plan. Human reason, in its Euclidean variant, is all-powerful, and the aspect of the city presents only straight lines, planes, right angles, and neat diagonals. The streets and the houses are of glass, and, like the Crystal Palace which was for Dostoevsky the symbol of scientific rationalism, hard, shiny and square. The inhabitants have never even seen a tangled, mixed-up structure such as a tree, or stepped on any surface that wasn't level and smooth.

Outside the Glass Wall there is only the debris of nature, wild, uncontrolled, free growth, and strange, imperfectly organized beings. It develops that a small remnant of the human race had been forgotten and left behind outside the wall, but these people have fallen in the scale and become like animals. While one part of the human race has developed entirely along rational lines, the other part has preserved primitive, instinctive impulses and feelings. Zamyatin's point in this novel would seem to be that only through the union of the two parts could a fully human being again develop. Zamyatin finds hope in the irrational creatures that had been left "outside the wall"—only they can revivify and rehumanize life within the wall. Revolutionists in the Only State propose to tear down the wall that separates them from nature. George Orwell develops a similar idea when he indicates that a part of the human race in 1984 has been left out of the regimented society. The *proles* in that novel, descendants of the proletarians of our day, have been allowed to sink to a prehuman level and are regarded as no better than slaves. But when a rebel from the civilized community looks for hope for the future of humanity he can find it only in the *proles*, who have maintained the old human feelings of love, desire, and honor, and still have some memory of poetry. O'Kelley and Didi in *Islanders*, with their fondness for song and story, also represent the human feelings that go on living "outside the wall."

In the regimented paradise of Zamyatin's *We*, the concept of an individual human being has already died out, and it is possible to speak only of "we." The citizens do not have names, but only numbers; they are called "numbers," or "unifs," a corruption of an old word meaning uniform. Politically the organization of the state is so perfect that no thought, no initiative, and no action is ever required of the citizens. The chief officer of the state, the Benefactor, is an iron-willed, mercilessly loving father image and god substitute. He strives always for the welfare of the "numbers," and their whole duty is to obey, honor, and—yes—worship him. His name, and pronouns referring to Him, are capitalized. The name is mentioned only in hushed reverence or in anger:

when the citizens swear, it is not by the long-dead gods, but "by the Benefactor." (It will be remembered that in Huxley's *Brave New World* Ford had become a deity to be sworn by.) The earthly paradise has need of security forces. They are called the Guardians, and they hover protectively over the citizen at all times, displaying the most benevolent interest in his reading habits, listening to his conversations, observing the expression of his face for evidence of thought. Every citizen expects a slight delay in the delivery of mail, since all letters must first be read in the Bureau of Guardians. And the Guardians operate a mechanism called "The Machine," a terribly modern contrivance for executing political criminals, wherein those who defy the Benefactor are atomized—an advance over "liquidation." D-503, the narrator, in his moments of rational calm, likens the institution of the Guardians, with its care for the welfare of every citizen, to the system of "guardian angels" in which the ancients believed.

There are elections, regularly held on the Day of Unanimity. The suffrage is universal, and the voting is open and above board. The good citizens of the Only State have no desire for the slinking secrecy in the voting process which the ancients favored, for each one wants everyone to know that *he* votes for the Benefactor.

All life is social life, and every moment is scheduled. D-503 regards the ancients as having been particularly primitive in this respect, and he finds it hard even to imagine how life would have been without precise regimentation.

> I have had opportunity to read and hear many improbable things about those times when human beings still lived in the state of freedom, that is in an unorganized, primitive state . . . How could a government, even a primitive government, permit people to live without anything like our Tables—without compulsory walks, without precise regulation of the time to eat, for instance? They would get up and go to bed whenever they liked!

He willingly admits that his own society has not yet attained complete perfection, since two hours out of the twenty-four in each day are set aside for the "numbers" to do as they please, but he derives comfort from the reflection that with the progress of science and reason in human affairs at long last all 86,400 seconds of the day will be organized and supervised by the state. "Let them call me an idealist and a dreamer, I believe that sooner or later we shall find a place in the general formula even for the personal hours," he wrote in his diary. He regards the most nearly perfect product of ancient twentieth-century literature to have been the railway timetable.

Love and its sexual expression have been controlled. Hunger and

Love no longer rule the world. The *Lex Sexualis* of the twenty-ninth century declares that "any number has the right to use any other number as a sexual article." This law ended the irrational situation (and unjust as well) in which there were some whom everyone preferred and others whom no one preferred. And it is easy to see how much mischief such a law eliminates from human life: the pang of unrequited love, the madness of jealousy, the suicides, the novels of Turgenev, "The Backbone Flute," all of these things have been rendered quite obsolete by the promulgation of this simple, healthful law.

One of the scheduled hours in the Table is the personal hour, the only time of the day when the "numbers," all of whom live in glass houses, have the right to draw their shades.

> The rest is only a matter of technique. You are carefully examined in the laboratory of the Sexual Department where they find the content of the sexual hormones in your blood, and they accordingly make out for you a Table of sexual days. Then you file an application to enjoy the services of Number so-and-so (or Numbers so-and-so). You get for this purpose a checkbook (pink). That is all.
>
> ... The thing which was for the ancients a source of innumerable stupid tragedies has been converted in our time into a harmonious, agreeable, and useful function of the organism, a function like sleep, physical labor, the taking of food, defecation, and so forth.

Literature and the arts have, like love, been freed of the irrational. Poets there are, and tons of poetry are produced, but it is unthinkable that a poet, a member of the Institution of State Poets and Authors, should write about anything that happened to come into his head. Poets have been domesticated and harnessed. They perform a state service, and their poetry is a commodity.

Music is produced entirely by mechanical means; tunes are turned out in the factory—the same ones for the whole population. George Orwell lived at a time when television and radio had reached a high level of development, and the *1984* "Telescreen" produces programs which are obligatory for all—there is only one channel, and you can't turn it off. Zamyatin could not know of the technological advances which would later in the century convert the media of mass communication into a terrible menace, but he does foreshadow the immediate future with remarkable insight in this repellent image of the Musical Factory producing soothing music to which everyone must listen.

Yet there is revolution brewing even in this perfectly regimented society, and the Number on whose diaristic notes the novel is based, D–503, finds its ferment inside himself. As he writes, his attitude toward life in the Only State subtly changes. He had thought that his relations with other human beings were coldly codified, but suddenly he falls in love—with a particular woman. His love is desperate, irrational and out of control. The turmoil in his mind shows itself in confused and dreamlike images in his writing. He develops a flair for original metaphors. (He could even have written "The Backbone Flute.") He dreams. As his illness grows worse, reality sometimes seems to fuse and flow; at other times the world seems fragmented. His thoughts occur not in ordered and logical sequence but in swift telegraphic impulses. And he finds that there are many rebels: his pink-cheeked girl friend O-90, who is below the maternal norm but wants a baby anyway; his friend and official poet, R-13; S-4711, a member of the Guardians, who is a secret revolutionary; and the object of his bursting love, I-330, who is actually a leader in the revolutionary plot to break down the wall and let into the city the primitive creatures from the surrounding woods. I-330 it is who initiates him into the secrets of life in the twentieth century. She sheds her uniform for a saffron-yellow dress, smokes cigarettes (very harmful!), and drinks a queer tasting greenish liquid with a heady effect. She takes him to a house of that era preserved in glass, the "Ancient House." There is the bust of a poet (Pushkin) in the house and furniture of irregular geometry. She takes him outside the wall where the hairy creatures on whom the future now depends have a meeting. And the builder of the *Integral*, D-503, infatuated with all of this, recovers his sanity only after an operation has removed from his brain the center of fantasy. Only then is he as good as a machine and capable of perfect happiness.

Zamyatin is not entirely pessimistic about the human future, and the novel simply does not contain the frightening prophecy which has been ascribed to it. The leader of the Only State, the Benefactor, only *seems* to have complete control; there are many revolutionaries—in fact almost all the characters we meet are in the movement—and rebellion is still in progress with the issue in doubt as the novel ends. As revolution rages on the streets of the city, D-503 finds refuge from it in the men's room of a subway station:

> I do not remember how I got into one of the public rest rooms, in a station of the subway. Above, everything was perishing; the greatest civilization, the most rational in human history, was crumbling, but here, by some irony, everything remained as before, beautiful. The walls shone; water murmured cozily; and like the water, the unseen, transparent music . . . Only think of it! All this is doomed; all this will be covered with grass some day; only myths will remain.

There is much in common between Mayakovsky's play *The Bedbug* and *We,* written about ten years earlier. No doubt Mayakovsky was consciously engaging Zamyatin in dispute over the importance of the values which, both agree, would probably disappear in a rational world. Mayakovsky ridicules Prisypkin's "heart strings," his individualism, and his dirty indulgence in cigarettes and vodka. For Zamyatin, in both *Islanders* and *We,* in the twentieth as well as the twenty-ninth century, these things are symbols of rebellion against social regimentation. The quality of Zamyatin's rebellion is neither political nor soundly philosophical. It is bohemian. The "Ancient House" where I–330 arranges assignations with her lover, the mathematician D–503, is an apartment in Soho, or a spot in Greenwich Village. And though his vision of future men serried into ranks of human anonymity may seem horrible to us, surely the hairy creatures "outside the wall" are more horrible. And Zamyatin must have known that primitives are never as free as civilized men and that a sense of individual worth has developed as civilizations became more complex.

Defective though it may be as an anti-utopia, Zamyatin's *We* is a truly great book which will probably outlive most of its relatives in the genre. With satiric scorn, it offers a quintessential image of any and all Establishments, religious or social, bourgeois or Communist, that seek to enforce their particular and temporary values on all human beings as eternal verities. D–503, in his period of naïve adjustment to the Benefactor and the Only State, had believed that the revolution that created that state was the last one. Zamyatin could observe in the Bolshevik revolutionaries of his own day evidences of a developing conservatism and hostility to change. The October Revolution, they thought, was the last one. The young woman I–330 challenges this doctrine of finality: "There is no such thing as a 'last' revolution. The number of revolutions is infinite."

Zamyatin's influence was felt by many writers of the Serapion Brotherhood, though probably no surviving member would admit this, and he was an esteemed and influential figure in the Writers' Union until attacked as a literary enemy in 1929 and relieved of his post as a member of the executive board. His work is hardly known to the present generation of Soviet readers, and his name is mentioned in the recent three-volume *History of Soviet Literature* only in order to characterize him as an anti-Soviet "inner *émigré*," who joined the "outer emigration." That work quotes his ironic survey of contemporary letters in 1921, *I'm Afraid,* in which he maintained that since proletarian literature was a "step backward," and the real writers, "madmen, hermits, heretics, dreamers, rebels, and skeptics," were silent, it followed that Russian literature had only one possible future: its past. His stories "The Cave" (1922) and "Flood" (1930) are mentioned only as indicating a certain reprehensible tendency. His tales of Petrograd in the grip of hunger— "Mamai," for instance, which catches in lucid metaphor the essence of life reduced to subhuman privation—are passed over without intelligent comment. His *Impious Tales* are not mentioned, nor are his early works *The Province* (1913) and *Far Away* (1914), set in the Russian backwoods, and featuring a *skaz* narrative style. Zamyatin's brilliant essays on Anatole France, and on the work of H. G. Wells, with whom he had many things in common, as well as his portraits of the literary men he knew, are evidence of fine human and literary sophistication. His own roots reach into the purely Russian style of Leskov, Remizov, and Bely, whose ornamental wordplay he admired. Zamyatin drew his strength as a writer from the Russian tradition, and at the same time had a lively appreciation of Western literature. The Soviet authorities who have decreed that he is to be ignored are defeating themselves. They have "thrown a pearl away, richer than all their tribe."[1]

Olesha's Critique of the Reason

The creatures who rule the world of *We* rely on the power of human reason to return that world, after its adventure in revolution, to predetermined logical shapes. They would deprive man of his fantasy, because that faculty is not always obedient to reason, containing an element of individual caprice. The man who lives by fantasy creates a private world of his own and may thus become a subject for medical attention.

Or he may become an artist. Indeed an artist by nature possesses and exercises the power of fantasy; this is the message contained in the work of Yury Olesha, who died in 1960 at the age of 61, having produced only his famous novel *Envy* (1927), a few magnificent short stories, a fairy tale for adults and children, *The Three Fat Men* (1924), one full-length play, *A List of Benefits* (1931), a number of movie scenarios, some critical articles and fugitive literary comments, and brief reminiscences of his contemporaries. His autobiographical novel, entitled *Not a Day without a Line*, was published in full in 1965. It combines reminiscence with intensely personal literary reflections.[2]

The "Complete Works" of Yury Olesha do not bulk large in Soviet literature, nor do they have a prominent place in the consciousness of the contemporary Soviet reader. After an explosive success with the novel *Envy* in 1927, Olesha fell silent and was largely forgotten during the thirties. The reason for his silence he stated himself with disarming frankness in a speech to the First Congress of Soviet Writers: "The First

Five-Year Plan was not my theme. I could have gone to a construction project, lived at a factory among workers ... but that was not my theme." What, then, was Olesha's theme? The principal object of his artistic interest is the particular and unique quality of every human experience: the individual flavor of a particular person, the shape of daylight at a given place and time, the unexpected look of a clock's face pointing to 3:15, the fantasy effect of long shadows in a northern latitude, sunlight reflected in a bronze vase or broken into its spectrum of color by a mother-of-pearl button. Olesha re-creates the world as a child might see it: a world of direct sense impressions which, unnamed and as yet uncatalogued, still have the freshness of surprise. The Formalist critics who influenced Olesha, Victor Shklovsky in particular, emphasized the importance for literary art of such devices as the "estrangement" and the "deformation" of reality. The artist, said Shklovsky, by breaking the fixed pattern of verbal or sensuous experience, forces the beholder of art to see again simple things which he had taken for granted, or to hear again the actual sounds of speech. Estrangement of reality in Olesha does not, except in the fairy tale, *The Three Fat Men*, consist in the construction of an unreal and nonexistent world. That is not the source of Olesha's fantasy. Rather it is the rich world of experience which the individual mind can create for itself out of the simplest reality, just by paying attention to it—a stone, for instance. In a wonderful story called "The Cherry Pit" Olesha introduces a fairy tale about a young man who was "in too much of a hurry to throw a stone." He threw it, but in throwing it—in treating it according to its definition as a "thing to be thrown"—he had lost forever its special and unique reality:

> With the stone in my hand I stood about four paces from the wall. The stone was supposed to fall into the niche and stay there. I swung my arm and let it go. The stone flew away and hit the brick. There was a short spurt of dust. I had missed. The stone fell in the bushes at the base of the wall. It was only then I heard the stone's cry, uttered while it was in my hand and before I let it go.
> "Wait!" it cried. "Look at me!" And then I actually remembered. I should have subjected the stone to an inspection. Why, really, that stone was a remarkable thing. And now it's disappeared there in the bushes! And though I held it in my hand I don't even know what color it was. But maybe it was a lilac-colored stone; maybe it wasn't a monolith but consisted of several separate parts; maybe something petrified was locked into it, the remains of a beetle, or a cherry pit; maybe the stone was porous, and maybe it wasn't a stone at all that I picked up but a weather-beaten bone.

The sudden metaphysical malaise felt by Olesha's young man when he threw the stone anticipates Roquentin's very similar experience with a stone in Sartre's novel *La Nausée*, written many years later. Roquentin has lost the faculty of separating one thing from another and organizing the items of experience into classes by the device of naming. The eyes of his mind are out of focus, and he experiences nausea. The stone, which he picked up at the seashore intending to throw it into the water, was by definition inanimate, but it seemed to touch him, like a live thing, and he could not throw it. The epistemological concern of Sartre is the same as that of Olesha: both men are examining the texture of the human mind as revealed in experience; for Sartre the detachment from naming and classification results in nausea; for Olesha it is a source of wonder and of new worlds.

In the story "Liompa," the old man Ponomarev is dying and in delirium. The world of things is gradually receding from him until at last he is left only with those things which directly touch his person: the bed, the blanket, the sounds in his immediate vicinity. For everything else he has only "names," arid concepts without weight, color, or texture:

> The vanishing things left the dying man nothing but their names.
> There was an apple in the world. It was shining amidst the leaves; it was seizing little bits of the day and gently turning them around: the green of the garden, the outline of the window. The law of gravity was waiting for it under the tree, on the black earth, on the hummock. Beady ants were scampering among the hummocks. Newton sat in the garden. There were many causes hidden inside the apple, causes that could determine a multitude of effects. But none of these causes had anything to do with Ponomarev. The apple had become an abstraction to him. And the fact that the flesh of a thing had disappeared while the abstraction remained was painful to him.

In the apartment with him is a little boy who rushes about greeting each new thing as a wonder, though he is already falling into the rational trap of classification:

> The little boy dropped in on Ponomarev. The child's head bounced around like a ball near the edge of the bed. The sick man's temples were pale, like those of a blind man. The boy came close to Ponomarev's head and examined it. He thought that it had always been this way in the world: a bearded man lying in a bed in a room. The little boy had just learned to recognize things; he did not yet know how to distinguish time in their existence.

For Ponomarev the condition in which he possesses only the *names* for things, only the rational tools for their manipulation and not the real things themselves, is the condition of death.

Envy and Rage

There are novels which catch and concentrate the essence of a particular historical moment. Such was Yury Olesha's novel *Envy*. Published in 1927, it was acknowledged by almost every literary faction as an important artistic statement. The literary critics reacted with interest and sympathy to the picture of an anti-Communist intellectual claiming to belong to the nineteenth century, reduced in the new world to sharing with a colleague a fat petit-bourgeois widow in a rococo bed. For them that image meant the degradation and death of the old values. The leaders of the Russian Association of Proletarian Writers admired Olesha's reduction of a dissident intellectual to basic ingredients of envy and adolescent rage. These critics, moreover, saw in Andrey Babichev, the Soviet businessman, a satire on power-hungry bureaucrats of the trusts and committees. Intellectuals tended to see themselves in the drunken poet Kavalerov, and they interpreted the novel as a plea for the rights of the individual against the mass pressures of the Communist regime. The mark of genuine greatness attaches to the novel. No one can fail to recognize in it a part of his own human reality.

The fundamental thematic structure of *Envy* is not original, but, rather, typical of its period in Soviet literature. Many novels and stories of the period deal with the conflict between old and new values and the dislocation of sensitive intellectuals in the collective society. Even some proletarian writers, perhaps influenced by Freud and Jung, explored subconscious, nonrational factors in the behavior of their characters. The debate of the intellectual with himself over "accepting" or "not accepting" the Soviet regime, a favorite theme of Olesha in both *Envy* and *A List of Benefits*, was already an established one in the work of the fellow travelers. Olesha's originality lies in his statement of the problem. He presents that problem in concrete literary terms as a conflict between a successful Soviet sausage manufacturer and two drunken and dissolute poets who envy, hate, and maybe at times love him. The theme when stated in these terms, and enriched with overtones of adolescent sexual attachment, takes on universal significance. One forgets that Olesha is describing the Soviet Union of the twenties and that the big breezy Babbitt of his story (he is actually named Babichev) is a Communist bureaucrat. The Babichev of Olesha's novel is a hard-headed businessman with big ideas and a purely utilitarian set of values. He has little use for intellectuals except as proofreaders and suppliers of interesting but useless bits of information, like the answers to such questions as "Who was Jocasta?" He has two overpowering projects on which he lavishes his wealth of efficient energy. The first is to create a sausage, firm, tasty, nutritious, and just juicy enough, that can be mass-produced for twenty-five cents a pound. His second and more alluring dream is to build enormous communal dining rooms where thousands of people can be served at a nominal price. This creation, which is destined to liberate women from slavery to pots and pans, is actually being realized as the novel opens. The "Ten Cent Piece"—as Babichev has named the dining room, after the low cost of the nourishing mass meal which it will serve—is in process of construction, and Babichev, its creator, rushes about in a fever of activity attending to everything. Modern critics with Freudian credentials have not failed to point out the possible meaning of the sausage as a metonymic extension of Babichev, especially in contrast to the "old, fat, and crumbly" widow Prokopovich, who is metaphorized as soft liver paste.

Andrey Babichev has a protégé, Volodya Makarov, a young man who represents the new. He is a famous soccer player, universally admired for his courage and skill on the field. He carries the aroma of sweaty athletic prowess, and when he smiles two rows of perfect teeth appear. He too is deeply involved in building the brave new world, and if he experiences envy, it is envy of the machine. He writes to Babichev:

> I am a human machine. You won't recognize me. I have become a machine. And if I am not really one yet, it is what I want to be. The machines in the workshops here are pedigreed! They are terrific, so proud, so dispassionate, nothing like the ones in your sausage factories. Yours are just artisans. All you do is slaughter calves. I want your advice. I want to be working-proud, proud of my work. I want to be indifferent to everything . . . everything that is outside my work. And so I have become envious of the machine, you understand? Why am I not just as good as it is? We invented it, designed and constructed it, and it turned out to be much harder than we are. Start it and it gets to work. And it won't make a single unnecessary wriggle. That's the way I would like to be. Understand, Andrey Petrovich, not a single unnecessary wriggle.

Opposed to the new and positive men are Nikolai Kavalerov and Babichev's brother, Ivan, both aliens in the new world, both poets of a sort, both engaged in a love-hate duel with Andrey Babichev, and both devoted to the unnecessary wriggle. Olesha devised the complex structure of the novel so as to present Babichev and his world through the eyes of the alienated pair. In the first part Kavalerov is the narrator, and it is his attitude toward Andrey Babichev that the reader experiences. Olesha consciously adopts for his character Kavalerov the irrational emotional attitudes of Dostoevsky's Underground Man, and he understands better than most of the commentators on Dostoevsky that the

Underground Man's hatred of the normal world is the outgrowth of adolescent rage, of the fury experienced by the unfledged young unable to place or define himself. Kavalerov, though not young in years, displays symptoms of a delayed adolescence and of homosexual attachment to his father image and enemy, Andrey. He is surprised, on seeing his own reflection in the mirror, to observe a general resemblance, no more than sexual, to his own father. His thoughts about Babichev, who has befriended and supported him, reveal hatred so special and particular that it is not far from love. His letter to Babichev is a distillation of wounded feeling:

> Andrey Petrovich:
> You took me in out of the cold. You took me in under your wing. I slept on your delightful sofa. You know how lousily I lived before that. Came the blessed night. You took pity on me, gathered up a drunk.
> You put me in linen sheets. The material was so smooth and cool, it was calculated to, and did, soothe my anger and ease my anxiety.
> Even mother-of-pearl pillowcase buttons came back into my life with the iridescent ring of the rainbow swimming in them. I recognized them at once. They came back from a long-forgotten corner of childhood memory.
> I had a bed.
> The word itself had a poetic remoteness for me, like the word "hoop."
> You gave me a bed.
> From the height of your well-being, you lowered upon me the cloud-bed, a halo that surrounded me with magic warmth, wrapped me in memories, nostalgia without bitterness, and hopes. A hope stirred that I could still have much of what had been intended for me in my youth.
> You are my benefactor, Andrey Petrovich!
> Just think: a famous man made me his close companion! A remarkable public figure settled me in his home. I want to convey my feelings to you.
> Strictly speaking, it's all one feeling: hatred.
> I hate you, Comrade Babichev.
> I'm writing this letter to bring you down a peg.
> From my first day with you, I felt afraid. You stifled me. You crushed me under your weight.
> You stand in your underpants giving off the beery smell of sweat. I look at you and your face becomes strangely enlarged, your torso becomes bloated—the lines of a clay idol curve out, swell. I want to shout out:
> Who gave you the right to crush me?
> How am I worse than he?

Is he more intelligent?
Is he richer spiritually?
Is he on a higher level of organization?
Stronger? More important?
Superior not only in position, but in his essence?
Why must I acknowledge his superiority?
These were the questions I was asking myself. Every day, observation gave me a fraction of the answer. A month went by. I know the answer. And now I'm not afraid of you. You're just an obtuse dignitary. And nothing more. It was not the importance of your personality that crushed me. Oh no! Now I see through you, look you over, having placed you in the palm of my hand. My fear before you has passed, like something childish. I have thrown you off my back. You're not much really.

At one time I was tortured by doubts. Can it be that I am a nonentity compared to him? I wondered. Can it be that for an ambitious man like me he is plainly an example of greatness?

The first part of the novel involves a straight presentation of Kavalerov's viewpoint, but in the second part the viewpoint is that of Ivan Babichev. There is an apparent shift to the third person narrator, but his narraton is based almost entirely on Ivan's memories, fantasies, notions, and dreams. Part Two begins with an account of Ivan's reminiscences of his boyhood, when he thoroughly frightened his father because of an incurable penchant for treating his daydreams as reality. Ivan perversely rejects the real in favor of his own fancies, and he abjures rational counsel if it interferes with feeling. When interrogated by the Soviet security police he announces that he is organizing a "Conspiracy of Feelings," those feelings, such as pity, tenderness, pride, jealousy, love, which he believes are being liquidated:

"I want to find the representatives of what you call the old world. I mean feelings like jealousy, love for a woman, vanity. I want to find a blockhead so that I can show you: here, Comrades, is an example of that human condition known as stupidity.

"Many characters played out the comedy of the old world. The curtain is coming down. The characters must gather on the proscenium and sing the final couplets. I want to be the intermediary between them and the audience. I will direct the chorus and the last exit from the stage.

"To me has fallen the honor of conducting the last parade of the ancient, human passions."

Ivan hates the machine-made world of Edisons, Babbitts, and efficient communal kitchens, but he himself is the inventor of a fantasy machine which will, he says, destroy them all. He has given his machine the sweetest and tenderest human name: Ophelia, the name of a girl who killed herself out of love and madness. His creation is the most human of all machines; it is the human source of the machine itself, and he places all his reliance on it. But Kavalerov in a dream sees this most human machine turn on him and destroy, not the others, but its own inventor. Perhaps Olesha wishes to suggest in this strange nightmare that human feelings would not really die in the new world but would only reject the Dostoevskian irrationalists who rely on them exclusively. The new generation, represented by the sun-tanned girl Valya, whom both Kavalerov and Ivan yearn to have on their side, rejects the old-fashioned poet and the dreamer. All the beautiful and good things in the world are garnered by the bustling bureaucrat and the young sports enthusiast, and the conspirators are left in the end with only their holy feelings of hatred and envy. Instead of the fresh and tender Valya ("Valya, I have waited for you all my life. Take pity on me!") the two settle on Annie, the petit-bourgeois widow, who has a small flat and a high, old-fashioned featherbed. The theme of thwarted manhood appears in the portrait of Annie's husband which hangs over the bed where Kavalerov possesses the woman:

> "You do remind me of him," Annie whispered ardently, leaning over him.
> The glass-covered photograph hung over the bed. In it there was a man, somebody's youngish grandpa, in formal attire, one of the latest cutaways of the bygone era. One could feel that he had a solid, many-hooped nape to his neck. A man of perhaps fifty-seven.
> Kavalerov remembered his father changing shirts . . .
> "You do remind me a lot of my husband," Annie repeated.

Envy, like *We*, contains conscious echoes of Dostoevsky's *Notes from the Underground* as well as of "The Grand Inquisitor." Both novels enter a plea for individual freedom and the autonomy of feelings in opposition to the rationalism of modern mass society. Like Dostoevsky, both novelists rebel against the imagined "Crystal Palace" of the future, where life responds only to logarithmic tables, and the individual human being, for the sake of happiness, gives up freedom. The principal literary text for Olesha's *Envy* is the passage in *Notes from the Underground* where Dostoevsky lashes out at the "Crystal Palace," the utopian vision of the communist future presented by the socialist critic Chernyshevsky in 1863. Poetry, the human personality, traditional Russian culture are shown in Olesha's farcical fantasy as degraded and discarded. The envious adolescent Kavalerov and the retarded old fool Ivan Babichev, neither of whom has a man's place in the new world, reflect Olesha's pessimistic view as to the fate of the nineteenth-century literary imagination in the twentieth century. Though Kavalerov and Ivan are defeated, Olesha has so contrived the telling of his story that the reader identifies himself with their disreputable human feelings, and never with the Buddha-shaped businessman in nose spectacles. The bizarre form of the novel conceals a defense of human values which Olesha felt were being trampled upon in the name of building socialism, and a plea for the right to existence of love, a sense of personal honor, and respect for oneself.

Yet Olesha is not without optimism for the future, even should it be socialist. This quality of essential hope, the conviction that organic human growth will break through iron and concrete, is characteristic of him. The feelings that now conspire against the state will continue to live though they may change their form. The nineteenth-century imagination may be dying but that does not necessarily mean the death of all imagination. The sausage manufacturer has a real affection for his young protégés, though doubtless different from the feeling of a father for his children. The sausage manufacturer, though presented through the eyes of those who hate him, is a sympathetic character. His sausages are the product of a kind of art, and the creation of the "Ten Cent Piece," his communal dining room, called for idealism and imagination. Olesha's novel seems to have a prescience of new feelings coming to birth as the old die out.

Thus in his story "The Cherry Pit," which opposes a fanciful young man living in the "invisible country" of artists and poets to a sober Marxist with a set of stable names for his predictable range of experiences, the last scene is an expression of Olesha's deep optimism. The fanciful young man has planted a cherry pit in a city lot in memory of his unrequited love. But he had not taken "The Plan" into account, and on that spot a huge concrete works was to be set up:

> Dear Natasha, I forgot about the main thing, the Plan. A Plan exists. But I acted without consulting the Plan. In five years a huge concrete establishment will rise on that spot where there is now only a vacant lot, a ditch, useless old walls. My sister, Imagination, is a rash creature. In the spring they'll start laying the foundation, and then what will become of my stupid cherry pit? But in the invisible country, a tree will blossom, dedicated to you. Tourists will come to see the mass of buildings. But they won't see your tree. Is it really impossible to make the invisible country visible?

The above is an imaginary letter. I never wrote it. I would have written it if Avel [the Marxist friend] had not said what he did:

"The buildings will be laid out in a semicircle. The interior of the semicircle will be taken up by a garden. Do you have any imagination?"

"Yes I do," I answered. "And I see it, Avel. I see it clearly. There will be a garden here. And on the very spot where you are standing a cherry tree will sprout."

4 The Intellectuals, I

Serapions

The Bolshevik terror of the Civil War years did not fully liquidate the prerevolutionary educated class—the sophisticated and finely cultivated Russian intelligentsia. The bearers of nineteenth-century culture in the Russian world rising from the ruins were young men who had roots in that class. Of those who were born near the turn of the century many took part in the Civil War—sometimes mobilized by the Whites, sometimes by the Reds—and after the advent of peace and the New Economic Policy in 1921 they tried to find a modus vivendi with a regime organically hostile to their traditions and their class. A number of hopeful young writers with no claim to proletarian origin or ideology found one another in Petrograd in 1920, and under the inspiration of two older men, Victor Shklovsky and Eugene Zamyatin, consciously sought ways to preserve the heritage of literary culture they had received. Under the patronage and protection of Maxim Gorky,[1] they met regularly in the House of the Arts in Petrograd to discuss literary problems and perhaps even more to develop a strategy for dealing with an unprecedented situation in which a tyrannical regime basing its power on the illiterate proclaimed itself the sponsor and advocate of cultural enterprise. When Lenin's liberalized New Economic Policy had opened the door to experiment in the production of a free and independent literature, these young men moved courageously into the field, at the same time insisting on their sympathy for the Revolution. This was the Serapion Brotherhood. The date of their first public meeting is an important one in Soviet literature, February 1, 1921, and their first collection of stories and articles came out early in 1922.[2]

Recognizing the anomalous position of these young men, Trotsky with real perception dubbed them, and others like them, "fellow travelers" of the Revolution. Their manifestoes were ironic parodies of the apocalyptic proclamations which proliferated at the time in the literary milieu. They proclaimed only freedom from proclamations and demanded only that art be allowed to exist and to develop independently of doctrines and parties, camps and classes. They rebelled against the tendency of nineteenth-century Russian literature, too, to serve the aims of ideology, and in this they reveal an affinity with the prerevolutionary Symbolist movement, with its insistence on the specific nature of literature:

> With whom do we stand, Serapion Brothers?
> We are with the Hermit Serapion. We believe that literary chimeras are a special reality, and we will have none of utilitarianism. We do not want to write for propaganda. Art is real, like life itself. And like life itself it has neither goal nor meaning; it exists because it cannot help existing.

It would be a mistake to think of the Serapions as one of the many literary organizations of the day. They were not organized in any way. They shared no conviction about literary style. Only in a very limited sense were they brothers, for they had nothing in common with one another except an organic revulsion against the *use* of literature for nonliterary purposes. Zamyatin, usually considered an elder of the society, maintained that there never was such a society. The Brotherhood "was invented," he said, "partly by myself." There could be no "Brotherhood" since the brothers all "had different fathers"; they had no common direction, since some moved west and others east; some were realists and some impressionists, while others cultivated Hoffmannesque fantasy. Independence was all they valued, and Slonimsky claimed that they feared only one thing: that some day a "Serapion Brothers Society" would be established in the People's Commissariat for Education.

Whether we think of it as a Brotherhood or not, the membership of the Serapions included the best literary talent of the day. They were violently attacked as enemies of the Revolution. They met in difficult times to find a way of adjusting to a strange and even repellent reality, and the majority succeeded in this, though eventually their success meant critical compromise with the state.

I shall here review briefly the careers and principal contributions to

Soviet literature of the Serapion Brothers, then deal in some detail with other important writers of the so-called fellow-traveler movement.

Victor Shklovsky (b. 1893) is one of the most important figures in the history of Soviet literature. A leading theoretician of the Formalist school of critics, he was active during the First World War in the Society for the Study of Poetic Language (*Opoyaz*) in Petrograd, which specialized in a study of the linguistic devices of poetry and engaged in a polemic with exponents of biographical and historical criticism, as well as with Symbolist aestheticians. After a career during the Civil War which still remains in shadow, though it is certain that he at one time fought on the side of the Socialist-Revolutionaries and against the Reds, Shklovsky appeared in Petrograd in 1920, and his authority was such that he immediately became a leader among the Serapions. He was a close literary friend of Mayakovsky, as we have seen, and when his rather clouded past, as well as his penchant for the use of metaphors and illustrations gleaned from erotic literature, led to attacks on him, Mayakovsky supported him as a critical intelligence whose ideas were important for Soviet literature. At a meeting called to negotiate an agreement between members of the Moscow Proletarian Association (MAPP) and Lef, the proletarian leaders demanded before agreeing to anything that Lef expel such doubtful characters as Shklovsky and Pasternak. Mayakovsky refused to do this, saying that "even Victor's dubious notions will enter into the history of Russian literature."[3]

And Victor Shklovsky's ideas are certainly stimulating, even when they are demonstrably wrong, whimsical, or fantastic. He is a specialist in paradoxes which, while they may shock or amuse, always point to the essence of a problem. When he says, for instance, that "art has always been free of life, and its colors never reflected the colors of the flag waving over the city," or that "new art forms are simply old and inferior genres elevated to the level of art," and that "Pushkin's lyrics come from album verses, Blok's from gypsy songs, Mayakovsky's from comic doggerel," or when he maintains that a literary work is simply the sum of its devices, Shklovsky raises in acute and original form important problems as to the genesis of art, or the succession of genres, or the nature of creative writing.[4]

Shklovsky's propagation of the notion of *ostranenie*, estrangement, of reality as a basic function of all literary art, even the realistic variety, had a pronounced influence on the work of Olesha and of many younger fellow travelers. The artist should, according to Shklovsky, break down the habit of automatic reaction to the outside world and force the reader to see and hear it. His own literary style is subjective

and impressionistic and, because of the personal and arbitrary movement of his thought, difficult to follow. Clarity is itself a kind of lazy
man's vice, he seems to think, and the reader who would follow
Shklovsky's turns must work at it all the time.

Shklovsky has not only survived, but managed a career in Soviet literature. He has long since lost the intransigent fire and recanted the
heresies of his youth. Critical reviews and books which he has published in recent years do, however, contain occasional flashes of the
early Shklovsky.

Lev Lunts (1901–1924) was a brilliant playwright and an associate of
Shklovsky. He produced much of the manifesto material which identified and described the Serapion Brotherhood and wrote four plays of
distinction. His essays deplore the indifference of Russian writers to
story structure, and his plays, *Outlaws* (1921), *The Apes Are Coming*
(1921), *Bertrand de Born* (1922), and *The City of Truth* (1924), have intricate and original structures. His slogan "To the West" meant that a new
prose revival should arise from the union of Western, particularly
French, storytelling art and the raw material of Russian life. Had he
lived Lunts might have made an important and original contribution to
Russian drama. Gorky regarded him as one of the most promising
younger men.

Nikolai Nikolaevich Nikitin (1895–1963) was a writer of singular power
and remarkable range of style whose stories about the Civil War, *Fort
Vomit* (1922), *Bunt* (1923), and others, are grotesques of moral and physical horror which the author presents calmly and almost without concern. His naturalistic scenes of sex or violence shock and stupefy the
reader, and they might also repel him except that the technique of narration places such things at an artistic distance. His characters tend to
be dominated by erotic drives.

Nikitin is different from Lunts in the kind of material he uses and in
the manner of narration, but he is like him and like other Serapions in
his self-conscious concern with the craft of narration itself, and in his
experiments with storytelling method. Nikitin is a practitioner of the
verbal somersault: the words normally used to describe a person or an
incident are often avoided as too hackneyed, and other words unprecedented in the given context are selected. The influence of Victor
Shklovsky is clearly in evidence here, but the effect of that influence is
not always happy.

Like the majority of the Serapions, Nikitin made a successful adjustment to the requirements of "Soviet reality." In a novel written in 1950,

Aurora Borealis, he deals with a conventional theme, capitalist intervention during the Civil War, in a thoroughly conventional manner. In
1958 he published a frankly political essay: *Taiwan—an Inseparable Part
of the Chinese People's Republic.*

Vsevolod Ivanov (1895–1963) was the product of an intellectual milieu,
but his biography is more like that of Gorky in the bewildering variety
of his experience on the lower level of life. Like Gorky he lived as a
kind of tramp from an early age. He had many occupations: composi-
tor, sailor, organ player, poetry reader, clown, sword swallower, and
dervish. He is unlike Gorky in that there is some doubt as to his sympathies during the Civil War. He fought with the Whites under Admiral Kolchak, was taken prisoner and sentenced to be shot. Pardoned, he
joined the Red Army and fought in its ranks until the end of the Civil
War. When he arrived in Petrograd in 1922 he joined a group of proletarian writers, the Cosmists, but he outraged the proletarians by joining
the Serapion Brotherhood at the same time. The proletarians apparently attributed this not to naïveté but to lack of principle.

And indeed how could a young man coming of age in 1917 find in his
world secure moral or ethical moorings? Ivanov's biography and his
stories betray the effect on young intellectuals of the catastrophic collapse of values experienced during those days. Something analogous to
this happened in the West in the postwar period, but nothing like the
Russian experience of being reduced to a bare subsistence level in morality.

His early stories, which brought him fame along with the misfortune
of being called "a new Gorky," which he certainly was not, describe
guerrilla warfare in Siberia and in the Far East, where Russia borders on
Mongolia and China. The setting of the stories is exotic, the cast of
characters a mélange of Russian peasants, Kirghiz nomads, Chinese
farmers, Mongol horsemen. They are dark and cruel, they have lost
normal human feelings of pity. A band of Russian peasant partisans destroys a Kirghiz infant whose mother is favoring it over a motherless
white child ("The Child"):

> "You want a Russian boy to die for that infidel? You want Vaska
> to die?"
> The peasants began to feel very sad.
> Selivanov said to Afanasii Petrovich:
> "Take the other one away. To the devil with him, let him die . . .
> We've killed a lot of them. Just one more."

A group of peasants driven south by famine and starving on the way
await the death of one of their number so they may eat him ("Hollow

Arabia"). The stories "Armored Train No. 14–69" (1922), "Colored Winds" (1922), and "Blue Sands" (1923) describe events of the Civil War. The basic human experience in Ivanov is of unbridled passion and violence, and when, as in "Colored Winds," the characters philosophize, what emerges is a kind of unlettered and ignorant pessimism.

Ivanov, too, in his early period is a conscious literary stylist. Plot and incident are less important in his stories than their lyrical atmosphere, though narrative structure is not absent from his work, as it often is from that of Boris Pilnyak. Even when the actions described are harsh and cruel, the language is musical and evocative, and scenes are depicted with an artist's sensitivity to line and color.

Ivanov, never a man to stumble, easily conformed to the new demands on literature which were made in the period of the Five-Year Plan. He was one of the first and most enthusiastic literary celebrants of the industrial achievements under Stalin, taking part in excursions and official visits to collective farms and industrial enterprises as early as 1930. His *Adventures of a Fakir* (1934–35) is a fascinating account of his experiences as a circus performer, full of action, color, and cynical amusement. *Parkhomenko* (1938) is a novelistic biography of a Civil War general, conventional in form and neatly tailored to the Party line. *The Fall of Berlin* (1945) is a long novel about the Second World War. Certainly it is fair to say that it lacks the stylistic interest of his early work as a Serapion.[5]

Mikhail Leonidovich Slonimsky (1897–1972) in his autobiography says that his father was editor of the magazine *Herald of Europe*, and that his mother was the sister of a famous professor. "My childhood," he wrote, "passed in an atmosphere permeated by literature and music." His earliest literary teachers were Zamyatin and Shklovsky and his work shows clear traces of their tutelage. *The Sixth Rifles* (1922) is a collection of stories dealing with war and revolution and like the work of Nikitin and Ivanov it presents in a subjective manner pictures of grotesque and senseless cruelty. His novel *The Lavrovs* (1926) depicts the fatal effects of the Revolution on values and on family life in the intellectual milieu. There is a note of compromise and conciliation even in the first version, where it seems clear that the hero will "become a useful Soviet citizen." *First Years* (1949) is a retelling of *The Lavrovs* with a more explicit ideological denouement. *Foma Kleshnyov* (1930) deals with the "re-education of intellectuals."

Venyamin Kaverin (b. 1902) is a former Serapion whose adjustment to "Soviet reality" has not always been successful. He managed to publish his skillfully constructed novels and stories in every period of Soviet history, and he has recently completed a major work, his trilogy, *Open Book* (1949–1956), dealing with the life and education of a Soviet scientist. Lunts he considered his best friend and acknowledged a debt to him for his own literary development. He shared with Lunts an attraction to writers of fantasy and adventure stories: Robert Louis Stevenson, Edgar Allan Poe, and E. T. A. Hoffmann were his favorites, and his early works *Masters and Apprentices* (1923) and *The End of a Band* (1926) reveal his interest in the carefully plotted tale. In the novel *Nine Tenths of Fate* (1926) he tried to present the psychology of the displaced intellectual of his day. His most famous novel of the early period, *Artist Unknown* (1930), develops a conflict between a serious artist and a realistic builder of the new world. The builder, Shpektorov, is contemptuous of ethical values and holds the product of art to be low on the list of requirements for the new state. The artist who insists on the need for a free art is defeated, but he has produced, nonetheless, a single deathless picture. His *The Fulfillment of Desires* (1935) and *Two Captains* (1939) are arresting, well-written, and nicely constructed stories, with just enough of the required ideological element to make them publishable in the Soviet Union.

Kaverin had a prominent role in the movement for liberalization in Soviet literature after 1956, and frequently ran afoul of the dogmatists. He was one of the editors of the collection *Literaturnaya Moskva*, II, which appeared in 1956. His novel *Searches and Hopes*, published in that collection, the final volume of the trilogy *Open Book*, dealt with a scientist's struggle for authenticity and honesty in her field. Kaverin has been an important figure in Soviet literature, both early and late.

Other writers who formed part of the Serapion Brotherhood and felt Shklovsky's influence will be dealt with later. Zoshchenko's humorous sketches have a special place in Soviet literature; Fedin and Pilnyak have made important contributions to the modern Russian novel and will be examined at length; Tikhonov was a successful poet and until 1946 president of the Union of Writers. Vladimir Pozner emigrated to Paris where he was active as a critic and poet; Elizaveta Polonskaya, the only woman among the "brothers," is known for her poetry. Ilya Gruzdev is a well-known critic and literary historian.

Almost all of the young intellectuals who found one another in Petrograd on the day after the Revolution have become eminent in Soviet literature. These men represented, it would seem, that segment of the old intelligentsia which either could not or would not emigrate, and elected rather to try to find an adjustment of some kind to the Soviet dictatorship. For the most part they managed to make such an adjustment. What that adjustment cost in terms of personal morale is difficult for an outsider to judge. In a literary sense, each successful accommodation meant the reduction of an individualistic literary idiom to common terms.

Boris Pilnyak: Biology and History

Boris Pilnyak was not one of those who successfully adjusted to Soviet reality. The Revolution he never accepted, though he pretended to welcome its barbarous violence as a cathartic process. With persistent irony he treats the Revolution as the blindly elemental deed of that old Russia of the steppes and deep provinces which never had a part in the Westernized culture of the cities, and now would burn out every trace of Europe, translating into Slavic terms even the socialist theories of Marx. Perhaps the most sharply discordant note in Soviet literature is the work of Pilnyak, and it is not surprising that he was regularly in trouble over certain of his published works. He was disgraced and dismissed from the Union of Writers in 1929; he disappeared during the Stalinist purges, and while his name is occasionally mentioned in the Soviet press he is one victim of the terror who has not been fully rehabilitated.[6]

A few passages from his autobiography are interesting for the light they throw on his background and personality:

> My real name is Vogau. My father was a rural veterinary whose family came from the German settlements on the Volga. My mother belonged to an ancient Saratov merchant family. She graduated from the Moscow Teachers College. Both my father and mother played an active part in the populist movement of the eighties and nineties.
>
> I carry in myself four blood lines: German with a touch of Jewish on my father's side, Slavic and Mongol (Tartar) on my mother's side. My childhood I spent in provincial towns . . . Mozhaisk, Bogorodsk, Kolomna, and in the home country of my parents, Saratov, and the village of Yekaterinshtat on the Volga.

Pilnyak emphasizes that his parents belonged to the radical intelligentsia and worked among the peasantry in rural areas. It is characteristic of him also that he attaches importance to facts not so much of his biography as of his biology: the mixture of races and "blood lines" in him. This bare autobiographical statement reveals more about his philosophy than about his biography. The Revolution he understands as a peasant revolt, and the setting of his stories is always the small provincial town, backward and barbarous in its ways. He is nationalistic, in fact he has been called a Slavophile, and he sees the Revolution not as a step toward the West but as a rebirth of some ancient Slavic quality in the Russian soul. The ancient past of Russia and its survivals far from the city and the centers of culture acquire a kind of religious mystique in the thinking of Pilnyak.

As a writer he was one of the most popular and certainly the most famous of the fellow travelers. His first published work after the Revolution appeared in 1920 under the title *Bygones,* a miscellany containing sketches and stories about events and characters of the Civil War. Most of these were later worked into the novel which made his reputation, *The Naked Year* (1921). Pilnyak later claimed to have been the first "Soviet writer," the pioneer of the literary revival of the twenties, and until he was discredited in 1929 it was a commonplace of Soviet criticism that Pilnyak was the leading figure in that revival. His style had a wide influence on contemporary writing. He is a writer's writer, and his mastery of a particular manner set a literary fashion. Though his style is derivative, owing very much to Andrey Bely, he displays original imaginative power both in the involved, symbolistic, nonrepresentational manner of *The Naked Year,* and in his more normal, stylistically more conventional stories, which are noted for vivid narration, "The Human Wind," for instance.

Pilnyak's characteristic language is a kind of poetic prose, at times personal and lyrical, at times featuring an epic solemnity, with frequent retardation and word for word repetition of key passages. We find also in *The Naked Year* a conscious reminiscence and echo of the Russian folk epic, a national creation, to which Pilnyak refers many times. Sometimes his style becomes ridiculously involved, in fact a kind of caricature of literary style, with intricate syntax, parades of exotic vocabulary items, subordinate clauses within subordinate clauses, and obscure, learned allusions. Such passages, read aloud and for fun, are surprisingly effective. At other times his style descends to coarse, vulgar simplicity. And he makes frequent use of the very simplest linguistic devices, the catalog, for instance, where he simply lists objects or words to create the effect of a particular social or natural environment. Pilnyak, in a word, inherited from his elders a literary style which suited him perfectly, and which he used with versatility and verve. To read him is not easy, but it is rewarding.

One of the characteristic devices of Pilnyak is the so-called *skaz* technique. This is a method used extensively in Soviet literature of the twenties, by Zamyatin and Babel and by the numerous imitators of Pilnyak. *Skaz* involves telling the story, or expressing certain feelings or ideas about the events of the story, from the viewpoint and in the speech style of one of the characters. We shall see how this device is used in Babel's *Horse Army* (sometimes translated as *Red Cavalry*), where shocking details of savagery are related by a morally obtuse character whom they do not shock at all. Pilnyak often tells what happened, not in his own idiom, but in that of a vulgar town character, a peasant, a criminal, or a newspaper. The predilection of Pilnyak for the *skaz* manner and the widespread use of the technique in Soviet literature of the twenties is probably explained by the fact that it made possible the inclusion in novels and stories of critical or satirical comments on Soviet life for which the author would not have to take responsibility.

It is not possible to speak of the plot of the novel *The Naked Year*, nor is it possible to speak of a single central idea. The work is made up of a series of episodes describing scenes of the Revolutionary period. They had been published separately, and are not worked into a coherent novel form. Some of the obscurity is the result of symbolic hinting at hidden meanings, but often enough it is caused by the author's failure to tie the parts neatly together. Sometimes, indeed, the obscurity seems deliberate; for instance, the use of the same name for Donat the Bolshevik and Donat the religious sectarian does something besides establish a symbolic connection—it quite literally confuses the reader and gives him a sense of actual participation in a whirlwind of events when it is impossible to know just what is happening or just who is who— was that Donat the Bolshevik, or Donat the sectarian?

The Naked Year presents a number of scenes from the famine year (1920) in the Russian interior. The decay of old values in the midst of hunger and misery is its central theme, and this theme gives rise to a medley of new ideas, borrowed notions, and old prejudice. Pilnyak's philosophy is frankly visceral. He belongs to that group of Russian intellectuals who called themselves "Scythians" and who insisted that Russians are not European but rather a half-Asiatic people with special characteristics of their own. The special traits of this Slavo-Tartar blood line have only been damaged by the contact with Europe, and Peter the Great, symbolized by the ponderous Bronze Horseman hovering over Russia, had inhibited the growth of native cultural forms. To this idea Pilnyak returns in the novel again and again, and some of the passages that express it have real emotional power:

> Once there was a native Russian painting, architecture, music, folk literature. Peter came—and after him, like an impossible clod of earth, that Lomonosov [the eighteenth-century classicist] with his Ode on Glass—and the national creative genius disappeared ... Since Peter, Europe has hovered over Russia, but under the

horse's hooves our people have lived just as they lived for thousands of years.

Certain characters who are the spokesmen for Pilnyak in the novel, the priest Sylvester, for instance, insist that in order to cleanse Russia of contamination the "holy blood bath" is a necessary and healthy thing. The Revolution is like a Russian forest demon whose weird cry Pilnyak hears in the new-fangled invented words of the Communists: *Glavbum, Kolkhoz, Cheka, Tseka, Gubkom*. These are the sounds of the submerged Slavic gods now sweeping over the land to drive out the Western carriers of contamination: priests, czars, landlords, and worst offenders of all, the intelligentsia. "Our days," he says, "are bitter, like wormwood. But with wormwood Russian women purify their huts of unclean demons." The "unclean," it must be remembered, include in their number the principal agents of culture in prerevolutionary Russia. Notions such as these are developed also in another early novel, *The Third Capital* (1923), which features a contrast of Russia and Europe, to the accompaniment of explicit allusions to Spenglerian ideas on the inevitable decline of the West.

An important argument of *The Naked Year* is that the old aristocracy has degenerated, and the Ordynyn family symbolizes this degeneration. Most of its members are diseased and childless: they suffer from syphilis, alcoholism, narcotics addiction, and in the case of the father, from religious insanity. Gleb, the artist, is a saintly figure, but he is virginal and without issue. Only Natalya is a complete human being, but she has joined the Bolsheviks and will marry the leather-jacketed Arkhipov, a Bolshevik leader wearing the beard of a peasant patriarch, and they will produce a new line of healthy children. Here Pilnyak introduces another of his favorite notions, the need for the nobility to regenerate itself through intermarriage with the lower classes, and once again we see his insistence on blood and genes. Pilnyak is at his best in some of the pages dealing with the aristocratic Ordynyns. Seldom has anyone given us the feeling of degenerative despair, of that "nowhere to turn" hopelessness, with such sympathy and skill as Pilnyak when he describes how Andrey Ordynyn is obliged to leave his ancestral home. Bunin and Chekhov had treated the same kind of tragedy, but Pilnyak gives it special and original emotional empathy.

Superimposed upon the Russia of degenerate aristocrats, anarchistic peasant villages, sectarians, and occasional saints Pilnyak presents another kind of human force called "leather jackets" from the conventional dress of Bolshevik organizers during the Civil War period. The leather jackets in Pilnyak meet the primitive and elemental forces of revolution and propose to harness and regiment them for rational purposes. His leather jackets are not Europeans in outlook or culture, but are Russians of the native soil who have the brains and the courage to ride the whirlwind, to control and direct the passionate hatred and cruelty released by the Revolution. They are uncompromisingly cerebral men—rational, purposeful, and ruthless. They undertake impossible tasks and succeed in them. Equipped with a foreign ideology, they are yet as thoroughly Russian as the religious sectarians, and are symbolically linked with the latter.

Arkhipov the Bolshevik, one of the leather jackets, spends his nights in study. He carries with him a *Dictionary of Foreign Words in the Russian Language,* and all foreign words he stubbornly Russianizes in pronouncing them. He is reading *Das Kapital,* and will no doubt translate Marx's ideas into a Russian idiom. His peasant followers have no notion of the niceties of theory: they love Arkhipov the Bolshevik (a native Russian word) but hate all Communists (an imported word).

The Naked Year is a virtuoso performance. It is a symphonic structure of themes and ideas—some of them, the Slavophile idea and the degeneration of nobility, for instance, traditional in Russian literature and some quite new. Passages of description or cerebration on the part of the author or his characters are packed with ideas both expressed and symbolically suggested. The ideas are not necessarily original or profound, and they may be fantastic or repellent, but Pilnyak has contrived to link them with the troubled characters of his novel in such a way that the reader experiences a kind of aesthetic empathy for each fragment in the philosophic medley. In thus personalizing his ideas Pilnyak is at times reminiscent of Dostoevsky.

The book displays an amazing stylistic versatility in the various levels of Russian speech which Pilnyak easily commands: that of the cultivated aristocrat, the radical intelligentsia, the simple peasant. It is a textbook of literary devices, and one from which Pilnyak's contemporaries studied their craft. It is one of the most *literary* novels of the period, in the sense that the author never conceals from the reader his function as a craftsman of words and a dispenser of ideas. The author is present in the narrative *qua* author. He comments on his own work and addresses critical remarks to the reader. The linguistic wealth of the novel is enhanced by the great variety of original documents included in it: records of court decisions, newspaper articles, ancient documents, diaries, and notebooks. One of the first Soviet novels, indeed *the* first, if we are to believe Pilnyak, *The Naked Year* is also one of the most versatile, and of the novels and stories which deal with the Civil War it is the one which, even with all its devices of estrangement and stylization, presents the most immediate, moving, and, if one may be allowed the word, realistic account of the period.

Pilnyak, like Olesha and Zamyatin, sees the Communists making a fetish of the machine and industrialization, and in Pilnyak's best work a struggle is taking place between biological, blind forces and the directing hand of rational, organized man—the leather jacket. In *Machines and Wolves* as well as in *The Naked Year*, Pilnyak seems to be entering an argument for the leather jacket, but this argument takes place only on the artist's rational surface. Pilnyak's organic subconscious sympathy is not with the Communists, but rather with the sectarians or the anarchists—with those who are seeking freedom from compulsion—even with disillusioned Communists who want to return to 1917, when everything was clear and simple.

His most telling protest against the effort to subject all life to a rational plan was a story bearing the curious title "A Story of the Unextinguished Moon," published in 1926 in the journal *New World*. This story expresses Pilnyak's feeling that the rationale of the leather jacket concealed a basic error. A Red Army commander and hero of the Civil War has fallen sick and the Party apparatus has ordered him to undergo an operation. The Commander has an instinctive feeling that he should not allow himself to be operated on, that the operation will end in death. He seems to sense the approach of death, and he reflects on the meaning of his own life. He remembers Tolstoy, particularly the desolation of Tolstoy's Ivan Ilych, who when dying found that a life lived according to the pattern of conventional *comme il faut* was no life at all. He converses with a little girl whose fantasy about blowing out the moon seems to him important, though it doesn't fit the fixed rational categories. His own free thoughts and the girl's fantasy are a pleasant contrast to the "apparatus," with its soldiers at stiff attention, giving out orders touching matters of life and death. The apparatus is operated by a *troika*, the number-one member of which is a ramrod man who sits constantly at a desk over papers and reports and whose speech is an instrument for the transmission of formulas. He is surrounded by soldiers and secretaries who, like himself, are automata. This dehumanized machine demands surgery "in order to repair a good workman," but the Red Army commander, as he himself had foretold, dies on the operating table.

The story when it appeared in print had the effect of holding a mirror up to nature. Stalin thought he recognized himself in Number One, and the incidents of the story suggested to him the fate of the Red Army Commander Frunze, who had died in very similar circumstances a year earlier. All issues of the magazine in which the story appeared were confiscated; Pilnyak and the editors of *New World* were forced to denounce the story as an error. Many years later Pilnyak tried to clear himself of blame by suggesting that A. K. Voronsky had given him the idea for the story.

But the story is probably not a topical political document. The fact that the characters and events in it are so much like reality is a tribute to Pilnyak's artistic sensitivity. The character "Number One" is most probably not drawn from any living example but is rather a typical image of the party bureaucrat. The soulless *apparatchik*, dead to feeling and sympathy, is a not uncommon character in literature of this period. Stalin's rage at recognizing the image must have been a source of surprise and gratification to Pilnyak.

Ivan Moscow, which appeared in 1927, develops the theme of an individual whose quirks of brain and personality unfit him for a part in the new industrialized society, in spite of his belief in it. Pilnyak's best statement on the inexorable passage of time is contained in this story. Time passing brings death to the old way of life with its superstitions and evil incantations, and brings a new way of life through the unlocking of atomic power. The dead, however, are slow to die, and remain among the living in mummified form. Ivan Moscow, the rational creator of the new world, is himself in the grip of the dead past: he has an incurable hereditary syphilis.

Mahogany (1929) features romantic, individualistic Communists for whom the finest hour was the Revolution itself and who cannot be at home in the tame construction work of the late twenties. The setting is the deep provinces, where modern mechanization confronts an old and semi-Asiatic culture. Ivan, one of the leading characters, lives in a dugout in the yard of a brick factory with a few honest followers who are still faithful to the Revolution as a "cleansing fire" and who practice a kind of basic Communism. This novel, published first in Germany, caused Pilnyak new and serious trouble.

The Volga Falls to the Caspian Sea (1930) is Pilnyak's effort to produce a novel about reconstruction and to make amends for *Mahogany*. Much of the material of that work appears in this new novel. Near the ancient town of Kolomna a great new dam is being constructed which will reverse the flow of the Moscow river, flooding the ancient settlement in order to create a hydroelectric plant and make the river navigable by ocean steamers. The theme is the familiar one of the struggle between "the old and the new," but it is characteristic of Pilnyak that he induces in the reader a lively sympathy for the old culture with its beautiful artifacts and its mysterious links with the deep past. As in *The Naked Year*, on the surface of his thought Pilnyak is drawn to the machine builders, but what fascinated him as an artist was the old and not the new: the old town of Kolomna itself, sluggish and seemingly asleep, with its ancient towers and its ruined Kremlin, is a more interesting place than the planned city that is rising near it. The mahogany collectors who seem peripheral characters in this novel symbolize, in spite of their grubby backwardness, the tender concern for old things: beautiful hand-wrought, carved things of fine-grained wood. Pilnyak has no real sympathy for the builders of the dam who, when they reverse the river's flow, will leave not a trace of the Russian past.

Pilnyak's work after *The Volga Falls to the Caspian Sea* is both sparse and undistinguished. There is the novel *O Kay* (1932), devoted to his travels in the United States, and *The Ripening of the Fruit* (1935), which continues his chronic, inescapable inner conflict over the disappearance of old values, old art, and all old things.

Pilnyak was the most important single influence in Soviet literature of the twenties, more important, probably, than either Zamyatin or Shklovsky, since he was a more productive writer, and his works, while often published first in Germany, did circulate freely in the Soviet Union. Those works set a fashion for the times. Cultivation of Pilnyak's literary manner was common, not only among the fellow travelers in the Serapion Brotherhood, but even among proletarians. "Pilnyakism" was a phenomenon recognized, named, and duly deplored by Communist critics, though some of these acknowledged Pilnyak's greatness. Pilnyak himself was not a retiring man, but was, on the contrary, energetic and active as a writer and as a literary politician. In spite of his generally bad political repute he was chairman of the Moscow executive board of the Union of Writers in 1929, a tribute to the high esteem in which he was held by the writers' community itself.

Precisely at that point he fell afoul of the Stalinist authorities in literature. We have seen that with the adoption of the First Five-Year Plan in 1928 the relative freedom of the twenties in literature began to be eroded. A focus of heterodoxy and free thought was the Union of Writers, which had continued to function as an organization concerned more with the economic welfare of its members than with their political indoctrination. This condition of the Union was symbolized by the fact that in 1929 Zamyatin was head of the Leningrad section, and Pilnyak of the Moscow section. The Russian Association of Proletarian Writers (RAPP), engaged in vicious warfare with "neobourgeois and kulak" literature, and enjoying the full support of the Party, turned its fire on the leadership and apolitical program of the Union of Writers. The "struggle against neobourgeois literature" was a 1929 euphemism for a campaign to oust the leadership of the Union of Soviet Writers. That campaign was carried on by RAPP, and took the form of an attack on Pilnyak and Zamyatin, two of the principal leaders of the Union, who had published abroad novels that could not be published in the Soviet Union.

The purpose of RAPP was to exert proletarian and Party leadership over the fellow travelers and to negate among them the influence of that group of writers whom it identified as right wing, or neobourgeois. The list of writers "out of tune with the times" was usually headed by Pilnyak, and it included Zamyatin and Fedin, Zoshchenko, Alexey Tolstoy, and many others. For a number of reasons the leaders of RAPP considered these men to be out of sympathy with the Revolution: Pilnyak had consistently talked and written against the prevalent tendency to write from the viewpoint of an ideology; Zamyatin's works were described as a polemic against the proletarian dictatorship; Fedin had been attacked for his story "Transvaal," which had portrayed a kulak of foreign origin as the only source of progress in a Russian village. Such writers as these were influential in the Writers' Union and had a large following among the fellow travelers.

The attack on Pilnyak and his reduction to recanting impotence might have served as a model for later literary campaigns and purges. The technique was the very simple one of associating him with enemies of the Soviet Union. His novel *Mahogany* had been published abroad, and though this was not uncommon in the twenties, this deed was represented as evidence of an alliance with the "White Guard." Headlines in the literary press screamed of his "criminal action," and that of his "fellow conspirator," Zamyatin. Under this attack Pilnyak's nerve seems to have broken. He defended himself by pointing out that the history of the publication of his novel abroad itself refuted the charge of "trafficking with enemies," but in his letter to the editors of the *Literary Gazette* assuring them of his loyalty to the Soviet system, he "explained" those parts of the novel which seemed to be critical of the Soviet regime. Pilnyak's prestige as a leader of Soviet literature was permanently damaged.[7]

After 1932, as we have seen, all separate literary groupings were disbanded. The literary groups that have been mentioned, Pereval, Smithy, RAPP, Lef, Constructivists, and others, were dissolved by Party fiat, and all writers were gathered together into a single Union of Soviet Writers with a single program and purpose in order to facilitate centralized control of writing and publishing. Factionalism, whether based on stylistic affinities or common political interests, was after that considered an unhealthy thing. Yet Pilnyak maintained during the thirties regular contact with a group of writer friends who met at a kind of literary salon in his apartment in Moscow. We know of this from the accounts of people who emigrated during the forties, accounts which are entirely credible.

Throughout the thirties, until the time he disappeared from view during the purges, this literary salon was a meeting place, apparently, where anything was allowed. There was stimulating and quite free debate on literary questions, sharp and at times violent discussion of the Soviet order, all of this mingled with heavy drinking and some debauchery. The meetings went on until the beginning of Stalin's purges. Those events thoroughly terrorized Pilnyak and his friends, and with reason: many of them were swept away in the wake of the trials in 1936, 1937, and 1938.[8]

Our admiration for Pilnyak's great gifts as an artist, and our sympathy for him as a human being crushed by a tyrannical regime, should not obscure the fact that his view of the world would probably be no more congenial to Western democrats than it was to the Stalinists. We may admire his courageous opposition to the Soviet dictatorship, but we should not forget his attachment to the old and primitive, his mystical belief in the Slavic soul, and his emotional distrust of Western scientific rationalism. Such atavisms occasionally appear in Soviet literature of the seventies and eighties, we shall see, as well as in certain segments of the emigration. In Pilnyak's career there is a double tragedy. He was kept from the full realization of his powers as a writer not only by the Soviet state, but by his own insistence on using the literary form to preach a set of sterile notions. The artistic level he might have reached is evidenced in powerful scenes from *The Naked Year* and in many beautiful short stories. But he always returned to the pretentiously cryptic statement of an arid philosophy.

5   The Intellectuals, II

Isaac Babel: Horror in a Minor Key

Prose fiction of the early twenties, whether written by proletarians or fellow travelers, had one overpowering and ever-present theme: the Civil War. Every one of the writers who created the literary revival of the twenties dealt with that experience from one viewpoint or another. The fellow travelers tend to be more concerned with the literary style than with the political or social content of their work, but they could not be indifferent to the latter. Thus it has happened that the Russian Civil War is thoroughly documented by literary works, some of them stylistically mannered and obscure, most of them featuring verbal and metaphoric ornamentation, all of them agreed on the need to study either in aesthetic or political terms the moral nakedness of the times. The generation of writers that witnessed the events of the Civil War felt the need of catharsis and found it, partly, in portraying with aesthetic detachment scenes of horror and blood. Sensitive children of a high culture, they had witnessed the ultimate degradation of human passions, and they had observed the actions of men more cruel than beasts. These writers seem to suffer a compulsion to present scenes of extraordinary violence in literary form.

The Civil War stories of the fellow travelers are interesting also for their geographic and ethnographic content. Their authors had been dispersed in the course of the war to all corners of Russia and even outside of Russia, and this dispersion is reflected in their stories, which deal with Volga settlements, Kirghiz tribesmen, Cossacks on the Polish border, Tambov Province, the steppes of Siberia, and Don country, as well as with the cold caverns of Moscow and Petrograd. The Marxist critic Kogan, defending the fellow travelers, pointed specifically to this feature of their work:

> In a very short time Russia was described more realistically and in more vivid detail than ever before. The majority of the writers had fought on numerous fronts, held responsibilities both in big cities and in the deep provinces, seen with their own eyes pictures of hunger and inhuman cruelty and also superhuman feats of bravery. They had seen sectarians, superstitions, the age-old customs of tribes and peoples scattered over that enormous expanse.

The principal work of Isaac Babel, a series of short stories concerned with incidents in the campaign of Budyonny's First Cavalry Army in Poland, is typical of Civil War literature in the variety of its characters—Cossacks, Polish lords and peasants, Jews, and Russians—and in the cruel reality which it depicts.

Babel was born in Odessa, the son of a Jewish merchant who educated his son in the Hebrew language, the Bible, and the Talmud. He records that life at home was difficult because of his father's insistence on serious study, but that he found relief from that in school. There he learned French, well enough to write short stories in that language, and he came to love French literature. In Odessa he witnessed the pogrom of 1905, an experience which figures in one of his most moving stories. Literary ambition and the need to escape at any cost from the narrow orthodox world took him to Petrograd in 1915, were he lived miserably in a cold cellar, constantly on watch for the police, since he did not have the residence permit required of all Jews. Only Gorky would accept any of his stories. The prominent Bolshevik editor printed two of these in his journal *Chronicle* in 1916. Because of these stories Babel was brought into court on the charge of subversion and pornography, but, as he reported ironically, the Revolution of 1917 saved him from prosecution. Of these early efforts, which combined eroticism and a certain wit, Babel wrote: "The complete absence of decency in them was rivaled only by their meager content. Fortunately for well-intentioned people, some of them never saw the light of day." Babel records that Gorky's encouragement was one of the most important events in his life, and he claimed to revere the memory of the famous writer.

After this literary misadventure Babel abandoned the effort to write fiction for a number of years, and though he attributes the ensuing period of varied activity to Gorky's advice it was more likely the result of the troubled times. He fought in the Czarist army on the Rumanian front, then joined the Bolsheviks. According to his "Autobiography," written in 1924, he worked with the Soviet security police (*Cheka*), was a functionary in the People's Commissariat of Education, and in 1918 took part in grain-collecting expeditions. He fought against the Whites on the northern front, did editorial work in Odessa, and was employed in the local Soviet administration there. He was assigned in 1920 to the First Cavalry Army, where he was primarily responsible for political indoctrination of the rough Cossack mass that made up Budyonny's army. Out of this curious assignment came his most powerful writing, the collection of stories known in Russian as *Konarmia* (Horse Army), a Soviet neologism for cavalry, usually translated as *Red Cavalry*.

The book on which his fame rests can best be understood if it is approached in the spirit in which it was written. *Konarmia* was intended as a series of anecdotes, each with an ironic twist. In the stories thoroughly absurd human beings in ridiculous situations are occupied with the slaughter of other human beings. We misread Babel if, searching for open or hidden commentary on the Revolution, or horrified by pictures of barbarism, we fail to see that each story is built around a grim incongruity. Consider these priceless anecdotes: A peasant soldier writes a letter to his mother regaling her with all the adventures of the campaign, including among them an account of how his brothers murdered their father; a Cossack remount officer reassures peasants to whom he has given worn-out nags in return for their healthy horses: "If the animal can stand up it's a horse"; a village artist offers to paint a picture of you as St. Francis and of your enemy as Judas Iscariot for a small fee; the same artist tells how Jesus lay with Deborah, a Jerusalem maid of obscure birth, and begot a son who was hidden away by the priests; a Cheka officer, sick of the Revolution and the war, asked to be reassigned to Italy where it's warm and sunny or at least to the Cheka headquarters in Odessa; the Jew Gedali wants to found an International of Good People, where every soul would get "first-category rations"; a mild intellectual assigned to a Cossack platoon earns the respect of his soldier comrades by taking and killing a goose that doesn't belong to him; the same intellectual, after spending the Sabbath with a community of Hassidic Jews, returns to his *agit-train* to finish an article for "The Red Cavalryman." After a town is taken a commissar encourages the stunned and plundered populace: "You are in power. Everything here is yours. No more Polish Pans. I now proceed to the election of the revolutionary committee." The hero is upbraided by a Cossack soldier for going into battle with no cartridges in his revolver: "You're a milk-drinking pacifist. You worship God, you traitor." A rabbi's son, who has rejected orthodoxy for the Revolution, still lives in his father's house, "because he doesn't want to leave his mother."

Ilya Ehrenburg, who wrote the Introduction to the one-volume edition of Babel's work published in the Soviet Union in 1957, claims that Babel's diary, which has not yet been published in full, contains entries proving that these sketches were based in the main on actual occurrences of the Polish campaign, and are therefore "highly realistic." It is possible to agree with Ehrenburg's statement that the sketches contain much firsthand experience, but the term realistic as applied to them is meaningless. On the other hand, Budyonny, leader of the First Cavalry Army (who appears as a character in two of the sketches), fulminated against Babel for his failure to show the heroism of the Cossack horsemen in their struggle for the Revolution. It would seem that Budyonny in rather naïve terms is criticizing the sketches for their failure as realism. But perhaps Ehrenburg and Budyonny both miss the point. The sketches do not purport to give a balanced picture of the Cavalry Army or the Polish campaign. They are a series of sketches or, as Babel called them, "miniatures" based on experiences of the author during that campaign, and held together by the deliberate injection into each one of the author's own personality. The picture of the Cossack fighters is impressionistic and subjective. We have to do with a kind of lyric apprehension of absurd violence, seen through the eyes, indeed through the spectacles, of a sensitive intellectual whose work for the Revolution has brought him into the company of innocent savages. And the Cossacks are innocent men: they shed human blood without reason but almost without malice. When the book is examined as a whole it appears that, far from offering a comprehensive treatment of Budyonny's cavalry or the Polish campaign, only a little more than half of the sketches have to do with that organization or its exploits in war. The rest tell of other things: Hassidic Jews in eastern Poland, the deserted Polish church at Novograd, an assortment of original local characters, old buildings and cemeteries, pogroms, and other matters. What is peripheral to the campaign in Poland becomes central in Babel's cycle of sketches. In a letter to a friend he revealed the anguished experience of human tragedy which dictated the eccentric shape of the cycle:

> I have gone through two weeks of total despair as a result of the fierce and constant cruelty I've seen, and also because I've realized how unqualified I am for the business of destruction. Well then, some will make the Revolution, but I . . . I will sing of whatever happens to be on the periphery, or of what is deeper down. I have the feeling that I will be able to do it . . . that I'll have time enough and room enough.[1]

Conventional Soviet criticism is no doubt right according to its own lights in finding that Babel's work is weighted with the details of brutality, and that he has missed "the rational principle in the Civil War, and the organizing role of the Communist Party." No doubt Babel himself could have constructed a final ironic anecdote featuring the Soviet literary critics who say such things. The great virtue of his stories is precisely their lack of political color, their apparently casual and fragmented structure. Not the least of Babel's ironies is the fact that the ideals of the socialist revolution, wrapped in facile phrases, have come into the possession of Russian peasant warriors incapable of understanding or realizing them. The stories are studded with such phrases as "no more masters," "heroic revolutionary army," "all are now equal," "the teachings of Lenin," "the revolutionary consciousness of the mass," and so forth. Such ideas might have been used by another writer, Furmanov, for instance, to justify and give rational meaning to the bloodshed of the Polish campaign. But in Babel's stories they are always given in mangled, misunderstood form by a moral illiterate who has just performed some needless piece of violence, such as killing an old Jew or shooting a woman in the back. Babel's stories are reminiscent of Blok's poem *The Twelve*, where the world is at the mercy of twelve Red guards who kill and plunder to the tune of revolutionary songs and slogans. The hopes and fears of the reformers, idealists, and revolutionaries of the nineteenth century, in *Konarmia* as well as in *The Twelve*, find distorted utterance in brutish mouths.

The narrator of the sketches in *Konarmia*, whose job is political propaganda, is present in almost all of the stories, and it is his personal view of things that the reader usually becomes aware of. The fact that he is a Jew is made explicit in some of the stories, and is suggested in others by the organic hostility toward him expressed by the Cossack soldiers. He is a man of peace—the only one, if we except Sandy the Christ, a mild syphilitic moron, who travels with the Horse Army—and he finds it almost impossible to adjust to the folkways of violence. He loses his best friend because he is unable to kill a comrade dying in misery.

> Silhouetted against the setting sun, Afonka Bida came galloping toward us.
> "We're pounding them a little," he cried out gaily. "What's the fuss here?" I pointed to Dolgushov and rode off.
> They spoke briefly, but I didn't hear the words. Dolgushov handed his papers to the commander. Afonka stuffed them into his boot, then shot Dolgushov in the mouth.
> "Afonka," I smiled pathetically as I rode up to the Cossack, "I just couldn't do it."
> "Get out of here," he said, and his face was white, "or I'll kill you. You fellows in specs have as much pity for guys like us as a cat has for a mouse." And he cocked his revolver.

I went off at a walking gait, without turning around, and I felt the cold chill of death at my back.

"Hey, you," Grishchuk cried out behind us, "are you crazy?" And he grabbed Afonka's arm.

"The filthy snake," Afonka shouted. "He won't get away with it."

Grishchuk caught up with me at a bend in the road. Afonka had gone off in another direction.

"You see, Grishchuk, today I've lost my best friend, Afonka."

He wins their friendship only by brutality, he loses it when he displays a civilized reluctance to kill, maim, or defile another human being. Saddened by his alienation from the Cossacks he "implores fate to grant him the simplest of skills, skill in killing human beings."

Konstantin Paustovsky's reminiscences of Babel and the latter's own stories about the anguish of the Jewish community during the pogroms in Odessa, "The History of My Dovecote," for instance, reveal with unusual clarity the sharpness of Babel's consciousness that he was a Jew. The scornful remarks of the Cossack about "fellows in specs" are anti-Semitic attacks, and therefore Babel was never allowed to forget the fact of his biography. Paustovsky wrote:

A tear gleamed behind the convex lenses of his glasses. He took them off and wiped his eyes with the sleeve of his drab patched jacket.

"I did not choose my race," he said suddenly in a broken voice. "I'm a Jew, a kike. Sometimes I think there's nothing I can't understand, but one thing I'll never understand: the reason for this black vileness which bears such a humdrum name as anti-Semitism." He fell silent. I too was silent and waited for him to calm down and for his hands to stop trembling.

"I went through a pogrom when I was a child and survived. But they twisted the head off my dove. Why? . . . I hope my wife doesn't come in," he whispered. "Lock the door. She doesn't like this sort of talk. And she might easily cry all night. She thinks I'm a very lonely man and perhaps she's right."

Not only do the stories describe peaceful orthodox Jewish communities, Hassidic rabbis and dreamers like Gedali who talk of an International of Good People, but also young Jews who like Babel himself had rebelled against the ghetto and "joined the Revolution." There were many of them in the Odessa Cheka and in the Red Army during the Civil War, and they often reached positions of leadership. This historical fact is beautifully etched by Babel in a single symbolic image:

Our foot soldiers were entrenched three versts from the town. Before the front line a stoop-shouldered youth in spectacles was walking back and forth. A saber dragged along at his side. He moved with a hopping gait and an air of irritation as though his boots hurt him. This "hetman of the peasants," whom they had chosen and loved, was a Jew, a near-sighted Jewish youth, with the thin, concentrated face of a Talmudic scholar.

Jewish characters and themes are an important ingredient of *Red Cavalry.* Maurice Friedberg has pointed out that the dusty towns through which the Cossack army passed may be peripheral to Russian history, but they occupy an important place in the history of East European Jews. The town of Zhitomir, for instance, was a center of the Hasidic movement, and three of the sketches deal with the Hasidic Rebbe, a follower of his, Gedali, and the Rebbe's son.

Babel had many faces: Chekist, soldier, reporter. The most real and the most important of his many roles was that of writer, and it is the one which he himself took most seriously. The reminiscences of his friend Paustovsky reveal the tortured perfectionism of his attitude toward the craft:

> What I do [Babel said] is to get hold of some trifle, some little anecdote, a piece of market gossip, and turn it into something I cannot tear myself away from. It's alive, it plays. It's round like a pebble on the seashore. It's held together by the fusion of separate parts, and this fusion is so strong that even lightning can't split it. And people will read the story. They'll remember it, they'll laugh, not because it's funny but because one always feels like laughing in the presence of human good fortune. I take the risk of speaking about good fortune because we're alone. As long as I live you mustn't tell anyone about this conversation. Give me your word. It is, of course, none of my doing that, I don't know how, a demon or an angel, whatever you want to call it, has taken possession of me, the son of a petty merchant. And I obey him like a slave, like a beast of burden. I have sold my soul to him, and I must write in the best possible way. I guess it's an affliction. But if you take it away from me—either my good fortune or my affliction—the blood will gush out of my veins and my heart along with it; I will be worth no more than a chewed cigarette butt. It's this work that makes me into a man, and not an Odessa streetcorner philosopher.

The trick of Babel's art is to find the stuff of life by indirection, almost by accident. The Cavalry Army itself is a kind of side issue in a world which includes a vivid array of individual peasant soldiers, plundered villages, trampled fields, and indifferent nature itself. The task of political education, of explaining what it means, is abandoned as a grim travesty. The superflux of suffering and violence seems really to serve no rational end, and, therefore, Babel takes the sensations of the moment and transforms them through art into aesthetic experience. One of the means for this transformation is an ornate and elevated style, the texture of which is variegated with elaborate and arresting metaphors: "Blue roads flowed past me like streams of milk spurting from many breasts"; "His long legs were like girls sheathed to the neck in shiny riding boots"; "And we were moving toward the sunset, whose foaming rivers flowed along the embroidered napkins of peasant fields"; "Crouching at the feet of huge estates were dead little Jewish towns"; "The orange sun rolled down the sky like a severed head"; "The deathly chill of eye-sockets filled with frozen tears"; "The stars put out by ink-swollen clouds"; "Between two and three o'clock of a spacious July day the rainbow web of heat shimmered in the air." By such lavish use of poetic language Babel screens himself and the reader from direct experience of violence. The device makes it possible to treat as matters for contemplation even Afonka Bida's empty eye socket: "In place of the left eye on his charred face there yawned horribly a monstrous pink bulge."

Ilya Ehrenburg in his reminiscences, *People, Years, Life,* devotes several pages to his memories of Babel and quotes from the diary Babel kept in 1920 during the Polish campaign the following passage, containing raw material which went into the story "Berestechko." The entry in his diary demonstrates Babel's method, the gathering of impressions which can be given artistic form but hardly reduced to a rational meaning:

> The ancient house of a Polish count, probably built about 100 years ago, horns, old-style paintings on the ceiling, little rooms for the servants, stone blocks, passageways, excrement on the floors, Jewish urchins, a Steinway piano, sofas torn open down to the springs . . . oaken doors, letters in French dating back to 1820.

Like Olesha and many other fellow travelers, Babel produced very little. At the Congress of Writers in 1934 he announced that he was working in a new genre, "silence." In addition to the stories in *Konarmia* he published *Odessa Tales* (1923–24) which describes in his characteristic exotic manner the Jewish half-world of gangsters and racketeers, a number of short stories, many of them autobiographical, and two plays. When he was arrested in 1939—"on a false charge," according to the Soviet edition of his works—he left behind the manuscript of a number of unpublished stories, some of which appeared during the 1960s and 1970s in various places. He died in 1941 at the age of forty-seven and was cleared of criminal charges in 1954.[2]

Konstantin Fedin: The Confrontation with Europe

Konstantin Fedin (1892–1977) describes himself as an early associate of Zamyatin and the Serapion Brothers, and he asserted in 1926 that the association had meant very much to him. His early novels in their experimentation with time sequence, in their transitions from one narrative tone to another, and in their complex plot structure speak eloquently of lessons learned in the school of Zamyatin and Shklovsky. But Fedin's relationship to the Serapions was solely one of stylistic affinity. He was hardly one with Lunts and Kaverin in their call "To the West!" nor did he belong wholly to the "eastern" or Scythian wing of the movement. His position, rather, is a uniquely personal one somewhere between the Westernizers and the Scythians. In the body of his work we find an original, even idiosyncratic statement of the problem which for him overshadowed all others—the relationship of Russia and Europe. This preoccupation of his, also one of the chief problems of the Brotherhood as a whole, has become involved in Fedin's work with a number of other questions: the problem of the individual in history, the fate of the old Russian intelligentsia, and the issue of "the superfluous man" in modern Russia.

A fact of prime importance in Fedin's biography was his civilian internment in Germany during the First World War, from 1914 to 1918. Impressions of the German bourgeois world form an important ingredient of his two most important novels, *Cities and Years* (1924) and *Brothers* (1928), and the profound disturbance engendered by long exposure to Western culture is reflected even in those stories and sketches which describe the deep provinces in Russia. Bourgeois individualism, progressive and rationalistic, is, according to an old model going back at least as far as Dostoevsky, contrasted, sometimes with the backwardness of rural Russia, sometimes with the collective organization of the new society. Fedin's basic sympathies seem to be confused and divided. One of his best stories, "Transvaal," describes a foreign "kulak" who holds Russia in contempt, and, because of his superior cultural background, has managed to gain control of a peasant village. As time went on and history unfolded, Fedin seemed to resolve his dilemma in favor of the Soviet version of socialism and to adapt his art to the precepts of socialist realism without fatally vitiating the former.

Fedin began to write in 1919, and in 1921 was "found" by Gorky and introduced to the Serapions. His first writing of consequence was a play, *Bakunin in Dresden*, conceived as dramatic scenes for reading and intended to present important events in the life of the Russian anarchist. The play was produced under the inspiration of Gorky, who as head of the publishing house World Literature had developed the grandiose idea of a cycle of dramatic works each presenting a crucial moment in human history. Fedin's dramatic treatment of Bakunin is interesting as an early effort to explore the psychology of a puzzling historical figure.

Fedin first attracted notice in the literary world with the short story "The Orchard," published in 1922. The story is direct and uncomplicated in both plot and style. Interestingly enough, the experimental touch of the young Fedin is absent from it, and it is no surprise to learn that he wrote it in 1919, two years before his introduction to the Serapion society. In its simple laconic realism it resembles the mature Fedin of *Early Joys* and *An Unusual Summer* rather than the self-conscious stylist of *Cities and Years.* A luxuriant orchard once part of a fine estate but abandoned by the owners has been converted into a Soviet Children's Colony. In the character of the old gardener, Silanty, who refuses to accept the ruin of his old master's estate by the new revolutionary regime, Fedin introduces thus early in his career one of his main themes: the resistance of old habits to the new. Silanty's revenge on the new takes the violent form of arson committed against the Children's Colony.

A collection of his stories under the symbolic title *Empty Land* appeared in 1923. These stories are the fruit of his boyhood and early manhood in the provincial towns of southeastern Russia. They deal almost exclusively with old and outworn habits, with characters and a way of life that ought to be, but, one suspects, are probably not entirely dead. The stories are told in an ornamental, mannered style, with frequent use of the *skaz* technique.

The novel *Cities and Years* (1924) is a study of the emotional vicissitudes of an intellectual unable to accept fully the Revolution and the new regime. The novel develops, in the life experiences of a single character Andrey Startsov, the complex of problems which beset the old intelligentsia during the twenties. Cultivated and sensitive, European in his education, Startsov is not so much an enemy of the new as he is a soul at dead center, unable to move in support of either the old or the new. He is an individualist to the marrow and as such cannot find an honorable way into the collective society, which seems to him to violate indispensable humanistic ideals. The novel somewhat resembles Olesha's *Envy* in its theme, though it has greater psychological realism than the latter novel. Like Olesha, Fedin seems to sympathize with his doomed hero, Startsov, whose doubts and misgivings may easily have been shared by the author himself. The determined and well-organized opposite to Startsov, Kurt Wahn, a Bolshevik in thought and action, whose ideas flow in simple prose and whose speech is constructed of proper phrases, lacks the human and individual touch and therefore may repel the sensitive reader. The conflict between the two men concerns the importance of individual human beings and the evaluation of one's ties to them of friendship, loyalty, or gratitude. Startsov, whose revolutionary enthusiasm has quickly cooled, spares the life of a class enemy to whom he owes a private debt of gratitude. Wahn, who had been Startsov's friend, hunts the latter down and coldly kills him as a traitor to the Revolution.

The structural ingenuity of the novel has often been commented on. The chronological order is exactly reversed, and the story begins in 1922 with its final act, the killing of Startsov by Wahn and the latter's exoneration by a revolutionary court. Time then turns back to 1919, when Andrey, already doubtful and dispirited, is assigned to the Petrograd front to help defend the city against Yudenich. The action then moves farther into the past, to Andrey's young manhood in Germany where, like Fedin himself, he was interned during the war. Thereafter the time sequence is observed with relative regularity and the knot of mystery and suspense created by the opening chapters is gradually untied, though not without frequent digressions on a variety of themes and with great versatility of stylistic cadence. The tone is sometimes elevated and tragic, sometimes emotionally lyrical, not infrequently ironic. There is real poetry in the prose of the early Fedin. He attempted to explain and justify the compositional eccentricities of his novel. The storm through which he had lived forced its will upon the structure of the novel itself. "The seething reality of war and revolutions obliged the writer to seek new and untried artistic methods."

Fedin's treatment of the German world, in spite of his apparent propaganda intent, reveals ambivalence in his attitude toward the two cultures. The neat, bright German towns with an abundance of all good things and a relatively free life are in striking contrast with Fedin's bare and primitive Russian towns. The hero, Andrey Startsov, is at first powerfully drawn to German culture and only as the novel moves toward its climax and World War I moves toward revolution does Andrey's—and Fedin's—attitude toward the West change. Under the proper veneer of bourgeois decency another Germany suddenly revealed itself, the narrow philistine Germany whose banal patriotism brought on the First World War. This, it turned out, was the Germany that really counted. And this Germany is fully documented in the novel, which includes diaries, editorials and articles from German provincial newspapers, and scenes of mass enthusiasm for the war which Fedin had witnessed. Fedin gives himself many opportunities for emotional declamation on the senseless suffering of war, and these passages are often beautifully written, though they come perhaps too frequently and are too long.

After *Cities and Years* Fedin turned his artistic attention again to Russian peasant life in areas far removed from contact with the centers of culture in Europe or in Russia. He spent the years from 1923 to 1926 in what he calls the "deep preserves of the old way of life" in the Smolensk area. The fruit of his sojourn was a collection of three stories which appeared in 1927 under the title *Transvaal*. The story which supplied the title for the collection had actually appeared separately in 1926 in a collection of stories and articles entitled *The Proletarian*. It is the most arresting of the three stories, and it gave rise to a prolonged and violent polemic in the Soviet press, for Fedin, as we have already observed, seems to portray an alien and unsympathetic kulak as the only source of economic progress in a Russian village. The contrast between the resourceful European, Svaaker, and the superstitious, childlike Russian peasants whom he easily controls produces in the story a dominant note of pessimism. Pessimism always disturbs the Communist critics, and Fedin was violently attacked for introducing such a note. But in the course of discussing pro and con its social implications, the real nature of Fedin's Svaaker and of his story tended to be forgotten. Fedin's Svaaker is a powerful creature of dubious past, who claims to be a Boer in origin, and his presence in Russia is mysterious. One-eyed and disfigured, he is a human grotesque, and he speaks atrocious Russian. A charlatan and a resourceful performer, he has won the complete trust of the peasants, who think he is a magician. He exploits not only the peasants but the Revolution itself in order to build a private empire. He disposes easily of the former landowner, marries his daughter, and through unconscious charismatic power and deliberate chicanery reduces the whole area to dependence on him. The story reveals no trace of any native force, Communist or other, capable of opposing this foreign influence.

In his second novel, *Brothers* (1928), Fedin returns to the theme and in part to the manner of *Cities and Years*. The novel deals with the maladjustment of a sensitive intellectual, this time a musician, in revolutionary times. The main character, Karev, is a lonely individualist and remains one to the end, but this seems to be justified by the fact that he is an artist and as such in need of creative isolation. Free from the pressure of social involvement, he may yet produce a great work, bearing upon it the stamp of his own time. Karev, after unsuccessful efforts to screen his own life from the socialist world, accepts the Revolution and tries to adjust to it. But even his artistic success, his symphony, bears on it the stamp of Europe and of the past, and its inspiration has been private and personal.

In Fedin's third novel, *The Rape of Europe* (1935), the confrontation of two worlds, Europe and Russia, is explicit in both theme and structure. The value of Fedin's observations of both worlds is diminished by the patent thesis of the novel, written during the Stalinist thirties, that the capitalist world is in decline and doomed to destruction, while the socialist world burgeons with new people and new strength. It is to be regretted that Fedin was obliged to work under motivations ulterior perhaps to his own purposes. He had traveled and lived for long periods in the West and he might have produced an important novel. As it is, *The Rape of Europe*, which draws on Fedin's long experience abroad, contains many pages of realistic description dealing with the crisis-ridden thirties in Europe, pages that in spite of the author's ever-present thesis do have artistic merit. Most readers and even Soviet critics agree that the pages in which he tries to express in a credible artistic idiom the successes of socialist construction in the USSR have much less merit.

His next novel, *Arktur Sanatorium* (1940), is based on his own sojourn as a tubercular patient at a sanatorium in a Swiss mountain valley. Again the setting and the characters are Western, and Soviet Russia is here represented by only one important personage. Fedin's purpose in the novel was, he said, to present a picture of Western society "crushed by the contradictions of those years."

This was the last in a long series of novels in which the character of European life, and its contrast with Russian, was Fedin's principal preoccupation. His next publication was his reminiscences of Russian literary life of the twenties, *Gorky Among Us* (1941–1944), a book which is not only honest and wise, but indispensable for the historian of that period. It was bitterly attacked in the Soviet Union for the objectivity of its tone when describing ideologically alien elements, and publication ceased after the appearance of the first two parts. In the autobiographical sketch written for the 1957 edition of his works, Fedin spoke of his intention to complete this work in the near future.

After the Second World War Fedin abandoned Europe as novelistic material and turned to the writing of a trilogy on purely Russian themes. The first two novels in the trilogy, *Early Joys* (1945) and *An Unusual Summer* (1948), were published soon after the war, and the third novel, entitled *The Fire*, was serialized in *New World* (1961–1967). The abandonment of what had been a favorite theme, Western Europe, may have been forced upon Fedin by the chauvinistic mood of the Soviet authorities under Stalin; but it is more likely that the experience of Russia—and Fedin personally—with the German army during the Second

World War soured him on the values of Western culture and brought about a decisive turn to Russian themes and a search for a Russian hero. Such is Fedin's account, and there is no reason to question the sincerity of his statement that "Western Europe obliged the Russians to think of many things in the course of the war." The obvious answer that it was not all of Europe but only German Fascism that made such havoc in Russia would probably seem to him beside the point.

Fedin, while he is probably not a great writer, did possess in a high degree the talent for communicating the atmosphere of a particular time and place. His best writing is reminiscent re-creation of his own experiences, and his memory is able to select and retain sensuous elements of long-past scenes which render their telling a rich experience. This quality is found in his memories of his youth among the German students and burghers, set forth in *Cities and Years* and *Brothers*, in the recollections of his boyhood contained in *Early Joys* and a number of beautiful short stories, and especially in the pictures of his early manhood among the doomed literary bohemians which one finds in *Gorky Among Us*.

Fedin's talent has been one of the casualties of the Soviet epoch, but it has not been a total loss. His career is unique in that it covers the whole span of Soviet literature. He was on intimate terms with the Serapions, but survived all the purges, and, though drawing criticism from time to time, he was never in serious trouble, and even won a Stalin Prize in 1948. His characteristic theme is the tragic dislocation of individual human beings in a time of catastrophic change, but his efforts to deal with this problem did not lead him into conflict with the regime. On the contrary, he managed very well as a reliable administrator of literature, becoming Chairman of the Board of the Union of Writers and one of the editors of *New World*, positions which he used to discourage dissident departures from orthodoxy. He will probably be remembered in literary history for the eloquent and utterly damning denunciation of his role in the Solzhenitsyn affair circulated in an open letter signed by Tvardovsky and Kaverin.[3]

Leonov and Katayev

Two men whose careers are alike in that both began as intellectual writers of an apolitical hue and eventually achieved acceptance and status as major Soviet writers are Leonid Leonov and Valentin Katayev. Both have originality and power, and both have experimented with the novel form. Leonov (b. 1899) began as a practitioner of ornamental prose, but in his first, and perhaps his best novel, *The Badgers* (1924), employed a more conventional style, saturated however with the speech turns of peasants. The novel deals with the impact on the village and the peasantry of the Revolution and symbolically pits brother against brother in the struggle. *The Thief* (1927) is a novel containing much powerful writing and full of the real substance of human character, but it is spoiled in execution by the self-conscious literary poses of the author and his transparent derivation of himself from the irrationalist Dostoevsky. Leonov nonetheless performs a shrewd psychological dissection upon his main character, a disillusioned commissar who has become a member of a gang of thieves. He produced a thoroughly reworked version of this novel in 1959. In *Soviet River* (1930) Leonov returns to the Russian interior to describe the construction of a paper mill on the banks of a river in the dense, half-civilized northern forest. This novel, Leonov's contribution to literature of the First Five-Year Plan, sets forth the obstacles both natural and human overcome by the Communist builders. *Skutarevsky* (1932), probably one of his best works in style and intellectual power, explores the psychological problems of an eminent scientist working in a socialist state and, in what is undoubtedly an autobiographical statement, traces his development from a skeptical critic of the new order into an enthusiastic supporter. *Road to the Ocean* (1935) presents a kind of philosophy of history in complex novelistic form, with a fantasy treatment of the Communist future and subtle variations on the expected time sequence. The hero, another embodiment of Leonov, meditates on the suffering he has caused and endured and tries to answer the question whether it was worth while in the total economy of history.

In *Russian Forest* (1953), as E. J. Simmons has said: "The majestic forest . . . stands as a symbol of permanence in an impermanent world . . . the eternal forest is Mother Russia embracing all of Russian life, its antiquities, its art, and culture." Leonov has been a versatile and prolific dramatist as well as a successful Soviet novelist. He is like Fedin a case study in the adjustment of an intellectual to Soviet society, and in his novels, though they contain the required admixture of "tendency," it is possible to study such an intellectual's image of himself and the historical problem.

Valentin Katayev (b. 1897) had a long career as a Soviet writer. His first successful novel, *The Embezzlers* (1927), is a Gogolian satire of the new Soviet bureaucracy. The embezzlers of the novel are two Soviet officials, conventional, philistine examples of the breed, who more or less by instinct or by accident conspire to defraud the Soviet state. They are thoroughly respectable and decent officials whose tastes and characters are petit bourgeois and who simply need money to satisfy these tastes. Elegance and style are not to be found in the Soviet Russia of the mid-twenties, and in their journey in search of fine ladies and titled gentlemen the embezzlers turn up only a drunken prostitute and a spurious Czar. They try to retain in their drunken haze the forms of bureaucratic propriety, carefully itemizing all the expenses of their trip.

Katayev, like Leonov, has been a successful playwright. His best and probably most famous play is *Squaring the Circle* (1929), a farcical satire of Communist marriage folkways and of the Moscow housing shortage.

Katayev's *Time, Forward!* (1932), one of the best of the construction novels, describes the building of the huge metallurgical plant at Magnitogorsk in the Urals. The title of the book was taken from a poem by Mayakovsky, and its theme is the speeding up of time in the Soviet Union where the historical development of a century must be completed in ten years. Katayev devised techniques which convey a vivid impression of time in movement. Objects are shown always in motion: inanimate things are blown by the wind, landscapes are seen through the windows of moving trains or from an airplane circling above. Quick cinematic techniques are used to confuse ideas of space and time: old space and time concepts are made to seem inadequate to the new historical period. And the central event of the story is the successful attempt of a brigade of workmen to break the world's time record for pouring concrete. *Peace Is Where the Tempests Blow* (1936), a novel laid in Odessa during the 1905 Revolution, is a warm and sensitive study of the psychology of children who witness the events of that revolution. It is the first in a four-volume cycle. Others in the cycle are *A Cottage in the Steppe* (1956), *Winter Wind* (1960), and *For the Power of the Soviets* (1951), a novel about Odessa during the Second World War.

During the sixties and seventies Katayev developed a style that departed sharply from Soviet standards, though it had been foreshadowed in some of his earlier novels and stories. Those experiments in recovering the past out of fragmented memory he ironically named *movizm* (from the French *mauvais*), and they included *The Holy Well* (1966), *The Grass of Oblivion* (1967), *Kubik,* (1969), *The Graveyard in Skulyani* (1975), and *A Fragmented Life* (1972).

Conclusion

"The Russian intelligentsia," says a character in Pantaleimon Romanov's *Comrade Kislyakov* (1930), "began with Belinsky and is ending with specimens such as us." The pessimism of that remark seems justified by the story of Kislyakov, an intellectual of the finest grain who found a place for himself in the new society only at the cost of degrading his intellect. Romanov's novel is an ironic treatment of a stock theme: the intellectual who accepts the Revolution. In that novel the remnants of a fine tradition, individualists to the marrow, are still devoted to the free mind, but this devotion they can express only in furtive conversations and in low tones. Their overwhelming needs are the simple ones: a job, an apartment, clothing. Kislyakov has a job on the staff of a historical museum which is directed by one Polukhin, a worker who believes in proletarianizing both the staff and the exhibits. Intellectuals on the staff who won't cooperate are faced with dismissal, but those who will he welcomes as converts and comrades. Kislyakov flatters the director, praises his ignorant ideas on reorganizing the exhibits to feature the working class and the movement, even pretending to hold views slightly to the left of Polukhin's. Having wormed his way into the Party cell, Kislyakov cleverly undermines his boss, and is at last appointed director of the museum to replace him. For Kislyakov conversion to the new order meant the disintegration of his intellect and character, and the acceptance, not of the Revolution, but of cynical self-service as a way of life.

No doubt Romanov's novel reflects some part of the truth about the experience of intellectuals under the Soviet regime. Not all of them, however, were able to make a successful adjustment. Zamyatin, Olesha, Pilnyak, Babel, and many others went their own way, and not the way of Comrade Kislyakov. A kind of conversion to the new order was the rule, however, for the great majority, and it would be a presumption to pass judgment on this conversion. The complex of forces that made good Soviet citizens out of rebellious individualists can only be partly understood by one who observes this process from a safe vantage. One may assume, however, that the struggle to survive as a writer called into play in many cases a cynical acceptance of what could not, at the moment, be changed.

The great tradition of the Russian intelligentsia found its best expression in the work of the Serapions, or those called fellow travelers, and the great majority of them did survive. They are men of broad education, at home in the languages and cultures of Western Europe. Zamyatin was on intimate terms with English literature; Fedin's work is seldom free of German associations; Babel was formed as a writer in part by his study of French literature; Lunts and Kaverin sought lessons in their craft "in the West"; Valentin Katayev knew English and French literature; Leonov's "plot play" suggests more than a passing acquaintance with Gide. The fellow traveler movement, if one can speak of such a thing, maintained contact through almost all its members (even the "Scythian" Pilnyak) with the literature and culture of Europe as a whole.

They were receptive to new method and content in art, and their literary work is, in almost every case, experimental. They avoided established and easy forms in favor of innovation. They wrote, not for a mass audience, but for readers with an intellectual tradition. Their work was published in relatively small editions and read by the culturally literate. Their roots in Russian literature go back through Remizov and Bely to Dostoevsky and Gogol, rather than to the conventional realists, Turgenev and Tolstoy.

What is most important, they have to some extent preserved the tradition of regard for the individual human being and respect for the untrammeled mind. The movement began as a reaction against the corporate and the collective in literature and continued to assert the existence and the rights of particular human beings. In this, too, they were, perhaps, more in the Western than in the Russian tradition.

6   The Proletarians, I

The term proletarian is now hardly ever used in the Soviet Union of Writers or in Soviet literary works and is used sparingly and usually without clear definition in other areas. Abandonment of the term in literature occurred suddenly in the early thirties as the result of the bad repute proletarian organizations had acquired through their arrogant efforts to dominate Soviet literature. A contributing reason for the disgrace which overtook proletarian literature under Stalin was the fact that proletarian organizations had close ties to the old Bolshevik leaders whom Stalin was determined to destroy, and proletarian novels were a frequent source of muffled dissension. When, in 1932, the Russian Association of Proletarian Writers was dissolved by Stalin's edict he accomplished the double purpose of destroying the influence in literature of an unreliable element and taking credit for liberalizing literary policy.

Yet the term proletarian literature, properly delimited, is a useful, indeed an indispensable one for the proper analysis of certain literary trends of the twenties. It is not used here to identify the class origin of writers or works. A proletarian writer is not necessarily one who has sprung from the working-class milieu or writes exclusively about factories and slums. While in the early twenties the class connections of a writer were important and biographical articles never failed to give some details as to social antecedents, an examination of those biographies reveals that with few exceptions there simply were no writers of properly proletarian background. Nor is this surprising, since proletarians were, in Trotsky's phrase, "the stepchildren of culture." The writers who belonged to proletarian organizations and prided themselves on the working-class essence of their writing were, as their biographies reveal, products either of the peasant village or of a lower-middle-class milieu, and many of them came from families belonging to the provincial intelligentsia. Because they were not proletarian in origin they found it necessary to give special importance to Marxist ideology, which was their chief claim to the term proletarian and thus to the material advantage and political mystique that the term commanded in the early days of the Soviet state.

The atmosphere of literary life in the proletarian world was the complete antithesis of that to be found among the Serapions. To the proletarian writer the *raison d'être* of a literary work was its social message. Though many of them showed traces of the influence of the Symbolists and of the radical experimenter Pilnyak, the dominant formal demand was for clarity and simplicity, and this meant in practice the cultivation of literary forms already well established and widely intelligible. The proletarians were deeply conservative, and looked with suspicion on the "tricky" writing of the Serapions and other fellow travelers. They were also committed to organization, and their theoreticians insisted from the start on the comradely pooling of collective strength rather than isolated individual effort. Zamyatin's *We* is a conscious satire of this collectivist tendency among the early proletarians.

The Proletcult

The earliest organization of proletarian writers was the Proletcult, an abbreviation for the Proletarian Cultural and Educational Organization. Founded in 1917 by A. A. Bogdanov (Malinovsky), for many years a theoretician of the Russian Marxist movement, it received warm support after the October Revolution from the Commissar of Education, Lunacharsky. The "literary studios" set up by the Proletcult served as the center and focus for creation of a literature which was to be an expression of the proletarian world view, just as bourgeois literature, now about to disappear, had expressed the world view of the bourgeoisie. It should be pointed out that Bogdanov had been one of the principal theorists of the so-called *Vperyod* (Forward) group of Marxist thinkers who between 1908 and 1917 engaged in a bitter polemic with Lenin over their program for "God-building," by which they meant the development by the proletariat of a new "religion" of socialist labor. Lunacharsky himself had been part of that opposition to Lenin and was therefore sympathetic to Bogdanov and the aims of the Proletcult.

Lenin was their implacable opponent. In order to produce at forced draft and as early as possible this new proletarian literature the new organization spread its network over the country, and during the terrible winters of the Civil War gathered into its heated studios thousands of ambitious proletarians eager to wield the pen. The First All-Russian Conference of the Proletcult passed a resolution which said:

> a) In order to acquaint [the members] with the literary heritage of past epochs courses should be given in ancient and modern literature, Russian and foreign . . . and in the history of culture, and at the same time all these courses should be given from the viewpoint of the working class.
> b) . . . The writer and working-class reader should become acquainted with the technique, with the practical skills and habits of literary creation, and for this purpose theoretical courses and practical exercises should be given in metrics, rhythm, and the general theory of versification, in the theory of dramaturgy, artistic prose, and criticism.

Bogdanov's theories on the origin and functions of art are an attempt to apply Marxism to the production of literature. Today they are a historical curiosity. He maintained, as do all Marxists, that literature is a social product conditioned by the class environment in which it arises, but he went beyond this in asserting that the principal function of literature has always been to organize the forces of the collective in which it arises. The proletariat, therefore, must have its own class art to organize its collective strength. In 1918 he published a lengthy article called "Art and the Working Class" in which he set forth his ideas in detail. Labor, he believed, was not only the source of all economic value, but also the source of all art. Poetry began in the cries of primitive people at work. Nor were their cries ever the pure creation of art for its own sake: "They were not simply an amusement or a diversion. The workers' songs united the effort of the group in a common task, gave to their movements order and rhythm, and in this way served to organize the collective." The same purpose is served by myth making in primitive societies and science today, the purpose, that is to say, of organizing the practical efforts of the group. Even pure lyric poetry has the purpose of communicating to a large group of readers inner moods and experiences which the individual author has known, by this means organizing the collective psyche, and eventually collective action, in a certain way. What the working class needed was the work of poets who take the viewpoint of the working class, who think and feel in the way that is peculiar to that class. As an example of a genuine proletarian poem, Bogdanov quoted the following, by the proletarian poet Gastev:

> When the factory sirens give forth their sound
>   In the Workers' quarter,
> It is no summons to toil
>   But a song of the future.
> Once we labored in poor little shops
>   And our work began at odd times
> But now at eight in the morning
>   The siren sounds for millions at once
> And at the same instant, the millions
>   Take hammer in hand—
> What are the songs of the factory sirens?
> They are the matins of unity.

In summarizing his views Bogdanov insisted that the distinguishing characteristic of literary work in the epoch of proletarian power would be "collectivity." In bourgeois times the division of labor and the high level of specialization made for individualism in the process of literary creation, but comradely collective work would be characteristic of the proletarian machine civilization. Thus individual creativity would tend to disappear and "we" be substituted for "I."

For a number of reasons, chief among them Bogdanov's pretension to independence of government authority, the Proletcult soon fell into disfavor. Lenin scotched its claim to independence, and Trotsky wrote with searing contempt of the grandiose but impractical theories and plans originating in its collective discussions. He argued that a specifically proletarian class literature simply did not exist and would not have time to develop, since the role of the proletariat in world history would be to do away with classes and create a socialist society throughout the world. Of the proletarian product he said:

> There can be no question that even weak, colorless and illiterate verses can show the political growth of the poet and his class and may have considerable importance as cultural symptoms. But weak, and moreover illiterate, verses do not constitute a proletarian poetry, for they are not poetry at all.[1]

The Blacksmith Poets

The Smithy (*Kuznitsa*) was formed in 1920, by a group of proletarian poets who seceded from the Proletcult and set up their own organization. Some of them had published before the Revolution. Poets such as Gerasimov, Lyashko, and Kirillov were among the pioneers of working-class literature. Like the Proletcult, the Smithy had a program embodied in a "Declaration of Principles." In a letter published in *Pravda* announcing their withdrawal from the Proletcult, this group of writers gave as their reason for taking this step that the Proletcult "is holding back the development of the creative possibilities of proletarian writers." The real motivation is not known, though it probably had to do with factional Party politics as well as concern lest creative energy be dissipated in mass cultural work.

In their declaration the poets of the Smithy announced that literature was a "weapon for the organization of the coming Communist society." They maintained that writers of the old bourgeois stamp were unable to use the new revolutionary material and that therefore the new literature must be the product of proletarians. In this the Smithy took the same ideological position as the Proletcult. They maintained, moreover, that proletarian art must be a monumental art, an art of large canvases.

The group further declared itself the one and only proletarian literary organization and thus initiated that clannishness which was a characteristic of proletarian literary groups. And yet, in its understanding of art as a means of organizing the new society, the Smithy group reiterates Bogdanov's basic idea, an idea which became an essential part of proletarian dogma. Their manifestoes are prone to statements which cannot be reduced to exact meaning, but do have important emotional effect. The Smithy, like the Proletcult, was another manifestation of early proletarian romanticism, and its literary ideas were cosmic but ill-defined. Only one thing was clear. Proletarian art must be like the proletariat itself: mighty, monumental, and merciless toward its enemies.

The factory and the working class, both highly idealized, are the central theme of Smithy poets. They found in the factory the source of the proletarian's might, "the cradle of a new world." The factory of the Smithy poets is not, however, a particular, earthly factory. Nor is their proletarian a man of flesh and blood but a romantic idea. The apotheosis of the proletariat led to the peculiar development in proletarian poetry known as "cosmism." The cosmic mystique appears not only in the cosmic swing of their poems and declarations, but in an effort on the part of the poetic imagination to go beyond the bounds of earthly life and to include sun, moon, and planets in the ecstasy of earthly triumph. According to the Marxist critic Kogan, the revolutionary cosmism of the Smithy was the result of "the poet's faith in the unlimited power of science and labor." Other observers saw in the tendency a more or less obscurantist effort to escape from this earth for another, purer world. Voronsky interpreted it as "quietism" arising from the need to "drown the living, feeling, seeing human being in a sea of cosmic and pantheistic emotions." A combination of influences made for cosmism in proletarian poetry: science fiction as well as Symbolist poetry.

The chief criticism leveled at the Smithy poets by the younger proletarians was that they were romantic and abstract, withdrawn from the world of living human beings and quite unconscious in their poetry of the real physiognomy of actual proletarians. Moreover, they developed no new proletarian forms, deriving their poetic rhythms from Briusov, Balmont, Blok, and other poets of the Symbolist movement. Their poetry was remote from the actual life of proletarians and was for the most part unintelligible to the working class. Their romanticism was ill-suited to the prosaic NEP period which followed hard upon the victory in the Civil War, and a new proletarian organization was formed by dissidents who wanted to "forget about the cosmos . . . and celebrate the earth and living people." One of the leaders of the new group was Yury Libedinsky (1898–1959).

Yury Libedinsky: Communists as Human Beings

When, in the early twenties, Party representatives queried the ambitious young proletarians as to what literature they were actually producing, they would point with enthusiasm to a short novel, Libedinsky's *A Week*, published in 1922 under the editorship of A. K. Voronsky in a collection of stories and poems called *Our Days*. For a time there was little else to which they could refer with satisfaction, but this work seemed a promise of future production. *A Week* remains, for all its passionate statement of a political point of view, and in spite of inept lyrical excursions in the modern manner, one of very few honest literary formulations of life in a Communist apparatus of the revolutionary period. The principal characters are members of a local Soviet organization isolated and defenseless in a rural area where the peasantry is murderously hostile to the regime. The Red Army detachment on which they depend has been dispatched to collect fuel to move the trains which will bring in seed for the spring sowing. While they are absent an uprising occurs in which most of the Communists are killed. To deprive the local Soviet of its troops was a hard decision, but it was the only correct one, as Libedinsky assures the reader:

> If the troops were to be taken out of the town, there would be no way to prevent an uprising; if they were not taken out the spring sowing could not take place. The correct path was taken—the contradiction was resolved at the price of heavy sacrifices. To sow the fields it was necessary to get seed; to get seed it was necessary to obtain fuel; to get fuel, and bring in the seed, it was necessary to take out the Red Army men; and this might be the occasion for an uprising. But it had to be done.

The violent uprising which followed is reported from the viewpoint of the individual human beings who made up the Communist organization. Libedinsky explores the personal life and the particular psychological problems faced by each of the more or less willing "sacrifices." The chief merit of the novel is this effort to show the operation of the Party from the inside, not only inside the apparatus, but inside the individuals who formed it. To the extent that it is possible for him, a youthful Party member emotionally committed to the cause, Libedinsky is objective. He tries to explore the experience of each of his characters in facing death or bringing death to others. He reveals the doubts and inner conflict which they experience. He is ruthlessly frank in communicating their sense of isolation in a "swamp," as one character expresses it, "of hatred."

A Week is an important event in Soviet literary history. It was the first of the proletarian novels, though Libedinsky himself was no proletarian, but the son of a provincial doctor. It was the earliest attempt to depict the workdays of the Communists from their own viewpoint. Though realistic in approach and basic method it still bears the stamp of Bely. It is laden with political doctrine, but expressed so naïvely and innocently as to be relatively inoffensive even to the non-Marxist taste. The didactic message is more than mere support of Soviet power but touches, even, upon internal Communist doctrinal disputes. The helplessness of the Russian Communists in the face of the hostile peasant mass suggests Libedinsky's support at that time of Trotskyism: the idea that the Revolution in Russia could gain significance only if supported by revolutions in the advanced countries of the West.

His next novel, *Tomorrow* (1923), is frankly Trotskyist in viewpoint. It describes the inner life of the Communist Party during the period of transition from war Communism to the "normalcy" of NEP. Disillusion and moral deterioration among the Communists are the motif of the novel. Hope for the Russian Communists, sunk in the swamp of NEP and bourgeois revival, is presented in the form of a Communist revolution in Germany, the only possible outlook for tomorrow in the mind of the old Bolshevik character in the novel. *The Commissars* (1925) takes up again the problem of neobourgeois influences on Communist leaders trained in that hard school of the Civil War. The novel is a valuable historical document, presenting, as it does, scenes from Party debates of the period, and showing the conflict between glamorized commissars and the routine discipline of Party machinery. *The Commanding Heights* (1929) is an excursion into playwriting, heavy with propaganda messages. Its value as literature is slight, and it adds little in the way of documentation to the history of the period.

The Birth of a Hero (1930) is Libedinsky's best novel. Vilified and forgotten by official Soviet criticism because of ideological deviation, it has gone unnoticed also outside of Russia because its author considered himself an orthodox Communist. The novel perhaps deserved a better fate, for it attempted to formulate in literary terms certain basic moral problems, and it was Libedinsky's relative honesty in facing these problems that aroused the suspicion of the orthodox. The themes he touches upon are all of them important, and they transcend the Communist milieu and the Russian locale. He explores the relationship of children to their parents, stating the problems in terms of characters and situations that would be recognized almost anywhere in the Western world. He attempts to eliminate the artificial alienation of one human being from another resulting from ideological or party differences. He deals with the problem of subconscious motivation and its relationship to the rational part of man. His novel reveals the growth of comfortable bourgeois complacency in his own Communist milieu. And the most important and pervasive themes seem to echo Zamyatin's *We,* for Libedinsky is concerned with the freedom and integrity of individual human beings and with the continuing and permanent revolution. Like Zamyatin, he makes the point that "there is no *last* revolution. The number of revolutions is infinite."

From this description it appears that Libedinsky's novel is a thesis novel, indeed a thesis-ridden novel. Libedinsky used the novel form to say a number of things which he felt very strongly and thought needed to be said. His thoughts, however, do not obtrude themselves in the nonliterary form of direct preachment. For each of his problems he has devised fully adequate human characters that are interesting in themselves. Influenced in his literary technique by the example of Tolstoy, he probes the minds and exposes both the ostensible and the real motives of his characters—and the tools of Tolstoy even in the hands of an imitator are effective literary instruments.

The Birth of a Hero is a muted protest against the hardening authoritarian structure of the Communist Party and the deadening effect of this development on Soviet life. It exposes conformism and stagnation in the intellectual life of the Party milieu, and it is a defense of the revolutionary attitude against the search for stability and comfort. The main character, an old revolutionary named Shorokhov, is in conflict with a new generation of Bolsheviks, whom he identifies in their standards of behavior as enemies of the cause he has worked for. These enemies include his young and beautiful wife, Liuba, whose interests are limited to family, home, and reproductive activity, all encased in the petit-bourgeois comfort of pleasant and pretty things. One of the enemies is his own daughter by an earlier marriage, Olga, herself married to a grim-faced young Communist named Gorlin, whose thought takes the form of rigid doctrinal assertion. The most important of Shorokhov's enemies, the one who stands as a symbol of the inimical element around him, is his assistant, a proper and well-organized young Communist named Eidnunen, an efficient administrator and conscientious clerk for whom each problem has its own patterned and symmetrical solution. Lacking a sense of human complexity, Eidnunen makes frightful mistakes in dealing with human problems, mistakes of which he is quite unconscious, for he knows he always has acted according to correct doctrine.

The key statement of Libedinsky's ideas as to the inner complexity of human beings and the infinite possibilities of variation among them is given in the interior monologue of a "young pioneer," Valka, who, doing his homework, makes up arithmetical problems which he works out and demonstrates with matches:

> Then Valka tried to make up a problem for some young pioneers. But the problem wouldn't work out. For he couldn't treat the pioneers as he handled the matches. With matches it was simple: you have 52 and you add 36; how many are there? Or you lay the matches out in 12 rows and the total is 240—how many in each row? But the young pioneers were different somehow: they were always doing something . . . He remembered something which had happened while the pioneers were at camp: some pioneers went to bathe and left some others to guard the camp. But here they are playing leapfrog, and there are so many of them: the problem wouldn't work out. All the pioneers were interested in their own affairs, each one had his own face, his own name, his own voice— and Valka's arithmetical problem just melted away into life.

Under heavy attack from various "Eidnunens" in the Party bureaucracy, Libedinsky acknowledged that his novel was a mistake soon after its publication, though he had earlier said at a meeting of proletarian writers that he considered *The Birth of a Hero* his most successful attempt to embody in a work of art the idea of the dialectic of history. At the same time it was discovered by the dogmatists that other works of his bore the virus of deviation. Some of his short sketches on the Soviet "heroes of labor," part of his contribution to literature of the Five-Year Plan, were criticized for delving too deeply into the psychology of those heroes, revealing with too much emphasis negative qualities, such as doubt and conflict. Libedinsky was in serious disfavor at the time of the dissolution of RAPP in 1932, and he was briefly expelled from the Communist Party during the purge of 1938, which he miraculously survived. *The Birth of a Hero* was his last attempt to produce a work of serious literature. His writing since that time suggests by its subject matter a long sojourn in the provinces, particularly in the Caucasus and

Siberia, the locales in which the novels *Mountains and People* (1947), *Dawn* (1952), and *The Morning of Soviet Power* (1958) are set. His reminiscences, published in 1958 under the title *Contemporaries,* are rather sentimental, especially where they touch on memories of his life as a young man devoted to the Revolution and deep in the struggle. The book is not without documentary interest, since it does deal with a variety of important figures in the proletarian literary movement. But Trotsky is not mentioned, nor is Leopold Averbakh, one of Libedinsky's closest friends. And the book sheds little light on the mysteries of Libedinsky's own career.

Tarasov-Rodionov: "Our Own Wives, Our Own Children"

Shortly after the appearance of Libedinsky's *A Week* in 1922 another young commissar, who had taken part in the Revolution and the Civil War and returned to Petrograd full of harrowing experiences, published a novel based in part on those experiences. *Chocolate* (1922), which appeared in the magazine *Young Guard,* was an immediate success with Russian readers, earned the admiration of some critics, and was for a number of years the focus of an embittered controversy. Alexander Tarasov-Rodionov in this novel faced without blinking the truth about "revolutionary justice" as meted out by the organs of state security, and with knowledge gained at first hand he revealed the methods used by the Cheka to maintain the Bolsheviks in power.

The novel *Chocolate* has a feature that most Soviet novels lack: an interesting and suspenseful intrigue. The story grows out of a sequence of events all interconnected in a narrative whose outcome is a matter of life or death for the principal characters. These events are presented in an order which gradually heightens the sense of danger to the hero, and his ultimate destruction comes about as an inevitable result of what might be called a tragic mistake: "a moment of pity for a class enemy." The pervasive influence of Bely and Symbolist prose writers is obvious again in this tale of life among the Communist secret police. There are three levels on which the main character is presented: his uttered speeches, his conscious but unspoken thoughts, and the unconscious dreamlike images of the life of blood and struggle through which he has passed. The *Chocolate* of the title stands symbolically for luxuries enjoyed by the bourgeois in the midst of proletarian starvation, luxuries which now tempt even the most seasoned of proletarian revolutionaries.

The main character, Zudin, is the chief of the local Security Police (Cheka) in a Russian provincial town not far from the front lines where the White Armies are advancing. His men have arrested a group of conspirators and along with them a beautiful young ballerina, Yelena, who happened to be present, but in the role of prostitute rather than that of conspirator. After questioning her Zudin is convinced that she knew nothing of the conspiracy and orders her released. He pities her, and allows himself moreover to be captivated by the upper-class charm exuded by the delicate creature. She pleads with him to let her work for the Revolution, and he hires her as a secretary in the Cheka office, where they have many lingering contacts. The liaison is never consummated, in spite of all her efforts, for Zudin's proletarian conscience at the crucial moment steps between them. He resists, not without a struggle, her passionate advances, then explains himself to her:

> You must not feel hurt. Naturally, I'm not a saint. The coarse and tender feelings, all the instincts peculiar to man are not foreign to me. But I have also something within me that you will not understand—how shall I explain it to you? Class feeling! It is an amazing, ever-living, and powerful spring. From it I derive all my strength, from it alone I drink my dearest and most precious happiness. How this feeling was born in me I cannot remember myself. All I recall is how, in the dark cellar where I lived with my mother, who was a laundress, watching through the window the feet of the passers-by, I, a ragged child, understood that in the world there were beautiful people in new boots but with hard, dirty little souls, and that there were many, many others who were always barefoot and dirty but who shone with sincerity and devotion.

Yelena is at the same time having an active affair with another dear friend, one Edward, an Englishman and a suspected spy wanted by the Cheka, who supplies her with chocolate and silk stockings. She makes a present of some of these things to Zudin's wife, who, in her thoughtlessness and hunger for the finer things, accepts them. Yelena then discovers that one of the bourgeois prisoners being held by the Cheka had actually been cleared of all charges three months before but, through an oversight, had not been released from prison. A simple order from Zudin is all that is necessary, but before calling the matter to his attention she extorts a heavy payment from the young man's family in return for his release, pretending to be acting in the name of her chief. At that very moment Zudin's assistant, Katzmann, is killed by a socialist revolutionary, and in a sudden passion of class hatred Zudin orders the immediate shooting of one hundred bourgeois hostages held in the Cheka jails. This is done suddenly, without a second thought, almost casually.

Yelena's operations are finally revealed to the Central Committee, and Zudin is involved in charges of bribe taking and collaboration with a class enemy. One of the heaviest ironies of the story is that no blame ever is laid upon him for the casual killing of one hundred innocent people, but the charge that he had accepted chocolate and several pairs of silk stockings is repeated by the investigators with venomous insistence. The investigating commission reaches its decision by a curious path of revolutionary logic. They doubt very much that Zudin is guilty—and of course the reader knows that he is innocent of the charges brought against him—but they decide that the question of guilt or innocence is unimportant, and the question of justice never enters their deliberation. Zudin had, on his own admission, made a mistake in pitying Yelena, he had compromised the Revolution in the eyes of the workers, whose mood because of him was rebellious. In order to win back their good opinion and their support in the struggle against the Whites, it is decided that Zudin must be shot, guilty or not. An old revolutionary comrade of Zudin's explains the decision to him, and he accepts it:

> We reasoned it out very simply, just as you did. There is no question of guilt here. But we have to do something, and something cruel, terrible, otherwise our whole cause will perish. You understand, not us, but our cause. What devil ever moved you to take pity on that wench? Haven't we inherited enough of that refuse? But you are an old revolutionary, and you should have looked at the most important things, and gone right past her. But we're all alike, with very few exceptions, and we don't blame you. You know we all have our very own wives, our very own children.

The sacrifice of a single human being without regard to moral considerations is justified in the supposed interest of thousands of human beings, of the mass of human beings. Such is the ostensible message of the story, but it provoked fierce opposition precisely because it exposed to public discussion the philosophical assumptions of the terror—both Red and White. It is impossible to suppose that the author did not realize the deadly nature of the questions he raised. The story is prophetic of the purge trials of the thirties, when, no doubt persuaded by arguments not unlike those offered to Zudin, and like him reduced to moral impotence by their own lives of terror and deception, the Old Bolshevik leaders delivered in court confessions of their own guilt—not for their real crimes, however, but for fabricated ones.

Tarasov-Rodionov wrote a second novel, *Linyov* (1924), which develops themes of the Civil War period with his characteristic irony and not without excessive verbal ornamentation, and he projected a chronicle of the Revolution in the form of an autobiographical trilogy, called *Heavy Steps*, which was never completed. He was accused of Trotskyism in 1937, and he disappeared from the Soviet literary scene. There is no record that he confessed to any crimes. He was posthumously rehabilitated.

Dmitry Furmanov: An Earnest Commissar

Another young man "of pen and sword" who served as a political commissar with Red detachments during the Civil War, then settled in the literary calling, was Dmitry Furmanov (1891–1926). His two most important works are *Chapayev* (1923) and *The Uprising* (1925). He also wrote a number of short stories, the story "Red Landing" (1923), and many propagandistic and critical articles. The Soviet edition of his works in four volumes contains his diaries and notebooks and the sketch for a novel about the literary milieu entitled *Writers*.

The novel for which he is most honored in the Soviet Union is *Chapayev*, and it is on this work that his claim to the status of classic depends. The novel, based on Furmanov's own experiences as a Party representative attached to the headquarters of the peasant guerrilla leader Chapayev, contains the central political idea that the Communist Party bridles and controls the anarchistic force of peasant rebellion. Chapayev is the leader of a senseless and violent "Russian revolt" such as Pushkin deplored in his novel about the Pugachev uprising; Klychkov, the young commissar assigned to Chapayev by Red Army headquarters, represents discipline and order. The practitioners of the latter turn out to be more ruthless and stronger than the elementally brutal Chapayev. Klychkov is an autobiographical character, and his experiences are derived from those of Furmanov himself.

Furmanov's brief autobiography, written in 1926, is a curious document, which throws much light on the character of this young representative of organization and plan:

> My earliest childhood, up to the age of eight years, I can remember only in sad fragments. But at that point the passion for reading hit me. I read a great deal, in a kind of hot fever for books. With particular interest and enjoyment I read Jules Verne, Conan Doyle, Maine Reed, Walter Scott, and things of that nature. Education: a public grammar school in Ivanovo-Vosnesensk. A trade school in the same city, and in Kineshma, a town on the Volga. I finished three years of a scientific secondary school. After that, Moscow University. I completed the course in Philology in 1915, but never managed to pass the state examination. I was sent as a medical

corpsman (*brat miloserdiya*) to the Turkish front, the Caucasus, to Persia, to Siberia, to the Western front . . .

In the middle of 1916 I arrived in Ivanovo-Vosnesensk and . . . I taught in workers' schools. Then came the Revolution of 1917. My fiery mood, together with a meager knowledge of politics, drove me to be at first a maximalist, then an anarchist. As it seemed to me then, the new and longed-for society could be built with the help of bombs, anarchy, and everyone's unlimited goodwill. But life pushed me into the Soviet of Workers' Deputies—and later into the Party.

It is evident from this that the young man who wrote the classic work on bridling the Russian revolt had himself a history of anarchism, and this history, while it may have served him as useful psychological material, caused him to overcompensate in the direction of discipline. The photos published in Soviet editions of his work show a young man of set jaw, whose eyes seem to look at one with grim certitude. His capacity for work amazed his comrades. He was First Secretary of the Moscow Association of Proletarian Writers, a position in which he demanded punctual production both from himself and from others. He could not endure literary bohemians who were irregular in attendance at meetings or who came to them late. He kept a diary and kept it systematically. Libedinsky, in his reminiscences, reported that "Furmanov's life moved constantly in a brave and happy rhythm of work. It was as though he was marching to the beat of music which came from inside his young and inspired heart." Any irregularity, independence, individuality seemed to him a symptom of bourgeois decadence. He believed passionately in the organization of literature. When some of the proletarian writers complained at a conference in 1925 that organizational pressure was "crushing the initiative" of individual writers, Furmanov stood firmly for collective literary work in which proletarian writers would help one another to develop creatively and protect one another from infection with alien ideology. The one-time anarchist, turned inside-out, had become the most disciplined personality on the literary scene.

Furmanov's own comments on *Chapayev*, in his diary and notebooks, reveal that he approached the task of writing with forethought and a high degree of literary interest. It is significant that he, almost alone among proletarian writers, was interested in the problem of literary genres and had asked himself the relatively sophisticated question, "To which of the established genres does *Chapayev* belong: (1) *Short story*, (2) *Reminiscences*, (3) *Historical record*, (4) *Fictionalized historical chronicle*, (5) *Historical ballad*, (6) *Scenes*, (7) *Historical sketch*. What would you call it? I don't know."

Further evidence of literary perception is his high opinion of Isaac Babel's sketches. Babel described people and situations very similar to those we encounter in *Chapayev*, but Babel's approach is the opposite of Furmanov's. Babel views his reality from a near vantage, where each detail can be brilliantly sketched; Furmanov, while not sparing himself the senseless violence of his characters, focuses attention, not on the details of bestiality, but on the rational historical development in which, as he believes, even Chapayev, that "wild horse of the steppes," had an appointed place. The two writers were as far apart in style as in temperament. Babel is ornamental, his style constantly calling attention to itself; Furmanov is laconic and matter-of-fact. Babel has no explicit ideological task to perform; Furmanov, in his own words, "set himself the practical, revolutionary aim of showing how we carried on the struggle in the days of the Civil War, of showing this without artifice or invention." Furmanov's appreciation of Babel as a literary stylist, attested to by a close friend, is, therefore, interesting evidence of a certain catholicity of literary taste in the man, and his own writing is not devoid of sensitivity.

The avant-garde critics of *Lef* and *New Lef* valued Furmanov as a writer whose works might serve as textbook illustrations of the modern literary mode. Brik and Shklovsky admired his uninvented narrative based on historical fact and constructed out of biography, diaries, notebooks, newspaper accounts, official orders, and other evidential materials. Such work was a perfect example of that "Literature of Fact" in which they believed. Perhaps the most important single factor in the formation of Furmanov's literary style was not his indoctrination with Marxist ideas but his labors in the field of Red journalism. The best pages of both *Chapayev* and *The Uprising* are those which bring to life the partisan movement in the southeastern steppe country. Chapayev himself and the members of his band are portrayed in simple vivid strokes as part of the primitive peasant milieu which produced them. If Furmanov had refrained from injecting his philosophy into the narrative—if he had not editorialized—*Chapayev* would have been a journalistic account of the war in the steppes comparable to the best of Western war reporting. His description of the guerrilla band as it unceremoniously takes over his own quarters is an achievement of some merit:

> Soon the boys who had come with Chapayev poured in, in a noisy gang. They tossed their stuff in every corner of the room. On the table, the chairs, the windowsills they threw hats, gloves, belts, laid out their revolvers. Some of them took off their bottle-shaped bombs and carelessly shoved them right among the caps and gloves. Tanned, stern, courageous faces; coarse thick voices;

clumsy, unpolished movements and speech. Some of them had such a strange way of talking that it seemed they uttered nothing but abuse; they asked questions curtly and roughly and they answered just as roughly, as though in anger ... The whole house hummed with their arguments and their conversation: the new arrivals had soon spread themselves out into all the rooms ...

In a few minutes Klychkov observed one of the guests spread himself out on the unmade bed, prop his legs up against the wall, light a cigarette and shake the ashes off to one side, aiming them directly at Klychkov's trunk which stood near the bed. Another slumped onto a fragile "dressing table," which crunched and cracked under his weight. One of them beat out a window pane with his pistol butt; another threw his dirty and stinking sheepskin coat over the bread laid out on the table, and the bread when it was eaten had a sickening smell.

Equally ironic is Furmanov's account of the mysterious power exercised by Chapayev over the peasants. It is to be doubted that the author had ever heard of the modern concept of the charismatic leader, but he has presented in Chapayev an excellent case history of such a leader. Chapayev's mastery of the rough peasant mass seems to Furmanov the result of some magical power, and the passages that depict him in action as a popular leader are written with mingled irony and respect:

We arrived at a village and stopped at the office of the local Soviet. The peasants, as soon as they heard that Chapayev had come, crowded into the building, all pushing their way forward, hungry for a look at the famous hero. Soon the whole village had learned of his arrival, and the streets were full of a thronging mob rushing to find him, to get a look at him. The entryway was blocked by the numerous throng: boys and old women, even bearded white-haired old men who had crawled out for the occasion. Everyone wanted to greet him, Chapayev, as an old and good friend, many called him by his first name ... Swimming on the faces of the crowd were pathetic honey-sweet smiles, and strange, gray faces suddenly sparkled with joy. Some gazed at him seriously and intently as though to be sure of getting the full satisfaction of seeing him and to imprint forever in their memory the image of the heroic commander ... The street boys stopped their hubbub and stood quietly, patiently waiting for something. And everybody seemed to be waiting for something—clearly they wanted to hear what Chapayev would say ...

"You might say something, comrade commander," the chairman of the local Soviet said to him. "You can see the peasants would like to hear a wise speech."

"What am I going to say?" Chapayev smiled.

"Oh, tell them how people are getting on—all around. You'll think of something."

Chapayev never liked to make a fuss. He could see the peasants wanted to hear him—why not say something? While the horses were being harnessed he made a speech. It would be difficult to state the central theme of Chapayev's speech. He simply repeated commonplaces about the Revolution, the great danger, the great famine. But even these things they liked, and why not? Wasn't Chapayev himself speaking? With strained attention they heard out to the last word his long and confused speech, and when he had finished, they nodded their heads sympathetically and whispered to one another:

"That's the right stuff!"

"That's the way to give it to them!"

"Boy, he's a great one!"

The story interest in *Chapayev*, as well as the central ideological theme, is the development of a working relationship between this ignorant and politically unversed peasant leader and his commissar, Klychkov. Klychkov's problem is to establish his ascendancy over Chapayev and to direct into predetermined channels his spontaneous revolutionary energy. He has little respect for Chapayev as a man and is dubious as to the Chapayev legend. The rational force in Furmanov's book masters and exploits the emotional energy generated by the peasant leader, and thus Klychkov, not Chapayev, is the real hero. Indeed the end effect of Furmanov's story is to deprive Chapayev and other individualistic swashbuckling Civil War heroes of the glamour that surrounded them. Freewheeling filibusters riding the wave of the peasant uprising—and Chapayev was such a one—are the objects of the commissar's cool and reasoned contempt. And individual deeds of spectacular courage, he concludes, are to be indulged in sparingly:

> That kind of thing is very good—*but* . . . and at that point he insisted on a *"but."* At that point he drew a logical, irrefutable, clear and convincing conclusion: a commander should never permit himself to be carried away by his own private action, but always have in view the welfare of the whole—of the total operation, and all his troops. Particular action he should assign to someone else. Yelan's personal bravery might have had a sad outcome for the whole brigade if he . . . had been shot and his replacement had been unable to manage the brigades.

On almost every page Furmanov insists on the solid factual basis of his narrative. Letters, telegrams, official orders, announcements, and the like are introduced as authentic documents: "Here is a note written by Klychkov on the spot"; "the following letter was then sent to headquarters, and it is given here word for word"; "This document has been preserved in the archives." Much of the content of *The Uprising*, which describes a rebellion of Red Army troops in the town of Verny against the local Soviet authorities, is given in the form of official archive material. Furmanov's method, which, as we have seen, was related to that "Factography" advocated by the Left Front of Art, has profoundly influenced Soviet prose. Gladkov, Serafimovich, Sholokhov, Polevoy, indeed the majority of successful practitioners of socialist realism, all lay careful claim to *historical truth* for their novels. They purport to deal with real situations and actual characters. Not all of them have succeeded in producing books like *Chapayev*, which can be read with pleasure even by a non-Marxist. Furmanov has the advantage over the socialist realists in that his sharp and honest intelligence draws a fine line between the actual *facts* and his own opinion about them. By presenting his ideas directly and without disguise he has produced works which have genuine value both as ideology and as literature.

A. S. Serafimovich: A Popular Saga

At the time of the Revolution, A. S. Serafimovich (1863–1949) was already an old and established writer, his first stories having appeared in 1889 and 1890, while he was living as a political exile in the far north. Those early stories are documentaries on the life of poor peasants and laborers in many parts of Russia and in various occupations. In 1902 he met Gorky at the home of Leonid Andreyev, and the first volume of his collected stories was published in 1903 by Gorky's famous Znanie publishing house, which was partial to books that described with sympathy and social purpose life on the lower levels. Thereafter Serafimovich, who had already received the accolade of political exile, was associated with the Marxist Social-Democratic Party in its Bolshevik variant, though he did not actually join the Party until 1918. He was thereafter active throughout his life in Red journalism, editing magazines and contributing regularly to *Pravda* and *Izvestia*. In 1921 he was chief of the literary section of the People's Commissariat of Education under the Commissar, Lunacharsky. In 1924 he published his principal work, *The Iron Flood*, which has become a classic of Soviet literature. He planned and labored over a second novel, *The Struggle*, which dealt in documentary fashion with peasant and worker life, but never finished it. His work from 1924 until his death in 1949 consisted of sketches, stories, editorials, and articles on contemporary political and social problems. He worked on an autobiographical novel during the forties. He was awarded a Stalin Prize in 1942 "for many years of service to literature."

Quite apart from its merits or defects as literature, *The Iron Flood* is a significant historical document. It is significant not so much for the events which form the core of its narrative as for the approach and method of the author. *The Iron Flood* has entered into the main arteries of Soviet literary life, and some of its "iron" is still to be found there. Its portrayal of the mass as the hero in history; its unconcern with individual personalities; its implacable optimism; its insistence on victory over terrible odds; its tendentiousness—all of these ingredients are to be found in the standard product of socialist realism. That standard product is, however, very inferior to the prototype, for Serafimovich does not shrink from the reality he has chosen to portray. The mixed mob of deserters, mutinous sailors, and Bolsheviks with their women, children, and household goods who marched north from the Taman peninsula, after escaping encirclement by the Whites, is shown as an unruly and bloodthirsty force. Atrocities committed against the enemy are not glossed over. For instance, the following actions are described as part of the capture of an enemy village:

> From the priest's house people with ashen faces and golden shoulder-straps were being led—part of the Cossack headquarters' staff had been taken. Their heads were cut off in the vicinity of the priest's stable, and blood soaked the dung.
> The din of the firing, the shouts, curses and groans stifled the noise of the river.
> The house of the village ataman was found. It was searched from basement to attic—he was nowhere to be found. He had fled. Then the soldiers called out:
> "If you do not show yourself we shall kill your children."
> The ataman did not appear.
> They began to slaughter the children. The ataman's wife crawled on her knees, with streaming hair, clinging to one of the soldiers' legs.
> He slashed at the little girl and then split open the skull of the wildly laughing mother.

The Iron Flood is a relatively honest book, but can anything be said for it as literature? Two writers, Zamyatin and Furmanov, who are nearly at opposite ends of the literary spectrum, have made definite pronouncements as to its merits. Zamyatin in his essay "On Today and the Contemporary" (1924) said the following:

> *The Iron Flood* is metal torn up out of the earth. Well, you might think, what could be better? But just send a bit of that iron to the laboratory and you'll find that it's been gathering rust for a long long time in the cellars of Gorky's Znanie publishing house. And just as one would expect from the tried and true custom of the

Znanie writers, for a solid page or two the workers sing: "Thou hast fallen in the brave and fateful struggle." And again according to the Znanie formula, this time inherited from Leonid Andreyev's *Red Laugh*, we find such locutions as: "the mad sun"; "the mother laughs with an inexplicably gay, ringing laughter"; "she wildly kisses her child"; . . . "madly the light trembles"; "above the sky-blue abyss." . . .

But there is something else there, too—something that wasn't in the Gorkyesque [Znanie writer] Serafimovich. When we read: "Toward the windmills there comes out of the throng with an inexplicably red face, with a black mustache just sprouting, in a sailor's cap . . ." in such a sentence without a subject we sense an unbridled "modern," almost Pshibishevsky. When we find phrases like: "Again among those people who were straining toward salvation there arose an overwhelming astonishment," we must suppose here the beginnings of a kind of instrumentation, almost in the manner of Bely.

And another thing: in Znanie there never was the cheap gilt that one observes on Serafimovich's iron, which he mined "from the Depths." The figure of that "rotten compromiser" Mikheladze is fashioned according to all the rules for gilding. And the gilt is especially thick at the end of the story, with the apotheosis of the hero . . . and the "tears streaming down the windworn faces of the crowd . . . and the young girls' eyes shining with tears."

The ore that Serafimovich used for his *Iron Flood* is so rich that even worked up into operatic stuff it is not completely worthless—we do remember a few scenes.

Zamyatin's casually devastating review of *The Iron Flood* was published in 1924, soon after the appearance of the novel. Furmanov's critical reaction was strikingly different and can be given much more briefly:

From his first story "On the Ice" to this last fine novel *The Iron Flood*, Serafimovich has always been a singer of the struggle of labor against capital, the struggle of a free order with the realm of poverty, violence, and exploitation . . . Serafimovich has no need to be "tendentious." It is enough that he is just himself . . . Serafimovich combines the mastery of an artist with the rich erudition of an ethnographer and the wise and sane approach of a sociologist-historian . . . Serafimovich shows reality in its revolutionary development . . . Through the darkest ignorance of the masses, through their barbarity and cruelty one can sense the new thing that will come to replace that ignorance, barbarity, and cruelty.

Furmanov speaks of "the symmetrical structure of the novel, its carefully planned composition, the balanced proportion of its parts, the author's economical handling of his material."

The confrontation of these two critics is an important one, for much more is involved here than the difference in literary method or literary taste. The chasm separating Zamyatin from Furmanov is one which probably cannot be bridged. One observes Zamyatin's easy, offhand sophistication, his expert knowledge of literary styles, his sensitivity to literary echoes, however distorted, his acute ear for the peculiar resonance of a political fairy tale, and his contempt for the hard-driving sentimentalist with "weatherworn" face and a "glistening" tear. Zamyatin's most caustic vitriol is directed precisely at borrowed ornaments in Serafimovich's style: the already hackneyed devices of Symbolists and populists which he uses to construct his propagandist tale apparently without fully realizing that they are devices and that they are hackneyed. But what of Furmanov's criticism? To dismiss it as the work of a partisan, as one is inclined to do, would probably be a mistake. Furmanov derived enjoyment which he would label aesthetic from the reading of *The Iron Flood,* and so did millions of people who have read it in the Soviet Union. These millions were probably not aware of any aesthetic lack in the book, since they, and Furmanov as well, do not have the critical sophistication of a Zamyatin or his sensitivity to the ring of falsehood. Zamyatin's remarks mirror the gently educated taste of an intellectual, Furmanov's the popular hunger for heroic sagas, especially those which claim historic truth. The word *bylina,* which came to be used for the Russian folk epic with its superhuman heroes and marvelous deeds of valor, meant originally "a true event." Those epic stories evoked an emotional credence which had nothing whatever to do with their credibility. In much the same way the modern Russian reader follows with sympathetic, suspenseful interest the epic journey of that filthy and ragged mob (the proletariat) in its relentless, iron-hearted march out of captivity through terrors both man-made and natural, moving with one will and a massive resolve into the promised land of the Soviet state. Their leader, Kozhuk, is more than human. He has no weaknesses, no doubts, and no hesitations as to the right path. There are no separate distinct personalities in the marching mass. The only individual portrait is that of the "rotten Mikheladze," the Menshevist traitor to the working class, whose egocentric stream of consciousness is presented only as a fitting prelude to his death. Furmanov and the Soviet reader find in Serafimovich what they put there themselves, a sympathetic identification with the mass hero. Zamyatin simply did not have it.

7   The Proletarians, II

Fyodor Gladkov: A Literary Autodidact

The unresolved problem in Soviet literary practice even to the present day is the problem of the individual hero. Questions that were asked during the twenties as to the area of private life and personal motive that might be allowed a proletarian character are still debated. This debate began, as we have seen, with the reaction against the abstract metallic proletarian of the Smithy, but the transition to prose fiction with a realistic thematic base only posed the problem in sharper form. *The Iron Flood's* total abstraction from the personal lives of its characters was the more striking for the fact that the work, in spite of its emotional charge, is a prose work about ordinary people. Other works of the earlier period exhibited the same indifference to individual character, for instance A. G. Malyshkin's *Fall of Dair* which relates, also in highly charged prose, the military feat of the Red Army in recapturing the Perekop peninsula from the Whites. In this heroic tale, as in *The Iron Flood*, there are no individuals but only a massive human force which seems to move according to predetermined historical laws. Similarly, a consciously Marxist view as to the relative unimportance of the individual in history is implicit in Furmanov's account of that "great man," Chapayev.

Critics both proletarian and bourgeois spoke of this neglect of individuals as a fault, and the proletarian literary organization in setting up demands upon its writers insisted on their cultivating a literary method which would avoid this particular fault.

The slogan for the presentation of the "living man" . . . on the one hand correctly orients proletarian literature toward the reflection of contemporaneity, and on the other hand expresses the necessity of struggle with stereotypes, with schematic portrayal, with "bare poster art," and of development in the direction of showing forth the complex human psyche, with all its contradictions, elements of the past and seeds of the future, both conscious and subconscious.

The campaign against "poster art" and stereotyped heroes was headed by Libedinsky, the leading theoretician of the Association of Proletarian Writers, and Alexander Fadeyev, a grim commissar of the literary world, who had the following to say about the faceless heroes of proletarian literature:

[Works which have recently appeared] represent an advance even over the novels of Furmanov and Serafimovich, where the "hero" was predominantly the collective, the workers' element, or the forces of history which move people. Concrete figures were portrayed in such novels not in their particular and individual traits, but only from the point of view of those qualities which helped them to fuse themselves with the collective.

Fadeyev found solid Marxist support for the idea that historical processes, however impersonal, find their concrete expression in individual minds and hearts, and should be portrayed in terms of the actual experience of particular persons.

The psychology of characters acquires great importance in our eyes because it is the psychology of whole social classes, or at least of social groups, and because, therefore, the processes taking place in the souls of individual characters are a reflection of historical movement.[1]

The appearance of two novels marked the emergence of the new emphasis on the real problems of actual people—Fyodor Gladkov's *Cement* (1925) and Fadeyev's *The Nineteen* (1927). It is instructive both to compare and to contrast the two works. Gladkov (1883–1958), a literary autodidact whose life story is like that of Gorky, was a Party man before the Revolution, suffered imprisonment and exile, and nurtured a bitter Gorkian hatred of the clean and respectable world. He read everything, but was particularly drawn to Lermontov, Nekrasov, and Dostoevsky. The influence of Dostoevsky, as has been pointed out, is evident in most of his early work, including *Cement*. Early tales which carry the clearest evidence of Dostoevskian influence in the handling of the characters, and of modernistic tendencies in style—*The Fiery Steed*

(1923) for instance—Gladkov finally rejected as alien to him in form and content. Figures of demonic wickedness, revolutionaries with "feverish" personalities, women with an "infernal" hatred of the double standard and their inferior position, families and communities torn by poverty and misery, all of these bear the impress, faint no doubt, of Dostoevsky's style. The presence of such types is likely to escape the reader's attention in the welter of Communist propaganda, topical thematics, and rousing speeches on socialist construction, but Dostoevsky's "infernal woman" is still recognizable in Dasha, the emancipated woman of *Cement*, fighting for the independence of her own will, though Dasha does wear a red scarf.

Cement is, like *The Iron Flood*, a popular saga, but it is a saga not of war but of reconstruction. It is a novel about industry, in which the machine is treated, in poetic prose reminiscent of Smithy poetry, as the proletarian's friend and savior. The hero, Gleb Chumalov, an industrial worker and Red Army commissar, returns to his home after the end of the Civil War, to find that the old forms of life have been destroyed but nothing new has yet taken their place. Zamyatin said of *The Iron Flood* that certain scenes are well done and memorable. The same thing can be said of *Cement*. Gleb's homecoming is one of these. As he observes the enormous cranes and huge blocks of factory buildings, Gleb experiences a thrill of recognition, but immediately senses something discordant:

> Very good! Once more, machines and work. Fresh work. Free work, gained in battle, won through fire and blood. Very good!
> The goats scream and laugh with the children. The ammoniacal stench of the pigsty. Weeds everywhere, and the paths besmirched by hens.
> What's this? Goats, poultry, and pigs? This used to be strictly forbidden by the management.
> Three women were walking towards him in single file, with bundles under their arms. In front marched an old woman with the face of a witch; behind, two young ones. One of them was fat and full-bosomed. The other with red eyes and red swollen eyelids, her face deeply buried in her shawl. Was she ill or weeping? . . .
> As he approached them on the narrow pathway he stood aside in the high grass and gave them a military salute.
> "Greetings! Comrades!"
> They looked at him askance and stepped past him. Only the last one gave a screeching laugh like a scared hen: "Get on with you! There's enough scamps like you about. You can't greet them all."
> "What's the matter with you women? Don't you recognize me?"
> Loshak's wife looked gloomily at Gleb—just as an old witch would do—then murmured to herself in her deep voice: "Why, this is Gleb. He has risen from the dead, the rascal!"
> And went on her way, silent and sullen.

In this scene of Gleb's rude greeting by an industrial compound overrun with barnyard animals and by emancipated impudent girls, Gladkov has, with a certain sense of structure, introduced the main themes of his novel: the restoration of industry along socialist lines and catastrophic changes in the family. Gleb's mighty socialist feat in making the factory work again, carried out against opposition from relics of the old regime, from bands of White terrorists, from traitors and weaklings within the fold, is only part of his story. He must also, as his wife Dasha pointed out, fight a civil war within himself to conquer the old morality and the old family relations. Dasha believes in free love and complete equality. She wants to work, organize, and fight in the same rank with her men. In a section of the novel called "The Cold Hearth," Gleb experiences the desolateness of this new life:

> At nighttime he came home and Dasha was not there. She was not waiting for him on the threshold as she used to in the early days. In those days it was cosy and hospitable in the room. Muslin curtains hung at the windows. The painted floor glittered like a mirror and the white bed and clean tablecloth beckoned to him. And a samovar . . . The clinking of the china . . . Here Dasha lived in every corner: she sang, sighed, laughed, spoke of tomorrow and played with her daughter Nurka.

Nurka, his daughter, is in a children's home, and Dasha insists she is no better than the others and should get the same treatment as any other child: "They're all equal here and they all are lovely." Nurka herself has almost forgotten her father and hardly recognizes the word "home":

> "Would you like to come home, Nurka? To play there like you used to . . . with daddy and mama?"
> "What home? My bed is over there. We've just had some milk, and now we're going to march to music."

In Gleb's public life he is a hero. In the course of realizing his dream of the reopened cement factory he conquers laziness and disorganization in his own proletarian comrades, and, an even greater triumph, he wins the loyal support of the bourgeois engineer, Herman Hermanovich Kleist, who was at first his enemy. The following scene, which probably can make no claim to verisimilitude, is a symbolic statement of the Party's policy toward skilled specialists inherited from the old regime:

> "Herman Hermanovich . . . now you are one of our best workers—a good head and hands of gold. Without you we couldn't

have gotten anything done. Just see what a fine job we have done under your guidance."

"My dear Gleb Ivanovich, I intend to devote all my knowledge and experience—all my life—to our country. I have no other life except that life with all of you; and I have no other task except the struggle to build our future."

And for the first time Gleb saw Kleist's eyes fill with tears . . .

"Well then, Herman Hermanovich, let's be friends."

"Right, Gleb Ivanovich, let's be friends."

In his private life Gleb is not successful, but that is not the important thing. As the novel ends he has not yet found the way to a socialist relationship with Dasha but is still blinded by jealousy and rage at her new life, and his daughter Nurka has died. Optimism in the face of personal tragedy is, perhaps, the leading motif of the novel, and in Gladkov's world the loss of a separate home, one's own child, and individual happiness counts for little. Gleb himself sensed that no individual could take credit for success in the really important thing, the reconstruction of the factory. Support for that came, he felt, from the mass of laboring men, and he would have been helpless without that support.

The expendability of individual human beings in the general economy of history is a variation of the main theme of the book. *Cement* represents an advance over *The Iron Flood* in that it does recognize the existence of private lives. Yet it does so only to show their insignificance as tiny units in a huge sum. Gladkov was influenced by Dostoevsky, but in *Cement* he debates with his master as to the moral weight one should attach to the suffering of history's guiltless, incidental victims. It will be remembered that Ivan Karamazov, in his dialogue with Alyosha, rejected God's world because he could find no way to justify the miseries visited upon the innocent: "If the sufferings of children must swell the sum of sufferings necessary to pay for truth, then I protest that the truth is not worth such a price."

The answer to Ivan Karamazov is given in the meditation of Sergey Ivagin, who has been unjustly expelled from the Party on the ground that he is "an intellectual, and a demoralizing element." Ivagin, still a devoted Marxist, reflects:

> Whether he would be readmitted or not made no difference; he, Sergey Ivagin, as a separate personality did not exist. There was only the Party and he was an insignificant item in this great organism. But that day he was going through his old pain once more.

A further stage in his melancholy thought process leads to the conviction that he as an individual owes all of himself to the Party and the historical process embodied in it:

Would he be rehabilitated finally or not? It was of no importance: it would not change his fate. He must work and only work.
If he were to be thrown out like refuse, then it meant that this was
necessary for the future. He was bound to the whole world, to all
mankind, by unbreakable ties.

Wandering and reflecting on his own and man's fate, Sergey finds
himself at a dockside and stops to look down at the pounding waves:

> Right at the seawall, placed among the refuse and seaweed there
> lay the body of an infant. A white scarf was tied about its head,
> there were stockings on its legs, and the arms could not be seen
> because of the swaddling clothes around it. It was a fresh corpse,
> and its waxen face was quiet, almost alive, as though it were sleep-
> ing ... Where did the infant come from? The warm hand of its
> mother was almost still upon it—in the scarf, the swaddling clothes
> and the little stockings on its chubby feet. Sergey gazed at it and
> could not tear his eyes away ... Where did such a pitiable human
> sacrifice come from? From a wrecked ship? Thrown overboard by a
> frenzied mother?
> He stood there, unable to tear himself away from the little body.
> People approached curiously, looked at the corpse and at once
> continued on their way. They muttered a question to Sergey, but
> he neither heard nor saw them. He stood there gazing without
> thought, sorrowful, his eyes full of astonishment and pain, and he
> felt a deep oppressive grief encircling his heart. Then uncon-
> sciously he spoke aloud, without hearing his own voice.
> "Yes ... It must be so ... A tragedy of the struggle ... To be
> born anew, one must die."

Cement lacks both verbal artistry and psychological power, yet it had
an emotional impact on the Soviet reader, and it became the model and
prototype for the vast novels of industrial construction written during
the thirties. It was a favorite of Stalin, and as such was circulated in
millions of copies. It contained an explicit statement of Marxist philosophy, and in successive editions it quite unsubtly reflected changes in
Party policy. Gladkov's fundamental indifference to his novel as a literary product is shown by the ease with which he altered both content
and style as times and fashions changed.[2] One example of these alterations is amusing evidence not only of the Soviet reader's changing taste
in the matter of naturalistic detail, but of the Party's changing doctrine
on the relative position of the sexes. The parallel passages are from the
1925 edition and the 1950 edition, and the later version reflects in a
brutal image the return to a more conventional relationship, in contrast
to the woman's struggle for emancipation in the early days:

1925 Edition

From the other side of the narrow street muffled drunken voices could be heard coming from the open window of a building. It was the heavy voice of the cooper Savchuk and his hysterical wife Motia, who was cackling like a hen. Gleb left his kit near the fence and crossed over to Savchuk's place. The walls of the room were filthy with soot. Overturned chairs lay helter-skelter on the floor, and clothing was strewn about . . . Because of the sun in his eyes Gleb could not immediately distinguish any person. Then he made out two dirty, convulsed bodies rolling and fighting on the floor. Taking a closer look he saw that it was the Savchuks, man and wife. The man's shirt was torn to bits, his back was bent and his ribs stuck out like barrel hoops . . . The woman's full breast heaved violently as they struggled together.

1950 Edition

On the othe side of the street the drunken cooper, Savchuk, was making a row. His wife Motia was screaming hysterically. Gleb listened to it a moment then sprang into action. He got up and went over to Savchuk's quarters. There was dirt and stench in the room. Stools and clothing were strewn about on the floor. A tin tea kettle lay on its side. Flour was scattered all over everything. Motia was lying on a potato sack and hugging it to her bosom, and Savchuk, in a torn and ragged shirt and bellowing like a bull, was punching Motia with his fists and kicking her with his bare feet. Gleb grabbed him from behind under the armpits and dragged him away from her.

A second example of political editing was applauded by a Soviet critic, and it illustrates Gladkov's responsiveness to the demand for intelligible and didactic prose even in the remarks of a character under emotional stress. A sudden sharp attack of White "bandits" has just been repulsed. Several workmen have been killed in the action, and Gleb, choked and panting, addresses the proletarian crowd:

1925 Edition

Again Gleb raised his arms on high.

"Comrades, listen! A sacrifice to labor . . . With our united strength . . . No tears or crying! The victory of our hands . . . the factory. We have won . . . We shall make ourselves heard with fire and machines. The great labor of constructing the Workers' Republic . . . Ourselves, with our brains and hands. . . . The blood and suf-

1950 Edition

Gleb shouted through his palms as through a megaphone: "Comrades! This has been a sacrifice in labor and struggle. No tears and sobs, but the joy of real victory . . . Soon the factory will begin to roar with its furnaces and machines. You and I are beginning the mighty construction of socialism. Yes, blood has been spilled, and there has been much suffering. There have been many trials on

1925 Edition	1950 Edition
fering of the battle—these are our weapons for winning the whole world."	our path and there will be many more. But this path of struggle leads to happiness, to the final victory over the world of violence. We are building our own world with our own hands. With the name of Lenin on our lips, with faith in unlimited happiness let us double and treble our efforts for the conquest of the future."

The earlier variants provide evidence that Gladkov's style possessed originally a kind of rude emotional power. In an article entitled "My Work on the Novel *Cement*" Gladkov describes the systematic "normalization" of that style undertaken so that the book's message might be intelligible and acceptable to as many Russians as possible. In successive operations on the text of the novel, Gladkov excised substandard vocabulary, vulgar language, and almost all traces of class or local dialect.

Gladkov's work after *Cement* falls into two main categories, socialist-realist works on topical themes and autobiography. The former are unreadable in the sense that they can be read neither as literary products nor as documentation nor even as honest propaganda; the latter are quite readable reminiscences of Gladkov's boyhood and young manhood with its wanderings and chronic hardship. In the first category, the massive novel *Energy* appeared in installments from 1928 to 1938, was published after extensive revision in book form in 1939, and after much criticism and further self-censorship by the author appeared in a new edition in 1947. It undertakes to describe the construction of the great hydroelectric power plant on the Dnieper river, Dnieprostroy. Gladkov, always responsive to the demands of the Party, spent several years at the construction site accumulating first-hand information on matters both technological and human. He produced during his visit a great many sketches on the great labor taking place at Dnieprostroy, and he seems to have become a kind of expert in the technical details of construction. The result is a formidable novel.

The Birch Grove (1941) deals with the industrial transformation of the provinces, and in it Gladkov attempts to strike a human note in the person of the schoolteacher Martin, who lectures the construction manager on the need to create, along with his new project, a more beautiful life for human beings. In *The Vow* (1944) Gladkov portrays the magnificent patriotism shown during the war by Russian workingmen in the rear, who carried out without flinching the collective vow made to the great leader, Stalin. Gladkov's autobiographical trilogy, *A Story of My Childhood* (1949), *The Free Way* (1950), and *A Hard Time* (1954), is not without interest, and in some parts, the first volume particularly, displays the power of language that Gladkov originally possessed.

Gladkov's novels, chiefly his proletarian "classic" *Cement*, are read in many parts of the world by the recently literate masses to whom the strictures of cultivated critics or the amused contempt of a Formalist writer such as Osip Brik are understandable, probably, only as evidence of their malice.

Alexander Fadeyev: The Search for a New Leo Tolstoy

Fadeyev (1901–1956), who was a native of Siberia and the son of a village doctor, joined the Communist Party at the age of seventeen, fought in Siberia against Admiral Kolchak, the Japanese, and Semyonov's Cossacks, published his first stories "The Flood" and "Against the Current" in 1923, and at last settled in Moscow to become a close collaborator of Leopold Averbakh, the leader of the Russian Association of Proletarian Writers (RAPP). Fadeyev was from the start a writer with a mission. Though his first novel *The Nineteen* (1927) was a success in the Communist and proletarian milieu, he early showed a preference for the writing of resolutions, speeches, and essays on the theory of proletarian literature. Under his guidance RAPP adopted an attitude toward Gladkov that was distinctly unfriendly, and however justified their criticism of artistic shortcomings in his works, the sharpness of their tone is mildly shocking. Gladkov complained that the critics of RAPP declared his novel *Cement* "beyond the bounds of literature," and he fought them with equal ruthlessness. In the archives of the Institute of World Literature, in Moscow, there are manuscripts in Gladkov's hand which refer to his constant struggle against the literary theories of Averbakh, Fadeyev, and other semibourgeois "aesthetes," as he called them, and to his punishment at their hands by silence, censure, or abuse. Like most devotees of a particular doctrine, Fadeyev believed that contrary doctrines were mistaken and harmful and that their carriers should be corrected. His sternness toward Gladkov was motivated by a conviction that, although *Cement* did reveal personal and family problems, its author had left untouched the inner lives of his characters.

Fadeyev's insistent emphasis on the portrayal of "living men" in their complex psychological reality was solidly based on Marxist doctrine. Marx and Engels had provided texts suitable for use in the ideological struggle against those relentless "human streams" and romanticized heroes of the early proletarian period. Because Marx, Engels, and Lenin had at times expressed a preference for writers of the realistic school, the words "reality" and "realism" came to be clothed with mystical authority. Fadeyev took upon himself the task of liquidating romanticism. He was an emeny, also, of formalism, stylization, "factography," anything, indeed, that smacked of modernism. He developed the argument that realism is the literary expression of materialist philosophy and devised a slogan to be used against romantics: "Down with Schiller!"

Fadeyev and his friends in their position as lawgivers to proletarian writers urged upon them the value of a realistic approach to individual psychology and prescribed models for them to imitate. The importance of the "classics" and the need to learn from them were a steady refrain. What classics did they have in mind? Not even the Proletcult or the Smithy had succeeded in producing a totally new literature, and all proletarian writers had in some degree been learning from past masters. The question clearly was which classics should be imitated, and for Fadeyev, the classics added up to one author, Leo Tolstoy. Rebelling against the modernism of Bely and Pilnyak, which had infected even proletarian writing, Fadeyev, and with him the leading proletarian writers, reverted to the style of their "grandfathers," the great masters of classical realism.

Tolstoy was made to order for the proletarians. His approach to character seemed rational in that his probing tended to reveal the motivation of behavior in terms of environment, memory, hidden needs, and desires. His method had solid sanction from the nineteenth-century socialist critic Chernyshevsky, who called him a "dialectician of the human psyche," and from Lenin, who admired his ability to "remove the masks" from social convention. And his artistic means are so simple and economical in appearance that it would seem anyone might use them with profit. Fadeyev reported that before writing his novel, *The Nineteen*, he reread *War and Peace* in its entirety.

The Nineteen reveals hardly a trace of "Pilnyakian" device. It is free of excited lyrical digression. Its language is a smooth instrument of communication featuring matter rather than manner. Syntactic distortion, verbal play, self-conscious ornamentation are scrupulously avoided, almost for the first time in Soviet prose. The important thing for Fadeyev is the political *idea* of the book, and he exercises what literary skill he has to express that idea in terms of individual human experience. The result is a novel which, in spite of its reversion to an earlier realistic style, struck the Soviet reader as a new departure, for it described real people rather than a clash of primitive forces or the inexorable historical march of masses.

The political purpose of the novel is to show, in a small band of guerrillas operating in parts of Siberia controlled by the Whites and the

Japanese, the nexus of relations binding together the social forces which made the Revolution. The band contains peasants, workmen, professional revolutionaries, "*lumpen*proletarians," students, intellectuals. The psychology of each class is presented in the inner thoughts and feelings of a particular representative. Thus the peasant has a violent hatred of former landlords, but so strong a love for his own little plot of ground that he fails to understand larger issues; the youthful intellectual Mechik has a romantic attachment to "the workers" and "the Revolution" but can't be relied upon in a crisis; the unruly proletarian anarchist Morozka develops loyalty and discipline in association with the band. And it is the "real" worker, the miner Dubov, who understands most clearly the great issues of the time, and the leader of the band, the Jew Levinson, lays his greatest reliance on Dubov and his men.

In Levinson, Fadeyev created a new kind of hero. Levinson has all the square-jawed ruthlessness of Kozhuk in *The Iron Flood* or Gleb Chumalov in *Cement*, and he presents to his men the image of unbreakable resolve. But he also has a secret inner life and a consciousness of his own weaknesses. The techniques for revealing the private as well as the public thoughts of his characters Fadeyev learned from Tolstoy. He confessed, "When working on *The Nineteen* I often found myself subconsciously imitating Tolstoy even in my choice of words and in the rhythm of my sentences."

Examples of the Tolstoyan technique of the inner monologue and other Tolstoyan devices are common in the novel. The young intellectual Mechik muses about his working-class girl friend, Varya:

> His thoughts carried him far away into the bright days of the future, and in consequence they were light and airy, dissolving of their own accord like the soft, rosy clouds over the plains of the taiga. He thought how he would return with Varya to the town in a cushioned, jolting train with open windows, through which they would see just such soft, rosy clouds sailing over the darkening chain of mountains in the distance. They two would sit at the window, very close to each other, Varya murmuring soft words to him, he stroking her head, and her braids would shine like gold, like the noonday sun . . . The Varya of his daydreams bore little resemblance to the round-shouldered woman of the pump at No. 1 Pit, since all his imaginings were remote from actual things and embodied only what he longed to see.

Mechik sees Morozka and Varya return from a tryst in the woods:

> When he saw Morozka again, returning so soon from the forest (the orderly was swinging his arms as he walked, his steps heavy and slow), Mechik, with the subconscious assurance which is

based on no concrete fact, but which does not permit of doubt, realized that "nothing had happened" between Morozka and Varya, and that he, Mechik, was the cause. An uneasy joy and an inexplicable feeling of guilt woke in him, and he began to be afraid of encountering Morozka's murderous glance.

The adjutant Baklanov involuntarily reveals his reverence for the leader:

> "What? . . ." Baklanov asked again in threatening tones, turning his whole body to the man in the way Levinson would (Baklanov thought that Levinson did this in order to emphasize the importance of his questions, but in point of fact Levinson twisted in this manner because he had been wounded in the neck and could not turn round in any other way).

Fadeyev's novel is simple in its plot and straightforward in its execution. Levinson's band, trapped and hopelessly outnumbered, is beaten and decimated. Only nineteen men escape, and they go on, defeated but not demoralized, ready to fight again for the Revolution. The revelation of that leader's human weaknesses, his fear in battle, his secret failures in self-confidence, and the near collapse of his strength and will in the face of disaster was the new touch that added to Fadeyev's proletarian novel the fillip of human verisimilitude. Fadeyev claimed to have created, in Levinson, not a saint but a "living man." He did succeed, in any case, in jolting the reader with this picture of an abject and miserable commander surveying the poor remnant of his band:

> Levinson's eyes remained fixed for several seconds on the men. Then all at once he somehow collapsed and shrank, and everybody at once noticed that he had become weak and much older. He was no longer ashamed of his weakness and he no longer tried to hide it; he sat huddled up in the saddle, slowly blinking his long wet eyelashes, and the tears ran down his beard . . . The men turned aside in fear that they might lose control of themselves.
>
> Levinson turned his horse and slowly went on ahead. The company followed him.
>
> "Don't cry! . . . What good . . . will that do?" Gontcharenko said humbly, raising Varya by the shoulder.
>
> Whenever Levinson forgot himself he started to look behind him in uncertainty; remembering that Baklanov was not there, he began to cry again.
>
> So they rode out from the forest—the nineteen.

Fadeyev's second novel was planned as an ambitious fictional effort to be published in six substantial parts. Only the first four parts had been completed at his death in 1956, and he was at that time engaged in writing the fifth part, of which one chapter was published. *The Last of the Udegs* has, like *The Nineteen,* an idea which gives it form and content. The Udegs, a remote nomadic tribe of the Russian Far East, whose contacts with twentieth-century civilization have been sporadic and brief and whose culture is still on the level of primitive communism, are suddenly confronted with the Communism of a modern world state. Fadeyev planned to demonstrate in telling their story the thesis that an extremely primitive people under the guidance of the Soviet government may experience a leap from tribal communism to the complex collective organization of the twentieth century, skipping over the intervening historical stages: family, private property, slavery, feudalism, capitalism and socialism. Lines from Engel's *Origin of the Family, Private Property, and the State* stood as an epigraph in an early edition of the novel. But to describe the novel solely in terms of ideology does less than justice to a work over which Fadeyev labored for many years and to which he gave his best as a writer. Uneven though it is, *The Last of the Udegs* contains some of Fadeyev's best pages, and the fact that he spent his energies on literary administration rather than on the completion of this novel is a minor tragedy. In concept it was to be, in a sense, an experiment in the juxtaposition and contrast of various stages in the development of human societies, and each stage had its representative in a particular person. There are a dozen or more clearly delineated characters, the merchant-capitalist, the radical intellectual, the peasant revolutionary, the proletarian socialist, the Chinese merchant, and, last, the members of the primitive Udeg community itself whose way of life was to be radically altered through contact with history in the form of collectivized farming.

When Fadeyev describes in translucent prose the simple way of life of the Udeg tribes, their adjustment to cruel seasonal changes, their hunting expeditions, the education of their young, their courtship and marriage customs, he covers very skillfully ground which has, no doubt, been gone over before. And yet the story of these simple but hardly innocent people abruptly confronted with the weapons and the violent issues of modern Europe has a power of historical drama not wholly dampened by the author's insistent Marxist message.

The Young Guard, Fadeyev's novel about the guerrilla resistance to the German occupation during the Second World War, has had a sorry fate. Published in 1945, it was awarded a Stalin Prize, first class. In the same year a dramatization was presented in Leningrad. Discussion of the novel took place in factories, at meetings of the Young Communist League, and in the Writers' Union. Defects were pointed out, the presence of which Fadeyev acknowledged in a letter covering his "errors":

I was criticized not because the underground fighters were poorly described, but because I should have given a broader picture of the activity of our Party in the underground, and because I should have shown not only Bolsheviks who were weakly organized and who failed, but chiefly such as were capable of organizing a genuine resistance to the German occupationists. The latter were of course more typical, and I shall take this advice.

A revised and enlarged edition of the novel was published in 1951. A comparison of the two versions shows that Fadeyev included new material giving credit to the centralized Party apparatus for a movement that had in the first edition been presented as a spontaneous manifestation in the young of Soviet patriotism.

The operation performed on *The Young Guard* damaged but did not destroy it. Fadeyev displays in it a stylistic virtuosity that was absent from both *The Nineteen* and *The Last of the Udegs*. An occasional note of romanticism recalls the early Civil War novels, and elements of the heroic national saga have reminded some critics of Gogol's *Taras Bulba*. As in so many of the Civil War novels, including his own *The Nineteen*, the most powerful scenes, those labored over with special devotion and skill, are scenes of disorganization and defeat. Quite possibly the best writing in *The Young Guard* is to be found in those pages which describe the retreat of the Red Army before the Germans and the confused and tragic evacuation of the civilian population.

A study of Fadayev's career as a writer and as a literary official would throw much light on Soviet society. He was another of the young Red Army commissars who entered proletarian literature in the early twenties with firm convictions and great plans. He was one of the principal leaders of the Russian Association of Proletarian Writers and, along with Averbakh and Libedinsky, devised its literary platform and fought its literary battles. When RAPP was liquidated in 1932 and his comrades fell into disgrace, Fadeyev himself wrote a series of earnest articles (*Old and New*) in support of the new regime in literature. He survived the purges of 1936–1938 while many of those same comrades were shot or sent into exile. His role during this period is difficult to assess on the basis of information we now have. From 1939 to 1954 he was Secretary of the Executive Board of the Union of Soviet Writers. He was thus directly involved in policies that led to the debasement of Soviet literature, and he was the official spokesman of its Stalinist period. He was not re-elected as Secretary of the Union at the Second Congress of Soviet Writers held in 1954, after the death of Stalin. There is evidence that he suffered from alcoholism, and had undergone hospital treatment for that ailment. In May 1956, early in the de-Stalinization period, he shot himself. Probably the most honest words spoken in public about him were those of the novelist Sholokhov at the Twentieth Congress of the Communist Party:

> Why couldn't someone long ago have said to Fadeyev: "The thirst for power is a contemptible thing in the writers' world. The Writers' Union is not a military body, nor is it a punitive battalion, and no writer need stand at attention before you, Comrade Fadeyev . . ." For a great many years Fadeyev was a "general secretary" and gave his time exclusively to such business. The result is that we lost a good writer, and now we have also lost a "general secretary" (*Pravda*, February 21, 1956)

Mikhail Sholokhov: The Don Cossacks

When the first installments of Sholokhov's *The Silent Don* appeared in 1928 in the magazine *October*, published by the Moscow Association of Proletarian Writers, it was as though some natural phenomenon suddenly burst forth outside the normal chain of cause and effect. Their author, who was just twenty-two, was relatively unknown, and his *Stories of the Don*, published in 1924 and 1925, had given no one reason to suppose that he possessed major literary talent. He was not one of the youthful commissars who had come to Moscow after the Civil War to produce proletarian literature but the son of an entrepreneur and administrator who had settled in the Don Cossack region and married a woman of partly Cossack origin. He was and always remained averse to the normal means of publicity available to Soviet writers: his name is not conspicuous in collections of autobiographies or of essays on "How We Write" or "The Nature of the Writer's Work." And as one installment of *The Silent Don* followed another the fascinated Soviet reader sensed that this new star hardly belonged in its proletarian constellation. The story contained no inept digression on the iron will of the proletariat—in fact the village characters were not proletarians at all in the generally accepted meaning of the term, but Cossacks, the traditional support of the government against the Revolution. One superb scene after another convinced the Soviet reader at last that no clear political thesis would emerge, that no commissar would appear to guide the "elemental forces," that no problems of Communist ethics would be raised and solved. *The Silent Don* became in a very short time the favorite reading of millions of Russians, and such it has remained. In the life-and-death story of a remote Cossack village on the Don the reader could experience the full tragedy of his own war and revolution unhindered by the verbal complexity of a stylist or the lucid commentary of a commissar. Events in the lives of ordinary human beings were in the center of Sholokhov's focus, and not from theoretical considerations, but because they entered organically into his design. For instance, a moment just before dawn when Gregor Melekhov is watering his brother's horse is completely captured:

> Aslant across the Don lay a waving, never-trodden moon path. Over the Don hung a mist, and above it the grain of stars. The horse set its hind hoofs down cautiously. The drop to the water was bad going. From the farther side of the river came the quacking of ducks. A sheatfish turned and darted over the water above the mud by the bank, hunting in the shallows for smaller fry.
>
> Gregor stood a long time by the river. The bank exuded a dank and sickly rottenness. A tiny drop of water fell from the horse's lips. A light, pleasant void was in Gregor's heart. He felt happy and carefree. The red-tailed dawn was pecking up the starry grain from the dove-colored floor of heaven.
>
> Close to the stable he ran into his mother.
>
> "That you, Grishka?" she asked.
>
> "Who else?"
>
> "Watered the horse?"
>
> "Yes," he answered shortly.

And the haymaking in the Cossack Village:

> The haymaking began immediately after Trinity. From early morning the meadow blossomed with women's holiday skirts, the bright embroidery of aprons, and colored kerchiefs. The whole village turned out for the mowing. The mowers and rakers attired themselves as though for an annual holiday. So it had been from of old. From the Don to the distant alder clumps the ravaged meadowland stirred and pulsed.

Or Aksinia filling her pails at the river:

> Her pails scraping, Aksinia went down to the Don. The foam serpentined along the shore in an intricate yellow lacework on the green hem of the wave. White seagulls were hovering and mewing above the river. Tiny fish sprinkled in a silver rain over the surface of the water. On the other side, beyond the white of the sandy headland, the gray tops of ancient poplars rose haughtily and sternly. As Aksinia was drawing water she dropped her pail. Raising her skirt, she waded in up to her knees. The water swirled and tickled her calves, and for the first time since Stepan's return she laughed, quietly and uncertainly.

And the husband when he is deserted by an unfaithful wife:

> He stared around the room, and at last he understood. He dropped the lamp, tore his sabre down from the wall, gripped the

hilt until the veins swelled in his fingers, raised Aksinia's blue and yellow jacket on its point, threw the jacket up in the air and with a short swing of the sabre cut it in two as it fell.

Gray, savage, in his wolfish yearning he threw the pieces of old jacket up to the ceiling again and again; the sharp steel whistled as it cut them in their flight.

Then, tearing off the sword knot, he threw the sabre into a corner, went into the kitchen, and sat down at the table. His head bowed, with trembling fingers he stroked the unwashed table top time after time.

When war and revolution come, they seem to enter these individual lives like drought, flood, and other natural calamities. The author's Marxist viewpoint can be discovered if one looks for it in his selection of detail and system of emphasis, but through most of the book this viewpoint is neither explicit nor obvious. The long and multiplaned story of his heroes' lives is told with objectivity and in a mood of reflective detachment. Political viewpoint becomes obtrusive in the later portions of the novel when the background of war and revolution must be given, and in the 1953 edition passages of an offensively tendentious nature were inserted under pressure from Stalin.

But those who in 1928 read the first volume of the novel as it appeared in *October* were struck first of all by its freedom from the familiar idiom of proletarian art. Surprise was expressed in many quarters at its originality and power. Serafimovich published a review in *Pravda* in which he likened Sholokhov to a baby eaglet who suddenly spreads enormous wings. Others were incredulous, and rumors soon began circulating that *The Silent Don* was actually the work of a White officer killed during the Civil War whose manuscript Sholokhov had appropriated and presented as his own. This accusation was so widespread and so persistent that it was felt necessary to answer it publicly. A statement appeared in *Pravda* in March 1929, signed by Serafimovich, Fadayev, and Stavsky, who claimed to have seen Sholokhov's own notes for the novel and the rough draft of his manuscript. But the story of plagiarism is still heard in Russia and in the emigration, and many still refuse to believe that the proletarian writer Sholokhov is the author of *The Silent Don*.

Two books published in the middle seventies once more called in question Sholokhov's authorship of *The Silent Don*, and one of them actually proposed an alternative author, the Cossack writer F. D. Kryukov (1870–1920). That book, *The Current of the Quiet Don*, was authored by an unidentified Soviet scholar using the pseudonym D*, and carried a supporting introduction by Solzhenitsyn, which argued that Sholokhov could not have been the author because he was uneducated, because he was too young to have witnessed the events described, and because Sholokhov as a strict adherent of the Communist ideology, could never have been as fair and objective as the author of *The Silent Don* often is. Those arguments are seriously flawed. Neither formal education nor direct experience of one's theme have ever been a requirement for the writing of good fiction. A case in point is the greatest novel about the American Civil War, *The Red Badge of Courage*, whose author, Stephen Crane, was born six years after the war ended. The early sections of *The Silent Don*, moreover, were written in the twenties, when many proletarian writers were trying to practice objectivity and even-handedness in the assignment of dark and light colors (see chapter 6). As for the possibility that the Cossack writer Kryukov is the author, Herman Ermolaev has carefully compared *The Silent Don* with Kryukov's published works and demonstrated that they are by different hands. Roy Medvedev's *Problems in the Literary Biography of Mikhail Sholokhov* (1977) supported the old charge of plagiarism, but Medvedev's book has been shown to contain both factual errors and superficial stylistic analysis. There is no evidence to support the suspicion of plagiarism, but Sholokhov's long history of endorsing repressive actions against literary men and his generally malodorous behavior make certain that the charge will surface again.

The vast design of Sholokhov's novel as it began to emerge in the published installments in 1928 was surprising. Prose fiction as it revived in the twenties had been largely confined to short, concentrated pieces centering on particular events and relatively few characters. None had yet attempted an epic of "war and peace" rivaling Leo Tolstoy's in the dimensions of its canvas and the number and variety of its characters. Sholokhov's "epic" in its final form consists of four volumes in eight parts totaling 1500 pages, and is thus somewhat longer than *War and Peace*. The first two parts deal with life in a Cossack village before the First World War, the action of the novel beginning in 1912. In its portrayal of the manners and mores and in its reproduction of the dialect of these Cossacks, the novel has some claim to merit as an ethnographic document, and as such it was read by many critics. Conversations are reported in the actual dialect of the speakers and even descriptive passages are laced with vocabulary and phrase-turns peculiar to the Don region. Because the novel was difficult reading for its Russian audience, it was provided, when published in book form, with a glossary giving the Russian equivalents of about three hundred local words.

The third part, which concludes the first volume, describes the intrusion upon the Cossack community of the First World War, and the disturbance in its normal life brought about by the loss of its men to the front lines. The moment of excitement and tragedy at the beginning of the war is given in the following image, where the late summer haymowing is interrupted by the news of war:

> As they crossed the field track Piotra glanced to his left, and noticed a tiny cloud of dust moving swiftly along the distant high road from the village.
>
> "Someone riding there!" he remarked to Natalia, screwing up his eyes.
>
> "Fast! Look at the dust!" Natalia replied in surprise.
>
> "What's up? Daria!" Piotra called to his wife. "Rein in for a minute, and let's watch that rider!"
>
> The cloud of dust dropped down into a hollow and disappeared, then came up again on the other side. Now the figure of the rider could be seen through the dust. Piotra sat gazing, his dirty palm set against the edge of his straw summer hat. He frowned and took his hand away; "He'll kill that horse—riding at a gallop like that."
>
> Now the horseman could be seen quite plainly. He was riding his horse at a furious gallop, his left hand holding his cap, a dusty red flag fluttering in his right. He rode along the track so close to them that Piotra heard his horse panting as it breathed the overheated air into its lungs. As he passed, the man shouted:
>
> "Alarm!"
>
> A flake of yellow soapy foam flew from his horse and fell into a hoof print. Piotra followed the rider with his eyes. The heavy snort of the horse, and, as he stared after the retreating figure, the horse's croup, wet, and glittering like a steel blade, remained impressed in his memory.

The second volume (parts four and five) describes the growth of discontent and the outbreak of revolution both in the army and in the village. The third volume (part six) deals with the struggle in the Don country between the revolutionary Cossacks under Podtyolkov and the Whites under Kaledin. The fourth (parts seven and eight) has as its central theme the uprising against the Reds in the Tatarsk area and its bloody suppression. In the last three parts much attention is given to the fate of individuals and of Cossack families torn apart by the changing fortunes of civil war. The central figure in the novel, its "hero" Gregor Melekhov, is a young man whose rebellious love affair with his married neighbor Aksinia Astakhova runs as a single thread through the narrative as its focus shifts from the village to the war fronts or to the capital in the days of the Revolution and again back to its structural center, the village.

Sholokhov's panoramic novel has been compared both to Tolstoy's *War and Peace* and to *Anna Karenina;* though there are similarities the comparison is not helpful, since the two writers are far apart in their style and in the kind of world they portray. Sholokhov's concept was undoubtedly influenced by *War and Peace,* and the movement of the story is reminiscent of Tolstoy's work: the fortunes of a few Cossack families are traced through upheavals of world-wide significance, the scene shifting back and forth from public to private events and lives. Like Tolstoy, Sholokhov introduces historical personages, the Cossack general Kaledin and the revolutionary Podtyolkov, for instance, as characters in the story, and actual historical documents, for example Lenin's statements on imperialist war, are worked into the text of the novel. The battle scenes, especially those seen through the eyes of Gregor Melekhov, owe much to Tolstoy. Sholokhov has learned the trick of using the viewpoint of the naïve observer to convey an impression of violent confusion, to produce, in Shklovsky's terms, an estrangement. And Melekhov's groping search for the right path to take in the confusing clash of armies and parties, his adherence first to the Reds then to the Whites, and at last to no party, does have a tenuous likeness to Pierre's search for truth. But the ways in which Sholokhov is simply himself and quite different from Tolstoy are more interesting and more significant.

Sholokhov was born in 1905 and grew to manhood in a period of constant bloody strife in which he himself was a participant. His sensitive artist's vision preserved and recreated innumerable scenes of violence. The novel opens with the savage stamping to death by the villagers of Prokoffey Melekhov's pregnant Turkish wife, suspected of being a witch, and Prokoffey's revenge on one of the instigators:

"Drag the bitch into the yard!" came a roar from the steps. A regimental comrade of Prokoffey's wound the Turkish woman's hair around one hand, pressed his other hand over her screaming mouth, dragged her at a run through the porch and flung her beneath the feet of the crowd. A thin shriek rose above the howl of voices. Prokoffey sent half a dozen cossacks flying, burst into the hut, and snatched a sabre from the wall. Jostling against one another, the cossacks rushed out of the porch. Swinging the gleaming, whistling sabre around his head, Prokoffey ran down the steps. The crowd shuddered and scattered over the yard.

Lushnya was heavy of gait, and by the threshing floor Prokoffey caught up with him; with a diagonal sweep down across the left shoulder from behind he clave the cossack's body to the belt. Tearing out the stakes of the wattle fence, the crowd poured across the threshing floor into the steppe.

Some half hour later the crowd ventured to approach Prokoffey's farm again. Two of them crept cautiously into the porch. On the kitchen threshold, in a pool of blood, her head flung back awkwardly, lay Prokoffey's wife; her lips writhed tormentedly back from her teeth, her gnawed tongue protruded. Prokoffey, with shaking head and glassy stare, was wrapping a squealing, crimson, slippery little ball—the prematurely born infant—in a sheepskin.

Violent emotion that issues in cruel attack upon the persons of other human beings is the stuff of which *The Silent Don* is made, and it is made with great skill. The action is punctuated at regular intervals with scenes of irreparable injury committed by one human being on the body of another. As Stepan Astakhov beat and kicked his faithless wife: "You would have thought, watching him from a distance, that it was someone doing the Cossack dance." Aksinia's father, after raping her, was beaten by her mother and brother, and they "went on beating him steadily for half an hour." The despised Ukrainians are beaten by Cossacks in a fight over a turn in line at the flour mill: "At the door of the weighing shed a young Ukrainian boy lay with a broken head in a pool of blood; bloody strands of hair fell over his face." A troop of Cossacks drag a young girl into a shed and rape her one after another, and afterwards: "She lay on her back, her legs crossing and uncrossing like scissors blades, her fingers scrabbling in the snow by the wall." Podtyolkov's men slaughter their captured White officers; Podtyolkov's men are themselves slaughtered and their bodies piled into a hastily dug hole. The Red Misha Koshevoi kills the father and grandfather of his enemy, Mitry Korshunov; Mitry Korshunov returns after the Whites recapture the town and kills all the remaining Koshevois, old and young: "And Mitry throws a rope around the old woman's neck and drags her along the ground, just as though she was a dog—and she, poor thing, doesn't make a sound."

Scenes such as these are recurrent in the novel, and the author dwells on them with detached horror. Tolstoy no doubt witnessed such events, but the conventions of Tolstoy's realism did not admit the literary treatment of such matter. Gorky, rather than Tolstoy, is here the model, but Sholokhov has left all his models far behind in mastering the techniques of raw naturalism.

Sholokhov probably has no masters in one other area: the expression in physical terms of overpowering human emotion. Sometimes the effect is humorous, as when Pantaleimon Melekhov, in a frenzy of rage at his sons, "slobbers his beard, and dances up and down in the field." And grief at the death of a loved person in Sholokhov's world literally strikes men to the ground: "Like a blind man he ran into the gate, gave a hollow cry, fell down . . . and crawled along the ground on all fours, moving faster and faster, his face almost touching the ground." And the onset of sexual love literally "moves" his characters: "A wave of rapture and heavy joy carried Bunchuk away. He bowed his head as though before a blow, and said, half seriously, half in jest: 'Anya, you're as good as someone's happiness.' "

His chronicle of human disaster Sholokhov projects against the background of nature—of the silent River Don flowing endless and unperturbed to the sea. Nature he perceives in moments of lyric clarity and reduces it to fresh and unusual, if at times somewhat strained, metaphors. The poetry in Sholokhov's roughly realistic prose is its most original feature.

The Silent Don is a much better book in its earlier than in its later chapters, and most commentators agree that there is a decline in imaginative power in the last two volumes, where it becomes necessary to tie together the threads of the chronicle. The novel then becomes an account of the victory of the Reds over the Whites, and the author, a conscious Marxist, includes documentary material and commentary intended to illuminate the historical significance of that victory. Unlike Tolstoy, who believes that there must be an iron necessity in history but does not claim to know the laws of its movement, Sholokhov has at his disposal in Marxism a scientific explanation of those laws, and a forecast of the future. His Marxism does not vitiate, however, Sholokhov's feeling for certain basic realities. His hero, searching for the right path, does not find it in Communism. He finds no answer to his questions, and after his tortured journey returns precisely to that spot which he had left as the novel opened and which remained for him the only reality, his own home and family.

> And now had come to pass that little thing of which Gregor had dreamed during so many sleepless nights . . . He was standing at the threshold of his own home, holding his son in his arms.
> This was all that was left of him in life and that still made him kin with the spacious earth that lay glittering under the chilly sun.

The final emphasis on a separate, individual existence independent of nations and history, so reminiscent of the ending of *War and Peace* on a note of family happiness, argues that Sholokhov is philosophically close to Tolstoy and that in him Marxist historical doctrine is less than skin deep. Though the Reds do beat the Whites (and indeed who in Sholokhov's world is not "beaten"), *The Silent Don* is not a happy or a hopeful book. Life's movement we sense in it, but (even though his

characters tell us about it in confident terms) we do not have a sure
sense of its direction. The interpretation of the novel according to
which Gregor's individualism is "wrong" and the outlook and behavior
of the Communist hero Koshevoi "right" belongs to the Soviet critics
rather than Sholokhov. The novel is so contrived that the reader identifies himself and sympathizes with Gregor and with no other character.

Yet Sholokhov has been responsive to Party demand upon his talent.
Recent studies have shown that the text of *The Silent Don* suffered during the Stalin period from emendations aimed at eliminating vulgarity
in its language or deviations in its politics. The most damaging alterations of the text occurred in the 1953 edition, but in the 1956 edition
older readings have in almost all cases been restored.

He was responsive to the Party's literary needs in 1930, when, on a
visit to Moscow, he was persuaded to interrupt the writing of *The Silent
Don* in order to produce a novel on the collectivization of agriculture in
the Don region. The first part of this novel, the title of which, *Podnyataya Tselina*, has been translated as *Seeds of Tomorrow*, or *Virgin Soil Upturned*, was completed in 1931. After publishing the first part Sholokhov
returned to the writing of *The Silent Don*, which he completed in 1940,
and the second and final part of the novel on collectivization did not
appear until 1960. The latter has been translated under the title *Harvest
on the Don* (1961). During the nearly twenty years while he worked on it
rumors were rife as to the reasons for the failure to finish it. There was
speculation abroad that Sholokhov was not in sympathy with the direction of Stalinist policy and that changes in the novel had been dictated which he refused to accept. Inside the Soviet Union scarcely
veiled charges were made from time to time that Sholokhov had not
been able to finish the novel because he did not "really understand" socialism on the land.

In the years from 1940 to 1960 Sholokhov published little. During the
war he traveled on various fronts as a correspondent, but found that he
had no skill in the writing of newspaper sketches. A short story, "The
Science of Hatred" (1942), has some historical significance in that it
shows the transformation of a good-natured Russian officer, disposed
to tolerate and even to like his fellow man, into a furious hater of all
Germans. Sholokhov in this story draws heavily on his resources for
the portrayal of extremes of emotion. Chapters from a novel about the
Second World War, *They Fought for Their Country*, planned as a major
production, have appeared. The short story "Fate of a Man," published
in *Pravda* in 1957, has been translated into many languages and made
into a distinguished film. The story is a powerful and tender treatment
of the resilience of human love under adversity.[3]

A Scatter of Minor Deities

Out of the Proletcult, the Smithy, and the RAPP organization there emerged a number of proletarian poets and prose writers whose very names have in many case been forgotten. The principal poets have already been mentioned. The prose writers are not without a certain literary and historical interest. P. K. Bessalko (1887–1920) belonged to the older generation of proletarian writers and spent many years in exile in Western Europe. A pupil of Bogdanov, he became a fanatical theorist of proletarian exclusiveness in the arts, and is the author of a work on proletarian poetry. In a series of autobiographical novels he traces the growth of a working-class child into a conscious revolutionary. N. Lyashko—pseudonym of N. N. Lyashchenko (1884–1953)—began to publish in provincial magazines before the revolution of 1905, and, like Bessalko, he sentimentalizes the worker in a manner peculiar to proletarians of the older generation. His most important work, *The Blast Furnace* (1924), is a predecessor of *Cement* in the depiction of proletarian reconstruction in industry, and it outdoes *Cement* in romanticizing the proletarian collective at the expense both of individuals and of other social groups. In this novel the toiling mass, heroic in its devotion and faith, brings to life again a decaying industrial plant.

V. M. Bakhmetyev (1885–1963) qualifies as a proletarian writer by early membership in the Bolshevik faction of the Russian Social Democratic Party. He is one of the best representatives of the proletarian school of psychological realism. His most important work, *The Crime of Martyn* (1928), is an interesting psychological study in the motivations of a Communist functionary, revealing the clash of his instinctive drives with carefully learned rules of behavior. It is a study in the dominance of instinctive behavior.

Alexander Neverov (1886–1923), whose promise for Soviet literature was ended by his early death, was closer to the peasantry than to the proletariat. *Tashkent, City of Bread* (1923) is an account of the search for survival by a young boy who during the famine year leaves his village on the Volga and, always displaying courage and cleverness, makes his way to the "city of abundance," Tashkent. Neverov was the author of numerous sketches and stories of peasant life, and his plays were awarded a prize in the State Publishing House competition of 1920.

A number of new writers appeared in the pages of the RAPP publication *October* at the end of the twenties. Some of these displayed the promise of new talent, but, in most cases, have been lost to Soviet literature. L. S. Ovalov (b. 1905) wrote a number of stories in which the central characters are rank-and-file Soviet workers whose lives and thoughts are honestly explored. The story "Chatter" (1929) is in the form of casual notes describing the everyday activities of a printer, a man of the older generation whose comments on the contemporary scene are pointed and sharp. A second story, "Hunters of Doubts" (1930), dealt with the underground Trotskyist opposition movement, and Ovalov took his readers inside that movement to reveal the kind of people who were drawn to it. He represents them as mistaken but honest revolutionaries, and his story documents the underground political life of the times.

A. Mitrofanov (1899–1951) is the author of stories and sketches on the life of the young Communists, and his best product was the story "June-July," the first part of which appeared in 1930. Mitrofanov in this story presents sympathetically a number of young people who are disillusioned with the direction the Revolution has taken. A cruel campaign against Mitrofanov as an apologist for such attitudes was launched soon after the appearance of the first part of his story.

An able and interesting proletarian writer, now largely forgotten, was Sergey Semyonov (1893–1942), whose best and most popular work was *Natalya Tarpova* (1928), a long novel dealing with the private and personal as well as the official lives of Communist party functionaries during the NEP period. Semyonov was one of the best practitioners of psychological realism, and his lancet frequently lays bare the inner lives and thoughts of his characters; in fact his chief skill is in reporting the stream of unspoken thoughts and desires that lie behind their actions. The central theme of the novel is the conflict inside a Communist woman between the natural affection she feels for a bourgeois engineer and her strict set of Bolshevik values. The novel is a valuable historical document in that it gives an entirely credible account of the problems of marriage and morality as they were examined at that time and in that milieu.

Finally, the proletarian novelist Fyodor Panfyorov (1896–1960), a very prolific writer, gave his principal attention to the collectivization of peasant life. The long novel *And Then The Harvest* (1928–1937), on which his fame largely rests, develops its thesis from the processes which militated against individualism and in favor of collective enterprise. Panfyorov is like Furmanov in the frankness with which his thesis is stated and developed, yet he gives vivid portraits of a great variety of village and Party types, showing the tensions that existed between the peasant who simply loved his land and the organizers possessed by a theory and a program. The novel, especially in its early chapters, is interesting and rewarding reading. The non-Soviet reader finds less rewarding those sections that describe the efforts of peasant leaders to overcome "petit-bourgeois individualism" in the village. Panfyorov has keen powers of observation and his peasants are real and interesting people.

The Struggle For Peace (1945–1948) is a long novel about operations behind the German lines during the war. *Mother Volga* (1953) returns to the theme of peasant life and the struggle for production. Panfyorov's frank realism in the treatment of peasant character and setting is one of the most interesting features of this novel, as it is of the story "In the Name of the Young" (1960). Like so many Soviet novelists his work is painfully uneven. Pages of excellent writing regularly yield to journalistic statement.

Conclusion

Few of the writers in the proletarian literary movement had ties either to the urban working class or to the intelligentsia. Many were of peasant stock, but the majority came from middle-class provincial families. This is true of the most prominent among them: Fadeyev, Sholokhov, Furmanov, Libedinsky, Averbakh, and Serafimovich. Their education was purely Russian. They had few contacts with Europe, and only rarely betray awareness of Western literature. Fadeyev speaks with great respect of Balzac, but that is no doubt an echo of Engels' favorable opinion, and there is no evidence that Fadeyev himself had any interest in French literature. Averbakh knew German and wrote about Goethe, but from a narrowly proletarian point of view. They were on the whole exclusively Russian in culture and outlook.

They settled easily into group work and placed their literary talents at the service of the movement. They welcomed the organization of literature. Libedinsky's satire of the soulless bureaucrat was directed more at his soullessness than at his bureaucratism. Even Sholokhov, who lived apart from the writers' hive, was, as a Party man in good standing, always available for Party tasks. And so were most of the others.

Narrowly conservative, they recognized only the established traditions of Russian realism. Some of them showed traces of Symbolist contamination, but that was superficial and accidental. They were uneasy with strangeness or originality of form, and preferred writing that was intelligible to the great mass of readers. They were influenced by Tolstoy rather than by Gogol or Dostoevsky, and they carried on the Russian tradition of literature as a social value.

Few of them were satisfied with the mass hero, and their tendency was to seek for individual human experience and to find in their characters thoughts and feelings that were particular and personal. Sholokhov reported that in his initial version of *The Silent Don* the novel was to center on "event" and on generalized portraits, on a historical panorama of Cossack participation in the Revolution. But he rejected that form, he said, and chose to reveal historical events through the lives of the leading characters, who then became the principal elements in the plot. Proletarian literature as a whole underwent an evolution similar to that described by Sholokhov. The idealized metallic sculptures of the first proletarian poets early gave way to Libedinsky's living and suffering human beings, and Serafimovich's faceless monolith broke up into the vivid likenesses of *The Silent Don*.

8   The Critic Voronsky
and the Pereval Group

Criticism and the Study of Literature

Literary criticism during the Soviet period has, paradoxically enough, produced a rich harvest of ideas and literary theories. It is true that original and independent criticism was more common during the twenties than in any other period, and that during the years of Stalin's ascendancy the Russian critical spirit was in a state of suspension from which it is reviving only very slowly. The most powerful stimulus to critical thought came from the Formalist school and writers close to it in spirit, whose activity predates the October Revolution. Shklovsky's contributions to literary criticism on the pages of *Lef* and *New Lef* have already been mentioned. His works on literary theory were equally important: *On the Theory of Prose* (1925), *The Technique of the Writers' Craft* (1927) and the collection of essays *The Knight's Move* (Berlin, 1923) contain some pregnant observations, ideas, theories, and critical *bons mots*. Formalists who are primarily literary scholars have contributed new ideas in a number of areas: Boris Eichenbaum, with his investigation of the works of Leo Tolstoy and his studies of romanticism; and Boris Tomashevsky, with his essays on Pushkin and on the theory and practice of verse making. Yury Tynyanov's collection of essays published under the title *Archaizers and Innovators* (1928) is a brilliant contribution to the study of literary evolution, the theory of parody, Pushkin, Blok, poets of the early twenties, and other things. Formalist ideas and projects were in a state of partial eclipse for many years, but in the sixties and seventies the Soviet Structuralists revived and developed them in new directions.

During the twenties a set of remarkable theoretical works appeared, all associated with M. M. Bakhtin and his school. The authors of these works attempted to free criticism from established and habitual clichés and to clear the ground for a new understanding of language and literature. The principal contribution of the group to literary study was their analysis of literary language in the novel as "dialogic." Bakhtin specialized in studies of dialogue both implicit and explicit, and in the varieties of "reported speech": direct and indirect discourse, quasi-direct discourse or *erlebte rede*, and *skaz*. His analysis is a brilliant contribution to our understanding of literature in the twentieth century: the work of Babel, Zoshchenko, Pilnyak, Solzhenitsyn, and others whom we shall study. He has also contributed an immensely influential study of Dostoevsky, as the author of a new type of novel, in which no single idea or voice dominates but rather a symphony of conflicting ideas is orchestrated.

V. N. Voloshinov's book on Freudianism concentrates on the verbal performance of the patient, considered as part of a social event—the psychoanalytic session. The same author's *Marxism and the Philosophy of Language* (1929) also studies verbal performance as dialogue: "The word is a two-sided act . . . I give myself verbal shape from another's point of view. The word is a bridge between myself and the other." Closely related to his studies of dialogic speech was Bakhtin's study of the carnival spirit in literature, which he first developed in *The Art of Rabelais* (translated as *Rabelais and His World*), written in 1940 but published only in 1965.

Marxist criticism has been more varied and stimulating than might be expected. There has never been, even among official spokesmen, full agreement as to the meaning for literature of Marxism; yet certain basic tenets are shared by Marxist critics who will disagree on almost everything else. They hold that the social structure of a given society depends on the manner in which that society satisfies economic needs. Upon the basis of production and the relationship of social groups to one another in the process of production there is erected, according to their theory, the "superstructure" of religion, art, and literature which constitutes the culture of a given society. If the society is divided into classes this cultural superstructure will reflect the view of life of the dominant class. Only after a classless society has been established will literature, for instance, express the thought and feeling of humanity as a whole. The critic who maintains that the Soviet Union is a classless society must also maintain that Soviet literature has general human significance.

Within this general ideological framework a number of schools of thought developed during the twenties and thirties. Strict application of sociological criteria in literary criticism was the method of A. Bogdanov (1872–1928), V. F. Friche (1870–1929), and V. G. Pereverzev (1882–1969). Bogdanov was the founder and leading theoretician of the Proletcult, whose purpose as we have seen was to develop through the training of working-class writers a specifically proletarian class literature. The dominance of the proletariat in all cultural fields was, Bogdanov believed, a prerequisite to the establishment of the power of the proletariat over society as a whole, and art is a "means of organizing its forces." This position found no sympathy among higher Soviet officials, who were concerned that the Russian proletariat acquire the barest elements of human culture before attempting to create its own literature.

V. F. Friche was a sociological critic who tended to reduce sociology to simple economics. Typical of his approach is an essay on the *Sociology of Literary Styles*, in which he accepts the idea (advanced by Spengler and others) of the unity of styles in all fields of culture during a given period, but rejects as idealistic any but the economic interpretation of this unity: "The first task of sociology in this field [literary criticism] is to work out the relationship of a particular poetic style with a particular economic style." Friche believed that in the coming socialist world man would become a purely rational being and that literary style would reflect the rationalization of his life.

V. G. Pereverzev was an exponent of strict economic determinism in literary criticism, though he rejected Friche's belief in the imminent rationalization of literature. He maintained that in order to understand a given writer the critic should direct his attention not to his biography or his conscious view of the world, not even to his social and political environment, but exclusively to the position occupied by the given writer in the process of production. Thus Dostoevsky's frequent split personalities he explained as so many projections of Dostoevsky himself, a declassed nobleman torn between the values and standards of bourgeois productive relations and his own aristocratic traditions and antecedents. Pereverzev maintained, further, that the process of literary creation is subconscious and that the writer cannot by taking thought himself or by responding to directives from the Party alter the class nature of his "system of images." Indeed the writer works within a "charmed circle" of images, subconsciously determined by his economic environment. If the writer is a proletarian his images are certain to be of proletarian characters. The writer of one economic class cannot even imagine a character of another class. Since the creation of literature is directly determined by productive processes and the author's place in them, such creation cannot be mediated by educational, political, or governmental bodies. Pereverzev thought that the proletarian state could affect literature only by silencing the literary voice of "hostile classes."

Even strict Marxists like Friche and Pereverzev when they analyzed specific works were sometimes able to see them in an original light and reveal important factors, both cultural and psychological, in their production. Pereverzev's work on Dostoevsky and Gogol is a contribution to our understanding of those writers, couched though it is in a strange and seemingly ritualistic Marxist idiom. Other Marxist critics have made contributions of a more modest nature. P. S. Kogan (1872–1932) and V. Polonsky (1886–1932) are the most competent literary historians of the period. N. Piksanov is a scholar who concentrates on the study of literary texts and the process of their production. And two critics associated with the Pereval group, D. A. Gorbov and A. Lezhnev, emphasized psychological factors in literary style.

Voronsky

A strikingly humane tendency in Marxist criticism was represented by Alexander Voronsky (1884–1943), the main object of whose study was the individual writer and creative processes not reducible to terms of economics or sociology. One of the most important literary groups of the twenties was that associated with his name, Pereval (The Divide), and the group is important because its members risked everything and lost in their effort to remain free of a vulgar and dogmatic Marxism. The history of Soviet literature offers some examples of heroism in the face of terror. One such example is the behavior of the Pereval group, and that story should be better known.

Alexander Voronsky, the most sensitive and genuine Marxist critic of the twenties, belonged to the group of Communist intellectuals who supported Trotsky and opposed Stalin. According to a survey of literary trends in the twenties Voronsky belonged to the Trotskyite opposition from 1925 to 1927.[1] He was a courageous man whose opposition, at first clear and sharp, may have been ill concealed even after Stalin's control of the Party was established. When the opposition was defeated in 1927 Voronsky was arrested and sent into exile with other members of that group. After a formal recantation he was permitted to return to Moscow in 1930, where he continued to write and worked as an editor in the State Publishing House but was never again prominent as a critic. He was arrested again in 1935 and, according to the 1958 edition of the *Small Soviet Encyclopedia*, he died in 1943. No details of his death have been published, but it probably occurred in prison or in a labor camp. His name has been posthumously cleared of criminal charges, though the influence he exerted on Soviet literature is still described as heterodox and harmful.[2]

The debt which Soviet literature owes to Voronsky is very great. He deserves more credit than any other literary man for the revival which took place during the twenties. As a Party assignment he edited the magazine *Red Virgin Soil* from 1921 to 1927. This magazine carried important essays on history, economics, and politics along with a generous assortment of contemporary poetry and fiction. The publication was a Soviet version of the so-called "fat" journals which served the Russian intelligentsia during the nineteenth century. As an editor Voronsky soon earned the suspicion of proletarian literary groups, and the reason would seem to be that the criteria he followed in the selection of stories and poems for publication tended to be literary rather than social or political. The result of his policy was that non-Communist and nonproletarian intellectuals were able to make their contribution to Soviet literature. Rigid dogmatists attacked him as a fool or a traitor because he had opened the pages of the Soviet press to an alien element. In the course of a long and bitter controversy Voronsky examined his position and that of his opponents, presented an analysis of the nature and function of imaginative literature, and defended his own activities—always with courage and sometimes with patient scorn.

Voronsky was, during most of his adult life, an active Marxist revolutionary, and his ideas about the nature and function of literature developed at first within the framework of Marxist thought. The defense of his own liberal publishing policy he based on the writings of Belinsky and Plekhanov, both acceptable in the Soviet Union of the twenties as authorities on literary questions, and in his polemic with the organizers of art he restated certain ideas that had long been current in the Russian Marxist milieu. These ideas are still recognizably Hegelian, even after having been filtered through the thought of Belinsky, Plekhanov, and finally Voronsky.

Voronsky maintained, first of all, that art provides knowledge of the world in the form of sensible images. The artist, the scientist, and the philosopher are alike in that they all deal with "reality"; but whereas the scientist investigates and analyzes its nature and the philosopher generalizes about it, the artist presents his knowledge of reality in the vesture of sensible form. Philosophy and science offer their truths primarily to the mind, art to the sensuous nature of man, but what all three offer is truth. It followed from this that any genuine work of literature, though conditioned by the social origin of the writer and the historical period in which he lived, has an objective value as "cognition of life." And Voronsky pointed out—as in that time it was necessary to point out—that the great literature of the past, though it may have been the product of slaveowners or feudal lords, was a revelation of human experience and, as such, a permanent possession of all mankind, including the Russian proletariat. The works of supposedly bourgeois social origin which he published in *Red Virgin Soil* should be judged, therefore, by their value as artistic products first of all, rather than as social commentary or propaganda. And the aesthetic value of a work of art depends, he maintained, upon the validity of the images presented in it, their faithfulness to the nature of that which is portrayed.[3]

Voronsky's basic views do no offense to Marxist ideology and need not have troubled the state. Indeed he carefully eschewed any claim to a possibly dangerous originality in propagating such views, maintaining that he was a more orthodox Marxist than were his opponents, the champions of proletarian hegemony in art. Many of the most important political figures of the day supported him in this contention, among them Trotsky and the Commissar for Education, Lunacharsky.

But to those government figures who saw in literature and art only weapons to be used in the service of the state, the activity of Voronsky both as editor and as critic seemed close to treason. Averbakh, one of the leaders of the proletarian literary movement, was one of the first to observe that though Voronsky protested his innocence of unorthodox views, he "seemed to find the Marxist uniform too tight and close-fitting." Indeed an ideological uniform, whatever its color, would not have fitted Voronsky, and Averbakh was no doubt correct in his observation that the critic sometimes introduced into literary discussion ideas which lacked adequate Marxist sanction, often enough leaving them unrefuted. There was a disturbing tendency in Voronsky to range freely over literary topics and to entertain ideas from a variety of sources. He maintained to the end that he was a Marxist; yet he valued the Indian philosopher Rabindranath Tagore, who was not; he had studied Freud, and acknowledged the Freudian contribution to the understanding of the unconscious; he had certainly read Bergson; he drew upon Tolstoy for insights into the nature of artistic creation; his own reminiscences of his childhood suggest the possible influence of Proust; and at the same time he could confute his opponents, if need be, by citing texts from Belinsky, Marx, and Plekhanov. The dogmatists were right to distrust him.

Views that seemed heterodox crept into Voronsky's literary essays whenever he attempted to explain the process of artistic creation, though he always maintained that there was Marxist precedent for

those views. The behavior of the artist was to him rather mysterious
and not fully explicable in terms of conscious rational purposes. While
his polemical articles stressed the role of literature as knowledge and
made confident use of Belinsky's definition of the artist as one who
"thinks in images," his theoretical essays explored the possibility of
unconscious psychological processes in the creation of art. He concluded that something he could only call "intuition" was an essential
part of this process. In propagating such a view Voronsky was, in the
jargon of Bolshevism, out of tune with his epoch. Such words as "creativity," "inspiration," "intuition," were suspect in the Soviet literary
lexicon of the twenties, as indeed they are now, for it was feared that
such concepts smacked of bourgeois mentality. The idea was widely
accepted that the new literature would be, not "created" but "produced," by verbal craftsmen cognizant of the facts of life and instructed
in Marxist ideology. Their products would be so fashioned as to satisfy
the social demand of the socialist epoch. As we have seen, the Left
Front of Art contended that the highest form of literary creation was
good factual reporting and that in the dynamic present the daily newspaper had already taken the place of the great epics of former ages. The
Left Front was no doubt extreme, but there were other groups which
spoke of the central importance of "device," literary technique and
method, and still others presented a theory of literature as the "making
of artifacts." The Constructivists spoke of planned literature, wherein
the verbal material would be loaded with the latest scientific and technical connotations. Eager bureaucrats in the literary field suggested that
the Party, when drawing up a resolution on collectivization, for instance, should add a final point directing that a certain quantity of poetry and prose on the given topic be ordered. With the adoption of the
First Five-Year Plan in 1928 it became official doctrine that literary men
must devote their talents to propagandizing the plan "in great works of
art." The idea that artistic production, both collective and individual,
could be directed by a rational plan received wide acceptance in the
Soviet Union of the twenties.

Against this current Voronsky argued that intuition, an activity independent of rational intention, was basic to the artistic process. He defined intuition as the sum of knowledge which we have arrived at without conscious analytic investigation. Such knowledge is not "contrary
to reason," but may consist of truths discovered by the human reason
in former generations and stored in the subconscious. These intuitive
truths reveal themselves in the consciousness of the artist suddenly,
unaccountably, and often contrary to plan. To illustrate his thought
Voronsky quoted a passage from Tolstoy's *Anna Karenina*, where the

painter Mikhailov finds that an accidental smear on one of the figures in a drawing gave him a sudden insight into his picture not revealed to experiment and analysis. From Tolstoy, Voronsky borrowed the phrase "removal of veils" to characterize the process of artistic creation. In moments of freedom from the control of his rational ego, the artist is receptive to "direct, childlike impressions" and, "removing the veils" from the real world, is able to see it as it is. Shortly before the end of his career as an editor, Voronsky developed the idea that reality is deformed by our conscious cerebral processes, the purpose of which is not to *know* but to *use,* and that the artist, by shedding his social integument, recovers fresh and unspoiled images of a world which is beautiful in itself.

It is obvious that Voronsky could lay no claim to originality as a theorist of aesthetic experience. Of course he never identified the main sources of his ideas on the intuitive activity of the artist, for they were suspect. It was eagerly pointed out, however, that he had an affinity with Kantian aesthetics and that he was indebted to both Freud and Jung; and a major article in the magazine *Literature and Art* in 1930 "unmasked" Voronsky as a follower of Bergson, which he may indeed have been.[4] Yet Voronsky claimed to be a Marxist, a title generally denied him not only by Soviet historians, but by some Western intellectuals who have admired his work. He maintained that his ideas on the importance of subconscious factors in art were quite consonant with Marxist philosophy, and had indeed been discussed by Plekhanov. If we conclude that his position is inconsistent with Marxism, it can only be that we accept a rigid definition of what a Marxist is. Voronsky did not regard Marxist philosophy as a closed and complete system of beliefs, and he reached out into the stream of Western culture for ideas in areas not adequately explored by the founders of Marxism, such as psychology and aesthetics. Voronsky was a Marxist; but he was also a man of great intellectual scope and wide human interest, and as such he has never been acceptable to those Soviet authorities on Marxism who tend to convert it into a set of dogmas.

Pereval

Along with Voronsky the group of young writers who had looked to him for support and encouragement were castigated in the official press of the early thirties and passed over in silence for two decades. Some of them were imprisoned or exiled for criminally subversive activities. (One of these, Ivan Katayev, was, like Voronsky, posthumously cleared of such charges in 1956, and a new edition of his collected works was published in 1957.)[5] Pereval, as the group was called, means literally "a narrow pass over a mountain range" and is usually translated as "defile" or "pass." By their choice of the name the writers of Pereval dramatized their own view as to the transitory nature of the reality they were describing. The Soviet state of the twenties was not, for them, a static and established fact, but a moment in human development, and they viewed their time as a difficult journey toward new horizons. Perhaps "the divide" best expresses the overtones of meaning suggested by the word *pereval*. The members of Pereval proclaimed their devotion to the Revolution and their intention to work for its aims. More than half of them were, in 1925, members of the Communist Party;[6] but they insisted that the individual writer must find his own social content and work out his own style. Accordingly, the group issued no directives and announced no program, confining itself in public to general statements favoring such unexceptionable qualities as sincerity and artistic realism and deploring the prevalence of literary stereotypes. Their statements of belief and policy, though cast in the apocalyptic revolutionary jargon of the twenties, declare that the writer as such must be free of programs and parties. Certain recurrent ideas and phrases in their public declarations betray a close relationship to Voronsky: they reiterate the special importance of the writer's inner world, of his subconscious, and of intuition in the literary process; and they emphasize the primary importance for the writer, not of "the Party spirit," but of "the human spirit."

This quality of humanism was admired by their friends and severely questioned by their political foes. There was a danger that the direct portrayal of real human situations might suggest to the unwary reader the inadequacy of certain desirable political stereotypes. Various class enemies sometimes emerged in their stories as complex human beings on familiar terms with suffering and death, while workers and peasants might be portrayed as culturally or morally underprivileged. The Perevaltsy were not—as their enemies sometimes claimed—engaged in conscious sabotage of the official ideology; but it is a fact that the images of reality which appeared in their stories and poems were presented as the product not of conscious cerebration but of immediate impressions, and it might have been difficult for the thoughtful reader to make those images fit the vulgar folklore of the state.

Voronsky's influence in this respect is written large in the work of the Perevaltsy. His sympathetic interest in human beings, regardless of party, is evident in his autobiographical works, in his literary essays, and especially in a casual article he wrote in 1920 about a chance meeting with a former member of the Social Revolutionary Party who had once violently opposed the Bolsheviks. This article, which makes certain political assumptions and contains definite political judgments, reveals at the same time Voronsky's zest for understanding human situations. He manages to convey the bitterness of the old man's opposition to Bolshevism, his defeat and destitution, and the fear of complete disillusionment with "the cause of socialism" which had brought him to embrace the Soviet state. Voronsky displays such power of empathic writing that in his account pathos touches not only the converted Socialist Revolutionary but even the Bolsheviks, themselves caught in the general tragedy.[7]

No doubt the most original of the Pereval writers, and a skillful practitioner of "Voronskyite humanism," was Ivan Katayev (1902–1939), and the best of his stories is "Milk," published in 1930 and immediately singled out for special disfavor by the editors of *Pravda*, who regarded with suspicion Katayev's portrayal of a class enemy as a sympathetic character. The story is told in the words of a Soviet organizer whose job it is to set up dairying collectives and who has just eliminated a clique of kulaks from control of a dairying community near Moscow. But the organizer, nicknamed "The Calf" either because of a certain softness in him or because he had raised the norms for calving in his district, he's not sure which, is disturbed by what had happened. He had grown quite fond of the leading kulak, a Baptist named Nilov, a handsome, intelligent, and highly civilized peasant, the most efficient dairyman he had ever met and also a kind of Tolstoyan religious philosopher who spoke persuasively about that "great unifying force, the universal milk of love and brotherhood." Such was the power and prestige of Nilov in the district that the efforts of the "poor and middle" peasants to dislodge him from control at first got nowhere. But during a crucial meeting there occurred a sudden act of violence—quite unconnected with politics—against Nilov's son, who was brutally attacked by a personal enemy. After Nilov's misfortune the peasants suddenly turned against him and overwhelmingly passed a resolution deposing him from the executive board and installing a "committee of the poor and middle peasants." The peasant mass appears in the story as primitive and inarticulate: "Our peasants don't have any respect for bad luck," says the thoughtful organizer, "and a man who's unlucky will never get their trust. You see, as long as you are strong and healthy, they'll honor you and believe in you and trust you. But just as soon as you slip a little they're disgusted with you . . ."

Such was Ivan Katayev's contribution, in the critical year for collectivization of 1930, to the literature which described that development. The narrator had not only expressed interest and sympathy for the kulak Nilov, but ended his story on a questioning note: "Lord! How dark and confused everything still is! You can't find clear boundaries or sharp lines anywhere . . . You can't understand the beginning or the end . . . and men and their lives are devoured in the torrent . . . It can't be helped. But still it's chilling and frightening."

Katayev's "Heart," published in 1928, is a story in a similar vein, the hero of which is a Communist functionary who has abandoned the various hammer-and-sickle stereotypes, whether of language or manner, in favor of a simple human speech and natural behavior. Like the narrator of the story "Milk," he has a spot of softness in him and is not impervious to feelings of compassion. There is more than a suspicion that Katayev is attempting in this and other stories to portray an alternative to the image of the Bolshevik as a "man of steel."

Eight collections of stories were published by the Pereval group between 1922 and 1932, when all autonomous literary groups were liquidated.[8] Among the contributors were a number of young writers whose talents have, in many cases, been lost to Soviet literature. In these stories the locale is frequently the small provincial town or the distant village, and the inhabitants of these places are portrayed with the prescribed artistic realism, but sometimes with a distinct undertone of moral horror. Yekaterina Strogovaya's "Country Women" deals with the working class in a provincial manufacturing town. The characters and events are presented as though from life, with no attempt to organize the material according to any preconceived social thesis. The style is harshly and laconically realistic. Ostensibly the story concerns "survivals of the old way of life" and the activity of "antisocial elements," the work of the Party cell and the factory committees; all the material for a tendentious social treatment is present, but somehow the thesis never appears. We see the peasant women now become workers as illiterate, ignorant, savagely bigoted and ready to persecute a fellow worker who has lost favor with the group. They are gossip mongers who poison life with suspicion and hatred. One of the younger girls is ostracized because of a rumor about "a rich kulak uncle," though she and her family are destitute. A girl of masculine build and manners is driven out as a "half-and-half." And through the fog of meanness and stupidity one can see moving and occasionally having an effect such strange organisms as "womansec" (*zhenotdely*), "partycell" (*partyacheiki*), and the people from something called the "faccommit" (*fabzavkom*).

Boris Guber's "Corpses" is the definitive treatment of the melancholy aimlessness of life in the deep provinces. The heroes of his story, two country schoolmasters, are Gogolian grotesques of vacant boredom. Sleep, adventure stories, and vodka fill their free time. They have forgotten how to want anything or do anything. One of them cannot mange to finish a letter and in several false starts makes deliberate semiliterate spelling mistakes.

Zuev's "Tien" describes a Russian peasant community of the remote north, where the chairman of a village soviet struggles in vain with old and rooted tradition. In the works of many of the Perevaltsy we become vividly conscious of the elemental, savage, and desperately poor villages of the deep interior, an aspect of Russian life which seems to have escaped the attention of nineteenth-century novelists, who, with some few exceptions, idealized the Russian folk—and this aspect, of course, is not emphasized either in Soviet literature. As one unfriendly critic of the thirties put it, their stories of village life demonstrate the triumph of "biology" over "sociology," of primitive instinct over the forces of reason.

Thus in their stories, as in their critical thinking, the Perevaltsy tended to lay stress on areas of human experience not easily susceptible to rational explanation or control. If leanings in that direction had been confined to a small splinter group, the authorities might not have been disturbed; however, the Pereval writers and critics commanded respect in the literary world, and their ideas and their manner of writing spread like an infection even into the proletarian literary organization. Ideas identified as "Voronskyite" began to appear, after Voronsky had left the scene, in the critical articles published by the leaders of Averbakh's organization, the Russian Association of Proletarian Writers (RAPP). These ideas often appeared in vulgar, sloganized form, but there could be no doubt of their origin. Thus Voronsky's "removal of veils" became "the tearing off of masks," and his phrase "immediate impressions" was used by Libedinsky in a statement of the proletarian platform in literature. The humanism of Pereval was expressed in the RAPP slogan "For the Living Man in Literature," a call to treat human beings as complex psychological structures. This curious development, in which the sworn enemies of Voronsky and the Pereval had begun to mouth their favorite notions, was described in ironic terms by Lezhnev, a critic associated with the Pereval group:

> Time has shown that we were right after all. The principles of Pereval have been embraced by those who fought against them most bitterly . . . These principles are being put out now by a new firm, under a new label. Many people seriously think that the idea of the necessity for psychological analysis, about "the living man" . . . or the thesis that we must do battle with stereotypes or mere sketches for the sake of a more realistic art—that all of these things were advanced by the Association of Proletarian Writers. But Pereval, of course, has never taken out a patent on its own ideas.[9]

The dangers, imagined or real, presented by Pereval were such that leading organs of the Party and press turned their attention to the group in 1930. When attacks were published, the Perevaltsy demanded a hearing, and a public "debate" was held in Moscow in May 1930. The printed record of this event, though written from a partisan point of view and unfriendly to the Perevaltsy, shows that the latter defended themselves with spirit against a succession of slanderous attacks on their Marxism, their loyalty, and their honesty.[10] A second discussion was held at the Communist Academy, the upshot of which was a resolution published in May 1930, condemning among other things their "humanistic phraseology." The language of the resolution marks a stage in the evolution of Stalinist intellectual patterns:

> The use of humanistic phrases is one manifestation of the vacillation and panic experienced by certain intermediate petit-bourgeois and intellectual groups, who, unable to keep up with the rush of events, cannot find their place in the ranks of the fighters for socialism.[11]

After the dissolution of all literary groups in 1932 Pereval disappeared as a separate entity, though a number of writers who had belonged to the group continued to write, even satisfying, occasionally, the socialist realist demand of the epoch. From the middle thirties until 1954 there had been, as far as I can determine, only occasional references either to Pereval or Voronsky, and these couched in vituperative terms. It is especially interesting to note, therefore, that the spokesman of the Soviet Union of Writers, Surkov, sensed in some of the post-Stalin critical writing—especially where it spoke of sincerity, directness, the immediacy of impressions—a recrudescence of long-silent thoughts. The Party is still vigilant against any autonomous, unorganized activity on the part of its writers. Yet it will soon become evident that the current of humanism associated with the name of Voronsky and Pereval did not dry up but became a major force in Soviet literature.[12]

9 The Levers of Control Under Stalin

Resistance

The history of Voronsky and Pereval is clear proof that Russian literature did not easily accept regimentation by the state for collective purposes. If writers and critics who were members of the Party openly resisted encroachment on the autonomous preserve of literature, it is clear that resistance was widespread in the literary world. Shklovsky's warning, "You cannot control the unknown," was fully understood and accepted not only by the Serapion Brotherhood and other individualists but by active Marxists, the recipients of official funds.

Even more surprising than the resistance of Voronsky was the behavior of the Russian Association of Proletarian Writers under the leadership of Averbakh, Fadeyev, and Libedinsky during the years of the First Five-Year Plan. Their "dialectical materialist method" in literature had given rise to a number of slogans reiterated constantly during those years for the benefit of proletarian readers and writers. Libedinsky, Fadeyev, Semyonov, Mitrofanov, and other writers who belonged to the school of psychological realism, provided in their works concrete examples of how these slogans should work out in practice.

RAPP, the mass organization of proletarian literature, was the lever upon which the Central Committee of the Party placed its chief reliance. But the Party did not find that organization amenable to a grossly utilitarian program. The leadership was narrow, doctrinaire, and dogmatic, but it did not accept the idea that literature could be produced by directive. Their first and basic slogan was that literature must provide honest pictures of the material world, and since that world is in a process of dialectic movement, since things develop by way of internal contradiction and conflict, these conflicts will be reflected in the individual human personality. Such conflicts, they said, take place inside every psyche. Even a proletarian Communist is not *all* good but has many traits that are historically backward, and the conflict inside him between good and bad should be shown in literature. The bourgeois, on the other hand, though a class enemy, should never be portrayed as *all* bad. That would not be true to life, since everyone has *some* good qualities working in his particular set of dialectical conflicts. Motives moreover are not always clear and simple. A man contains subconscious irrational drives which may be just as important as his rational surface. The writer should never glorify or romanticize his heroes; positive heroes, models of desirable behavior, might be the material of propaganda, but never the material of literature. All of this they summed up in the slogan: "For the Living Man."

Other slogans of the late twenties were "Against the Varnishing of Reality" and "For the Removal of Any and All Masks." The proletarian leaders insisted that it was the right and the duty of literary men to expose vice and corruption wherever they found it. Incompetence in the bureaucracy, corruption and hypocrisy in the Party, brutality and ignorance among the workers—all of these things should be revealed by the writer wherever he found them. The actual world should be shown as it "really is." The proletarian theorists, it will now be obvious, owed much to Voronsky. Many of the slogans they mechanically repeated were vulgar capsule versions of his leading ideas.

Under the guidance of these slogans the proletarian writer sometimes behaved in strange ways. A fairly common object of his artistic attention was the disillusioned Communist, who regrets the passing of the period of strife, when life held promise and the world revolution seemed near, and who is disappointed at seeing life settle down into conservative and respectable ruts. Another negative type they portrayed was the ignorant and complacent Communist bureaucrat, capable only of thinking in terms of the latest slogans and of expressing himself in the language of the latest official statements. They occasionally wrote novels and stories in which the sordid side of Russian life was not glossed over. But literature of this kind was not at all what the Party wanted during the period of the First Five-Year Plan. It wanted books about construction and collectivization; it wanted positive heroes, and bright, hopeful perspectives; it wanted literature not to reveal what people are like and how they experience life at a given moment, but to inculcate lessons, to propagandize very simple ideas, to inspire and mobilize the workers, to "put across" to them in quasi-literary form the current propaganda line of the Party. The proletarian organization, narrow though it was in its devotion to a few simple slogans, was not narrow enough for the Party. So the Party's own organization had to be liquidated in 1932, and all writers, proletarian and others, were gathered into a single Union, the first Secretary of which was Shcherbakov, a political man close to Stalin. "The Dialectical Materialist Method in Literature" was rejected as a very dangerous approach. The slogan "For the Living Man" was buried; the slogan "Tear Off the Masks" was condemned as potentially counterrevolutionary because, as one Party representative said: "One must not raise such a slogan without indicating from whom the masks are to be removed." A new slogan and a new method became compulsory for all Russian literary men. That slogan was "Socialist Realism." From 1932 until the present socialist realism has been the required style for Soviet literature. Though the term did not appear until 1932, the method of socialist realism was actually applied during the First Five-Year Plan. Once the Politburo severely censured a publishing house because the books it had published did not show the *"heroism* of socialist construction." An editorial in *Pravda* in 1930 asserted that "literature, the cinema, the arts are levers in the hands of the proletariat which must be used to show the masses positive models of initiative and heroic labor." The writer was expected to draw inspiring pictures of the great enthusiasm and heroism displayed by the Russians working on the Five-Year Plan. He was expected to show how magnificent the future would be, even if he couldn't get excited about the present. Writers went out in brigades to visit and report on construction or agricultural work in a given district. A typical brigade promised that it would present "not less than four plays dealing with the completion of the spring sowing." Agitation vans were sent out to the collective farms to recite poems, sing songs, and present plays intended to inspire greater efforts on the part of the farmers. Most of the literature produced in this campaign was of low quality. It was admitted several years later by the head of the State Publishing House that seventy-five percent of the output of this First Five-Year Plan period was worthless as literature. But the Party didn't care about that. What was needed above all was a literature which would publicize and propagandize the program. It was a practical program engineered by practical men who neither knew nor cared much about literature. If there were Russians around who could write, they could write about the Five-Year Plan. And they'd better write in a simple, down-to-earth style, so the workers would understand them. It was a cynical and brutal program. What these practical men tried to do was take Russian literature in their hands and force it into a mold of their own making.[1]

The Purge

The great reform of 1932 involved the liquidation of all independent organizations in favor of a single Union closely tied at every level to the Party itself. From the viewpoint of the fellow travelers the reform was not unwelcome, for it meant the end of the arrogant pretension to authority of the Russian Association of Proletarian Writers and of proletarian orthodoxy as interpreted by the leaders of that organization. The reform could have meant a liberalization in the literary world, but in practice it did not. For the Union took over not only the defense of the material welfare of writers, but their ideological guidance as well. At the First Congress of Soviet Writers in 1934, which inaugurated the new Union, the leading literary figures, both proletarian and fellow traveler, took the platform to speak of literary problems, and though there were moments of the old controversial fire the keynote of the meeting was harmonious agreement on all essential points. The assembled writers heard the bright sallies of Bukharin at the expense of proletarian poetry, the sophisticated commentary of Radek on Western literature, the honest self-questioning of Olesha, and the cryptic phrases of Pasternak, but the tone of the meeting was set not by them but by a representative of Stalin, Andrey Zhdanov, who made the principal speech. In terms that could not be mistaken he voiced the concern of the Politburo with the content and form of Russian literature. He said:

> Our Soviet literature is not afraid of being called tendentious, because it *is* tendentious. In the age of the class struggle a nonclass, nontendentious, apolitical literature does not and cannot exist . . .
>
> In our country the outstanding heroes of literary works are the active builders of a new life . . . Our literature is permeated with enthusiasm and heroism. It is optimistic, but not from any biological instinct. It is optimistic because it is the literature of the class which is rising, the proletariat, the most advanced and the most prospering class.

No one could doubt after the First Congress in 1934 that the Stalinists were in control of Russian literature, and the direction in which they sought to move that literature was clearly marked out. No one could doubt either that they would deal firmly with opposition, but until the purge trials of the middle thirties it was impossible to guess how far they would go.

In the course of the three public trials held in Moscow in 1936, 1937, and 1938 the most important leaders of a former political opposition to Stalin were denigrated as spies, traitors, and Fascists. With some notable exceptions, and in one case only after an initial frantic denial of any guilt, all these former leaders of the Bolshevik movement confessed their crimes and threw themselves on the mercy of the court and the "Soviet People." Most of them were sentenced to be shot.

They were men who had held positions of great power. Zinoviev and Kamenev had been rivals of Stalin; Radek was a brilliant political writer; Bukharin had been a member of the Politburo since the early days of the Soviet state, and was the author of widely circulated works on the theory of Communism; Tomsky as leader of the trade-union movement had been a potent figure; Yagoda had, as head of the security police, organized such trials himself.

The episode in the history of the Russian Communist Party is now well known, and the real nature of the trials has been documented in the Soviet Union since the death of Stalin. What is perhaps not so well known is how deeply the purge extended into the ranks of the Communist Party itself. Each of the major victims at the trial had a numerous following of small-caliber bureaucrats, and thus a large group of minor Bolsheviks was discredited as the result of the moral and physical destruction during the thirties of their friends, comrades, and sponsors. With the head of the opposition severed at the trials no doubt this body of dissident intellectuals, fallen minor officials, Marxist but not Stalinist theoreticians, proletarian writers, and the like would have faded from view naturally and quietly. This, however, was not allowed to happen. Watchdogs at the lower levels were soon at work. One of the areas that attracted their attention was literature. Here was a rewarding field for the work of investigators and accusers. The opposition to Stalin, now firmly branded as disloyal and traitorous, had included at one time the most prominent of the Party intellectuals, many of whom had been active in literature or literary criticism. One of them was Trotsky, among other things a brilliant literary critic, whose influence in the early days had helped to hold in check the intolerant proletarianizers of literature. Another suspect was Alexander Voronsky, who had once been a member of the Trotskyite opposition (see chapter 8). Voronsky's literary enemy, Leopold Averbakh, had himself bridled at Stalin's raw intention to make literary men into obedient propagandists of Party policy. There were many young writers whose loyalty to Stalin's ideas was at best doubtful, and many of them had been discovered or fostered by Trotsky, Voronsky, or Averbakh. A few of these were very good writers. One of Voronsky's protégés was Ivan Katayev, whose picture of collectivization in the Russian village had aroused the official ire of the highest literary authority, the newspaper *Pravda.* Occasionally a talented writer emerged from the ranks of Averbakh's proletarian organization, and one of these, Libedinsky, had depicted the progressive ossification of the Party mind and the intellectual cowardice spreading among orthodox Party men.

Reverberations began in the literary world soon after the close of the first trial in 1936. The chief investigator, accuser, and judge at meetings of writers' organizations was a proletarian writer of peasant origin named Stavsky, the author of Party-oriented stories and sketches about collectivization. Grimly loyal to the Party program, Stavsky had gained a reputation as early as 1932 for savage denunciation of straying colleagues, and by 1936 he had advanced to the post of Secretary of the Board of the Union of Writers. Fearing neither truth nor falsehood, he publicly branded a score of writers as Trotskyites and traitors, and his accusations were fully reported in each issue of the *Literary Gazette,* which, as leader of the Union, he controlled. The men he named disappeared from the Soviet scene, and many of them were hardly remembered when, in the period of de-Stalinization, they were rehabilitated. One was Voronsky; another was Ivan Katayev. Most of the crimes charged to them had been committed much earlier. For instance Katayev had, in 1928, visited Voronsky while the latter was in exile "in order to get directives from him." What directives was never stated nor indeed was the question ever asked, for when two such prime suspects come together could they have any but an evil purpose? Boris Guber and N. Zarudin, also of the Pereval group, were caught in the net of accusation along with their colleagues. And the net swept wide enough to drag in even Semyon Rodov, a proletarian intransigent and one of the bitterest enemies of Voronsky and Pereval. Still another victim was Tarasov-Rodionov, whose novel *Chocolate* (1922) had raised serious questions of Communist morality (see chapter 6).

The end result of Stavsky's campaign against unclean writers was an editorial in the *Literary Gazette* which pointed out that a number of "Trotskyite bandits" and "agents of Fascism" had in the course of many years entrenched themselves in literature. The agents and bandits had wormed their way into important positions as magazine editors, publishing executives, and leaders of literary organizations. From these positions they had plotted to turn Soviet literature onto a false and fruitless path.

Early in 1937 a second trial was held and another batch of former oppositionists held up to public obloquy before being sentenced to death. Again the literary repercussions were immediate and violent. Alexander Fadeyev gave an ominous hint of things to come in a public speech to a gathering of writers. Fadeyev declared that there were still "enemies" active in the literary field. He warned that these elements carefully mask themselves and are not easy to detect. He demanded that great vigilance be exercised in dealing with all writers, for it is not easy to tell the bad ones from the good. He offered as a good method for making this distinction the investigation of those who express uncertainty or doubt as to the Party program. The carriers of such moods should be sought for and rooted out, he said.

Soon the editors of several literary periodicals were called to task because they had not exercised sufficient vigilance in the selection of articles for publication. The unhappy editors were obliged to explain why they had so often in the past printed works by writers now unmasked as "enemies of the people." Their defense was necessarily weak. One of them nervously pleaded that it was impossible to detect in all cases the subconscious intent of an article or story. This was characterized as "political blindness."

It soon developed that one of the chief literary villains was Leopold Averbakh, who from 1927 to 1932 had been the leader of the Association of Proletarian Writers and had exercised considerable power as interpreter of the current literary line of the Party. Averbakh had fallen into disfavor himself as early as 1932, chiefly because he had not shown enough enthusiasm for the regimented production of a literature glorifying the achievements of the Five-Year Plan. Many of his literary protégés had revealed disillusionment and degeneration in the ranks of the Party itself, and Averbakh had stoutly defended them on the ground that "Bolsheviks are not afraid of the truth." His association had been liquidated in 1932, and all the Party's literary sins had at that time been heaped on his not always guilty head. Now, in 1937, he was "unmasked" as an agent of Trotsky, whose literary ideas he had always opposed, and as a brother-in-law of the notorious chief of the Security Police, Yagoda, which indeed he was. One of his accusers, the popular and patriotic playwright Vishnevsky, offered as evidence against him that Averbakh's first book, published in 1923 when the author was eighteen, had appeared with a preface by Trotsky, proof that Averbakh, out of gratitude, had always followed Trotsky's line. No other evidence was offered to convict Averbakh of Trotskyism. Averbakh's part in the plot had been to persecute the "best Soviet writers," the nonproletarian fellow travelers, always, of course, at the behest of Trotsky. Stavsky contributed his mite to these accusations, too. He maintained that the errors for which Averbakh's organization had been liquidated in 1932 were actually a pattern of Fascist subversion in Soviet literature, a dark, underground plot against the Soviet Union itself. It was unnecessary to argue this point or to produce evidence to substantiate it. Pavel Yudin, head of the Institute of Philosophy of the Academy of Science and since 1931 a literary activist, published a violent personal attack on Averbakh mingling accusations of treason with snarling caricatures of Averbakh's speech, gestures, and manner of movement. The accent of anti-Semitism could hardly be missed. There could be no defense against such charges as: "It is now known to everyone that Averbakh and his paltry literary school were an agency of Trotskyism in our literature," for by this time the word "Trotskyism" had lost all denotative value and had become an ugly weapon with which to beat the alien, the dissident, or the unpopular.

Once Averbakh had been blackened as a devil of disloyalty, those who had been closely associated with him during the six years when he was a leading literary authority were under terrible pressure to divert suspicion from themselves. His best friends and closest collaborators rose in public to condemn him and excoriate his name and to assure the Soviet people that they had long since severed all ties with him. Libedinsky, a novelist who owed his public success in no small part to Averbakh, and who had been very close to him in the leadership of the Proletarian Association, was implicated in the "plot" by innuendo. One man suggested that there were "many dark places in Libedinsky's personal and political biography"; another suggested that certain proposals he had once made for the formation of a literary bloc "looked very suspicious"; another called upon Libedinsky to be frank and open with his comrades, to "tell all he knows." It was revealed as a suspicious circumstance that he had lost interest in the Party and had been remiss in paying his dues. Under pressure of this kind, Libedinsky at last took the floor at a meeting in Moscow where he dissociated himself from Averbakh, condemning him in language very much like that used in the *Literary Gazette* editorial. This was part of the price Libedinsky paid for survival.

Others were not so fortunate. The playwright Kirshon had grown up with Averbakh in RAPP. He was the author of highly successful plays on Soviet life such as *Bread, The Rails Are Humming,* and *Red Rust,* the last of which was produced on Broadway. He was fanatically devoted to the idea of developing new writers "from the work bench and the plow," and had never wholeheartedly accepted the decision of the Party in 1932 to liquidate the Proletarian Association. He had never attacked Averbakh and had often defended both himself and his friend when they were jointly accused of errors and heresies. When in 1932 the dialectical materialist method in literature came under an official interdict, he defended the method as sound and helpful. Once Averbakh had been identified as the devil himself, Kirshon was attacked as a minor demon. The instrument of his undoing was Vishnevsky, author of the revolutionary drama *'Tis the Final Conflict* and *First Cavalry Army*, written as a corrective to Babel's *Horse Army*, in which the heroes of Budyonny's cavalry are shown as men of high morale who knew what they were fighting for. Vishnevsky and Kirshon had been rivals as playwrights and members of opposing literary factions.

Vishnevsky demanded at a public meeting that Kirshon explain how it had happened that for fourteen years he had been associated with an "enemy of the people"—Averbakh—without ever having had a serious disagreement with him and had aided him in the management of literary affairs with complete and unbroken harmony. Why had he, five years before, criticized the decision of the Politburo to liquidate the Proletarian Association? How did it happen that sixteen years ago, when the Party was debating the role of the trade unions, Kirshon had voted against Lenin's motion? Why had he supported Averbakh in 1934 as a delegate to the Writers' Congress? How would he explain the circumstance that he once recommended for employment in the Soviet film industry a man who later left the Soviet Union and refused to return? Why had he, in addition to all these things, used his influence to promote his own plays and thus hindered the development of rival dramatists?

Kirshon attempted to defend himself. In his desperation he appealed to facts and reason, but such an appeal could hardly stand up against the gathering momentum of charges, epithets, innuendoes, suspicion, and hatred. Kirshon was expelled from the Party and soon disappeared for good from Moscow. And a few weeks later at a meeting of the wives of members of the Writers' Union it was heard that his relations with his wife had always been very bad and that his behavior toward her had been abominable.

Another playwright whose work had been favored by the leaders of RAPP was A. Afinogenov. His plays *Fear* (1931) and *A Far Place* (1936) were immensely successful with Soviet audiences, and he is distinguished among Soviet playwrights for his interest in personal psychological problems. He, too, fell into the nets cast by Vishnevsky and Stavsky. He was expelled from the Party in 1937 but restored to membership a year later. His recently published notebooks give us some idea of his experience:

> I kept walking around, then came home tired out and fell asleep, then I got up and went out to walk some more, and I kept this sort of thing up just so I wouldn't have to think about my fate, about what had happened to me, so unjust and unfair. I grew up an honest Soviet artist, a Party man and an activist, and now . . . they've thrown an orange skin under my feet, they've tripped me up and I've fallen and broken my head and other people stand aside and

watch and laugh and they think: There's another one knocked off his feet—and he won't get up again, or if he does get up he'll be a wounded enemy . . .[2]

Each of the accused reacted in his own way. Some attempted to divert suspicion from themselves by confessing former errors and implicating others in them. Such a policy was adopted by novelist Chumandrin, and he, too, saved himself for literature. Some managed to live through the storm without saying much of anything. Others tried to defend themselves, and of all the suspected and accused these last seem to have suffered worst. One such was the literary historian and critic Prince Dmitry Mirsky, who had fought in the White Armies until 1921 but had later become converted to Communism and returned to Russia under the patronage of Maxim Gorky. Yudin dredged out of his past the fact of his service in the White armies, characterizing him as "nothing but a filthy White-Guard officer." Several speakers publicly accused him of being a traitor and a spy on the ground that he had had many contacts with foreigners from the West. It is a fact that he was frequently seen in the company of Americans and Englishmen. A rather naïve visiting American Communist who was present at this meeting sought permission to defend Mirsky against these vicious charges, but the chairman of the meeting, Stavsky, would not give him the floor. Mirsky took the floor to defend himself but was so shaken that he could produce only weak and incoherent phrases.

Even in the Soviet Union hysteria is finally mastered. By the end of 1938 the purge of the little men had run its course, and Zhdanov admitted at the Congress of the Communist Party in 1939 that there had been excesses and errors of judgment as a result of which many innocent people suffered. The excesses were explained as the work of Trotskyites who had wormed their way into Soviet organizations and were using the purge as a weapon to discredit the Soviet Union. But Stavsky and Yudin were never punished for their terrorization of the literary world. In fact they stood higher than ever in the estimate of official histories. The novelist Sholokhov, at the same Congress which heard Zhdanov deplore the "excesses," made a fervent political speech in which he maintained that the ranks of Soviet literature, now cleansed of "enemies," were stronger and healthier.

The Literary State

A nearly universal literacy had been achieved by the policies of the Soviet dictatorship at about the time of the literary purge in the thirties. Practically everyone can read today, and most Russians do at one time or another. The question of what is to be written, published, and read—and why—is a rather complicated one. It is answered in an open society by the operation of a relatively free market. A writer in such a world when he sets to work has to aim at producing something that somebody will want to read, and the publisher as a general rule will publish only what a fair number of people will buy and pay for. Admittedly this arrangement falls far short of any ideal. As a practical matter it limits the creative artist to writing for a particular audience, an audience whose tastes and demands he must—however perfunctorily or subconsciously—take into account. The audience with which he must successfully communicate is the writer's cabin, crib, confine. He can escape from it if he likes by abandoning the writer's trade—by going up into the garret or by writing for himself alone.

We in the West are fortunate however in having not one but many audiences, and there is a place for writers of many and various colors, and off colors. Even though the variegated and motley nature of our audience may have changed in the direction of greater sobriety and uniformity of hue, the fact remains that there are different kinds of readers interested in different kinds of writers. Moreover, the writer can still create his own audience—with luck and persistence.

As a result we in the Western world still have some variety. We have a literature that does many things for many kinds of people. There are various levels of skill and artistry. One can buy and read books and stories which inculcate important civic and moral lessons, which, for instance, inspire patriotic and emulative respect for the heroes who fight our battles and lead our armies; or, one can occasionally buy and read a book expressing cynical contempt for the military life and its practitioners. There is a widely read periodical literature which has as its chief purpose to inculcate moral lessons; and this is balanced by an equally vast and growing product which seems to inculcate immoral lessons and foster feelings of violence and sadism. We even have—though only occasionally and for a limited audience—a literature that explores the world of human beings, their loves and hatred, death and forgiveness. We are rich indeed if the vast gray flood of our published books and stories occasionally deposits a work of art on our shores.

When we turn to look at the literary situation in the Soviet Union, however, we find that it is not like this at all. One lesson has been burned into the Soviet intellectuals through successive purges of their ranks: it is dangerous to be alone. And indeed it is almost impossible to be in any way lonely—in idea, in style, in subject matter—if one is a professional writer in the Soviet Union. Probably no other state in history has exercised such active and pervasive control of the literary product. At no point in his career does a Soviet writer lack the support, encouragement, and active inspiration of the collective. He must of course belong to the Union of Writers, which cares not only for his material needs, but for his ideological improvement as well. The Union supplies him with an apartment in town, a villa out of town, trips to the seashore, journeys around the country to gather material, and generous allowances while at work. Through the Union of Writers the collective watches over the growth of a Soviet novel from its conception in the writer's mind to the moment of its birth and after. How does this work? Themes for novelistic treatment are regularly suggested in speeches and reports by leaders of the Union. It was not just a happy accident that in 1955 and 1956 a number of novels, plays, and stories appeared in which an inventor with a new and vital idea is shown in conflict with authoritative officials whose interests are narrow and selfish. At the same time there were editorials in the newspapers and cartoons in the humor magazines with a very similar tendency.

A member of the Soviet Writers' Union, once he has begun to write, has the benefit of consultation with fellow writers and committees of the organization, and his manuscript before it is submitted may be carefully scrutinized for artistic and political shortcomings. This the writer willingly submits to, for it is known in the Soviet Union as "comradely criticism," and the result usually, but not always, is that the writer is placed firmly on the rails of established ideological and artistic practice. Occasional individual deviations from the norm are—ideally—ironed out in prepublication conferences. After the first publica-. tion, usually in a magazine, the novel is criticized and changes are often made before it is brought out in book form.

One would think that once the novel is in manuscript form and finds a publisher—say a monthly literary magazine—the author's worries would be over. Quite the contrary. He must then face the editorial office of the publisher, and the editor, blue pencil in hand, normalizes the style (strange, colloquial, substandard, nongrammatical or overly original language is usually questioned), and since editors are thoughtful Marxists, well-grounded in the Party program, they look for evidence of hostile influences, alien philosophies, decadence, pessimism, or other occasional peccadilloes which show themselves in the work of writers. Very often they find these. A young boy in a novel submitted for publication explains that he has a hobby—the raising of pigeons—and explains to a comrade that "hobby" is something that has nothing to do with your chief interest in life. "Just think about that word 'hobby,' " said the editor. "Isn't a 'hobby' characteristic of the philistine who lives in his own little world separate from the collective?"[3]

One must admit that in the Soviet Union, though literary experimentation has been officially deplored, something really new under the sun has been discovered: the novel of collective authorship. Literature as we understand it is traditionally the product of an individual human being—conditioned, it is true, by his or her own social existence as part of a group. The necessary characteristic of a piece of literature—a novel, a play, or a poem—is that not a group, not several persons, not an organization, but *one* man or woman has something to say about life—a writer has an idea, a feeling or a vision which he or she expresses in concrete literary images. During the Stalin period in the Soviet Union, and to some extent even today, that kind of literature tended to become outmoded, and to an astounding extent the collective replaced the lonely and often tragic writer of our own Western world. A. Kron in his "A Writer's Notes" observed: "The administrative method of guiding the artist has not aided in the development of an individual style."

The history of Russian literature during the Soviet regime is the record of a ruthless campaign, wasteful of people and of talent, to impose upon writers and critics this collective viewpoint. But Russian literature, let me repeat, did not easily submit. The resistance of Voronsky and Averbakh, the underground opposition of many other figures and of literary groups opposed to literary policy of any kind, the fierce purge of intellectuals in the thirties, all of this gives evidence of will and courage in the opposition. Most writers and artists think of themselves as individuals of a particular and precious vision, be it tragic, ironic, or humorous; the Soviet state insists on regarding them as employees who purvey approved doctrine to the literate citizenry. To reinforce this lesson it was found necessary after the end of World War II once again to cleanse the ranks of "cultural workers." The man who, not unwillingly, undertook this task was Andrey Zhdanov, and between 1946 and his death in 1948 he castigated deviationists in all the arts: not only writers, but clowns, composers, and movie directors felt his ideological scourge.

Andrey Alexandrovich Zhdanov (1896–1948) belonged to the generation of Party men who rose to power as creatures of Stalin and who encouraged his maniacal tendencies. After the mysterious assassination of Kirov in 1934, Zhdanov became Stalin's deputy as the Party Chief of Leningrad. The destruction and subsequent rebuilding along purely Stalinist lines of the Leningrad Party organization had been Zhdanov's chief task, and when it was completed he was elected to full membership in the Politburo (1939). When the German armies besieged and blockaded Leningrad from 1941 to 1943 he defended the city with brute courage, maintaining a labor force in the factories and troops at the front while half a million citizens died of starvation. Stalin regarded Zhdanov as his successor, and the fact that he was made a kind of commissar for cultural affairs is evidence of the importance assigned to that area. Zhdanov was a Soviet bureaucrat and was typical of the breed. A closer look at him can help us to understand the people with whom a Soviet writer must deal.

As the war ended, the people of Russia looked forward with intense hope to an end of their prolonged ordeal and to a release from regimentation. There were signs that pointed to such a development. The Western democracies and Russia had been allies against Fascism, and if they should remain allies in the postwar world a softening of the Soviet dictatorship might result. During the war years there had been an apparent dilution of the Party's ideology as a result of the need to cooperate with democracies and to enlist all the forces of "Mother Russia" against the invader. This dilution might result, it seemed, in some tolerance for opposing ideologies. The mood of the people in 1945 has been eloquently recalled by Boris Pasternak in *Doctor Zhivago*. Zhivago's friends Dudorov and Gordon are holding a book of his writings and looking out over Moscow:

> And Moscow, right below them and stretching into the distance, the author's native city, in which he had spent half his life—Moscow now struck them not as the stage of the events connected with him, but as the main protagonist of a long story, the end of which they had reached that evening, book in hand.
> Although victory had not brought the relief and freedom that were expected at the end of the war, nevertheless the portents of freedom filled the air throughout the postwar period, and they alone defined its historical significance.

Magazines and writers' organizations reflected the demand for a rest from the grim rigors of socialist realism even before the war's end. Fedin's freely ranging reminiscences of the twenties, *Gorky Among Us*, appeared in 1943; *Before Sunrise*, Zoshchenko's novelistic search through childhood experiences for the sources of a chronic and peculiar melancholy, appeared in 1943; and after a long silence Anna Akhmatova was able during the war to publish again her reflective lyric poetry. At meetings of writers' organizations a new spirit of liberalism was freely expressed, and bureaucratic interference in the creative process was openly deplored by writers of unquestioned loyalty.

But the fragile hopes of the people and of the writers were very soon destroyed. Stalin and his men were so acutely aware of Russia's mortally weakened condition after the war that they became convinced a new attack would be launched against them, and that, therefore, relaxation could not be allowed. Stalin's speech on February 9, 1946, warned the Russians that the days of their harsh trials had not ended: "As long as capitalism exists there will be wars," he said, "and the Soviet Union must be prepared." Relaxation of effort was unthinkable, and he announced a series of three new Five-Year Plans to raise production in basic industries. Not long after this speech attention was given to events in literature, and Andrey Zhdanov came forward to read the Party's indictment of those writers and editors responsible for the laxity of recent years.

An edict of the Central Committee was published on August 14, 1946, condemning two literary magazines, *Zvezda (Star)* and *Leningrad*, for having published the "shallow and insipid" works of Zoshchenko and the "decadent, apolitical" verse of Anna Akhmatova. Both writers were expelled from the Union, the editors of the magazines were replaced, and Tikhonov was removed as Secretary of the Executive Board of the Union of Writers. In articles and public speeches Zhdanov explained the necessity for these actions. Zoshchenko's story "The Adventures of a Monkey," which had been published in *Star*, received his special attention:

> If you will read that story carefully and think it over, you will see that Zoshchenko casts the monkey in the role of supreme judge of our social order, and has him read a kind of moral lesson to the Soviet people. The monkey is presented as a kind of rational principle having the right to evaluate the conduct of human beings. The picture of Soviet life is deliberately and vilely distorted and caricatured so that Zoshchenko can put into the mouth of his monkey the vile, poisonous anti-Soviet sentiment to the effect that life is better in the zoo than at liberty, and that one breathes more easily in a cage than among Soviet people.
>
> Is it possible to sink to a lower political or moral level? And how could the Leningraders endure to publish in their magazines such filth and nonsense?

Zoshchenko had of course done nothing to deserve this lethal abuse, nor could he rightly be called "a vile hooligan," a practitioner of "filth and obscenity," or the "dregs of literature." Zhdanov had simply not understood his whimsical story about a monkey who escapes from a zoo and, after many misadventures in a Russian town, is finally adopted by a wonderful little boy who undertakes to educate him, teach him to blow his nose with a handkerchief, to refrain from stealing grandma's candy, to eat meat with a fork, in short to behave like any cultured person—and better than some. Devoid of humor and burdened with official crime, Zhdanov could see in the farcical events of this children's fable only a projection of his own guilt and suspicion.

Turning to Anna Akhmatova, Zhdanov quoted one of her love lyrics:

> I swear to you by all the heavenly angels
> By the wonder-working ikons I swear
> And by the sweet delirium of our flaming nights—

and commented on it:

> Akhmatova's subject matter is individualistic through and through. The range of her poetry is pathetically limited. It is the poetry of a half-crazy gentlelady who tosses between the bedroom and the chapel ... Half-nun and half-harlot, or rather both nun and harlot, her harlotry is mingled with prayer.

Zhdanov's criticism of Akhmatova reveals both the man and the society. It reveals his hatred of the sensitive, cultivated gentry who should all have been destroyed but still find readers among the Soviet people. It reveals his coarse, puritanic revulsion at the frank expression of a woman's experience in love; it reveals his disastrous lack of literary sense or taste. It reveals the pathetic state of a society whose cultural life could stand at the mercy of an ignorant and violent clown. His positive demands on literary men can be briefly stated. They must produce an educational literature, intelligible and acceptable to the people, saturated with the ideas of the Party and loyal to the program of the Party.

The results of his intervention were immediate. Yarmolinsky's study of the period, *Literature under Communism* (1960), reveals that editors who had contracted with writers for fiction on historical themes scrapped their contracts and their publishing plans to concentrate on novels dealing with the one theme of reconstruction. Similar events occurred in the theaters: plays already part of the repertory were dropped in favor of hastily written pieces of more obvious propaganda intent. Semyon Babayevsky's novels *Knight of the Golden Star* and *Light over the Earth* (1948–1949) were awarded three Stalin Prizes but were rejected as dishonest propaganda after Stalin's death. The hero of these novels is a young Party member who returns to his collective farm village after the war with ambitious plans for electrification according to the goals laid down by the Central Committee. The chief obstacles to fulfillment of the plan are the individualistic leanings of the farmers, who prefer to work for private goals, and personal ambition in Party leaders. All such obstacles are overcome, however, when the collective will is at last awakened, and Semyon's own dream of success is realized when he is elected Secretary of the District Committee of the Party. Chakovsky's *Here It Is Dawn Already* (1948) deals with the life of fishermen on the island of Sakhalin. Any rebellion of the individual against the collective is resolved in favor of the collective, and the villains of individualism are converted to healthy ways in the end. In Pavlenko's *Happiness*, the hero, demobilized after the war, comes to the Crimea to find a life of peace and contentment in a home of his own but is drawn into the agricultural work of the district where he finds that "happiness" is indivisible and that he can enjoy it only as a member of the larger group. Plays of the period hammered the same lesson. Sofronov's play *Moscow Character* (1950) recounts the conversion of a plant manager who has fallen into the vice of regarding the plant as *his* enterprise and ignoring the workers' interest, other plants, and society as a whole.

After socialist economic development, the second major theme of the Zhdanov period was anti-Americanism, or, more broadly, antiforeignism. Dangerous thoughts from the West might have entered the heads of Soviet citizens during the period of collaboration, and the regime was concerned over the admiration for Western achievements and Western culture which it had itself encouraged during the war. K. Simonov's play *Under the Chestnuts of Prague* (1946) carried the grim lesson that behind the spectacles and under the capitalist hat of every Czech burgher there might lurk a Fascist enemy. Simonov's *Russian Question* (1946) shows the American newspaper world as the source of anti-Soviet bias in the United States. *The Mad Haberdasher* (1949), by A. Surov, attacks President Truman as a Hitler-like warmonger. Many of the books, stories, and plays that appeared during the period warned the good Soviet citizen of the treachery he would find in Western politicians, journalists, and scientists, and "exposed" the cultural poverty of Western life.

Zhdanov's campaign on the front of Russian music devastated an area that was rich in new talent and original creation. The story has been told in detail in a number of books and articles. The Politburo itself condemned modernistic tendencies in Russian music, especially the works of Shostakovich and Prokofieff; and the language of its resolution suggests that it was probably written by Zhdanov himself. The Politburo said of Shostakovich and the modernists:

> The characteristic traits of such music are the denial of the basic principles of classical music, the propagation of atonality, dissonance, and disharmony, as though disharmony were an expression of "progress" and "innovation" in the development of musical form; the rejection of the all important bases of music, such as melody. The modernists are carried away by confused, neurotic

combinations, which transform music into cacophony—into a chaotic conglomeration of sounds. This is the spirit of modern American and European music—which reflects the decay of bourgeois culture . . .

Many Soviet composers . . . have become alienated in their music from the demands and the musical tastes of the Soviet people, have shut themselves up in a closed circle of specialists . . . limiting [the function of music] to the satisfaction of the depraved tastes of individualistic esthetes.

At meetings of the Composers' Union Zhdanov himself appeared to explain the Party's needs in music as he had already explained its needs in literature. At these meetings an effort was made to represent him as an authority on music, too. His enthusiastic supporter, Zakharov, a writer of popular songs, pointed out that while Zhdanov was not a professional musician he was a great authority on the folk song, and he reported the following conversation with Zhdanov:

"Is it true, Comrade Zhdanov, that you know six hundred folk songs?"
"No, it is not true. But I suppose I do know about three hundred."[4]

The effects of Zhdanov's campaign were not long in appearing. The novels and stories written to the recipe of a rigorous socialist realism failed to engage the attention of the Russian reader. Literary works in which conflicts are attenuated, suspense eliminated, language normalized, and endings standardized left him bored and indifferent. The Party program had inhibited the production of good literature and (what was far worse!) did not even produce good propaganda. In 1951 and 1952 a reaction set in, and the Party press for those years revealed that floundering efforts were being made to correct a disastrous situation. Editorials and critical articles called for the injection of "new life" into literature, spoke of the need to portray "living men," demanded that writers show life "as it is," featuring the "bad" as well as the "good," and deplored the "varnishing of reality." The reader of such articles is appalled by the break in cultural continuity of which they give evidence: their authors show no awareness of laboring over ground already covered in the controversies of the twenties about Voronsky and the RAPP program.

10 Zoshchenko and the Art of Satire

The proliferation in the Soviet state of Stavskys, Yudins, and Zhdanovs suggests that a fertile field has existed there for the satirist. Yet these very characters, the natural objects of satiric attack, have been in a position to discourage the labors of the satirist. Satire has shown the same pattern of growth as other literary forms: it developed richly in the twenties, then settled into a domestic routine as a handmaiden of the state, directing its barbs at preselected bourgeois or imperialist targets. And even in the twenties the satirist could expose the stupidity of evil fools only at some risk, and usually he chose to avoid prime targets in favor of generalized vices, fantastic rogues, or the ever-present "philistine."

An exception to this rule was Zamyatin's *We*, which contained, as we have seen, a satire, not on the Communist future, but on the prophets of the collective who held forth in his own time. Mikhail Bulgakov resorted, like Zamyatin, to science-fantasy in *The Fatal Eggs* (1924) and *Devilry* (1925). In *The Fatal Eggs* a Soviet scientist has invented, but not yet thoroughly tested, a "red ray" which will greatly increase the growth rate of living organisms. No sooner has he announced his discovery than a leather-jacketed commissar appears in his laboratory with an official order to make immediate practical use of the ray in poultry breeding on the state farms. Over the scientist's objections the order is carried out, but the wrong eggs are used, and huge snakes and crocodiles are grown on the farms instead of hens. The life of the republic is threatened by those ignorant and premature attempts to apply scientific knowledge. *Devilry* (1925) mingles reality and fantasy in telling the absurd troubles of a Soviet clerk who has fallen afoul of the paper apparatus. Bulgakov's play *Zoya's Apartment* (1926), the setting of which is a fashionable bawdy house catering to the needs of the "new class" of entrepreneurs and officials, was considered too pointed in its satire and was closed. Bulgakov's satire was, like that of Zamyatin, unpalatable to the Soviet authorities. His work will be dealt with fully in a later chapter.

Other satirists of the twenties were more careful in their selection of targets. Ilya Ilf and Evgeny Petrov, whose *Twelve Chairs* (1928, also known as *Diamonds to Sit On*), *The Little Golden Calf* (1931), and *Little Golden America* (*Odnoetazhnaya Amerika*, 1936) have been popular with the Soviet readers and only during the Zhdanov period were suspect to the authorities, directed their ridicule at rascality of a bourgeois stamp. Their satire is akin in spirit to that of Valentin Katayev in *The Embezzlers*, and their finest creation, Ostap Bender, is an engaging and ingenious adventurer with the lofty ambition of becoming a millionaire. The two earlier novels describe his travels and farcical misadventures in a society where it is impossible to satisfy such a simple aim. *Little Golden America*, based on a transcontinental tour of the country, is basically satirical, but favorable to many aspects of American life, and it provides fresh and illuminating views of American society.

Mikhail Zoshchenko is sometimes included among the satirists, and I have already mentioned that Zhdanov understood his "Adventures of a Monkey" as ridicule directed at Soviet reality. And perhaps his work does fit in a general way the concept of satire, but it is in no sense a humorous attack on a specific social organization, or on particular contemporary characters, or on a way of life. There is no evidence in his work that Zoshchenko believed in Soviet values. There is no reason to think that he held firmly to beliefs that ran counter to those values. He feels neither anger nor scorn as he observes his contemporaries, but only perverse pity and baffled amusement both at them and at himself.

For the Russian humorist Zoshchenko sadness was a way of life. His life style is an intentional caricature of the melancholy clown. The fact that both his sadness and his humor were organic to him is demonstrated by the autobiographical novel *Before Sunrise*, which is a search for the explanation of his chronic melancholy. All his life Zoshchenko had suffered, he said, from fits of depression, which at times became so acute that he could not function. He was unhappy, and he could not understand why. He concluded that in this respect he was different from other people, and therefore sought in his own life some cause or explanation of a condition peculiar to him. The novel begins with this explanation of how it happened to be written, then moves to an investigation of significant memories beginning at the age of sixteen, each one a self-contained unit of experience. In the selection of memories lies the ironic meaning of the story. Zoshchenko recalls his attempted suicide over a low mark in composition, his experience of wounds and gas poisoning during the war, a succession of ridiculously unsuitable occupations from cobbler to detective from 1917 to 1920, and incidents of his life as a literary man in Petrograd. His brief, bare account of the literary great whom he met among the Serapions is in its way appalling. The face of the poet Blok expressed only sadness and apathy; Yesenin recited his poetry dressed in a velvet blouse with lips and eyebrows made up; Gorky wearily expounded truisms on literature and culture while someone behind him carefully wrote it all down; the editor and poet Kuzmin turned down Zoshchenko's funny stories because they were "exaggerated"; his girl friend, also a writer, asked him to wait for her on the embankment while she visited another lover "for just twenty minutes" and came back feeling wonderful; Mayakovsky turned out to be a hypochondriac, excessively afraid of infection from drinking glasses, forks, and spoons. These and other memories are told in short clipped sentences which lack the rational organization imposed by syntax. They are presented as raw, untreated items of memory and while there is no explicit reflection on their meaning, the sum of all the memories covering the years from 1912 to 1926 is a picture of a lifetime of quiet desperation. But with a detached air of scientific curiosity and with his tongue in his cheek Zoshchenko asserts that he cannot find in any of this the reason for his melancholy, so he decides to carry the search farther back into his childhood. The section dealing with memories from the age of five to sixteen is entitled "A Terrifying World," and it relates memories of family and childhood, each one in some way sad. Still not satisfied that he has found the answer, he carries the search back "before sunrise," to the dawn of consciousness, the earliest years of life. But still he cannot explain his sadness. He proceeds then to study the psychologists and gives the reader a brief elementary statement of the Pavlovian theory of the conditioned reflex and of the Freudian sexual theory. He looked for the specific event which caused his unhappiness in "associations" arising from dreams and found that in them water frequently had an association with strong emotion. Certain, he said, that he was on the track of the early conditioning process that had made him an unhappy man, he promised in the sequel to tell of this, but the publication of *Before Sunrise* in the journal *October* was aborted in 1943, and the full text appeared only in 1972. It is a fascinating account of a man's effort to come to grips with his own neurosis.

Although Zoshchenko's humor arises from his observation of the general human situation it is obvious that the Soviet predicament provided the data upon which he worked. Situational and linguistic absurdities from Soviet life are the subjects of his hundreds of short tales. Zoshchenko is himself authority for the statement that he introduced the language of the street into his stories, but as Soviet linguistic scholars have pointed out, that statement is itself an absurdity. The stories are stylized both as to language and form, and only in fairy tales or narrative folk songs do characters speak with the intonation, the pauses, the retardation and repetition, and the mock-pithy asides that characterize Zoshchenko's people. No one has ever spoken the language of Zoshchenko's heroes. It is an invented speech made up of newspaper rhetoric, the pronouncements of Stalin and other heroes, misunderstood fragments of Marx or Engels, all mixed up in a weird linguistic brew and laced with the catchwords of popular prejudice. Zoshchenko's technique has been labeled as *skaz*, and his work has been compared to that of Damon Runyan and Ring Lardner, whose stories are told in the speech style of a character who represents a particular milieu. But Zoshchenko is radically different from other practitioners of *skaz*. His narrator is not the Soviet man in the street, nor is he a representative of the Soviet lower middle class or any other social group. He is not a character at all. He is the mask through which Zoshchenko himself speaks to the reader.

Each of the stories is told—one might almost say confided to the reader—by the absurd narrator, who, like the wise fools of folk stories, says much more than he seems to know. The device of the wise fool enabled Zoshchenko to comment on Soviet life without attracting fatal attention from the state. His fool is pompously loyal to the latest and most grandiose Soviet notions and full of obvious wisdom on such subjects as the decay of the intelligentsia, proper management of public baths, civilized behavior on streetcars, health, true love in Soviet conditions, the housing shortage, and correct grammar. But the items of reality that he selects as illustrations offer a ridiculous contradiction of his wise pronouncements.

The stories are frequently constructed according to a pattern which can be studied in a few examples. Following a somewhat pompous formalistic scheme, the stories may be divided into three parts: (1) exordium, (2) epic narration, (3) moral conclusion. "Not All Is Lost" is typical. In that story the exordium consists of general comments on "melancholics" who have no interest in this "teeming" life: "All around us are various entertaining facts, a struggle is in progress, various events are, you know, unfolding . . . accidents, thefts. All around us nature with a lavish hand distributes her free gifts. The sun is shining, the grass is growing, the ants are crawling." The narrator reflects that such melancholics are "rootless intellectuals" suffering from overeducation, who would have been miserable under any regime. So you can't blame current events. The epic narration begins with the self-critical comment that perhaps one should forget all this "empty philosophy" and get down to the case in hand, one Innokenty, an intellectual who found new interest in living and stopped being a melancholic. The change in Innokenty's life occurred when the chairman of his apartment house committee announced that additional tenants would be assigned to live in his apartment, and Innokenty went off to the housing office to complain. While he was away his apartment was burglarized and some things stolen. As a result he had to visit the police station twice a day to get help and look around in the secondhand markets to see if his stuff had come up for sale. One day as he hurried about this business he fell downstairs and dislocated his arm and then had to go regularly to the doctor's office for examination and massages. So he had many things to occupy him: mornings the business of tracking down lost articles, afternoons the clinic, and evenings discussion of the day's activities with friends. And this rootless intellectual began to take an interest in things and changed radically for the better. Then comes the moral conclusions, with the fool's comment on the meaning of the story:

> Of course it's impossible to say whether he will continue to possess such spiritual boldness all his life. But maybe he will possess it all his life. It all depends on how his affairs develop. Maybe the house chairman will take him to court for nonpayment of rent. And then again maybe the Criminal Investigation Department will summon him about those goods that were stolen. And then again, maybe, as he rushes about on his affairs, Innokenty will break another arm, or dislocate his leg. And then, maybe he will die happy, in full contentment. And, dying, he will reflect on the affairs that filled his life, and on the struggle that he bore on his shoulders with honor.
>
> Not without reason did Comrade Budyonny once exclaim: "Our whole life is nothing but struggle."

Zoshchenko wore the fool's mask in almost everything he wrote—in his essays and novels as well as in his short stories. In an article published in 1922 as part of a symposium by the Serapion Brothers, he wrote:

> In general, it's kind of hard to be a writer. Just take ideology. Nowadays a writer has got to have an ideology.
> Here's Voronsky (a good man) who writes ... "It is necessary that writers have a more 'exact ideology.' "

But that's downright unpleasant. How can I have an "exact ideology," when not a single party among them all attracts me?
I don't hate anybody—that's my "exact ideology."

The mask served him well. He was attacked from time to time, but
those attacks, even Zhdanov's vicious assault, did him no permanent
harm. Serious charges could hardly affect a writer who offered no serious target. After his eclipse during the early fifties he reappeared again
in 1956 as the author of skits performed by the popular Moscow satirist
Raikin at the Hermitage Theater, and he published a few rather weak
stories in the literary magazines. He died in 1958.

Zoshchenko's style is a reduction to the absurd of solemn hypocrisy
in whatever form. It exposes the false and trivializes the pompous. It
brings to the ground all lofty sentiment loftily expressed. It reveals the
vulgarity under official heroism. Through the mask of his clown-hero,
Zoshchenko uttered judgments on the Soviet variant of modern life
that, coming from a serious man, would have been an offense to the
majesty of the state.

11 After Stalin:
The First Two Thaws

Pomerantsev, Panova, and *The Guests*

Evidence of deep unhappiness among Soviet intellectuals and of the Party's dissatisfaction with them in their unhappy state antedates by three years the death of Stalin. The first effort to mitigate distrust and regimentation of the intellectual world—a condition especially acute in the Zhdanov years—was made by Stalin himself in 1950 when he intervened in the specialized field of linguistics to smash with his ineffable "hammer blows" a sterile dictatorship which the Party had itself established in that field. That the orthodox Marxists in control of language faculties in universities and in scholarly societies were both dictatorial and unproductive may no doubt be taken as a fact, since we have the evidence of Stalin's own words for it. And Stalin was anything but mild in dealing with them: in fact one feels that his condemnation was perhaps a little too severe. "An Arakcheev-like regime" was what he said existed in the area of linguistic studies, with this ugly name evoking the shade of a nineteenth-century political general and martinet remembered chiefly for his brutal barrack-room attitudes and personal cowardice in battle. Even the mildest attempts at criticism of the dominant regime in linguistics had been persecuted, and Stalin deplored that. He enunciated on this occasion an important truth, that "no science can develop and flourish without a struggle of opinions, without free criticism"—brave words and true, even though Stalin's own. Yet Stalin's intervention did not result in the development of free and vigorous debate in Soviet linguistics.

It was obvious that the Party-State had failed to produce a controlled literature, though they did produce the appearance of loyal uniformity. Crippled and terrorized though it was, the writers' community maintained a separate existence and still cared for variety and individuality. Indeed, Soviet literature, when freed by his death from the worst rigors of Stalin's winters, revived the major theme of Russian literature since the Revolution: the fate of the individual human being in a mass state.

One of the first statements was an article by a young student of cinematography, Olga Shmarova, published in May 1953, only three months after Stalin's death, in which she deplored the absence of love from Soviet films. She complained that the theme of love had been replaced almost entirely by the theme of labor and construction and that the conversation of a pair of lovers in a film instead of being full of lyrical nothings was about bulldozers, tractors, generators, and dynamos. She complained of the depersonalized characters: that problems of production take precedence over individual life and individual experiences of all kinds, even the common human experience of falling in love. She quotes dialogue typical of recent Soviet films: "If you exceed the production goals for the spring quarter I'll be your wife." Such dialogue, she says, is not "true to life."

In November 1953, in the official Soviet publication *Soviet Music* an article appeared by the famous Soviet composer Aram Khachaturyan, an article which was amazing and encouraging by its frankness. It, too, contained much Soviet jargon, expressions of obeisance before the Party and devotion to the idea of the socialist content of music; but the main import of the article was that a stifling bureaucratic regime was making the production of good music nearly impossible. The article is a plea for the rights of the individual composer. Khachaturyan calls upon the authorities to take the small risk of trusting him: "Let the individual artist be trusted more fully and not be constantly supervised and suspected." He revealed that Soviet composers work "with a worried glance over their shoulder, always afraid that something bad may happen to them if they make a mistake." He describes how the heads of bureaus and directors of theaters interfere with the work of the actual composers, so that the latter refuse to take the responsibility for anything. "For instance, if the composer delivers a song to some institution everyone considers it his duty to 'advise' him about it . . . And strange as it may seem the composer usually agrees to all the changes suggested. Only if individuals are allowed to work out their own musical styles, free of bureaucratic intervention, can Soviet music thrive," said Khachaturyan.

At about the same time others began to speak of the dismal prospect offered by Russian prose and poetry. A Soviet poet, Olga Berggoltz, in "Discussion of Lyric Poetry," complained that in searching through recent issues of the literary journals she had not been able to find a single poem on the theme of love. And she found that the lyric note, the expression of particular and personal emotion, was nowhere to be found. Even a bulldozer operator, she reflected, has a personal life, and the people engaged in construction projects are, after all, *people*. Her article was a plea for consideration of the individual human being—for "the living man"—apart from the life of the collective. One reflects that in the Soviet Union the rediscovery of alphabets is a regular occurrence.

This was soon followed by the remarks of another Soviet poet, Alexander Tvardovsky, an editor of one of the leading literary journals and an official poet of some note and considerable skill. One of his best known works is a poem celebrating collectivization, "Muraviya Land." The main import of one section of his long poem *Horizons beyond Horizons* (1960) was that the mass of Russian readers hold writers in contempt for their insincerity. The main criticism of the readers who had spoken to him frankly was that Soviet literature does not reflect life, that it is "contrived and unreal." Tvardovsky went on to declare most eloquently that Soviet literature had everything that was required of it. It was full of social motivation, construction, the new socialist man, positive heroes of labor and defense, the new life—but unfortunately, it was a dead product.

Finally, lending greater prestige to these complaints, one of the deans of Soviet literature, a spokesman for Stalin and the Party line for many years, an apologist for all the crimes of the Soviet regime, Ilya Ehrenburg, spoke out loud and bold to the effect that Soviet literature is pale and uninteresting, and that a Soviet textile worker prefers to read, not modern novels, but *Anna Karenina*, which she reads not because Tolstoy tells her about the latest victories in socialist construction but because he understood and could convey the reality of childbirth, death, and love, and because he gives her living human emotions. There is only one area in which a writer must be an expert, says Ehrenburg, not in describing construction, but in creating the inner life of a particular human being. "Such books cannot be ordered or planned. They can only be created. Can anyone imagine *ordering* Tolstoy to write *Anna Karenina?*" Ehrenburg when he wrote that sentence was probably unaware that in 1924 a very similar thought had been uttered by Bukharin in the form of an ironic question directed at a proletarian organizer: "Did a Politburo of the nobility order Pushkin to write *Eugene Onegin?*"

How far would writers and critics be allowed to go in stating boldly such obvious truths? Indeed they went very far. In December 1953, a major article, "On Sincerity in Literature," was published in the magazine *New World*. Its author, a writer of prose fiction named V. M. Pomerantsev (b. 1907), registered his impressions of Soviet literature, interposing pregnant and humorous comments on life and people. The article was remarkable for its style. He abandoned the rigidly paragraphed and patterned system of the didactic critic to present his ideas impressionistically, moving gently from one idea to another without apparent ulterior purpose, and giving the effect of immediate contact with thought in process. The article was like an electric shock to the Soviet reader. Instead of a series of good points well taken, leading to inevitable conclusions, Pomerantsev provided something new: ideas of his own about literature. Pomerantsev became the center of a controversy, and though it was never admitted publicly, the approach of the author and his style, rather than the actual content of the article, were most likely what really disturbed the pontiffs. Sincerity, said Pomerantsev, is lacking in many novels and plays. Boldyrev's novel *Decisive Years* is a poor novel because the author's heart is not in it: there is nothing either new or exciting in that story of the struggle to make blast furnaces more efficient. What is wanted is a statement of what the writer has really felt and thought instead of constant preachment and propaganda. Readers are bored by lessons and arguments. Elementary psychology cries out against those contrived novels and plays, because they have no effect on anyone. People do not believe our writers because they varnish life, they try to slick it up, make things look better than they really are. Sanctimonious critics are not alone to blame for this. The writers do it willingly. The habit of improving on reality, Pomerantsev continued, has become deeply ingrained in Soviet writers. They have become their own best censors. They gild reality by presenting pictures of prosperity and well-being. Writers should not try to transport people into a dream world. Any scene in a newsreel tells a great deal more about our prosperity than a scene in the feature film because screenwriters are incapable of expressing in it the truth to be found in the newsreel. We writers suppress the real problems. Do not carefully spell out conclusions, and do not let yourself write a single line that you do not feel. Be independent.

In an imaginary colloquy with an author Pomerantsev says:

> Your heroes are carried by the ideas, not the other way round. They even dream only logical dreams. Normal confused dreams are not for them. And how they talk to one another! In their conversations your characters sound like radio announcers. Is human

conversation like that? Do speeches and harangues pour forth like that, especially when there are no more than two people present? Do you remember how one of your heroes gave his daughter a watch because, as he said, "his living standard had risen?" This is a phrase straight from the columns of a newspaper: the man who wrote it forgot that in the family circle a man would never say "his living standard had risen"; he would say that he was better off or that he had more money now.

"In my opinion," wrote Pomerantsev, "the primary task of criticism today is that of leading writers toward a broadening of themes and a change in the treatment of problems. This is the chief thing, because the reader must be able to get something from literature that he can't get elsewhere."

Pomerantsev's article was a cause for consternation. At first the official bodies seemed not to know just how to take it or even whether to condemn it. An article appeared criticizing it, then shortly after, another appeared defending the point of view it expressed. There was an interval, not of freedom, but of vacillation in the high councils of the Party, and during that interval a number of things were published which departed radically from the established patterns of Soviet literature and threw light on the realities of Soviet life.

During this first period of "thaw" the publication of Vera Panova's novel *The Four Seasons*, Leonid Zorin's play *The Guests*, and Ilya Ehrenburg's novelette *The Thaw* marked a change in the weather. The first of these, *The Four Seasons*, is the work of a woman whose powers as a writer are very great, but who has, so to speak, emasculated herself for the sake of the Party. She has written both fact and fiction for Communist newspapers since she was seventeen. She has tried her hand at verse, and had some success with drama. Her first successful novel, *The Train*, was written as a direct assignment from the Union of Soviet Writers. It describes in simple, utterly convincing language life on a hospital train behind the front lines during World War II. The human suffering and courage she portrays in that novel have the taste of truth, a truth which is not wholly negated by her Party-oriented selection of character and incident.

In her novels about the constuction of new industries and building the new life Panova (1905–1973) has somehow managed to maintain the immediacy of experience. Her characters are concerned not only with industry but with their private homes and real problems; the textbook scenes she includes are often a harsh interruption of human drama. Panova sees life from a woman's angle of vision: to her the home is important, and children are important. Her best writing is about children, their problems, and their way of looking at the world. Her "good" characters do say the right things, and her "bad" ones are likely to be converted to better ways, or, if *too* bad, defeated by the good ones. Yet the accident of sex lends to the work of Panova a warmth and sympathy which is not denied even to the negative characters and improves her insight into the positive ones.

Because of Panova's pervasive femininity some important Soviet literary leaders have never understood or fully accepted her. When her novel *The Four Seasons* appeared in 1953 it was an immediate success with the reading public and was selected for translation into foreign languages, but there was some distress at the highest level. An attack on the novel appeared in *Pravda* over the signature of V. Kochetov, who compared it to novels published in the twenties during the NEP period and attempted to kill it with a label:

> If the author of *The Four Seasons* undertakes simply to show "how things are in life sometimes," without passing any judgment, then she has taken the direction of naturalism. And naturalism explains nothing. Naturalism can entertain, astound, arouse emotion, but it cannot ever make profound and true social and artistic generalizations.

This is a fair criticism because what Panova is trying to do in her novel is to give, without preachment or propaganda, an immediate sense of the Russian experience. Each of the characters has an accent and an inner life of his own, each is different from the others, each one experiences life in his own way. They fall in love, or out of love, they marry, have children, work, find friends, and think uncomplicated thoughts—on life in the Soviet and outside of it. Panova does succeed in capturing some part of the reality, in giving us, as Kochetov puts it, some sense of "how things were."

The unifying idea of the novel is that power corrupts those who wield it. One of the leading characters is the top-level Communist bureaucrat, Bortashevich, a scoundrel and a grafter who lives in fear of exposure. But this scoundrel is treated sympathetically, and the reader does not, as he reads the novel, blame him very much. He is a good fellow who has fallen into crime because of the effect of environment: specifically the environment of upper-class Communist society. His criminal activity had begun very gradually, almost imperceptibly, with nothing more than a wink, just because he needed money in order to live in a style better than that of his colleagues, and after a few years he was so deep in crime that he couldn't get out no matter how much he wanted to. He was the victim of social evil, and Panova identifies this evil as the atmosphere of irresponsible power. At one point this is carefully spelled out.

Another character with a problem is Dorofeya, a peasant girl who has risen in the course of an adventurous life to be a high Communist official. Her son, Gennadi, is a lazy wastrel who expects to take from life but never give anything back. Through selfishness and weakness he falls in with some gangsters, Soviet version, and Panova's novel reveals the activities of the Soviet criminal underworld, a form of life hardly ever touched upon in approved novels. But Panova is sympathetic even to this spoiled and selfish young criminal, whom she portrays as basically good, but the victim of bad environment and bad education.

The Four Seasons ends on a note of indomitable feminine optimism. In contrast to her novel *Kruzhilikha*, in which the builder Listopad meditates on the marvels to come in science and industry, Panova in *The Four Seasons*, sensitive to the demand for attention to individual human beings, ends her novel with a lyric apostrophe to her characters:

> We'll soon be feasting. Even nondrinkers will have a drink tonight. When the Kremlin bells ring out at midnight, who would not drink a toast? Let's drink to the happiness of Sasha and Yulka and their friends, to the success of their plans, to the well-being of the town of Ensk. Let us wish Dorofeya courage in facing her new trials. Let us wish a great success to comrade Kosykh and the whole machine-building factory, and to all those who honorably work for life, for eternal, ever-young, ever-renewed life.
> Happy New Year, Comrades!

The novelist Panova is a sensitive person, whose interests are those of a woman, and whose comments on life have feminine gentleness and tact. She is a Party writer, but one with sentiment. She wears the "leather jacket," but hers has, one could say, yellow ribbons on it. Her work is important because she introduced and insisted upon some of the most important themes of the immediate post-Stalin thaw. Her chief themes are those that traditionally have had special interest for women: love, the need for human tenderness and consideration, the reality of private emotion, the family, the education of children. Her cycle of stories, *Seryozha* (1955), is concerned directly with children, their special character, their psychology, and their education.

The Guests, a play by Leonid Zorin (b. 1924), published in the magazine *Theater* (no. 2, 1954) and presented in Leningrad and Moscow, is a direct attack on the Soviet bureaucratic state. In this play the contemporary rulers of the Soviet Union were held up to public obloquy for having turned their revolutionary inheritance into a source of bourgeois comfort and power. The message of the play is radical: it is a frankly aimed attack at the Party and the government in the name of the lost ideals of the Revolution. The Ministry of Culture lost no time in condemning such a thing and in terms reserved for genuinely subversive material.

The play is built around a single character, a high official of the Ministry of Justice, who has the speech, the manner, and the way of thinking of a man habituated to arbitrary power. The action takes place in a summer house owned by the father of the minister, an old revolutionary toward whose ideals the son feels a kind of tolerant contempt. "Old granddaddy" with his ideas that go all the way back to 1917 seems foolishly old-fashioned to the new generation. For Pyotr political power is the only reality, and he uses his to build advantage for himself. He and his family are full of possessions: a car (with chauffeur), a fine summer house, a luxurious apartment; and to all of this they are jealously attached. The minister himself in his vulgar pursuit of privilege has learned to hold ordinary citizens in contempt. The action of the play revolves around a miscarriage of justice which Pyotr and his cronies intend to conceal because exposure would be a threat to them. The innocents who had been condemned and ruined must stay ruined, the wrong would not be righted.

Three generations are represented in the cast of characters: the old revolutionary, his son the minister, and the minister's son. The minister belongs to the generation of "careerist" bureaucrats, and his father directly accuses him of having betrayed the Revolution. "There is something alien and insulting in their life," comments one character, "a life in which the important thing is not labor, but pride of place." And when the minister's family are discussing a newly acquired piece of property one of the good characters says: "How I hate these filthy little bourgeois." The minister's family and his social set are exposed in the play as an uncultivated and arrogant ruling class. An optimistic note is struck when, near the end of the play, the minister's own son turns on him:

> "I hereby declare war on you. Wherever I meet you—in whatever guise you may appear, wherever you show yourself, whatever name you bear—I will recognize you and I will fight you to the death."

No doubt this is rhetoric, and not very skillful rhetoric, but the sentiment expressed was perhaps the most powerful indictment of the Stalinist bureaucracy published in the Soviet Union. Directed ostensibly at "criminal elements" in the Ministry of Justice whose crimes were investigated and exposed after the execution of Beria, the playwright subtly contrives that the portrait of these elements resembles a whole new class of criminal careerists.

Ilya Ehrenburg and Alexey Tolstoy

The novelette which gave a name to the post-Stalin period was Ilya Ehrenburg's *The Thaw*, published in the first months of 1954. Ehrenburg in this work provided a concise guide to the themes and theses of post-Stalin literature; as a matter of fact his work sums up so neatly in credible artistic form the main points of "de-Stalinization" that one is obliged to assume a degree of political guidance, direct or indirect, in its writing. The argument of *The Thaw*, taken up again by many authors in subsequent works, runs as follows: (1) Soviet life has become cold and rigid; let us warm up toward one another. (2) Soviet political and industrial heroes are often tyrants indifferent to the popular weal; let us expose them. (3) People are important, and they exist as individuals; let us cherish each one. (4) Emotions are real and cannot always be neatly catalogued and contained in rational categories; let us feel them: love, pity, fear, envy. It is a fine argument, indeed, but it is so well organized that one can sense in it a remnant of ice under the "thaw."

Ehrenburg (1891–1967) was after 1954 the most important advocate of liberalization in Soviet literature, and he made a not inconsiderable contribution, even though the points he laboriously hammers on the nature of artistic creation and the needs of literature are generally so obvious as to induce either laughter or tears. But in Soviet literature someone is always obliged to stress truisms.

Ehrenburg's biography is itself a kind of commentary on the Soviet regime. His personal history is interesting, not only as the development of a complex and cryptic personality under the pressures of the twentieth century, but as a commentary on the relationship to the Soviet regime of intellectuals whose education and outlook is individualistic and West European. A brief biographical digression on Ehrenburg is indispensable for an understanding of Khrushchev's thaw and may throw some light as well on the history of the Soviet state.

Ehrenburg was born into a bourgeois Jewish family. His father was the first of his line to break away from the folk and the faith, "to leave the ghetto," as Ehrenburg phrased it, and had received his own father's curse for the crime of attending a Russian school. His Jewish family origin has been, all his life, one of the most important factors in Ehrenbrug's view of the world. In an autobiographical sketch written in 1926, he said:

> I was born in 1891. A Hebrew. Spent my childhood in Moscow, Khamovniki, near a brewery. Warm, sour beer. The workers curse and fight in the barracks . . . In the spring we went to visit grandfather in Kiev. Imitating him, I prayed, my whole body swaying, and

I sniffed clove from a silver vessel. Then the First Moscow Gymnasium. The boys around me said: "The little kike sits on a bench, we'll sit the little kike on a fence." At home I raised mischief—more than was necessary. Set fire to a summer house.

The effect on a growing boy of such experience may easily be imagined. The fact that he was a Jew, and as such the object of a special, inevitable, and undeserved injury, goes far to explain Ehrenburg's career. The traumatic effect on him of the boyhood shocks he met with is borne out by the fact that he referred to such matters again in his more recent autobiography, written in 1960; but the years had mellowed his memories, and though he mentions the *numerus clausus*, the pale of settlement, the resident permit, and the pogroms, he would have his readers believe that "things were not really bad," and he provides a new version of that first day in a Russian school:

> I had somewhere read that the Jews had crucified Christ; uncle Leo told me that Christ was himself a Jew; aunt Vera told me that Christ taught us to turn the other cheek. But I didn't care for that teaching. When I first entered the gymnasium one of the preparatory students began teasing: "The little kike sat on a bench, let's sit the little kike on a fence." Without a moment's hesitation I hit him in the face. But soon we became friends. And no one insulted me again.

Note that an important mnemonic revision has occurred in the account of that boyhood incident written in 1960. In the first version, a number of boys sang the intolerable ditty; in the later account it is only one—a preparatory student at that—and Ehrenburg immediately silenced him. He goes on in that passage to insist that there was no great anti-Semitism among the Russian intellectuals of that day. But the experience of life symbolized by the obscene ditty was really unbearable, and Ehrenburg never became reconciled to it. The culture that contained such injustice has been, most of his life, the victim of his cynical mockery. His consistent support of the new regime in Russia was motivated, perhaps, by his contempt for the values of European bourgeois culture, and a certain fellow-feeling for the new barbarians. His occasional doubts as to the latter appear in a number of works, and after the death of Stalin he undertook to correct some of the damage that had been wrought in literature and art. His voice since 1954 has consistently championed individualism and artistic integrity, and in his reminiscences, *People, Years, Life,* published in 1960 and 1961 in the magazine *New World,* he tried to revivify those ties with modern European art which were a normal part of the Russian cultural tradition. Like the theses advanced in his novelette *The Thaw*, the points he gently emphasizes in *People, Years, and Life* have a programmatic ring.

The refusal to treat with due seriousness the alternatives offered by the bourgeois world is amply illustrated in Ehrenburg's biography. He was a student agitator during the 1905 Revolution and was imprisoned in 1907, at the age of 16. From 1909 to 1917 he lived abroad, spending much of his time on the Left Bank in Paris, talking and working at all hours in the Rotonde, the Closerie des Lilas, and other Montparnasse cafés. From 1910 to 1914 he moved in French Symbolist circles, was overcome with admiration for Francis Jammes, discovered Paul Claudel and Leon Bloy, became a convert to a kind of mystical Catholicism, and seriously considered entering a Benedictine monastery. The latter thought was perhaps his most respectable attempt at rejecting the values of the bourgeois world. When the war came in 1914 his reaction was original—he tried to enlist in the Foreign Legion, but was rejected as physically unfit. His first response to the October Revolution, "A Prayer For Russia," was a stylized poetic exercise in the neo-Catholic vein on the mystic agony being suffered by *"la pieuse Russie"* at the hands of infidels. He spent the years 1918 and 1919 in Kiev, Tiflis, and other southern localities where he barely escaped on the one hand the Cheka and on the other the pogroms. He returned to Paris in 1921 on an official Soviet "artistic mission," but was expelled by the French police and went to Brussels. There he wrote *The Extraordinary Adventures of Julio Jurenito and His Disciples*, a book of which he said: "This is the only book I wrote 'in earnest.' Neither the critics, nor the readers, nor even myself can tell in that book where the mockery ends." Without doubt Ehrenburg's best work, *Julio Jurenito* relates the adventures of a nihilistic philosopher who undertakes the mission of destroying finally the culture of Europe. His instruments of destruction are, ironically enough, typical products of that culture: an American Bible-thumping business man, Mr. Cool; a methodical and ruthless German, Schmidt; the French *rentier*, M. Delhaie; a melancholy Russian intellectual in search of his own soul. Auxiliary instruments and positive characters are an anarchist Bambucci whose only purpose in life is to violate all rules, and an African savage who believes absolutely in his own gods. Bourgeois culture is scathingly attacked in the novel, but the new order in Russia does not escape Ehrenburg's barbs.

During the twenties and thirties he lived for the most part abroad, producing stories and journalistic articles for the Soviet Press. *Trust D. E.: The Story of the Ruin of Europe* (1923) deals with the conquest of Europe by American capitalism. The novel *The Adventures of Lasik Roitschwantz* (1927) is a mockery of the bourgeois—and Communist—world given in the idiom of a poor Jewish tailor who is arrested by the Communist police and imprisoned, then escapes from Russia and travels in Western Europe where he is mistaken for a Bolshevik, and at last dies of starvation in Palestine. Lasik's amused contempt for both West and East is expressed in homely Jewish wisdom, and the novel is peppered with proverbs, sayings, Talmudisms, and the like. *The Summer, 1925* (1926) and *A Street in Moscow* (1927) give a depressing picture of society in the days of NEP, when the Revolution seemed to have reached a dead end. *The Conspiracy of Equals* (1929) is a historical novel about the life of Gracchus Babeuf. *The Factory of Dreams* (1931) is a satire on Hollywood. *Out of Chaos* (1933), Ehrenburg's contribution to Five-Year Plan literature, is second only to *Julio Jurenito* in importance and interest. It represents for Ehrenburg a decisive step beyond the nihilistic mockery of his earlier work. It is more "in earnest" than *Jurenito* and represents an effort to establish a rational basis for Ehrenburg's pro-Soviet position. The scene of the novel is the great Kuznetsk metallurgical combine in the days of its construction. It preaches the usual moral of Five-Year Plan literature, that a new Communist world will grow out of the industrialization program. The novel is important because of the main character Safonov, a young intellectual and a confirmed individualist, whose ideas at times echo *Jurenito* and who is certainly Ehrenburg himself. Safonov's sophisticated intellectual conscience is outraged by the crass materialism of the new collective. He cannot accept the world being created by the Soviet Five-Year Plan. In Safonov's private diary Ehrenburg pronounced an indictment upon the "anthill" culture being built in the Soviet Union, and in the personal history of Safonov he illustrated the helplessness of the lone intellectual before the onslaught of that culture. That feeling of helplessness was reinforced by Ehrenburg's conviction that no confidence could be placed in intellectuals either of the West or of the East.

Safonov's imagined speech to the "collective" confided to his diary expresses the thought and summarizes the tragedy of Ehrenburg himself:

> You are accustomed to silence. Some are silent because you have frightened them; others because you have bought them . . . As in the days of Galileo simple truth can be spoken only at the stake. You want to discuss the question of culture. It is unlikely, however, that anyone among you understands what culture is. For some, culture is blowing one's nose in a handkerchief; for others it is buying the Academy publications, which they do not understand, cannot, indeed, understand. You've established universal literacy and equally universal ignorance. After this you gather to-

gether and prattle about culture. Of course your not blowing your nose through your fingers deserves praise. But it has little to do with culture. You build a thousand blast furnaces and you are still ignorant. The anthill is a model of reason and logic. But it already existed a thousand years ago. Nothing in it has changed. There are ant workers, and ant specialists, and ant leaders. But there never was an ant genius . . . The Acropolis was not built by ants. The law of gravitation was not discovered by an ant. Ants have no Senecas, no Raphaels, no Pushkins. They have a hill, and they work. They build, they carry twigs, they lay eggs, they devour one another, and they are happy. They are far more honest than you are—they don't talk nonsense about culture.

Safonov did not deliver this speech before the collective, but another and thoroughly acceptable one. And Safonov's symbolic suicide had its real counterpart in the demise of Ehrenburg as a satirist. His work during the thirties need not concern us since it is for the most part patterned strictly and skillfully to the Party line.

In his journalistic articles during the Second World War he attacked all Germans so violently that the Soviet authorities found it necessary to check him, pointing out that there were both Fascist and anti-Fascist Germans. Immediately after the death of Stalin the most fruitful period in Ehrenburg's life began, the period of *The Thaw* and of his articles in defense of a literary and artistic culture that seemed threatened with extinction in the Soviet Union. The cynical nihilism of his young manhood had no part in the campaign he now waged, with a sure sense of the Soviet environment, to educate the recently literate but still uncultivated "Soviet man."

The shock produced throughout the world by Ehrenburg's novelette when it broke the long winter of Stalinism should not be forgotten. In the year 1954 the story seemed a miraculous occurrence, a fantastic piece of writing which gave a glimpse behind the Iron Curtain and revealed Soviet life in its real colors and contours. In this work Ehrenburg wrote according to a recipe which he had himself drawn up in the article "On the Writers' Work," which I have already cited:

Let us suppose that the novel deals with Ivanov, the reader's next-door neighbor. Neither Ivanov's appearance nor his everyday life is a secret to the reader. The reader has often seen Ivanov, heard him speak at meetings of the *aktiv*, perhaps even dropped in on him from time to time. Yet Ivanov remains unfamiliar and undiscovered territory to him. If the writer is able to show what this distant neighbor is thinking about, how he bears grief, how he works, loves and makes mistakes, the reader will feel enriched by reading this novel; he has come to know Ivanov and therefore has become better acquainted with himself.

The "inner world" of each character is the subject matter of *The Thaw*, and in this it is a conscious polemic against official Soviet literature and a return to the methods advocated in the twenties by Voronsky and the theorists of RAPP. The story is told in a succession of episodes, each presented from the viewpoint of a particular character, whose personal idiosyncrasies and unspoken thoughts are basic to the narrative pattern. Zhuravlyov, an industrial manager and an autocrat who destroys those who disagree with him, is a complex character. The chief villain of the piece, he is still not entirely a villain. He even has feelings. He is in love with his wife, Lena, and cannot reason himself out of such foolishness. Lena is in love, too, but not with her husband, whose faults she sees too well in spite of his production miracles. Sokolovsky, a lone eccentric who thinks his own thoughts, has had a bitter disappointment in love that accounts for his bristling nature. Vera Scherer is a doctor who, like Sokolovsky, lives alone with her sardonic reflections on life. Volodya Pukhov, a cynical artist, paints large canvases ("Feast on a Collective Farm") to order for the government, but secretly envies his colleague Saburov, who has given up success for the lonely path of true art. And other characters are presented in terms of *private* rather than *public* life.

The technique adopted by Ehrenburg effectively conveys the main idea of *The Thaw*. Each character seems to warm up a little toward the others, each becomes less hard and rational, more sympathetic and understanding. Each feels the need of giving and receiving love.

Ehrenburg was attacked for his revolutionary departure in *The Thaw* by no less a figure than Konstantin Simonov, who found objectionable his portrayal of the artist Vladimir Pukhov as a hack and a careerist. Simonov, with remarkable perspicacity, felt that Pukhov represented all of Soviet art and discerned Ehrenburg's intention to show him as a good character corrupted by environment: "As seen by the author," said Simonov, "Pukhov . . . is a victim who loves real art but is forced to do hack work because he has not the moral strength for heroic opposition to some enormous machine which mercilessly drags him down." Ehrenburg answered Simonov and others who attacked him, and he was at no time forced to recant or repent, but he did, in 1956, publish Part II of *The Thaw*, in which the incongruities of Soviet life as reflected in Part I tend to disappear: the true artist Saburov at last gains public recognition; the plant director Zhuravlyov has a new assignment and, while he may not be an entirely new man, he has learned a few lessons.

Having once said the important things, Ehrenburg seems to have been willing to appease his critics by the relatively optimistic tone of Part II. He was awarded the Order of Lenin in 1961, on the occasion of his seventieth birthday. He died in 1967.

In order to see clearly the quality of Ehrenburg, an intellectual who, though he compromised, at last threw his weight onto the side of cultural freedom, we should compare him to Alexey N. Tolstoy (1883–1945), who was also highly successful as a literary supporter of the Stalin regime. A scion of the aristocratic Tolstoy family and a distant relative of Leo, he bore the title of Count, and though he had served with Denikin and emigrated to Paris in 1919, he was welcomed back to the Soviet Union in 1923, where his career moved forward with only occasional hindrance from those proletarian critics who attacked him as a "gentleman" and a "White Guardist." His return to the Soviet Union has been explained in various ways. Some say that, lacking principle, he abandoned the ascetic rigors of the emigration for the fleshpots of Soviet fame; but it was not as simple as that. Others explain that he belonged to the "Change of Landmarks" group of scholars and writers who accepted the current Russian regime while rejecting its Marxist ideology; but Tolstoy was much less cerebral than the "Change of Landmarks" intellectuals. He probably returned because of a special feeling for Russia which one can detect in his novels and which might be called "patriotism." Russia was still Russia, even under the Bolsheviks, and if Tolstoy could upon his return live as a kind of "workers' and peasants' Count," what was even more important for him was that he could remain a Russian "Count."

Tolstoy as a writer had a brilliant narrative flair combined with thematic versatility and a command of pellucid prose, but it is probably fair to say that he had no serious intellectual concerns. He proliferated interesting stories form Russian provincial life, and Wellsian fantasies like *Aelita* (1922), which tells of a visit to Mars by a sensitive intellectual and a crude Russian proletarian who wants to annex the planet to the Soviet; *Engineer Garin's Hyperboloid* (1925–1926) in which a scientist who has invented a death ray seeks to impose his own brand of Fascism on the world; and *Blue Towns* (1925), another kind of fantasy in which a romantic idealist, the architect Buzheninov, is defeated in his conflict with philistines. *Nikita's Childhood* (1920), written while he was still in Germany, is widely regarded as his best and most genuine work. A fictionalized account of his childhood on a Russian estate, it is permeated with the charm of distant, remembered places and people, and conveys a kind of naïve joy in the recall of the most ordinary events. His most ambitious work, *The Road to Calvary*, begun in the emigration and not completed until 1941, relates the vicissitudes of a group of intellectuals who at first reject the Revolution, then learn to "accept" it. The earliest sections of the novel contain fascinating accounts of the years of hunger and war as they affected intellectual bohemians and artists, and many vivid pictures of people and events: an unforgettable portrait of the peasant anarchist leader Makhno, for instance, with his entourage of cutthroats and intellectual "idea men." The last volume shows a distinct drop in originality and power, and the novel ends on a depressing note of Soviet affirmation. His unfinished historical novel, *Peter the First* (1929–1945), is the fruit of an intensive labor of love over a vast body of Russian historical evidence. Tolstoy in this novel re-created Peter and his period in concrete, realistic images which, as a result of his long study of historical sources, he easily commanded. Its power as a work of historical fiction is not vitiated by the parallels Tolstoy sees between Stalin's and Peter's Russia, nor by his conscious rehabilitation of the cruel Czar. Tolstoy's deep and real feeling for Russian history converts this book into genuine art, just as his feeling for the distant motherland made *Nikita's Childhood* a thing of real beauty.

Tolstoy secured a place for himself with Stalin through conforming to the dictator's literary tastes and prejudices, and he made no effort to defend himself or other writers against the insane persecutions of the thirties. Ehrenburg tells of Tolstoy's behavior when in 1936 the sudden onset of a campaign against "formalist distortions" and "cynicism" created tortured consternation in the whole writers' community. Tolstoy's reaction was one of decisive and complete acquiescence in the charges and ready repentance for having himself written a formalistic play. Ehrenburg explains that Tolstoy wanted only "peace and quiet," and implies that Tolstoy would go to great lengths to achieve them (*New World*, no. 4, 1962, p. 61). How far he would go became clear in 1937 when, as insurance against the purge, he produced the novel *Bread*, which falsified history in order to present Stalin as the heroic defender of Tsaritsin (Stalingrad) during the Civil War. Stalin's successors have stigmatized this work as shameless flattery, and they have even changed the name of the city to Volgograd.

Tolstoy lived well, enjoying, we have been told, the good food and fine wines that belonged to his station in life and his title. Ivan Bunin described him as "the Bolshevik poet laureate." He is supposed to have been so rich that Soviet banks granted him an open account upon which he could draw without limitation. In return for all this he placed his talent at the total disposition of the regime and of Stalin personally. He was a shallow man even in comparison with Ehrenburg, and compared with Pasternak his work and his thought are only ankle deep.

The Second Thaw[1]

The works I have discussed were published in the period from March 1953 to about March 1954. By that time the reaction of the conservatives was already under way. Their counterattack began deviously, taking the form of a series of attacks on writers for ethical and moral lapses, for scandalous behavior, public brawling, drunkenness, and other such peccadilloes. The writers attacked may indeed have been grafters, brawlers, and drunkards and a disgrace to the writers' profession, but the interesting fact is that the campaign for an improvement in their morals took the more general direction of warning writers against individualism, bohemianism, and the like. Several writers, whose conduct may have been open to censure, were disgraced and expelled from the Writers' Union.

By August of 1954 the leaders of the Party had apparently decided that matters on the literary front had gotten out of hand, and vigorous action was taken to bring the writers to heel, especially since the Second Congress of Writers was scheduled to take place in the near future and all doubts about the correct literary line had to be resolved before that public event. The editorial board of the magazine *New World,* which had published much dubious material, was censured and the editor Tvardovsky removed from his post. A meeting of the collegium of the USSR Ministry of Culture was called to consider Zorin's play, *The Guests.* The Ministry of Culture condemned the play because "it presented an important Soviet official as a rascal and as a typical representative of the whole Soviet apparatus."

At the Second Congress of Soviet Writers held in December 1954, the chief spokesman of the Party, Secretary of the Union A. A. Surkov, reasserted the rigid Zhdanovite line on ideological purity and insisted on the use of literature for socialist purposes. Surkov, poet, patriot, and Stalinist to the core, from his tribune of authority, announced that the Party would continue to guide the work of writers and deplored certain recent "manifestations." But Surkov's rigidities did not fully characterize the Congress. Many writers in their own prepared speeches spoke out freely and with surprising frankness. And the reliable Simonov, who had replaced Tvardovsky as editor of *New World,* seemed for the moment to have joined the dissidents. He called for a broadened socialist realism within which greater variety might appear; he deplored the constant revision of old novels in the light of present needs; he called for a republication of Soviet satirists of the twenties, such as Ilf and Petrov. There was no wholesale punishment of the dissidents, nor were there any public apologies. And the poet Anna Akhmatova, who had been outraged by Zhdanov, reappeared at the Congress. Simonov's conversion was evidence that strong forces within the Writers' Union were moving in the direction of liberalization, although the organization itself was still controlled by old-line Stalinists. The issues between the two factions had not at that time been settled, and the highest authority in the Party, for the moment, held aloof from the contest.

At the Twentieth Congress of the Communist Party in February 1956, the Congress at which Khrushchev's speech on the crimes of Stalin was delivered before a closed meeting, there were two speeches on literature. The first, by Surkov, contained the time-tried formulas on the educative function of literature, but the second, by Sholokhov, was a humorous and at times obscene attack on the pretensions of Soviet writers and on all literary generals and general secretaries. "There isn't anything," he said, "that a writer can learn from Surkov. Why do we need such leaders?"

During the year 1956 the liberals seemed confident of their own strength, and that year witnessed the publication of a number of poems, plays, and stories subjecting the Soviet way of life to critical examination. Nineteen fifty-six has been called the "Year of Protest," and that it certainly was, though it was also a year of high optimism among Soviet writers as to the prospect for literary freedom. The revelation of the crimes committed by the Party and government under Stalin was the catalyst. To many Russian writers it seemed incredible that men who had accused themselves of such crimes that no moral credit was left to them would presume to guide the creative labors of poets and novelists. The Soviet writers did make an effort to free themselves from Party tutelage. During 1956 the magazine *New World*, which had earlier offended with Pomerantsev's article, published Dudintsev's *Not by Bread Alone*. Pasternak submitted his novel *Doctor Zhivago* to the editorial board of *New World*, apparently in the expectation that it might be accepted and published. This was perhaps the highest point of optimism reached during the year, and Pasternak received, not a reprimand, but a politely worded though stern letter of refusal from the editors. The second volume of the collection called *Literary Moscow* was published. *Day of Poetry, 1956* appeared. And a young writer named D. Granin published his story "One's Own Opinion." The literary product of that brief interval, which ended with the Hungarian revolt in October 1956, deserves careful scrutiny. Since the twenties Soviet writers had never been as free of official direction as they were during that year.

Neither the first nor the second thaw released any serious rebellion against the Soviet state, and it would be fruitless to look for evidence of a radical rejection of Communism or even of the basic forms of Soviet society. Though there may have been exceptions to the rule, the writers who produced the dissident literature of 1956 were loyal to the ideals of Communism and in rebellion only against practitioners of power who had debased those ideals. Like Zorin in *The Guests,* these writers suggest that the apparatus of the movement has fallen into the hands of opportunists who despise the people and degrade the state. An individual human being—even an individual Communist—can preserve his integrity only if he holds himself apart from a collective dominated by careerists and criminals. Such is the theme of Dudintsev, Granin, and a dozen or so poets and prose writers whose material was published in the collections already mentioned. The nature of their message explains the fact that in all of these works emphasis is placed on the freedom and responsibility of individual human beings. "You yourself must find the answer," said the poet Semyon Kirsanov. And when you have found the answer, the dissidents insist, you must take the responsibility of acting—even if you are alone. There is in all of this a tragic irony, for the ground these young men traveled with so much courage was country already discovered and explored. Thirty years earlier a controversy had risen over the so-called "Sten Letter," published in *Young Communist Truth* in 1929, which urged the young to "check and verify on the basis of their own knowledge and experience, every decision and every policy of the Party." Sten, a publicist and educator, was accused then of inviting the young to cultivate Trotskyism and other vices. There was no reason to expect a different kind of answer in 1956.

Dudintsev's *Not by Bread Alone* is not really a very good novel. The style is simple, direct, and competent, but it is also undistinguished, and over long stretches it is flat. We expect mediocrity in Soviet writings of the postwar period, yet Dudintsev has less verbal power than a number of his contempories: Panova's style has lucidity and charm, and both Ehrenburg and Granin have an ear for the rhythms of contemporary Russian speech. With the exception of the careerist villain, Drozdov, Dudintsev's characters do not emerge as visible images, nor can we recognize them by the sound of their voices or the inner movement of their thought and feeling. Lopatkin, the lone inventor who carries on an eight-year fight against the system, is a fine idea but not a living being, and it is difficult to sympathize with his fanatic devotion to the centrifugal casting and mass production of large-diameter iron drainpipes. The plot has a kind of textbook simplicity; suspense is not maintained; accident or coincidence plays a vital part in the development of the story. Things happen in the novel as the result of the inner needs and purposes not of the characters but of the novelist himself, who has very much to say and manages to say it all honestly and forthrightly.

It is at first sight not easy to understand why this novel was singled out for special censure and condemned by Khrushchev for overemphasizing the negative features of Soviet life. Dudintsev's central theme was already standard fare in Soviet literature: the scientist-innovator who must fight for a new idea against vested interest had appeared in the work of Kaverin, Ehrenburg, Granin, and others. In their treatment of the lone inventor at grips with monopoly these Soviet novelists have many points of contact with Mitchell Wilson, author of *My Brother My Enemy*, who is widely read, admired, and imitated in the Soviet Union. And the literary attack on petty dictators had already been accepted in such things as Korneichuk's *Wings*, a popular play of the period, as part of the de-Stalinization program.

Dudintsev's call for love and mutual understanding among human beings, his insistence that the powerful must consider the rights of men lower in the scale, his dictum that a man must speak his mind regardless of consequences when the right is at stake—all of these ideas had formed the principal substance of Soviet literature since Ehrenburg's *The Thaw* appeared in 1954. Where, then, did Dudintsev go off the ideological rails?

Dudintsev's novel presents a conflict between an individual who has a vital idea and a Soviet collective dominated by men whose chief interest is in protecting their own preserves and furthering their own careers. And the novelist, discarding approved literary clichés, honestly faced his hero's problem. Drozdov and his cronies who dominate the collective are able to frustrate Lopatkin at every turn and even imprison him on fabricated evidence. He is ultimately freed through the efforts of individuals who act independently, and in one case violate Soviet law, in order to see justice finally done. The official euphemisms which cover the abuse of power are resolutely abandoned in this novel. The phrase "cult of the individual" does not appear even once, and when a character, in order to account for a bureaucrat's behavior, uses the formula "survivals of capitalism," the effect is clearly ironical. Careerists and opportunists appear in this novel as an indigenous Soviet growth and as creatures of the Soviet power system. To present the problem in these terms was Dudintsev's first mistake, and the Soviet writers' collective, the Union of Writers, dominated by A. A. Surkov, insisted that Dudintsev "see" his mistake.

Not only is the novel a defense of the rights of the individual against entrenched and irresponsible power, but it also exposes to ridicule and shame the vulgar materialistic standards and low cultural level of the barbarians who wield this power. In the best tradition of Russian revolutionary literature Dudintsev derides them for their bourgeois attachment to creature comforts, for their fine clothing, lavishly furnished apartments, television sets, sleek black limousines, and all the rest. The hero Lopatkin could have had all of these things if he had been sensible, given up his original idea, and joined the "collective," but he chose instead his own way, the "endless, austere road" where he remained poor but independent, and free to work out his own thought. There are some interesting remarks on independence and freedom in the novel. Speaking of his trip to the Siberian labor camp, Lopatkin says: "No need to fear journeys. Anyone who is afraid of travel of course will not go. But in that case he will not get far either." And again, "The words *deprivation of liberty* are inaccurate. Whoever has learned to think cannot be completely deprived of liberty." Dudintsev's second mistake was that he portrayed the managerial group as a kind of "new class" with values that set them apart from the people and interests that have nothing to do with basic human values, such as freedom, equality, individual integrity. The exceptions to the rule are occasional idealistic individuals who refuse to conform to the values of "vulgar Communism." And the ending is not a hopeful one. The Drozdovs are still in power and the issue is in doubt.

Perhaps the most damaging accusation brought against the Drozdovs is that they are "worker ants" who jealously guard their anthill against the intrusion of strong and original individuals. In a speech which might be an echo of Sutyrin's remarks to Mayakovsky upon his entrance into RAPP, Drozdov expressed his distrust of "cranks and geniuses":

> "You know, Comrade Lopatkin, if I were a writer, I would write a novel about you. Because you are a truly tragic figure. You are the impersonation of a whole epoch, and one which has irretrievably disappeared into the past. You are a hero, but a solitary one ... We can see through you, but you don't understand us. You don't understand, for example, that we can get along without your invention, even if it is a genuine and great invention. We can do without it, and, just imagine! without suffering any loss at all ... Our designers' and technicians' collectives will find a solution. And this solution will be better than yours, because collective efforts always lead to the quickest and best solution of any problem. The collective is more of a genius than any individual genius ... We worker ants are necessary, while you solitary geniuses with your great ideas standing on feeble legs are not necessary."

Dudintsev's novel caused a sensation in Moscow, and when it was translated into Western languages it was widely read throughout the world.

There were many heated discussions of the novel in the days immediately following its publication, evidence that the issues it raised went to the heart of Soviet life. Many of the arguments turned on the question whether "the Drozdovs" were presented in the novel as typical or as exceptional, and the final authoritative judgment, pronounced by Khrushchev himself, was that Dudintsev had exaggerated and "generalized." But before the official mind was made up, the public discussion of the work occasioned some frank speaking. The writer Konstantin Paustovsky's speech on "the Drozdovs" was the high point of that discussion:

> This is a new group of acquisitive carnivores, a group which has nothing in common either with the Revolution, or with our regime, or with socialism . . .
> There are thousands of these Drozdovs and we should not close our eyes to their existence. Dudintsev's great merit lies in the fact that he has struck a blow at the most vital link in the chain. He speaks of the most terrible phenomenon in our society, a phenomenon to which we cannot at any price close our eyes, unless we are willing to allow these Drozdovs to overrun our entire country.

The collection of fiction, poetry, and criticism published in *Literary Moscow*, II (1956) was a deliberate reproach to the forces that have dominated Soviet literature since the thirties. In it were published a story of Ivan Katayev, who perished in a labor camp; the notebooks of Yury Olesha, who had been silent for almost twenty years; Ehrenburg's sympathetic introduction to a projected volume of verse by Marina Tsvetayeva, who committed suicide in 1941; some sharp commentary on Soviet drama and literary criticism by Mark Shcheglov and Alexander Kron; the short stories "Levers" by Alexander Yashin and "A Journey Home" by Nikolai Zhdanov, which expose the effects on human beings of life in the "apparatus"; and many other disturbing items.

Daniel Granin's story "One's Own Opinion," published in *New World*, dealt in a single sharply focused episode with the demoralizing psychological effects of conformity under the pressure of power. Granin has been concerned in most of his writing with the lives of scientists and engineers and especially with the struggle of inventive spirits against hardened dogma and estabished authority. His novels *Seekers* (1955) and *The Eye of the Storm* (1963) are particularly important.

A number of poems published in *Literary Moscow*, II, in *Day of Poetry* (1956) and in other literary magazines embodied like themes: Semyon Kirsanov's "Seven Days of the Week," an allegory on the need for honest human hearts, Yevgeny Yevtushenko's examination of his own conscience, *Stantsia Zima*, and his poem of hope for the future, "I Know

Not." The most passionate statement published of the revulsion felt by the literary community at the debasement of literature was V. Goncharov's poem, "I Hate":

I hate the retouchers,
There's nothing more horrible
Than their work—
For money they'll put
Truth itself to death.
A child is weeping—
But always ready at hand
Is a sly scalpel,
And the boy
Suddenly
To everyone's joy
Is smiling.
There's a dwarf
Who never grew up.
But that's no matter.
It's all quite easy.
Here he is!
Bigger than life
And higher than
The poet's honor.
And there's the dull face
Of a murderer and scoundrel;
Again the instrument
And whose portrait is it?
Our friend and comrade!
I hate the retouchers
Of the day's own light.
They're ready
To mask
The planet itself.
But what about us?
We laugh and cry—
We are the children of light.
The planet
Is dear to us
Without ornament.
No matter how you retouch it
The earth
Is still the earth.
You know the truth,
And like your own heart
It's always with you.

The last line of Goncharov's poem might serve as an emblem of the literary thaw. "The truth is like your own heart—it's always with you" states in a single image the thought that pervades the works of that period. The writers who produced them felt anger, not only at the deception that had been practiced on them, but at themselves for allowing it, and they appeal to individual human minds and hearts to judge truth hereafter for themselves and act on their judgment. This new thought in Soviet literature seems a belated echo of French existentialist thought. It was perhaps inevitable that the idea of an individual human being as both free and responsible should have occurred to many thoughtful people when the crimes committed in their name by the collective had become known, just as in France during the period of national degradation under the Nazi occupation an escape from collective guilt seemed to offer itself through individual will and action. The fact that, during the Stalin period, men of talent and reputation had supported oppressive policies that damaged literature as a whole and destroyed human beings could be explained only by the absence from Soviet life of a sense of individual responsibility. The latent purpose of the works examined here was to revive in individuals a feeling of involvement in collective deeds. The message is insistent. The managers of collective farms should not be levers in the hands of a higher echelon, but human beings with minds of their own; a man who insists on his own idea may be valuable, even though he seems a crank and troublemaker; it is important not only to have "one's own opinion," but to express and defend it; and the real heroes are those who even though alone carry the good fight against the Drozdovs—whose number is legion.

The Drozdovs soon reacted. Khrushchev's program to denigrate Stalin and those who had been close to him in the recent past had required a certain latitude for criticism, but there was always a danger that criticism would get out of hand, that negative characters might be treated not as deviations from the norm but as something inherent in "our Soviet reality," and that demands for radical reform of that reality would then be heard. The delicate power balance in which the leadership found itself explains the pattern of vacillation which we have observed: the relaxation of 1954 was followed by reassertion of control and the branding of certain kinds of criticism as out of bounds; the new relaxation following the Twentieth Congress, which reached its high point in 1956, was ended soon after suppression of the Hungarian revolt in November of that year. The fact that Hungarian Communist intellectuals had a prominent part in that revolt was not lost on the Party leadership, and Khrushchev, in talks with Soviet writers during the early months of 1957, assured them that if anything of the sort happened in the Soviet Union "he would know what to do with them, and his hand would not tremble."

At meetings of the Writers' Union the limits of permissible criticism were more or less clearly marked out, and writers who had overstepped those limits were named and invited to recant their errors. Among these were Dudintsev, Granin, N. Zhdanov, Yashin, and the editors of *Literary Moscow*, II (1956), Margarita Aliger and Venyamin Kaverin. They were not easily brought to heel. They sat silent at meetings called for the express purpose of "clarifying their position." As late as May 1957, Khrushchev complained that Dudintsev and Aliger had not reacted "properly" to criticism. The fact that they remained free and unharmed was evidence that there had been real changes since the days of Stalin.

Events, however, did not favor the dissidents. After the first sputnik was launched in October 1957, the authority of the Party in literature was to some extent rehabilitated. Some of the rebels of 1956, the poet Aliger, for instance, who had incurred the displeasure of Khrushchev for her failure to acknowledge errors, submitted declarations of complete loyalty only a few days after the launching. Evidence of astounding scientific progress, provided by the first artifical satellite, seemed to weaken the case of those writers who had attacked the bureaucracy as hostile to new ideas and an impediment to progress. The answer to Dudintsev's novel was given by Victor Shklovsky, the Formalist critic of the twenties, when he said: "The earth's gravity has been overcome, and signals are coming to us from the first cosmic laboratory in history . . . What we find in Dudintsev's novel is directly contradicted by the great scientific events which followed its publication."

Yet the struggle for the right to write one's own thoughts continued. The year 1957 saw the publication of the novel *Cruelty,* by Pavel Nilin, which has been translated into English under the title *Comrade Venka.* That novel, which relates the adventures in Siberia of two young Soviet detectives, is a well-made, exciting adventure story. We find in it something only rarely provided by Soviet literature: a thoroughly absorbing plot structure. And it is interesting, also, on the moral plane. Nilin's hero, Comrade Venka, is an idealistic young Communist whose simple idea of justice and human decency comes into conflict with the cynical cruelty of the power he serves. Rather than go on serving it Comrade Venka, a warm and appealing character, ends his life.

The Khrushchev regime felt it necessary to discredit the liberals of 1956 with the Russian masses. It did this in a number of ways. In 1958 a novel appeared in an important literary magazine, authored by the editor of the *Literary Gazette,* V. Kochetov. *The Yershov Brothers* was not only an answer to Dudintsev's *Not By Bread Alone* but a primitive and savage attack on the liberal intellectuals who perpetrated the rebellion against Party controls in literature. Its devices are so transparent, and its dishonesty so palpable and repellent, that even *Pravda,* while approving its ideological position, complained that it lacked artistry. The author underlines his thesis on every page. He sees two tendencies struggling in the Soviet Union, the socialist tendency which promises a bright future for all mankind, and the dark forces represented by the "intellectuals" and "aesthetes" who are at war with the future and who preach individualism, egoism, and hatred of humanity.

Khrushchev indicated that affairs in the literary world had reached a satisfactory posture in his speech at the Third Congress of Soviet Writers in 1959. He casually rehabilitated several writers who had been under a cloud and announced that "angels of reconciliation" were on the wing. His new liberalism was based on the assumption that those writers who had taken false ideological positions had abandoned them. In calling for an end to attacks against writers like Dudintsev who had "generalized the negative aspects" of Soviet life Khrushchev emphasized that those writers had seen the error of their ways and said "you shouldn't kick a man when he's down." Khrushchev's speech to the writers was offhand, rambling, studded with proverbial wisdom, and cheerfully ignorant of all literature. It was liberal in Soviet terms, but it contained a crudely dogmatic statement of the Party's demand for ideological support from the writers and betrayed no sympathy for their recent examination of conscience.

The Way of Pasternak

Boris Pasternak, whose world renown was one of the accidents of the thaw, stands as a refutation of Lenin's famous dictum: "It is impossible to live in a society and be free of it." To a degree he did preserve his inner freedom while managing to live as a Soviet citizen. Yet, at the same time and paradoxically, he is vitally bound to Soviet history and to contemporary Russian literature. Pasternak cannot be imagined apart from the Formalists and the Futurists, and his fate as a writer is bound up with the tragic misadventures of the Stalin period. He has influenced many accepted Russian poets, and the better ones have been ready to acknowledge that influence.

The literary historian Prince D. S. Mirsky, writing in 1926, maintained that Pasternak was at that time acknowledged among Russian poets as the greatest living member of their fraternity, and Bukharin, at the First Congress of Soviet Writers in 1934, called him "the greatest poetic master of our times." Displaying great insight, Bukharin went on to say that Pasternak's subjective apprehension of the world enabled him to produce original but overly personal images and metaphors. Chastely secluded within the poetic laboratory of his own mind, the poet, according to Bukharin, labored meticulously over the verbal form of his thoughts, memories, and associations, and produced poetry rich with intellectual experience, but necessarily narrow and individual.

Bukharin's analysis of Pasternak was both perceptive and fair, though the Marxist theoretician mistakenly sets up an implicit requirement that any poet, even a "laboratory worker," be consciously involved in social life. Pasternak's "noninvolvement" was a necessary condition of his own, possibly more important, work. Early in life he embraced poetry, not as a trade but as a vocation, not to produce useful linguistic artifacts but to discover new truth and new beauty. He not only worked at this calling but lived it, and this meant a certain estrangement from the world of immediate relevance, the world, that is, of established truth and old beauty. He was odd; he did and said strange things. Ehrenburg records that when he attended a Writers' Conference in Paris, Pasternak maintained his own eccentric daily schedule, with breakfast at two and very late dinners. He once took the floor at a meeting of the Russian Association of Proletarian Writers in the early thirties to make a speech in defense of genius and to chide the organization for tending to reduce all writers to common terms. In his autobiography *Safe Conduct,* his experience of the cataclysmic years from 1914 to 1920 is covered in three words: "Six years passed." His Zhivago-like noninvolvement in the external events of his time had in it, perhaps, an element of purely Russian *khitrost,* that cynical wisdom which makes for survival in difficult times. For Pasternak not only survived the cruel warfare of his time, but, unobtrusively and as though by accident, he prospered. Many stories have been told to explain this, but the basic reason was no doubt his unfeigned indifference to all significant issues of the immediate present. Charming and childlike in manner, Pasternak did not fit anyone's notion of an enemy, and his friends are as one in testifying that his warmth of human love was broad enough to include even the cruel maniac Stalin, grieving over his dead wife. Had he been in touch with the real world in the period of the literary thaw he would probably not have submitted his novel, *Doctor Zhivago,* for publication in the Soviet Union. That novel, while it was a triumph of poetic creation, fell short at precisely that point where Pasternak abandoned his subjective stance and commented directly on events and issues. In those pages of direct commentary he betrays the effect of his long exile inside himself.

Pasternak records in his autobiography that his first love was music, which he gave up for philosophy, and that his interest in poetry grew out of his experiences in Marburg as a pupil of the neo-Kantian philosopher Cohen. Like the young Blok, whose flirtation with *Sophia,* the Divine Wisdom, was an adventure in epistemology, Pasternak's concern as a poet is with the nature of knowledge. The *method* of Pasternak's quest for truth and beauty was not consonant with philosophy as a discipline. He belonged as a younger member to the generation of Russian artists—Scriabin, Bely, Blok—who seek ultimate truth not through the strict mediation of the reason, but through intuition, association, suggestion, image, and metaphor. Through the medium of poetic language Pasternak investigates, invents, and foreshadows new paths in the human apprehension of truth. He unlocks possibilities in the mind that may not yet be reducible to the categories so far discovered. "Locked in his laboratory," to paraphrase Bukharin, Pasternak carried on research, so to speak, in the nature and extent of the human resources that are available in the quest for truth. Pasternak's description of the room in Marburg where he wrote papers on philosophical themes suggests (as he would say) his method:

But from my very ardor an experienced observer would have said that I would never make a learned man. I lived through the learning of a subject much more intensely than the theme warranted. A kind of plantlike cerebration took root in me. Its characteristic lay in the fact that any secondary conception unfolding excessively in my interpretation would begin to demand nourishment and care, and when, under its influence, I turned to books, I was drawn to them not from any disinterested attraction for knowledge, but for literary quotations to its advantage. In spite of the fact that my work was accomplished with the aid of logic, imagination, paper, and ink, I liked it best of all because the more I wrote the more it became overgrown with a constantly thickening ornamentation of bookish citations and comparisons. But since a time limit compelled me at a given moment to renounce written extracts and as a substitute simply to leave my authors open at the places I needed, a time arrived when the theme of my work materialized and could be reviewed at a glance from the threshold of the room. It lay outstretched across the room rather like a tree fern which spreads its leafy coils over the table, the divan and the windowsill. To disorder them meant to break the thread of my argument, but a complete tidying up would be equivalent to burning an uncopied manuscript. The landlady had been strictly forbidden to lay a hand on them. Towards the end my room was not even cleaned. And when I imagined the appearance of my room . . . I really saw my philosophy incarnate and also its probable fate.

In his autobiographical remarks and prose works Pasternak frequently reverts to the definition of art. The following concerns the genesis of art:

We cease to recognize reality. It appears to us in some new category. And this category seems a condition belonging to it rather than to us. Apart from this condition everything else in the world has been named. New and unnamed is it alone. We try to name it. The result is art . . .

The clearest, most memorable and important thing about art is its inception, and the finest of the world's production, dealing with the most diverse things, are really telling of their own birth.

One of the basic features of a work of art is, therefore, the question that called it forth, the new form or quality or condition, whether in reality or in ourselves, presented to the mind as a problem of naming. Pasternak's literary life is a record of concern with such problems, and that is why he is important. Pasternak does not describe what is already known and named—that he leaves to the writers of socialist novels. Instead he concerns himself with naming what is as yet unnamed. His work as a "Soviet writer" is like Olesha's tree that grew out of concrete, or, as Hugh McLean suggests, like a mastodon perfectly preserved in a cold Siberian waste, or like a rich jewel in an Ethiop's ear.

The novel that crowned his artistic labor, *Doctor Zhivago*, had an original fate. He completed it at the end of 1955, after working on it for about twenty years. A chapter had been published in 1938 in the *Literary Gazette* under the title "Fragment of a Novel." No more was seen in print until 1954 when there appeared in the magazine *Znamya* (*The Banner*) the set of poems which make up the last chapter of the novel. Early in 1956 Pasternak submitted it to the Soviet magazine *New World*, the editors of which, as we have seen, politely but firmly rejected it. Considering the nature of the novel, their criticism was a model of restraint. Since he could not publish it in the Soviet Union Pasternak offered it to a Milanese publisher, Feltrinelli, who brought it out in an Italian translation in 1957. Urgent messages reached Feltrinelli from Alexey Surkov of the Union of Soviet Writers and from Pasternak himself asking that it not be published but returned for, as they put it, "revisions." These messages the publisher ignored.

The novel was then translated from Pasternak's Russian manuscript into French and English, and it was published in the United States in September 1958. Finally, by arrangement with the Italian publisher, who holds the rights to the manuscript, the novel was published in Russian by the University of Michigan Press at Ann Arbor. The history of publication of *Doctor Zhivago* parallels in many respects that of Zamyatin's *We*, which was never published in the Soviet Union, published first in an English translation, then translated into Czech, partially translated from Czech back into Russian, and finally published in its original Russian in the United States. Pasternak was awarded the Nobel Prize in 1958, *Doctor Zhivago* became a *cause célèbre* in the West, and, like Dudintsev's *Not by Bread Alone*, was employed as a psychological weapon in the Cold War. Pasternak, like Dudintsev, publicly deplored this outcome, and there is no reason to doubt the sincerity of his statements. Indeed, the last irony of his life was this use of his finest literary art for political advantage.

Zhivago is a poetic novel. The body of the work, written in poetic prose, relates the misadventures of the hero on the stage of history and his tragic fate; the last chapter is a collection of poems, which constitute Zhivago's real work. The hero is Hamlet-like in his refusal to undertake official actions or to involve himself in public affairs that need to be set right, so the plot of his life is spun by the actions of those others who thirst for mundane power. In every important crisis Zhivago temporizes, yields, retreats from action. His life in historical terms is a failure. Even his doctor's skill has not been put to use. He has had two families but has taken care of neither, and the woman he loved he surrendered to a scoundrel who could save her life. Yet Zhivago's testament, his thin volume of poetry, is assembled and reserved as a special revelation by his friends and followers. The life that he lived had little importance; the life that he created in art was a priceless treasure bequeathed to all men.

Zhivago is, then, a final statement by Pasternak on his own life and creation, and it is no wonder that he risked much in order to have it published. The poet insists that creatures like himself who produce nothing of immediate utility do have a use. The originality and strangeness of the poet's view of things may contain the germ of new thought. Yury Zhivago's power of *intuition* is underlined in the novel; he is a "thinker, and a seeker, a man of a creative and artistic frame of mind," but one whose thoughts do not move along direct, logical lines. In order to think thoughts that are his own Zhivago holds himself at a distance from state, community, and family; he finds a refuge from movements and parties, with their purposeful and ephemeral jargon. And perhaps everyone needs a "Siberian retreat," such as Zhivago's *Varykino,* where the poet gives birth to thoughts and images which are themselves pregnant with new birth. But then a problem arises. If you cut yourself off from the social body how will you survive? How can the individual human being, however precious his unrepeatable experiments in the laboratory of thought, survive outside of society? Pasternak's answer is a poet's answer and is rather whimsical. He suggests that there are more things in heaven and earth (Horatio!) than are dreamed of in your philosophy. Magic and miracle are not to be ruled out, and marvelous coincidences may alter history or save a life. In his autobiography *Safe Conduct* Pasternak relates that his own life was saved in Moscow in 1920 when an old Marburg friend miraculously turned up, and, an even greater miracle, as a member of the Party and an official in a commissariat. "Time is permeated with the unity of life's events," he wrote of another such occasion, "that is, with the crisscross movement of the hypnosis of being." Magic and miracle are "the Lord's way" of providing. Zhivago has, not *one* guardian angel, but two, who can provide for him because in some mysterious way they have power with the regime. San Donato (of which Samdeviatov is a corruption) turns up when needed to take care of Zhivago's material needs, and Zhivago's half-brother Yevgraf, who gives him spiritual advice and preserves his testament, was sent to him from above, as the account of his first appearance makes very clear:

> Footsteps sounded above him. Someone was coming down the stairs, stopping frequently, as though hesitating. At one point, he actually changed his mind and ran up again. A door opened some-

where and two voices welled out, so distorted by echoes that it was impossible to tell whether men or women were speaking. Then the door banged, and the same steps ran down, this time resolutely.

Yury Andreievich was absorbed in his paper and had not meant to look up, but the stranger stopped so suddenly at the foot of the stairs that he raised his head.

Before him stood a boy of about eighteen in a reindeer cap and a stiff reindeer coat worn, as in Siberia, fur side out. He was dark and had narrow Kirghiz eyes. His face had an aristocratic quality, the fugitive spark and reticent delicacy that give an impression of remoteness and are sometimes found in people of a complex, mixed parentage.

Thereafter Yevgraf also is at hand when needed, and at the end, at no loss to his saintly character, he has become a major general in the Red Army and a figure of real power. A symbolic meaning in Yevgraf has been seen by most of the commentators on *Zhivago*. Edmund Wilson, for instance, constructs a system of religious symbolism out of the details of his characterization. Whether one accepts or not the religious symbolism suggested by the American critics of *Zhivago*, both Yevgraf and Samdeviatov stand as symbols of a force that maintains and cares for us and toward which every human being should feel gratitude.

In Pasternak's world miracles do take place, and that is the simple explanation of the fact that there are in the novel *Zhivago* many coincidences of low statistical verisimilitude. Pasternak is not concerned with mathematical but with symbolic truth. The miraculous chances on which the plot of *Zhivago* turns symbolize the intertwining of all lives in the common human web; they represent also the role of the unpredictable in human life. Not every chance can be foreseen and worked into a rational plan for "remaking" the world, as the Bolsheviks would have it. Every new individual is an unforeseeable accident. Life, like art, is autonomous and rich in chances

Zhivago's poems, which make up the final chapter of the novel, are the Doctor's real and substantial contribution to life. Some commentators have attempted to show a connection between the poems and specific events and characters of the novel, and ingenious efforts have been made to tie certain poems to particular passages in the novel. Labor such as this remains unrewarded. Pasternak himself provided the key to the poems when he introduced them in 1954: "Zhivago's thoughts are expressed in a set of poems which constitute the final chapter of the novel." Those poems are Zhivago's created vision. The central and persistent thought in them is the renewal of life, symbolized by the passion and burial of Christ and the triumph of resurrection.

The prose of Pasternak is a poet's prose, as Jakobson insists. Rich with metaphor and symbol, it grows out of the normal rhythms of spoken Russian. Pasternak suggests through subtle variations of diction and idiom distinctions of personality, changes of mood, personal idiosyncrasy, geographical differences, class gradations. There is a language typical of Bolsheviks, formal, logical and tending to the "dead letter"; and that language is contrasted with the live rhythms of poetry and of untrammeled thought.

In *Zhivago* Pasternak has given us God's plenty in the form of an infinite variety of "names." Like the first man in the Garden of Eden, he names everything he sees. And the novel *Zhivago* creates an apprehension of love and beauty, and joyful optimism at the prospect of living.

12 Into the Underground

The Literary Parties

One important change in the literary world after the death of Stalin was the tolerance, within certain narrow limits, of disagreement and debate. This was apparent in spite of Surkov's authoritarian pronouncements on socialist realism, or Kochetov's primitive novelistic patriotism,. or Khrushchev's crude demands. When Ehrenburg's *The Thaw* was published in 1954 there were differing opinions as to its merits, public debate took place, and Simonov enunciated the principle that "the author has a right to argue with his critics." The publication of Dudintsev's *Not By Bread Alone* in 1956 was the occasion for violent disagreement. A discussion of the novel was held in a jam-packed auditorium, and, according to reports, those who could not get into the auditorium climbed ladders placed against the walls and listened through the windows.

The existence of more than one "party" and more than one idea in Soviet literature was recognized at the Twentieth Congress of the Communist Party in 1956, when reports from the literary field were delivered to the delegates by Alexey Surkov and Mikhail Sholokhov. Sholokhov not only took issue with Surkov, but covered him with ridicule, to the loud amusement of the delegates, whose "laughter and prolonged applause" is immortalized in the stenographic report. This was the first time since 1930 that two opposing viewpoints in literature had been represented at a Party Congress. At the Sixteenth Congress in that year a report on the state of literature had been presented by a leader of

RAPP, Kirshon; then a poem attacking the slogans of the leadership was read to the delegates by a member of an opposing literary faction, Bezymensky. Revived in 1956, the practice of recognizing and presenting to the delegates two opposing viewpoints in literature was again in evidence at the Twenty-second Congress of the Party in 1961, when contrasting reports were given by Vsevolod Kochetov and Alexander Tvardovsky, a leader of the liberals who had been removed as editor of *New World* in 1954, mainly for publishing Pomerantsev's article "On Sincerity in Literature." It is significant of the political trend that he was restored to the editorship in 1958 and awarded a Lenin Prize in 1961. Tvardovsky's speech at the Congress called for a literature sincerely engaged with the life of real people and free of political tutelage; Kochetov's rejoinder reminded the delegates of the past achievements of socialist realism and demanded a literature permeated with Communist ideas and presenting heroic perspectives.

The debate continued and the parties formed. By the early sixties the two main factions were clearly identified as to personnel and principles. Literary publications tended to belong to one or the other party. At opposite extremes were the very conservative and neo-Stalinist *Neva* and Tvardovsky's liberal *New World*. The magazine *Youth* was generally liberal and published excellent stories by new writers, while *Moscow* and *October* were generally conservative and in their criticism deplored the "bare realism" and "naturalism" of much contemporary writing. Novels and stories dealing with contemporary life sometimes offered evidence that the lines of dispute were well established and factional symbols widely recognized. In a novel called *The Ends of the Earth* (1961), by Ivan Shevtsov, the positive heroes visit the Russian Museum, which is devoted to Russian art, read the magazine *Neva*, and bear simple Russian names. The negative character prefers the Hermitage (the post-impressionists), reads *New World* and *Foreign Literature*, and has a name that is not quite Russian, along with thick brows and a slightly hooked nose. The liberal wing is thus crudely identified with intellectual sophistication and "cosmopolitan" tastes.

The existence of factions explains the apparently vacillating literary policies of the Party since 1954. Probably for the first time since the twenties opposing literary groups were able to make their influence felt, and Khrushchev leaned first toward one, then toward the other.

I had an opportunity, not long after the Twentieth Congress of the Party, to meet leading representatives of both the liberal and conservative parties in literary administration at that time. On successive days interviews were arranged in the Writers' Union with Boris Polevoy and A. A. Surkov. It was evident that Polevoy, the author of *The Story of a*

Real Man, who is usually regarded as a routine socialist realist if not a hack, wished to be regarded as a liberal. Surkov, of course, clearly identified himself with a firm policy of control.

Polevoy was at that time an important member of the Executive Board of the Union of Writers, while Surkov was First Secretary; the allotment of these posts seemed also to reflect a split in outlook and policy within the Party itself.

Polevoy's personality was a surprise. His books prepare one to meet a competent but dull purveyor of heroic personalities and perspectives, but he was quick, clever, and breezy in manner, a combination of Jack London (his favorite writer) and a proletarian Jim Tully. His hair was recalcitrant to the comb; his suit, though of excellent material, was casually worn and somewhat crumpled; he wore no tie, and his shirt— also of fine material—was open at the neck. Very friendly to foreign guests, he produced a bottle of Armenian cognac for their entertainment. Refreshments appeared. He invited "tough questions" and "abuse." He defended his novel *The Story of a Real Man* against the charge that it lacked human verisimilitude. Everything in it, he said, was based on accounts of actual events given him by living people. Images of selfless devotion to work in Soviet novels—the example he used was Krymov's *Tanker Derbent*—he insisted were "realistic," and would not seem exaggerated to anyone who knew the desperate poverty of those days and the need to give oneself completely to labor. The transformation on the tanker *Derbent* of a shiftless gang of individualists into a disciplined crew was not an exaggeration: such things happen to people, he said, when they are under great emotional pressure. Among Soviet satirists Polevoy thought highly of Ilf and Petrov but disparaged Zoshchenko. Challenged on his statement that Zoshchenko "satirized Soviet life from the viewpoint of the philistine" by the argument that it is precisely the Soviet philistine that Zoshchenko satirizes, Polevoy did not pursue the argument, saying that many people, even in the Writers' Union, did not agree with him on Zoshchenko, and "everyone has the right to his own opinion." His remarks and gestures betrayed honest indifference to Zoshchenko, who did not take "an advanced socialist position." "But," said Polevoy, "he's being republished, and people read him." Yury Olesha's allotment of "criticism" was an indifferent shrug. He had never accepted the role of educator; his theme was the lost intellectual in conflict with the new order and his work has little interest for the new generation. But "he's being published, too." Toward those writers whose sophisticated literary style has attracted attention in the West, Boris Polevoy expressed not distrust or contempt but only indifference. He thinks of himself as an educator of the masses. Realism he understands as an effort not only to portray reality but to influence its development. Of literature as a craft or a vocation he apparently has no notion whatever. Yet the views he expressed were, by the standards of the Soviet literary administrator, liberal in the extreme, especially his insistently tolerant statement, "You have your opinion and I have mine."

Alexey Surkov was a very different man. He fitted well his two roles of Party poet and implacable critic. He tended to be strict and correct in speech and manner. Rather short and neatly dressed in a blue-gray business suit properly buttoned, he wore a tie and gold-rimmed spectacles. His greeting was stiffly formal, complete with quick bow and brief, cold handshake, and almost, but not quite, a heel-click. The military attitude intruded itself in his bearing and conversation. There was no cognac for us and no refreshments. He waited for the first question, an easy one about the discussion then going on regarding the "varnishing of reality," then gave his answer in the form of a speech suitable for platform delivery and not to be interrupted. While Polevoy had invited objections, Surkov allowed no time for them. The tendency to "pretty up" reality he explained as a symptom of the youth both of Soviet literature and of the Soviet state. For a young and struggling society *affirmation* is more important than criticism. He thought American literature "in its period of youth" exhibited the same tendencies. Rapidly changing "reality" explained the difficulty Soviet writers found in orienting themselves. The fact that for so many years the Soviet Union had been at "war" explained its need for a positive, affirmative literature. The war against "imperialist intervention" lasted until 1921, the war against the neobourgeois lasted through the twenties, the war against the kulaks began in the early thirties, and these violent campaigns were only a prologue to the great war against Fascism and, though he did not say this, the Cold War against America. The note of military urgency was strong in the content and manner of his talk. His metaphors and illustrative examples were taken in many cases from the military life. "Soviet literature is loud and assertive because in time of war one doesn't urge on the soldiers with Brahms melodies." The difficulty some Soviet writers had in accepting the liquidation of the kulaks arose from the fact that they did not understand "we were at war with them."

Surkov, like Polevoy, was hospitable in his way, but his long and vigorous speech, delivered without interruptions to two Americans in a small room, was somewhat chilling. Even during the great Moscow thaw, with the theme of every slogan "peace and coexistence," one felt the presence of narrowly intransigent ideological forces, for whom that thaw was a temporary and probably unwelcome diversion of their strength. This very same emphasis in literature as a weapon in the struggle is to be found in the novels of V. Kochetov, published in 1958 and 1961.

Both Polevoy and Surkov impressed one as equally loyal to the Party program, but Polevoy seemed to move in circles that have knowledge of the outside world. Surkov, and those like him, can preserve the purity of their faith only by isolating themselves in their own world.

The Trouble with *Gosizdat:* End of a Thaw

The literary situation during the early sixties was shifting and precarious. The contest between liberals and conservatives continued, with sharp and unpredictable variations in the policy of the Party toward the two groups, and many serious casualties on the liberal side. Yet many still had the courage and the optimism to take action against censorship and control. Early in the decade Nikita Khrushchev, then Chairman of the Council of Ministers of the USSR, visited an exhibition in Moscow featuring contemporary artists, a few of whom offered nonrepresentational canvases. The visit was a planned move against "decadent" tendencies in Soviet art, and Khrushchev was accompanied by several members of the government, including Comrade L. Ilychev, the head of the Party commission on ideology. Khrushchev's remarks at the exhibition (reported in *Encounter*, April 1963) revealed his aggressive cruelty and his lack of information or taste, but they also signaled a broad campaign against liberal tendencies in all the arts. Here are some samples of his commentary:

On jazz: "When I hear it, it's like gas on the stomach."

On Nikonov's painting "The Geologists": "Are we going to take these blotches into communism with us?"

A question to the painter Zheltovsky: "Are you a pederast or a normal man?"

On the modernists in general: "Judging by these experiments, I am entitled to think that you are all pederasts, and for that you can get ten years."

Soon after Khrushchev's excursion into art criticism there were a number of meetings between Party leaders and literary men, the central purpose of which was to mount a propaganda campaign against modern art in all its manifestations. Ilya Ehrenburg was a special target of criticism, since his reminiscences, *People, Years, Life,* published serially in *New World* during the sixties, was a conscious attempt to revive the ties with modern European art that had once been a normal part of the Russian cultural tradition. Rambling, garrulous, and chronologically irregular, his reminiscences are at times fascinating, often dull, and usually a bit obvious in their commentary on people and events. But they were, nevertheless, a revelation to young Soviet intellectuals, for whom the recent past had become a terra incognita. Ehrenburg's work is a casually organized directory of modern art during the early part of the century; it rehabilitated Russian artists who were part of the modernist movement; it provided a plethora of names, both Russian and foreign: Burlyuk, Baltrushaitis, Tsvetaeva, Léger, Malevich, Meyerhold, Mandelshtam, Tatlin, Rodchenko, Apollinaire, Roman Jakobson, Braque, and scores of others. As such, it offered a prime target for the conservatives in the campaign of 1963.

A dependable wielder of the official hatchet, the critic V. Yermilov, was chosen to demolish Ehrenburg with the charge that his favorable presentation of cubism and surrealism tended to subvert the basic principles of Soviet art. Yermilov's article (*Izvestia*, January 30, 1963) was vicious and destructive, but his intended victim wrote a courageous reply, which was published in the same newspaper. The fact that Ehrenburg never recanted is evidence that the movement he represented had wide support, and perhaps even a measure of political power.

A series of meetings organized by Party leaders and the Executive Board of the Union of Writers during 1963 did, however, lead to recantations, or at least to expressions of loyalty to the Party's leadership, by a number of writers and artists. The sculptor Ernest Neizvestny, the composer Dmitri Shostakovich, the poets Robert Rozhdestvensky, Yevgeny Yevtushenko, and Andrey Voznesensky, among others, published statements to the general effect that they had learned useful lessons during the discussion inaugurated by Khrushchev, and that they recognized the educative role of the artist.

A harrowing statement of how that recantation process actually worked is contained in Anatoly Gladilin's *The Making and Unmaking of a Soviet Writer* (1979). Gladilin was one of a group of young writers who had surfaced in the early sixties and seemed to offer the promise of a new vitality and variety in Soviet literature. Writing in exile, he described the brutal tactics adopted by party officials in dealing with young and unconventional writers. At "Meetings with the Creative Intelligentsia" in 1963 some of those writers were subjected to vile and barbarous threats, and warned by Khrushchev: "Work with us and we'll help you. Work against us and we'll cut you to pieces." Gladilin, whose prose was a distinguished contribution to the literary movement of the sixties, records the disgust and gloom that he and his young comrades felt at that moment.

The one event of the sixties that reveals most about the condition of

Soviet literature was the Fourth Congress of Writers, which took place in Moscow during the last week of May 1967 as one of many functions celebrating the fiftieth anniversary of the Soviet state. That Congress was drastically different from earlier ones in the quality and interest of the reports presented at it. Although it is true that all four Congresses were marked by outward unanimity encouraged by the strong hand of Party control, the record of the First Congress, in 1934, offers stimulating and sometimes controversial statements by Bukharin, Babel, Olesha, and Pasternak; at the Second, in 1954, literary problems were to some degree discussed, and there was debate over the merits of certain works; the Third, in 1959, featured the ramblingly ignorant and overbearing speech by Nikita Khrushchev in which he discussed recent troubles in the literary world and restored to grace certain writers who had "repented" of errors. But the Fourth Congress differs from the earlier ones in that there was, as far as one can judge from the printed record, a dead calm at all of the sessions. There was no debate; there was no discussion of problems and difficulties; there was no serious discussion of literature, though long speeches were devoted to the ritual recitation of approved titles and names, accompanied by impassioned exhortations to produce a socialist literature for the people. Georgy Markov, Secretary of the Union, made a report on Soviet prose in which he mentioned about forty names. He brushed lightly on vexed questions. He mentioned Vasily Bykov's much discussed novel, *The Dead Feel No Pain,* but his remarks were only gently disapproving and were calculated to assuage the polemical bite of that powerful story. He seemed determined not to raise any embarrassing issues. In a similar spirit the critic Leonid Novichenko, who reported on the development of criticism, softly chided the liberal journal *New World* for "mistrust of the heroic and lofty, and attempts to justify theoretically a dismal and prejudiced carping." But in the very next breath he partially removed the sting from this by the comment that the archconservative journal, *October,* was also guilty of something—oversimplification.

The keynote speech was made by the novelist Konstantin Fedin. He touched ever so slightly on the disputes that rage beneath the surface of Soviet literary life. His speech, if one reads it with careful attention to its interlinear content, reveals that there were two distinct currents in Soviet Russian literature: (1) official socialist realist literature, and (2) a literature not yet clearly defined, partly underground, and struggling for a free development of literary styles and genres. The speech also reveals that the traditional concept of the realistic novel was being subjected to critical analysis. But though he distantly alluded to such problems, Fedin did not discuss them; his speech struck an untroubled major chord of pride in the "positive achievements," the "successes," of fifty years. It was a speech given in a jubilee mood.

All of the other statements but one followed more or less the pattern set by Fedin. The one exception was the speech of Mikhail Sholokhov, who had recently been awarded the Nobel Prize for literature. Sholokhov's speeches at such gatherings were as a rule offbeat and somewhat indiscreet, even though they usually supported the most backward tendencies and ideas. At the Party Congress in 1966 he branded as traitors Andrey Sinyavsky and Yuly Daniel, who had just been sentenced to long terms at hard labor for publishing their works abroad under the pseudonyms Tertz and Arzhak, respectively. At the Writers' Congress Sholokhov broke through the bland façade arranged by the organizers and talked about certain portents of sedition. A careful reading of his crudely but cryptically worded speech reveals that three unpleasant recent developments were troubling Sholokhov. He was disturbed in the first place by the fact that a number of writers were not taking part in the Congress. One of these was Ilya Ehrenburg, and with heavy sarcasm Sholokhov deplored the absence of that former stalwart comrade: "I don't know how the other Congress delegates feel, but I for one am greatly distressed by the absence of my dear old friend, Ilya Grigorievich Ehrenburg. I look around and look around and I feel something is missing; I feel a certain malaise, a gnawing at my insides, and sadness settles down like a black cloud on my otherwise cloudless mood. Where is Ehrenburg? It turns out that on the eve of the Congress he departed for Italian shores. Somehow this was not a nice thing for my friend to do."

The record shows that there was laughter in the hall. Sholokhov singled out Ehrenburg, but his remarks no doubt reflected concern at a much more serious defection from the Congress. According to a report in *Pravda* (May 26, 1967) 525 delegates had been elected to the Fourth Congress, and 473 were present. This can only mean that for one reason or another 52 elected delegates found it inconvenient to attend. Ten percent seems a rather high rate of absence from such an important affair, and we may be sure that Sholokhov was exercised at the absence of many others, whom he chose not to name. It does seem that the self-congratulatory ritual of the Congress was boycotted by a substantial number of writers.

The second matter troubling Sholokhov was the disaffection of an undetermined number of young writers, and this he laid at Ehrenburg's door. "Bad example," he said, "is infectious." He spoke very sternly to the young writers: "They have on their consciences a certain defiance, a rejection of generally accepted norms of behavior, and *some other things*" (italics mine). One notes the menace in the final phrase, "some other things." One can only speculate as to exactly what kinds of behavior Sholokhov had in mind: perhaps the public protest at the conviction and sentence of Sinyavsky and Daniel. Perhaps he was also concerned at a kind of boycott of official Soviet literature by the young writers. At any rate he cited some interesting statistics in his speech which, he said, "make one pause and think." In 1934 at the First Writers' Congress 71 percent of the delegates were under forty; at the Second, only 20.6 percent; at the Third, 13.9 percent; and now at the 1967 Congress only 12.2 percent of the total were under forty. Commented Sholokhov: "The average age of the delegates to this Congress is almost sixty, and that makes a rather sad impression." Sholokhov's remarks amounted to a tacit admission that official Soviet literature in its organized form—the Writers' Union, publishing houses, journals—had been losing the support of the younger writers. It is clear, therefore, that the voice of this Congress was not at all a boyish falsetto or a young man's confident tenor but a complacent middle-aged bass-baritone—complacent, but not really confident.

Still a third matter troubled Sholokhov: the demand of some Soviet writers—he does not name them—for "freedom of the press." Here too it is necessary to decipher his remarks a bit. He said: "Recently quite a few voices have been raised in the West in favor of 'freedom' of creation for us Soviet writers. These are uninvited cheerleaders, who include the CIA . . . some United States senators, rabid White Guards, the defector Alliluyeva, and the notorious Kerensky, who has long been a political corpse. It is in this bizarre company that our zealots of freedom of the press find themselves."

This was the most reprehensible passage in Sholokhov's speech, and it is not too difficult to guess the object of his attack. These remarks are his answer to a letter circulated at the Congress by Alexander Solzhenitsyn, author of *One Day in the Life of Ivan Denisovich*. In this letter, addressed to the Presidium of the Congress and all Soviet writers—a letter that had not been officially acknowledged—Solzhenitsyn demanded a measure of "freedom of the press" and an end of that "oppression, no longer tolerable, that our literature has been enduring from censorship for decades" and that the Union of Writers "should not accept any longer."

The third cloud on Sholokhov's mood, then, was Solzhenitsyn's eloquent letter, with its defense of freedom for all writers and its evidence that repression, injustice, and official slander of dissident writers were still the rule rather than the exception in the Soviet Union. The obtuse state of Sholokhov's ethical sense and the spurious character of his remarks at the Congress become evident when we realize that he implicated Solzhenitsyn, and all others who complain of the Soviet censorship, with CIA plots, White Guardist bandits, and even the old man Kerensky. They were all, in Sholokhov's mind, enemies or traitors to their country. Nevertheless, Sholokhov's speech did the service of giving the delegates a look behind the scenes and helped them and us to see some of the things that the bland surface of the Congress was intended to conceal.

There is clear evidence that the bureaucratic structure of Soviet literature as it was developed by Stalinist administrators during the 1930s was in real danger of collapse, and could be shored up only by police action. The trial and sentence of Sinyavsky and Daniel aroused angry indignation and even led to public protest on the part of eminent Soviet writers—not all of them young. The most interesting of several such protests was a letter addressed to the presidium of the Twenty-third Congress of the Communist Party and signed by sixty-two writers. This letter, like Solzhenitsyn's later one, complained of the narrow limits within which literary men were allowed to work, and asserted that the trial of Sinyavsky and Daniel had already caused more damage than all of their mistakes. Among the writers who signed this letter were Korney Chukovsky, Ilya Ehrenburg, Victor Shklovsky, and Venyamin Kaverin, all of them old and established, and three of them over seventy. Sholokhov's imputation of rebellious defiance to youth and inexperience was a deliberate misrepresentation: the disaffected group included both old and young writers. The older writers were joined in signing this statement by some of the most talented younger ones: the poets Bella Akhmadulina and Bulat Okudzhava; the promising prose writer Vladimir Voinovich; a scholar whose reputation is substantial, A. A. Anikst; the gifted playwright L. G. Zorin; and many others. It should be difficult, even in the Soviet Union, to turn aside such a document with the slander that it is the work of CIA agents and traitors.

A number of actions undertaken during and immediately after the Writers' Congress of 1967 provide evidence that some writers were ready to take resolute steps in order to end their automatic subservience to the Party and the state. The immediate and harsh reaction of the Writers' Union and the Security Agency (KGB) in almost every case revealed the Party's concern over any erosion of its authority and its determination to punish those who question its policies. Among those who defended Solzhenitsyn was the poet Andrey Voznesensky, who proposed that all of Solzhenitsyn's work be published in a new edition. As a result of his action Voznesensky's long-planned visit to New York for a poetry reading in June 1967 was abruptly canceled by the Union on the ground that the poet was "ill." He answered with a letter of protest to the Executive Board of the Writers' Union in which he said, among other things, "I am ashamed to be a member of the same Union as these people." This letter was never published in the USSR, but it reached the West, like so many other documents of this period, by uncharted underground channels.

One of the organizers of the public protest against the trial of Sinyavsky and Daniel was the young writer Alexander Ginzburg, who compiled a "White Book" consisting of the trial proceedings and a collection of statements, signed by many outstanding people, protesting the verdict. The "White Book," too, found its way to the West, and was published and widely read. Ginzburg, along with his friend Yury Galanskov and two others, was himself brought to trial in January 1968 and sentenced to five years in prison. Equally brutal and uncompromising was the treatment of Vladimir Bukovsky, who had been arrested for the specific offense of organizing a street demonstration in September 1965 to demand a fair trial for Sinyavsky and Daniel. His heroic speech to the court in defense of freedom of speech and of the press as rights guaranteed to Soviet citizens, recorded and sent abroad by Pavel Litvinov, the grandson of Maxim Litvinov, the former Soviet foreign minister and ambassador to Washington, was published in the *New York Times* on December 27, 1967. "What the prosecutor would like to hear from me he won't hear," said Bukovsky to the court. "There is no criminal act in our case. I absolutely do not repent for having organized this demonstration. I find that it accomplished what it had to accomplish, and when I am free again I shall again organize demonstrations, of course with complete observance of the law, as before." Soon after these events both Litvinov and Bukovsky were expelled from the Soviet Union. The latter has published an extraordinary account of his life as a dissident, convict, and mental patient: *And the Breeze Returns* (1979).

Other statements complaining about the travesty of justice in the trials of the writers were directed to Soviet organizations, to the Supreme Court of the USSR, and to Communist publications in the West. The most startling of these was a letter sent to the Presidium of the conference of Communist Parties held in Budapest in 1968, signed by twelve Soviet citizens, among them Pavel Litvinov, Larisa Daniel, the wife of Yuly Daniel, and Piotr Yakir, son of a Red Army general executed in the 1937 purge of the Army. This letter called attention to "the danger which results from the complete disregard of human rights in our country," and it revealed the harsh administrative measures that had been taken against many of those who had signed letters of protest:

"Those who were most active in their protests received replies in the form of notices terminating their employment, summonses to the KGB with the threat of arrest, and, finally, the most shocking form of punishment, compulsory confinement in a mental asylum."

The events of the middle sixties, fully described and well documented as a result of the boldness and civic sense of many Soviet citizens, clearly reveal that a cruel struggle takes place beneath the official surface of Soviet literature, a struggle whose outcome it is difficult to predict. Once this is realized, it becomes perfectly clear why the leaders of the Union of Writers, in the jubilee year, organized their Congress in such a way that there could be no public discussion of the issues that agitate Soviet intellectuals in private. Yet the façade they arranged concealed nothing. Solzhenitsyn's letter and Sholokhov's indiscreet remarks ruined some well-laid plans.

Buried Treasure: Platonov and Bulgakov

Solzhenitsyn's letter to the membership of the Union provided in a lengthy register the names of writers whom official Soviet literature had persecuted or neglected over the years, and whose works had either been forgotten or never published. Among those he mentioned were Mikhail Bulgakov, Isaac Babel, Boris Pilnyak, Andrey Platonov, Osip Mandelshtam, and Anna Akhmatova.

An "underground" activity, if I may bend the metaphor somewhat, is the officially sanctioned excavation through the archives of departed writers in the search for unpublished manuscripts of value. Encouragement for such enterprises was provided during the 1960s, when selections from the correspondence of Maxim Gorky with Soviet writers was published (in *Literary Heritage* and the *Archive of Maxim Gorky*). The letters revealed that Gorky had great admiration for unorthodox writers such as Platonov, Bulgakov, Pasternak, and Babel, while expressing cool reserve toward some who followed more closely the precepts of the Party. Since Gorky's authority is not questioned, there is no doubt that his favorable opinion of certain writers had much to do with the decision to republish their works.

If the Soviet Union were an open, democratic society, the works of Andrey Platonov (1889–1951) would have been found in this survey in their chronological place in the literature of the twenties and early thirties, the period when Platonov wrote and published many things. But he was an eccentric writer and both his style and his substance disturbed wary readers and outraged literary authorities in the late twenties. He was apparently never jailed or exiled, but he lived under a cloud of disapproval and was frequently under attack; much of his writing remained unpublished during his lifetime. In the middle sixties he was rediscovered, and collections of his prose were published in 1965, 1966, and again in 1977, thus introducing him to a generation that hardly knew him. But some of his most impressive writing, the novels *Kotlovan* and *Chevengur* for instance, remained unpublished in the Soviet Union, though they circulated widely in *samizdat*. The Russian text of the former was first published in the West in 1969, and the second has had a complicated publishing history. As Anthony Olcott puts it: "*Chevengur*, the book published in 1972 in Paris, is actually only part of a longer work bearing the same title, of which *Origin of a Master* [published in the Soviet Union] is the first part." Moreover, some parts of *Chevengur*, which was probably written in 1927–1928, were published at various times in the Soviet Union as separate stories. The complete novel was finally published abroad, in English translation, only in 1978.

The trouble with Platonov was that he provided honest, desolating, and at the same time stunningly beautiful pictures of peasant life. The weird action of his stories and novels, their imagery, and his style itself, all have the effect of cutting through the harsh encrustations of a sloganized language whose function was to screen Soviet reality. The story which aroused the ire of Stalin himself, "For Future Use" (1931), deals with the breakdown of production and the impoverishment of the land during collectivization. In the novel *Chevengur*, the poor peasants drive out the propertied people, then stop working and wait for communism to come. And why shouldn't it. They've "driven out the kulaks" and now have a "classless society." But nothing happens; things get worse; "the future" never comes. In Platonov's world the letter, the written formula or directive, receives absolute authority and takes precedence over observable fact. For instance, in the story "Gradov City" (1976), a biting satire of the Soviet bureaucracy, a traveler arriving in that miserable dry hole does not know he is there until he has asked a native, who will simply point to a two-story building labelled "Province Executive Committee"; this has to be a city.

The novel *Kotlovan* treats, in symbolic images mixed with folklore, the party programs for collectivization and industrialization, which were in full swing at the time it was written. The industrial foundation of the future is a vast hole in the ground dug for the colossal edifice of communism. Only the hole exists, however, and nothing in the environs suggests that a building will ever rise above it. But there is much energetic work, many orders and directives from above. Great action is carried on under the aegis of the Plan, ostensibly for the sake of the little orphan girl Nastya, who will inherit the communist future. The bone-breaking labor of the working class, the hunger, and the suffering are for the sake of the next generation, but little Nastya, its representative, is thin and sad and she lives in a coffin. She dies sadly in her coffin, but not before her native language had been debased into the lowest form of propaganda argot. The one who had taken over responsibility for her education is a repulsive cripple named Zhachev, who was mutilated in the war and is full of spite and hatred; everybody fears him because he is an informer. That deformed moral monstrosity had assumed a kind of father role with regard to Nastya—and other young girls.

Industrialization and the education of the young "in Communist ideals" are painted in dark and ominous enough colors, but Platonov's picture of collectivization is gloom unrelieved by any mitigating light. The peasants value their coffins more than anything else, and when the coffins are dug out of their hiding place by the excavators, the peasants demand that they be returned: "Give us back our coffins . . . We are lacking dead inventory. The people are waiting for their property. We got those coffins through self-taxation. Don't take away from us what we have earned."

The peasants, rather than surrender their animals to the *kolkhoz* (collective), slaughter them, and there were so many that the flies lived on through the winter. To get rid of the "kulaks" the Party activist simply loads them on barges and ships them down the river. A recurrent feature of Platonov's style, which adequately represents in language the human situation itself, is what I have called the "violent *non sequitur*":

> "Unexpectedly!" declared Chiklin and he struck the yellow-eyed peasant a blow in the face *to make him begin to live politically aware*. The peasant would have fallen but he was afraid to deviate too far lest Chiklin think him to be a prosperous peasant, so he moved up even closer to Chiklin, desiring to be the more seriously maimed and subsequently to petition for himself by means of his torment the rights of the life of a poor peasant; Chiklin, *because he saw before him such a creature*, mechanically hit him in the stomach, and the peasant fell down, shutting his yellow eyes [Italics mine.]

Platonov's language is no doubt his most original creation. In *Kotlovan* the story is told by a narrator whose speech has been infected by the Soviet ambience, and whose use of it serves both to estrange and expose a tortured and degraded idiom. It is a deliberately roughened style, one that calls attention to itself. Normal word choice and smooth word order are abandoned for the sake of strange lexical items and a ruptured syntactic pattern. Platonov's style favors jargon, bureaucratese, Soviet clichés. It embodies and satirizes a style of speech and of writing that obscures, rather than reveals, the truth. Iosif Brodsky has beautifully characterized that style: "Platonov speaks of a nation which in a sense has become a victim of its own language; or, more precisely, he speaks of this language itself—which turns out to be capable of generating a fictive world and then falling into grammatical dependence on it."

Platonov is devilishly hard to translate, but the following should give some impression of the language in question:

> The womb-excavation for the apartment house of the future life was ready; and now foundation stone was to be laid in the foundation pit. But Pashkin kept constantly thinking bright thoughts, and he reported to the main person in the city that the scale of the house was too narrow, for socialist women would be replete with freshness and full-bloodedness, and the whole surface of the soil would be covered over with the sown seeds of childhood; would the children then really have to live out in the open air, in the midst of the unorganized weather?

The most startling rediscovery of the period was the prose fiction of Mikhail Bulgakov, who has already been mentioned as the author of satiric fantasies and as a playwright. Two of his novels, which had lain unpublished for almost thirty years, appeared in 1965 and 1966 and were immediately acknowledged as the work of a superb literary craftsman. A third novel was published for the first time in an English translation in 1968. The first of these, entitled *A Theatrical Novel,* was published in *New World* (no. 8, 1965) and has been translated under the title *Black Snow* (1968). Written during the thirties, it was based on Bulgakov's experiences as a playwright and a member of the famous Moscow Art Theater, then presided over by Stanislavsky, the renowned originator of "the method." The novel succeeds in bringing the sacred institution and its director firmly to the ground. Its central character is Maksudov, a promising Moscow writer who has fallen in love with the theater and who pursues his mistress with constancy in spite of suffering and disenchantment. Maksudov is an autobiographical figure, and many of the incidents reflect Bulgakov's own experiences with the Soviet theater. The novel is important and interesting, not only as a deft deflation of a revered theater and its sainted leader, but also as an intimate account of a playwright's creative processes. Bulgakov conveys his enthusiasm for the theater and for the complex art of writing and producing plays.

The appearance of the second novel was an event of prime importance in Russian literature. *The Master and Margarita* has had curious misadventures in the history of its publication both in Russia and abroad. Published first in the literary journal *Moscow* (no. 11, 1966, and no. 1, 1967), it immediately caught the attention of literary critics as a magnificent accomplishment, especially since Bulgakov wrote it during the Stalinist thirties, when he was suffering from chronic rejection as a writer alien to the Soviet mode as well as from uremia and partial blindness.

The story is a fantastic tale featuring the devil and his retinue, Christ and Pontius Pilate, numerous characters from the literary and theatrical world of Moscow, the "Master," and the woman who loves him, Margarita. Its satire of contemporary life is aimed chiefly at the pharisaic mediocrities who dominate the Soviet literary world and whose official function it is to discourage literary talent. Like *A Theatrical Novel, The Master and Margarita* is concerned with the creative process itself. The Master has conceived and written a novel about Christ and Pilate, the creation of which gave him great joy, but he is driven to distraction when bigoted officials attack him for "dragging in the Christ theme." In a fit of desperation he destroys the manuscript, then has himself committed to a mental asylum.

This story about the strange destiny of a book contains a series of complex and bewildering involvements with the devil himself under the medieval name "Woland" and a number of his traditional minor demons—Behemoth, Azazello, and others. The devil plays infernal tricks on bureaucrats, time servers, and literary hacks, and he throws Moscow into a state of hysteria, but he figures paradoxically as a source of good. His magical tricks at the Variety Theater expose the petty avarice of the citizenry, especially their attachment to such bourgeois matters as fine clothes of foreign manufacture and to money. He interferes with base projects, he frees the Master from confinement, he reconciles Pilate with Christ, and, most important, he is the messenger who first tells us of Christ and who reconstitutes the manuscript of the Master's novel. *The Master and Margarita* is a kind of philosophical meditation on the nature of good and evil, and Bulgakov gives as its epigraph a quotation from Goethe's *Faust*: "Say at last—who art thou?" "That Power I serve which wills forever evil yet does forever good."

The story of Pontius Pilate and Jesus Christ we learn from the devil, from a madman's dream, and from a mad artist's manuscript. The rampant fantasy of the scenes in Moscow is skillfully counterpointed by the story of Jesus (Yeshua Ha-Notsri) and Pilate, which is given directly in human and natural terms. The details of Yeshua's character are both strange and appealing. He has a fanatical idea that "all people are good"; he sympathizes with those who torture him; he offers Pilate good advice; and his physical suffering in the process of crucifixion is frighteningly realistic. Bulgakov has given us an adaptation of the gospel story which renders the figure of Christ tragically human and utterly lonely. The cross on which he hangs is cordoned off by a detachment of Roman soldiers, and no one can approach it. Except for one half-mad disciple who loves him but garbles and misunderstands his message, he has no followers. The great sin is that of Pilate, who allows an innocent man, a good and generous if somewhat strange character, to be executed because Pilate can allow nothing to threaten the advancement of his own career. His sin is cowardice.

The Master and Margarita has often been acclaimed as one of the great novels of the twentieth century. Judged in the context of Soviet literature, it is certainly a magnificent tour de force and a demonstration of what that literature may still accomplish.

Bulgakov's third rediscovered novel, *The Heart of a Dog*, written in 1925, develops a satiric theme in a science-fantasy setting. A Soviet specialist in the transplantation of organs selects for his experiments a mongrel dog from the Moscow gutter. He successfully transplants in the dog the testicles and pituitary gland of a human being, with the result that the animal rapidly takes on the semblance of human form and acquires something like human speech. But he remains a dirty, slothful, mean, and lascivious animal. His speech is an amalgam of curses, abuse, and slander; he reads approved Marxist works and mouths slogans; he learns of his "rights" and demands a share of his master's goods; he acquires some skill at writing denunciations to the Secret Police; he becomes an employee of the state. Like George Orwell's *Animal Farm*, the novel provides a satiric picture of vileness and stupidity grasping for power. The setting and the idiom of this particular story happen to be Soviet, but its satiric reach is broader than that. Indeed, the bitter point of the novel is that a dog's heart is "human, all too human."

The Exodus into *Samizdat* and *Tamizdat*: Sinyavsky

The result of renewed and even more brutal repression was the withdrawal into *samizdat*—self-publishing—and thence into *tamizdat*—publishing abroad—of some of the best contemporary Russian writers. Another potent factor in this exodus was the Soviet invasion of Czechoslovakia in 1968. When the Soviet regime liquidated the "Prague Spring" and killed the hope it offered for democratic socialism in Eastern Europe, that regime undermined any remaining sympathy for itself in a large sector of the Soviet educated class. Hope for gradual improvement at home disappeared, and dissident writers turned more and more to writing for clandestine circulation, or for publication abroad.

Samizdat was not the invention of contemporary Russian dissidents, but a time-honored tradition of Russian and Soviet literature. The first Soviet *samizdat* author was Eugene Zamyatin, whose novel *We*, written in 1920 but never published in the Soviet Union, was widely distributed and read before being published first in English translation in New York, in 1924. Similarly Pasternak's *Doctor Zhivago*, along with some of his poetry and other things, was widely known in the Soviet Union before being sent abroad for publication. As a matter of fact this honorable tradition goes far back to the very beginnings of Russian literature in the early eighteenth century. The poet Antioch Kantemir (1708-1744) composed a number of satires aimed at ignorance, superstition, and vice among the Russian nobility. The satires circulated for many years in manucript but were first published only in 1749, in London, in a French translation; the first Russian edition appeared in 1762, long after the poet's death. One of the most important documents in Russian cultural and intellectual history was *A Journey from St. Petersburg to Moscow* (1790), but its author, Radishchev, was obliged to print it himself on a press he installed in his home, and when the 600 copies of the first edition appeared Radischev was arrested and sent into exile. The Empress Catherine ordered all copies of the book confiscated and destroyed, but some few escaped and circulated widely, as did copies in manuscript form. Griboyedov's famous play *Woe from Wit* (1825) was widely read in manuscript long before it could be published, as were Pushkin's epigrammatic sallies at the expense .of the Czar and Czarist officials. The critic Belinsky's eloquent and inflammatory attack on the serf system and the landowning class, his *Letter to Gogol*, was known to every literate Russian soon after it was composed in 1847, and the novelist Turgenev described it as an "article of faith" for him. But it was not published until twenty years after Belinsky wrote it.

Samizdat is a characteristically Russian phenomenon—well established, traditional, and so much a matter of history and habit that the Soviet authorities found it extremely hard to control. But they tried. Visitors to the Soviet Union have often been struck by a purely Soviet phenomenon, the meticulous search of baggage at points of entry by customs officers, but not for smuggled jewelry or narcotics. Andrey Sinyavsky comments on this grotesque official performance, calling attention to the abundant literary activity that made it necessary:

> The new upsurge in Russian literature can best be researched at customs inspection points. What are they looking for most of all? Manuscripts. Not gold, not diamonds, not even blueprints for Soviet factories, but—manuscripts! And what are they mostly look-

ing for when you enter the Soviet Union? Books. Books in Russian. What that means is that Russian literature, travelling in and out, has value. They have to set up an earth barrier, a dam, even a huge hydroelectric dam to keep manuscripts and books from getting through.[1]

And Sinyavsky in the same essay comments on "literary life" in the Soviet Union:

> The Russian writer who refused to write under official directive moved into a position fraught with risk and the fantastic: he became an underground writer, in other words he embarked on a career regarded as criminal by the government, and against which it provides the most severe measures of prevention and punishment. Literature became a forbidden area and dangerous, and by that token all the more fascinating.

For many writers literary life in the Soviet Union became a double-edged game, an adventure which might itself, as Sinyavsky put it, "be the subject of an intriguing novel." Indeed his own life story provides ample material for such a novel, and some of his "fantastic stories" are, as we shall see, subtle allegories of his own life.

The ever flowing stream of *émigré* manuscripts contained prose items of high literary quality and some of the best poetry being produced in the USSR. The first stories of a writer who called himself Abram Tertz came to light in 1959, and it was not revealed until 1965, when he was arrested and put on trial, that "Tertz" was Andrey Sinyavsky, a literary scholar and critic of distinction. Under his own name he had published in the Soviet Union a number of critical articles, the best of which is his sensitive and sophisticated introduction to the poetry of Boris Pasternak. His short novel *The Court Is in Session* (*Sud idet*, usually translated as *The Trial Begins*), was first published in a French translation in the journal *Esprit*, then in an English translation by Max Hayward in *Encounter* (January 1961). This story had been preceded by an ironic essay "On Socialist Realism," which provided a devastating argument against the term, the concept, and the practice of socialist realism. There followed six *Fantastic Stories*, the short novel *Lyubimov*, translated as *The Makepeace Experiment* (1965), and the volume of aphorisms *Random Thoughts* (*Mysli vrasplokh*, 1966). After a scandalous procedure—misnamed a trial—Sinyavsky was sentenced in 1966, together with Yuly Daniel, another writer of the underground, to a term in a labor camp. He was released in 1971, and in 1973 left Moscow for Paris, where he lectured on Russian literature at the Sorbonne. After his departure from Russia he published in London a volume consisting of excerpts from letters to his wife from prison, *A Voice from the Chorus* (1973) and two fascinating and original explorations of Russian literary figures: *In the Shadow of Gogol* (1975) and *Strolling with Pushkin* (*Progulki s Pushkinym*, 1976). His magnificent short story "Tiny Tsores" (*Kroshka Tsores*) was published in 1980. Sinyavsky is one of the great figures in contemporary Russian literature.

Sinyavsky had a sophisticated knowledge of literature, and he had a program for Russian Soviet literature which, in his isolated Soviet underground, he had worked out both in theory and in practice. The theory is more or less clearly stated in the essay "On Socialist Realism," and the stories serve as its practical demonstration. Sinyavsky maintained that Soviet literature has been dominated since the thirties by the great "Purpose" of building the socialist future, and that its "positive heroes" are ideal types intended to show the way to that future. But he points out that under socialist realism a certain hypocrisy also entered literature, in the pretense that these ideal types were true and typical representatives of the "Soviet Man." There was no escape from the lie; socialist realism was never realistic nor did it frankly or honestly romanticize the socialist hero. He sees a possible way out only in the abandonment both of the Purpose and of realism, and in the development of a "phantasmagoric art, with hypotheses instead of a Purpose, an art in which the grotesque will replace descriptions of ordinary life. Such an art would correspond best to the spirit of our time." He would seek truth in a new dimension "with the aid of the absurd and the fantastic." Literary art, he seems to say, must seek truth through distorting the given reality and inventing its own.

The stories illustrate his own program. They contain grotesque caricatures of Soviet police operatives, naturalistic scenes of Soviet upper-class debauchery flavored with the weird or the fantastic, dream sequences of brilliant power, frequent and frank treatment of sexual activity, usually with overtones of impotence or perversity, and, in the story "You and I," an exploration of both paranoid delusion and confused sexual identity. The stories contain many pages of superb writing, and they do succeed in evoking the political and cultural reality of the Soviet Union without resort to realistic treatment of character or situation.

The short novel *The Court Is in Session* offers an array of characters who can only be called typically Soviet and reduces them all to frustration, defeat, and literal impotence. The fatal cultural flaw they all share is that they think only of goals and purposes and are indifferent to the means they use. Sinyavsky's point is fairly clear: as with the practitioners of socialist realism, their vile and immoral means vitiate the noble

Purpose and in fact themselves become the final reality. The prosecutor Globov thinks only of the bright future of communism, and for the sake of that future he is willing, in a reversal of Jefferson's famous dictum, "to see dozens and even hundreds of innocent men suffer, rather than let a single enemy escape." The brilliant future keeps receding, like the horizon a weary traveler struggles toward, and Globov, a relatively honest Soviet prosecutor, is left only with his innocent victims and the system that victimized them. Globov's young son, Seryozha, is an idealistic boy who asks his father embarrassing questions about Soviet history and philosophy, and himself forms a secret society to struggle for a genuine Marxism and communism "with a human face," so to speak. He concludes that a world revolution is necessary, after which there will be justice, and everyone will treat everyone else decently. And anyone who doesn't will be shot. Clearly little Seryozha too has the infection, as has his trusted girl friend Katya, who turns him in, in the name of "our future" and to save Seryozha from himself. Karlinsky, a cynical lawyer, believes in nothing but himself and can't sleep for thinking of the death that will surely put an end to him. As a cure for his insomnia he decides he must have intercourse with Marina, the most beautiful woman he has ever seen, the prosecutor's wife. When at last after a successful campaign of flattery and maneuver he lures his beauty into bed, Karlinsky is totally impotent. "He gritted his teeth and made an effort. It was like lifting hundred-pound weights. Finally he remembered a packet of pornographic postcards he had hidden away and turning over the most obscene of them in his mind he prayed to God: 'Lord! Help me!' " He had used Marina as a means and not as an end in herself and richly deserved his misery and frustration. Sinyavsky's fiction provides little direct evidence of the religious faith we know he has, but Karlinsky's prayer rising out of the depths is the author's ironic comment on the failure of atheism in the clutches.

The novel *Lyubimov* has puzzled most commentators, and some have in desperation tried to find in it a literal allegory of Soviet history, with one character representing Marx, another Lenin, a third Stalin, and so on. Great ingenuity would be required to defend such a reading and some others that have been suggested. It is true that the fantastic events depicted offer ironic commentary on the Russian character, the behavior of Russian rulers, the materialist philosophy of the Soviet state, and, at the very end but without a trace of irony, on Russia's religious alternative to her present misery; in style and structure, however, the novel departs from consequent development of idea or plot, and no neat statement can be made concerning either. The action takes place in a provincial Russian town named Lyubimov (the *lyu-* root suggests brotherly love), where a bicycle mechanic named Tikhomirov (the roots from which his name is constructed suggest a serene and peaceful world, hence the use of the word "makepeace" in the title of the translation) gains access to a volume on the magical control of mental processes written in the last century by one Samson Proferantsov. He considers that volume a useful supplement to Engels' *Dialectics of Nature.* Armed with his magic powers Tikhomirov displaces the local representative from Moscow, induces in the populace a belief that he is their only legitimate ruler, declares Lyubimov independent, and guarantees freedom to all the citizens. Tikhomirov, like the young Seryozha in *The Court Is in Session,* plans an immediate leap into full communism, and his initial intentions are totally good. But he is obliged to hypnotize the populace into believing that there is a surplus of everything when the town is as a matter of fact dirt-poor, that the river water is flowing champagne, and that toothpaste is a tasty *pâté.* Reality asserts itself stubbornly, Tikhomirov loses his hypnotic power, and tanks from the "center" encircle the town where his ill-timed experiment in brotherly love had failed.

But such a dry recital gives no impression at all of this richly Gogolian masterpiece, whose dominants are humorous word play and narrative perversity. The specifically Gogolian feature in *Lyubimov* is the presence of a self-conscious narrator always striving for literary effects, ostensibly scrupulous about getting his facts right, but prone to hyperbole, oxymoron, and delightful digression. The Gogolian narrative situation is complicated here by the presence of *two* competing narrators, Savely Kuzmich Proferantsov, Tikhomirov's officially appointed historical chronicler, and Savely's supposed ancestor, Samson Proferantsov, the nineteenth-century discoverer of "magnetism," who collaborates with and often corrects his descendant. To this absurd narrative pair Tikhomirov delivers the soberly Leninist command: "Be our mirror, Proferantsov, be our Leo Tolstoy . . . Look at life around you, soak yourself in it, and be its living reflection in your memoirs." Gogolian *skaz* is, as Donald Fanger puts it, "a mannered narration in which the speaker unwittingly vies with his story for attention and vivid manner overshadows ostensible matter." And Sinyavsky's double narrator cannot refrain from upstaging the narrative. In order not to overburden his literary text with "excessive realistic detail" he relegates certain matters to footnotes: "Thus if any reader wants to he can take a breather and look up the details that interest him. But if he can't be bothered let him by all means push ahead as fast as he likes." He discusses with the reader various possible styles, offering occasional trials of his pen in different registers, setting the high poetic style resonant with periods and "metaphors" against the "civilized restraint of a Feuchtwanger or a Hemingway: 'The gunner pressed the lever. Period. His brains spilled out. Period. Buttoning his fly he heard the water flushing in the toilet bowl.' " He permits himself so many digressions that the narrative thread gets hopelessly tangled. There is one on the touching theme of his own love for a melancholy Jewish woman (Proferantsov is a bit of an anti-Semite, by the way), another is a rollicking irrelevance on the career of the nineteenth-century Proferantsov, a masterpiece of inconsequence and verbal flourish. And there is a lovely digression, *within* the digression on Proferantsov, about Lenin baying the moon:

> Thoughtfully, methodically, Lenin bayed at the moon—he bayed at the moon, our Ilych, knowing that he was soon to die. Every moonlit night it was the same. He howled, then he stopped and listened, and he howled again until he began to feel chilly and turned and ran as fast as his legs would carry him, his green eyes flashing in the dark, back to his writing and his calculating and his planning of the path we were to follow in life . . .
> You'll ask me what relevance this has to my story. None at all. Except that if even Lenin, even Vladimir Ilych, could have his moods, then why not a fine Russian gentleman who had never done any harm to anyone?

The distanced, or *skaz*, narrator has been a staple of Russian literature at least since Gogol. We see him in Leskov, in Remizov, in Bely, and we know that since the Revolution the *skaz* technique has been brilliantly developed by Zamyatin, Babel, and especially by Zoshchenko, whose pretentiously semiliterate narrator is probably the nearest model for Proferantsov, who is nonetheless a thoroughly original creation. Like Zoshchenko's narrator in such things as *What the Nightingale Sang*, Proferantsov is a master of the pseudoliterary cliché: "Truly a picture worthy of the artist's brush!" His language is replete with incongruities: "There was the yellow hospital shaped like a coffin, and, next to it, the brownish-red rectangle block of the prison." He creates oxymoronic and sometimes purely moronic combinations: Nicholas I (sometimes confused with Nicholas II) and his retinue are referred to as "courtier-commissars," and the ancestor who told Nicholas where to head in "was quite a Bolshevik." Tikhomirov, trying to get to the bottom of things, says: "Go on and tell all the lies you like. I've got to get at the truth."

Sinyavsky is part of a long Russian literary tradition, but he also owes a heavy and fully acknowledged debt to E. T. A. Hoffmann, from whom he learned, among other things, the ironic juxtaposition of prosaic everyday reality with magic. Both artists feature the philistine caught and surprised by fantastic happenings, but Sinyavsky's are dreary Soviet philistines, like the group of Soviet policemen sent out to infiltrate Lyubimov disguised as a hiking club with balalaikas, hunting and fishing gear, and a few machine guns, who are lured by magic deep into the forest and cannot get out.

We have seen that *Lyubimov* has thematic links with *The Court Is in Session.* Two strolling and tailing gumshoes, Vitya and Tolya, who in the earlier novel discuss the need to develop a "mindscope" for monitoring thought, reappear in *Lyubimov* furnished with the surnames Kochetov and Sofronov, real names of two reactionary and thoroughly repulsive Soviet writers who may indeed be police operatives. Vitya Kochetov manages to "penetrate" the town of Lyubimov but he becomes an abject convert to Tikhomirov's system of mind control which he welcomes as the mindscope he and Tolya had fervently hoped for. The glorious experiment of Lyubimov thus promises only a refinement of techniques developed in the center.

In the last chapter of *Lyubimov,* entitled "Finale," Tikhomirov's old-fashioned mother travels to a church "at the end of the world" to pray with an ancient priest who is still at his work because he knows that "even if his church were the last on earth he must stay at his post and continue to work for the salvation of impious men." In a marvellous transition to a major key, untroubled by Sinyavsky's usually dominant ironic note, the priest intones a solemnly eloquent prayer in Church language, asking mercy for all suffering humans: "Grant thy peace, O Lord, to all who have died bereft, lonely, destitute, and have no one to pray for them." If we exclude Karlinsky's brief prayer in *The Court Is in Session,* this is, as Rufus Mathewson says, "the only time Sinyavsky's religious views find overt expression in his fiction."

Perhaps the best of the *Fantastic Stories* is a strangely moving and mysterious piece entitled "Pkhentz." Its central character is a being who lives in Moscow, speaks its language, and functions as a bookkeeper there while totally alienated in spirit from Russian, and indeed from all terrestrial, life. The outward form his body takes is that of a hunchback, which further separates him from common humanity. He bathes with fanatic frequency, and is so chaste that he drives Veronika, a woman who pursues him, to the desperate measure of undressing herself in front of him: "It was awful. It turned out that all over she was the same unnatural white as her face, neck, and hands. In the front a pair of white breasts hung down. At first I thought they were a second pair of arms, cut off at the elbows."

His revulsion at the sight of the female body might suggest latent homosexuality, but this character's isolation runs far deeper than mere sexual inversion. The male human body is no less repellent to him: "If I were like them, I would never take my suit or even my overcoat off, day or night." His own body, when released from the straps and halters that hold it in a near-human shape, spreads out freely like a graceful palm tree, with many eyes and a multiplicity of hands and feet. He is, as it turns out, a native of some planet in a far-off galaxy who had been shipwrecked on earth many years before and lost all hope of returning to his homeland. The story is an original modern treatment, with an admixture of science-fantasy, of an old romantic theme: the human consciousness of an origin beyond the spatial confines of a particular planet. It is also a poignant symbolic treatment of spiritual isolation, and it expresses, as Sinyavsky has said, some part of the loneliness that he himself feels.

The works of Sinyavsky allude to or resonate with one another, and Vera Dunham remarks that "his oeuvre is so centripetal, cohesive, tightly interwoven that breaking it up into periods, even into *before* and *after* seems both impossible and wrong." "Pkhentz" registers an experience of fatal disaccord between the self and the surrounding philistine world, and that same experience is treated again in "Tiny Tsores." The latter story is dedicated to E. T. A. Hoffmann, whose *Little Zaches, Surnamed Zinnober (Klein Zaches, Genannt Zinnober,* 1819), provided the germ of an idea which Sinyavsky fashioned into a poignant statement of his own. In Hoffmann's tale the little dwarf is an odious and misshapen excrescence whose own mother cannot endure the sight or sound of him. She gladly gives him up to the fairy Rosabelverde; she brings it about that credit for the good deeds and talented behavior of others is given to the dwarf, who eventually becomes a minister of state. Sinyavsky turns Hoffmann's hateful dwarf into a figure of deep human pathos. Tsores—whose very name means grief—arouses contempt and suspicion in others by the very fact of his freakishness, his *difference* from all of them. Among his five brothers only *he* bears the name Sinyavsky, a device which, along with other things in the story, underlines a personal pain. He brings misfortune to others. Each of his five brothers died as a result of something he did, though he was not strictly to blame for any of the deaths. His mother abandoned him, and even his dog went away and never came back, because of the harm he brought, all unwittingly, on other people. Poor little Tsores compares his case with that of other terrible sufferers who have brought harm to those they loved: Vadim, who accidentally killed his sister, a mother who killed her boy. "Tiny Tsores" communicates the agonizing experience of guiltless guilt, of the murderer by accident who can never be certain there was not a modicum of intent in his action. It is a wonderful state-

ment of the guilt all humans to some extent experience—for being separate from others, for *self*hood, somehow for all the world's evil: for
Hitler, for Stalin. It's the guilt Dostoevsky's *Brothers* felt—all of them.
"Sinyavsky" itself is a guilty name, for it is the name of Tsores's father,
the author of this book, whom his brothers held in contempt as a
"scribbler." Brought back to life by magic those same brothers blame it
all on Sinyavsky, father and son: "Offal . . . Suicide . . . Dog . . . Enemy
of the people . . . He'll get his . . . Ought to be in jail . . . Degenerate,"
and the like. Sinyavsky has said that when all around "accuse you of
various crimes it's hard not to feel guilty of something," especially since
each of us harbors a little original sin. The dwarf Tsores put it much
more strongly: "We're all responsible for everything, in the last analysis."

Hoffmann's good fairy Rosabelverde appears in Sinyavsky's story as
the pediatrician Dora Alexandrovna, who attends Tsores as a child, and
whose handbag hanging on his bedstead smells of perfume—a mark of
her fay nature. Before her visit he was a stammerer, but she grants him
his heart's desire, to speak clearly and beautifully, and later brings him
as a gift a tall bookcase full of volumes that hold the gifts of eloquence
and fantasy. He calls the bookcase "E. T. A. Hoffmann on four legs."

Sinyavsky's religious view of the world is implicit in many of the
stories, but only reached clear expression in the volume *Random
Thoughts*. The thoughts are offered as occasional, accidental, and intuitive *aperçus*, somewhat in the manner of Rozanov's *Fallen Leaves* (*Opav-
shie listya*). However, the thoughts are not totally random in their structure. The book has three main themes: death, religion, and sex. About
death Sinyavsky says that it is nothing to be afraid of, a thought that he
develops in a number of fervent passages:

> How do you dare fear death? You know that's the same as cow-
> ardice in battle. Look around you, they're dropping everywhere.
> Just remember your old parents, who are now dead. Think about
> your cousin Verochka, who died when she was five. She was such
> a little thing, and she went off to die, strangled by diphtheria. But
> you—a healthy, educated adult—and you're afraid. Come on—
> stop trembling! Joyfully! Forward, March!

The first and almost the last entries talk of the need to face and embrace death as the crowning event of life. Thoughts on religion motivate a joyful confrontation with the "crown" of life by stressing the in-
evitability of God. Without Him there is nothing:

> It's possible to believe in God in many ways. It's possible to
> think about him endlessly: He encompasses everything and exists

everywhere. He is that Most Important Thing that can't fit into any other thing.

His thoughts on sex are at best ambivalent and at worst puritanical, and remind us that images of sexual confusion and frustration are common in his work: the Pkhentzian finds women (men too) sexually repulsive; that connoisseur of pornography, Karlinsky, is impotent; Tikhomirov has "no time" for his wife, who looked elsewhere; Tiny Tsores repels Dora by reaching directly for her buttons, the way he had been taught to do by hooligans ("Don't be so literal," she says); and the structural principle of "You and I" is the confusion of sexual roles, even of sexual equipment and function. In that story, moreover, the narrator's one climax in bed with Lida is associated with his own suicide. It is not surprising then to find in this book "random thoughts" in which Sinyavsky abjures the anatomical location of sex in the place of excrement and filth, and to read a hymn to the act as a "rapturous transgression," requiring for the renewal of rapture many different objects and new forbidden boundaries to cross. Freudian readers have found meat to their taste in all of this. A literary critic should surely point out that the motif of sexual ambivalence is one of the strands that link together all of Sinyavsky's fictional works. Most of his male characters would find congenial the aphorism we find in *Random Thoughts:* "If one could only be a castrato, how much one would accomplish." Other characters would prefer more pessimistic thoughts, such as: "The possibility is not excluded that life on earth is hell. Then everything is perfectly clear. But if it isn't? My God, then what?" And Pkhentz-Sinyavsky would find the following particularly apt: "What is the body? A kind of outer envelope, a diving suit. And it could be that I, sitting in my diving suit, just keep wriggling and coiling!"

A second volume of random jottings, *A Voice from the Chorus,* consists of excerpts from Sinyavsky's long biweekly letters to his wife from the labor camp. Probably because the letters were censored they contain no direct revelations of prison life, though misery is hinted at in many ways. There are references to his own utter loneliness even in the noisy and overcrowded camp, and reflections on the special clairvoyance provided by a life stripped of every amenity and every convention. The book comprises thoughts on a number of themes, fugitive reflections and observations together with many fully faceted gems of thought. Among the matters broached are: the activity and function of the artist, especially the writer; love and sex, usually from an unashamedly male point of view; many accidental, ephemeral, and unrepeatable experiences: "The rain falling hard and not stopping gives you a feeling of coziness ... even when you're freezing and wet through; you get a strange sense of hopelessness animated a bit by tenderness—no knowing toward whom or what—maybe toward this savage wetness, and this rain that has no care for people. Let it rain!" The book deals with sleeping and dreaming as simple and precious activities; religious experience and the sense of God's presence; the direct and artless style of the Gospels; religious characters among the prisoners, brilliantly sketched. Among the most interesting passages are his critical comments on a great variety of writers—Akhmatova, Swift, Mandelshtam, Shakespeare, Khlebnikov, Gogol, and Pushkin—passages which are always striking, original, and given from a surprising perspective. They remind us of Sinyavsky's earliest career as a writer of criticism.

One cannot read the multifarious product of Sinyavsky without a sense of revulsion and horror at the thought that so magnificent a writer was so cribbed and confined in his native land that there was nothing for him to do but leave it. And there were so many others like him.

The works of Sinyavsky's codefendant, Yuly Daniel, who published abroad under the pseudonym Nikolay Arzhak, gave offense to the state, as the record of the trial shows, chiefly because of satiric barbs aimed at the Soviet way of life. The judge, the prosecutor, and what appears to have been a selected audience were outraged at satiric scenes of everyday life in the Soviet Union, and in particular at one of Daniel's stories, "The Man from MINAP." That story features a young Communist student who claims he can determine the sex of his offspring at the moment of coitus. His services are in great demand among Soviet wives, some of whom wish to conceive sons, and some, daughters. When the Party discovers his talent and queries him as to his technique, he explains that for a male he thinks of Karl Marx at the crucial moment, and for a female, of the revolutionary Klara Zetkin. The young man is promptly employed by the state for the sake of accomplishing a new leap in Marxist-Leninist genetics and encouraged to exercise his talent under the most favorable conditions. The objects of Daniel's satire include Soviet housewives, puritanical Comsomol leaders determined to defend the Soviet family, and Party scientists eager to establish control over a still unpredictable area of human activity.

Daniel sent other stories abroad during the 1960s. In the story "Hands" the hero undertakes to explain why his hands are "constantly shaking" by recounting his experiences as a member of the Cheka, when those hands were involved in the execution of condemned prisoners. "Atonement" deals with the guilt and isolation experienced by a man who is suspected of having denounced people under Stalin. Perhaps the best of his stories is "This Is Moscow Speaking," a macabre invention which opens with a sober official announcement on Moscow Radio that August 10, 1960, has been declared "Public Murder Day," and that between the hours of 6:00 A.M. and midnight on that day any citizen will have the right to kill any other citizen. The story explores the reactions of various institutions and individuals to this sudden, inexplicable decree of the Supreme Soviet. The official newspaper *Izvestia* greets the announcement with a shower of Soviet clichés: "the rising level of life . . . genuine democracy . . . for the first time in history . . . the bourgeois press." A careerist Party man characterizes the decree as an important step in the direction of developing the "creative initiative of the masses." Another Soviet citizen understands the measure as evidence of democratization, in that the state is now granting certain of its functions to the people themselves. The hero's mistress suggests that they do away with her husband on "Public Murder Day." Even the hero and first-person narrator, whose moral level is relatively high, has a violent daydream in which he imagines a mass killing of those responsible for the purges of 1937 and for Russia's other agonies. An artist friend of his has already produced a picture celebrating and illustrating the Day. So inured are they to official murder that it occurs to hardly any of the characters that the whole idea should be rejected on moral grounds.

The trial of Sinyavsky and Daniel cast a new light on the Soviet literary underground and helped us to understand what motivates its members in sending their manuscripts abroad. Sinyavsky insisted at his trial that he was not moved by anti-Soviet sentiment or by any desire to damage the Soviet image abroad, but simply by the imperative need of a Russian writer to find readers somewhere for his most characteristic work when that work cannot be published in the Soviet Union. Sinyavsky's defense of himself at his trial was brilliant. He offered his judges many elementary lessons on the nature of the creative process, and his final words to them reveal the tragic isolation of the Soviet underground: "In my . . . story 'Pkhentz' there is a sentence that I feel I can apply to myself: 'Just think, if I am simply different from others, they have to start cursing me.' Well, I am different. But I do not regard myself as an enemy; I am a Soviet man and my works are not hostile works."[2]

13 Solzhenitsyn and the Epic of the Camps

The two great figures in the Russian emigration of the seventies (the so-called third wave), Sinyavsky and Solzhenitsyn, were in all important respects polar opposites. Sinyavsky as a writer favors fantasy, the grotesque, sexual deviation, opaque structure; Solzhenitsyn is concerned to convey the direct reality of experience: his art is ascetic and pure of the extraneous. Sinyavsky invents a fantasy world through which real Soviet characters and the Soviet ambience are perceived in grotesque displacement; Solzhenitsyn locates, documents, and describes a terrible world, grotesque in its real lineaments and in no need of phantasmagoric embellishment. Sinyavsky traces his lineage to Gogol, and his immediate stylistic predecessors were Bely, Pilnyak, Babel, and Zoshchenko; Solzhenitsyn emphasizes his own affinity with Tolstoy and Dostoevsky. Both men spent many years in "strict regime" labor camps, yet Sinyavsky's *A Voice from the Chorus* offers very little direct evidence of the inhuman conditions he had survived; Solzhenitsyn's major work in life and literature is a mountainous documentation of those conditions and a sustained and beautiful anathema against the evil that spawned them. The two men are opposites also in their style of thought: Sinyavsky in *Random Thoughts* and *A Voice from the Chorus* is an explorer of his own sensations and thought processes as territory full of paradox and surprise; Solzhenitsyn in many passages of the *Gulag* and in other things is a powerful dialectician, his thoughts arrayed in battle with cosmic evil. Both men are religious and deeply so, but Sinyavsky, whatever his affiliation, seems to me to be a tentative Christian without dogmatic reflexes; Solzhenitsyn is a convinced adherent of the national church and Russian orthodoxy. As we shall see, the two were natural antagonists in the many disputes that agitated the third wave.

Alexander Isaevich Solzhenitsyn (b. 1918) was a captain of artillery in the Red Army when he was arrested in February 1945. He had been decorated twice for valor in action. The charge against him was that he had spoken disparagingly of Stalin and the Soviet leadership in private letters written to a friend. The story of his arrest and removal to the NKVD headquarters in Moscow is told in the first part of *The Gulag Archipelago,* and his interrogation in the Lubyanka provided the material for certain key scenes in *The First Circle.* He served eight years at hard labor, an experience on which *One Day in the Life of Ivan Denisovich* is based. After his release in 1953 as a "perpetual exile" he was stricken by cancer and sent for treatment to a hospital in Tashkent. That hospital is the setting of *The Cancer Ward.* The treatment seems to have been fully successful. Released from exile in 1956, he was rehabilitated in 1957; in other words, the charges against him, after eleven years of prison and exile, were withdrawn as unsubstantiated. For the next six years he worked at his writing with little hope, as he tells us in *The Calf and the Oak,* of seeing any of it published. Finally in 1962 the miracle happened.

One Day

One Day in the Life of Ivan Denisovich burst upon the Soviet reader in 1962 like a shot in the night. As a revelation of the daily misery experienced by the inmates of Stalin's concentration camps, the novel had an immediate and sensational success. Solzhenitsyn transmits an intense, particular, and awful human experience. This account of one day in the life of a prison camp—and not one of the worst days—brings to life in the vivid four-letter language of the inmates themselves (the editor of *New World* in his note introducing the story felt it necessary to explain the presence of so many vulgar expressions) an array of characters: on the one hand the supervisors, guards, and their toadies, brutalized by the terror they themselves employ; and on the other hand the prisoners, some of whom may have been guilty of something, though most are innocent of the crimes charged to them. All of them, however, have been stripped of liberty, dignity, and elementary human rights. The story gives a credible account of life reduced to an animal level where "it was every man for himself," and everybody has his own little racket and expects his "own little cut." The very existence of the camp, and the level of life of the inmates, is a tragic irony in a land supposedly motivated by socialist ideals.

Solzhenitsyn has given us in *The Calf and the Oak* a fascinating account of the poet and editor Tvardovsky's heroic efforts on behalf of *One Day* and of Khrushchev's personal intervention, which assured its publication in *New World*. Khrushchev was surely deaf to the novel's artistic power, but he did identify with the peasant Ivan Denisovich and warmly approved his image as an efficient worker who "economized on building materials." And of course Khrushchev was at the time deep in a struggle with the dead Stalin and his many beneficiaries in the Party. Solzhenitsyn's story of the camps was one of many weapons he used against them, along with a massive rehabilitation program and the removal of the monster's material remains from the tomb on Red Square.

Solzhenitsyn's works are so full of matter and message that the critic may be tempted to speak only of such things and to forget that in these works sense is inseparable from structure and that Solzhenitsyn is primarily an artist, quite possibly one of the great ones. He is a serious artist, moreover, one who consciously involves his art with human problems—issues of the day as well as moral and philosophical problems. Like Dante—he himself invites the comparison—he accommodates in his inferno immediate political enemies whose policies he abhors along with poets and philosophers who reflect on man and the universe. Solzhenitsyn is quite conscious of himself as an artist, and he believes in art as a means of renewing and purifying life. In his famous Nobel lecture he offered as a fundamental tenet the statement of Dostoevsky that "beauty" will save the world, asking: "Could not . . . art and literature in a very real way offer succor to the modern world?"[1] The character of Solzhenitsyn's art should, therefore, concern us in the first instance.

A structural feature common to all of Solzhenitsyn's fictional works is the collapse of both space and time into a severely constricted area—a labor camp, a *sharashka* (special prison), a cancer ward, a particular battlefield—and a limited segment of measured time. The tiny area of confinement exercises enormous attractive power; like a "black hole" in space it has drawn into itself everything—both good and bad—from the outside world. The history of the Soviet Union, the fate of Russia, the great moral issues of the twentieth century, are concentrated for a moment of time at a single point. To a degree the distinction is lost between the world outside and the world inside, since the whole world has undergone a sudden implosion, a violent inward collapse. In *One Day* the stylistic sign of this collapse is the reader's total immersion in the viewpoint and the language of the prisoner, the *zek.*

As a result of this structure there are in *One Day* two levels of time as well as space, the limited time of the actual prison-life day, and the sweep of history—with a suggestion of eternity—conveyed in the prisoners' memories, reflections, and autobiographies. To take the inside plot first, the action of Ivan's "one day" is no different from the other three-thousand-plus days of his sentence. It begins as usual with reveille and frost *inside* the barracks. The first event is something like what Bruno Bettelheim calls an "excremental assault," the removal of the heavily laden toilet bucket. Ivan is sent to mop the floor at headquarters, and manages to screw the bosses by doing a poor job and slopping freezing water over their path. Breakfast follows, then an assembly for counting and re-counting of the prisoners and careful frisking. Then comes the march to the work site under the repeated warning "Step out of line and we shoot!" All of this leads up to the novel's climax, the high point of Ivan's day: the exquisite pleasure of building a wall straight and true and not wasting any mortar. That climax makes of *One Day* a kind of hymn to productive labor as the quintessentially human activity, a source of satisfaction for itself alone even when performed in an evil cause. (It is not hard to understand why the film *The Bridge over the River Kwai* had a stunning effect in the Soviet Union, especially on former prisoners. Its basic theme, the beauty and delight of productive labor even for an enemy, is closely related both to *One Day* and to *The First Circle*.) After the building scene the prisoners are again assembled, re-counted, and refrisked. Then they march "home" to the compound, but this time they have something to live for: food, however poor and scanty, a warm place, though crowded, and sleep. Once more it is the barracks and lights out, as Ivan develops his modest definition of prison happiness:

> [He] went to sleep fully content. He'd had many strokes of luck that day: they hadn't put him in solitary, they hadn't sent his squad to the settlement; he'd swiped a bowl of kasha at dinner; he'd built a wall and been happy doing it; he'd smuggled that bit of metal through . . . And he hadn't fallen ill. He'd got over it. A day without a dark cloud. Almost a happy day.

Such is the meager record of events at the level of that one day, but each of the prisoners projects another story, and those stories taken together are the real, the outside, plot of the novel. Ivan's letters from his wife reveal the poverty—material, cultural, and spiritual—of life on a collective farm. The story of his own imprisonment tells us of the thousands of returning prisoners of war who, far from being welcomed in the motherland, were rounded up and sent to labor camps:

> According to his dossier Ivan Denisovich Shukov was in jail for high treason. He'd testified himself that, sure, he'd surrendered because he wanted to betray his country, and he'd come back from captivity because he was carrying out a mission for German intel-

ligence. What sort of mission neither Shukhov nor the interrogator could say. So they just left it that way—a mission. In Counterintelligence they beat Shukhov a lot. So he figured it out: you don't sign a confession, it's the wooden kimono, you sign, you might live a little longer. He signed.

The prisoner Tsesar's remarks and his discussion of Eisenstein and the art film are a deft allusion to the fate of the avant-garde—including Eisenstein himself—in the Soviet Union. The brigade leader Tiurin's story is an item out of the immense tragedy of collectivization, "the destruction of the kulaks as a class":

> I got home late one night and entered by the back garden. Father had already been deported, and mother and the kids were waiting for a transport. A telegram had come about me, and the Village Soviet were already after me. We put out the light and sat trembling up against the wall under the window, because activists were going around the village peering in at the windows. I left again the same night and took my kid brother with me . . .

Captain Buinovsky's story is futher evidence of moral idiocy on "the outside." He had been assigned during the war to work with the British, and had made some friends among them, but when those friends later sent him presents and good wishes he was arrested as their agent. The meek Christian Alyosha, sentenced to twenty-five years for Christ's sake, is the only truly happy man in the camp. Bruno Bettelheim, whose *The Informed Heart* tells of life in the Nazi camps, remarks that the best adjusted prisoners in those camps were Jehovah's Witnesses, for they took seriously the biblical injunction to "rejoice and be exceeding glad, for so persecuted they the prophets." Alyosha's story and his message threw a bright beam out of hell itself onto a different plane of existence: "You should be glad you're in jail. Here you have time to think about your soul. You know what the apostle Paul said: 'Not only do I want to be in prison, but I am ready to die for the sake of the Lord Jesus.' "

One Day is remarkable not only for its structure but for its language and style, and there is little doubt that Solzhenitsyn's first published work had an impact on Russian writing in the sixties and seventies. After the long drought of socialist realism with its bland affirmation and transparent language, *One Day* was like a sudden flood of genuine speech, long dammed up but now flowing free. To a generation raised on the controlled and labored puristic banality of the Soviet literary journals Solzhenitsyn offered a prose saturated with the authenticity of a language free from all official norms: the obscene idiom of the *zeks* themselves, who are thus more honest than the clean world even in the way they speak. Some of the best criticism of *One Day* deals with its character as a linguistic artifact. Its style is one widely favored in modern literature and variously known as *style indirecte libre, erlebte rede,* represented speech, quasi-direct discourse, or, the term preferred by Dorrit Cohn, "narrated monologue." The technique, briefly, combined third-person past-tense narration with quasi-direct representation of a particular character's thought or speech in his own characteristic idiom. The passage already quoted on how Ivan got to a Russian prison after returning from German captivity reveals the rich possibilities of the technique. We note that Ivan's statements and thoughts are neither quoted nor given indirectly, but rather are embedded in the account of a narrator who also speaks the prison lingo and is wise to the camp system. The statement "Sure, he'd surrendered because he wanted to betray his country" represents ironically Ivan's willing admission of guilt after unbearable pressure, the nature of which the narrator feels no need to elaborate. Ivan's own calculation is given in the statement: "You don't sign a confession, it's the wooden kimono, you sign, you might live a little longer," to which the omniscient narrator adds only the laconic comment: "He signed." Obviously the technique has a wide range of uses and possible effects. Solzhenitsyn uses it in *The First Circle,* we shall see, as an ironic device in the portrait of Stalin and as an enhancement of pathos in the tragic story of the peasant Spiridon's life. It is in all of these cases also a device of estrangement, in the Formalist sense. In *One Day* its principal function is to provide for Ivan's story a broader narrative framework within which the fate of a simple peasant takes on historical and human dimensions.

The leitmotif of *One Day* is survival, not just of the physical person but of his respect for himself. A number of formulas for such survival are developed in the simple terms of Ivan's camp experience. For example, you never eat with your hat on. Hungry you may be, but you never fall so low as to lick a bowl, nor do you eat detached fisheyes floating in a soup bowl. You may crave a smoke and hope to be given a butt when the smoker is though, but you *never* look at the smoker's mouth while waiting; only people who have "lost themselves" do that. And of course you never rat on anybody: "You'll never survive if you lick bowls or rat on your comrades" is a fundamental rule.

Ivan is resourceful, even though the camp life frustrates every initiative. He treasures each morsel of bread and knows how to get the most out of every movement of mastication. Ivan is a primitive tool maker: he can invent a cozy face mask out of a piece of rag and some string or fashion a general purpose instrument out of a stray piece of metal. But if he's caught with it they'll send him to solitary. A most important human quality does survive in Ivan, as we have seen: love of labor and the pride of a good workman. At the high point of his work on the wall he felt himself for a moment to be independent, inner-directed, fully human, and almost free.

The First Circle and The Cancer Ward

There are two versions of *The First Circle*, one published abroad in 1968 while Solzhenitsyn was still in the Soviet Union, and another bearing the imprint "Vermont-Paris, 1978." The 1968 version, though first to be published, is according to Solzhenitsyn a *later* "self-censored" version; the Vermont-Paris version, he has explained, is the full, authentic text begun in 1955 while he was living in exile, revised in 1958, and revised again, definitively, in 1962. When it developed in 1964 that the novel might possibly be published in the Soviet Union, he softened and shortened it with an eye to the Soviet censor, and that self-censored version was sent abroad and published in 1968. The changes were radical, so much so that the 1968 edition is really a different and, as some believe, artistically superior product. I will discuss that version first, then deal with the text published in 1978, the "Vermont version."

Solzhenitsyn as an artist is an adept and resourceful organizer of his material. The central narrative of *The First Circle* covers just three days during Christmas week, the season of joyous tidings brought to men. The main thread of interest and suspense is a kind of detective story in which the reader knows who the guilty party is but the police do not, and all our human sympathy is with the hunted criminal, a man whose crime was that he once, quite unaccountably and on Christmas Eve, did a single good deed, a good deed in a dark and naughty world. He made a phone call to warn a man that he was about to be framed. But how far indeed—to continue the paraphrase of Shakespeare—that little candle sent its beams. The recondite scientific activities in the *sharashka* are made to revolve around the police problem of running that criminal to earth, of finding the man who did the deed; out of that chase, and in a way incidental to it, grow in incredible profusion the biographies of a score of prisoners, each of whom himself has a history of pursuit and capture by the police, and most of whom—there are some notable exceptions—now devote their talents either to catching another one or to protecting the conversations of the archjailer, Stalin. And the outcome of this detective story is unique in the history of the genre. The voice identifier that will pin the crime on the real criminal is never perfected, and the police never know for sure that Volodin is guilty, though the prisoner responsible for developing the voice identifier, Rubin, believes that he has narrowed the list of suspects down to two. Now the rules of the genre would seem to require that the police have been foiled, and the story has reached a dead end, since the evidence is insufficient. But the police in Stalin's Russia operated in an impenetrable world of their own. They arrest and destroy both suspects, and we learn that they need not even have gone through the farcical police chase at all. They had already arrested several young chaps who happened to be standing around at the phone booth where the call had been placed, and since they have been arrested they will surely be sentenced; the police were ready to arrest all the other suspects and convict them anyway. Why take chances?

While the actual plot of the novel is almost bare of events, the life histories of the characters—each one a kind of sketch for a possible novel—are rich in every kind of vicissitude. (We have noted this structure in *One Day*, and will find it again in *Cancer Ward*.) Those biographies reveal in terms of firsthand experiences the overwhelming tragedy of Russian life during the Stalin period: the bloody and senseless horror of collectivization in the peasant Spiridon's wonderful narrative; the sacrifices and hopes of the First Five-Year Plan in the story of the engineer who built the dam on the Dnieper River, then was imprisoned for much of his life; the destruction of the Old Bolsheviks, summed up in the scene from the Kharkov inner prison in 1937 when thousands of imprisoned comrades sang the International and other revolutionary songs; the Second World War with its heroism and frustration, in the biographies of the prisoners Nerzhin and Rubin. The biographies reveal every level of Soviet life: student life and the shabby dormitories of the university in the story of Nadya; artists and art workers in the experience of Nadelashin, a genuine artist who tries to but cannot satisfy the cheap tastes of his *nouveau-riche* clients; the dull workdays of policemen and jailers: Shikin and Myshin at the idiotic job of reading and hearing denunciations; the plush apartments and vulgar ambience of those who have "made it" in Soviet life: the prosecutor Makarygin worshiping at his expensive "tobacco altar"; the glib vacuity of Stalin laureates in literature and their critics: the writer Galakhov—who interviews a Soviet diplomat to elicit such details of his life as may be suitable for inclusion in a new novel on the heroism of Soviet diplomats. The essence of Solzhenitsyn's art, I would suggest, is the exposure of what has heretofore been hidden from view.

It may not be perverse and it may be instructive to compare Solzhenitsyn with Kafka, and particularly with two of the latter's works that deal with trials, prisons, and punishment, *The Penal Colony* and *The Trial*. In both of those works a man is punished through the operation of some law that is either completely arbitrary or inscrutable, and he is caught in a penal system which assumes his guilt. No one has ever suggested that the events described in *The Penal Colony* and *The Trial* could have happened. But Solzhenitsyn's stories not only could have happened but literally did happen to so many millions of people that we may be tempted to apply to *The First Circle* the old Marxist bromide about realism as "typical characters in typical situations." Solzhenitsyn is a realist writer raised on the Russian classics and probably not in sympathy with modern tendencies, but the reality he depicts is itself fantastic; his fantastic world closely imitates the real lives of actual people. In one other respect Solzhenitsyn is radically different from Kafka. Kafka's books are laden with a sense of guilt. As modern critics have noted, he shows us a world in which modern man, burdened by his feelings of guilt and isolation, seeks vainly for salvation. Solzhenitsyn's prison characters are actually much happier: they *know* they are *innocent*; they recognize clearly the features of the law that violates them, and they abhor it. For them salvation is ready at hand: a prisoner can be true to himself, refuse to cooperate, *not* work on a device that will help to ensnare innocent people, preserve his own moral nature against the massive pressures of the Stalinist system—indeed the fact of incarceration itself offers evidence that the man at one time had a measure of courage and inner integrity. Solzhenitsyn's world is much brighter than Kafka's; it is far more cheerful than the world we experience in modern fiction as a whole. And the last irony of his work and his career is that, execrated though he is by the Soviet literary bureaucracy, he has beautifully embodied in his work their precept that the writer must take an optimistic view of things. We note that he writes not of Ivan Denisovich's prison life as a whole, but of *one day* in that life, and a good day at that; that his hospital scenes are laid not in any ward but in a cancer ward, where men are obliged to ask themselves the essentially moral question, "What does one live by?"; and that the prisoners in his greatest novel are in the *first* or *top circle* of hell. Indeed everything is for the best in the worst of all possible worlds, and in chapter 47 of *The First Circle* we even hear a fervent prayer and have more than a flicker of hope for the "resurrection of the dead."

Solzhenitsyn's characters are realized with great precision and economy of means but without obtrusive literary artifice. His great strength lies in his power of empathy, his insight into the experience of human beings who are totally different from himself, even antipathetic. The Soviet police bureaucrat Rusanov in *Cancer Ward*, who built himself a career by writing denunciations, in order to distract his thoughts from the tumor that may kill him, meditates upon the good things in his life:

his orthodox children who have the expected problems, his predictable dog "Dzhulbars" lying on his little rug in the hallway. Everything would seem to be in order in his stuffy little philistine world. And the thoughts of Rusanov suddenly take the form of a kind of mental tape recording, exactly reproducing the man's trite and dismal idiom in a masterful narrated monologue.

But thoughts of home provide him no consolation in his misery, and when Rusanov turns his meditation to affairs of state a mind unfolds that looks like a matrix for any day's edition of the newspaper *Pravda.* A cerebral cortex is exposed that harbors only such neural activity as is proper for a Soviet man of the responsible class. Rusanov is a human mechanism seemingly devoid of ideas, morality, or honor, existing in a tightly curtained void impenetrable even to the thought of death. The exposure and perhaps ultimately the liberation of such curtained, or, to use Czeslaw Milosz's term, "captive" minds, is the principal business of Solzhenitsyn as an artist.

Solzhenitsyn in an interview with a Slovak critic once described the technique of his novels as "polyphonic," perhaps suggesting thereby an affinity with Dostoevsky. The novels are polyphonic in the sense that there are frequent shifts from one dominant viewpoint to another: they are structured out of many competing centers of attention. In *Cancer Ward* attention shifts from the inward experience of one character to that of another, and as the viewpoint shifts, the style of thought and expression—the gestures of language—also change in keeping with the character. We are told that Solzhenitsyn was once ambitious to be an actor; the frustrated actor found an outlet for his talent in multiform linguistic mimicry, which ranges from Stalin's harsh and alien accent to the sing-song, proverb-prone speech of Auntie Stepha and the beautiful peasant speech of Spiridon, which is curiously interlaced with history and politics.

Linguistic mimicry is one of Solzhenitsyn's methods for setting a character before us, but his treatment of persons involves another kind of mimicry, one that is paradoxical and almost perverse. Solzhenitsyn is unlike any modern writer that I know of in sheer descriptive power and in the importance he gives to visible, objective details of the real world. Solzhenitsyn's descriptions of characters in their completeness of detail ironically mimic the police record and the security questionnaire. For each character we learn in meticulous detail his age, his height, the color of his hair, even in many cases the color of his eyes. We are told of peculiar distinguishing marks: Nerzhin's deeply wrinkled face and the furrows on his forehead, Rubin's black beard, Spiridon's round face and thick reddish brows, and Sologdin's speech peculiarity. The purpose of the police record is identification, and Solzhenitsyn's detailed descriptions are such that every character is not only vividly presented before us, but is easily recognized—identified—every time he appears. There is still another type of record—the security questionnaire—the contents of which for each character we learn in considerable detail. Answers to questions such as social origin, activity during the Civil War (where applicable), Party status, various occupations, war service, number and location of relatives, friends and associates, lists of addresses where resided—all such questions are answered in the biographies of Sologdin, Spiridon, Nerzhin, Rubin, Pryanchikov, Ruska Doronin, and many others. Solzhenitsyn has transformed the kind of information you find in Soviet police records into a set of variegated individual stories, each one of which is restored its own rights as a private, intimate, individual experience.

At the various levels of this inferno there are a few consolations. Work is one—solving problems, making things. But the matter that can transcend misery is sexual attraction. It needn't necessarily involve any activity, just the proximity of people belonging to different sexes, and the hope or dream of some kind of fulfillment makes it possible to endure either the cancer ward or the first circle. One of the cruellest aspects of imprisonment is precisely its monastic feature, and the heavenly aspect of the first circle of hell is the presence of women. We note that the free workers who have to deal with the prisoners receive a careful indoctrination in inhumanity. They are taught to fear, suspect, and hate them, and for the most part this indoctrination takes effect. The one point of weakness is the sex difference. Serafima and Clara each fall in love with a prisoner, and when that happens human communication suddenly becomes possible. Simochka is a simple girl with nothing in her head that the authorities have not put there. She believes that the prisoners are enemies of the human race, and particular enemies of the Soviet Union, that they are mad dogs in the pay of imperialism and the White House, that they are capable of the most heinous crimes; but she knows also and with complete fervor that there is *one* exception to the rule: her own Gleb. It is almost a pathetic paradigm, a primitive model of true love. And even this reliable vessel of human feelings is fractured in Solzhenitsyn's world. When they are deprived of women, men are also deprived of humanity, of human warmth and human dialogue, and this is the tragic fate of Kostoglotov in *Cancer Ward* who has the grim choice of death by cancer or emasculation by the hormone he must take to cure the cancer. Solzhenitsyn in his treatment of sex and love is far out of phase with the modern accent, and a glaring contrast to his countryman Sinyavsky. He seems to have discov-

ered that normal, heterosexual love unencumbered by complex or deviation is a wonderful thing, and quite suitable for treatment in literature.

There is in both novels a steady contrast between the free people and
the prisoners. With the exception of the wives of the prisoners and the
women who make love to the prisoners, the free people that we meet
tend to be shallow, stupid, and mean, dishonest with themselves and
others, cheap and gaudy in their tastes, or, like Yakonov, the Soviet scientific official, thoroughly compromised in their inner being. The gen-
eralization is suggested that in Stalin's Russia all the decent people were
in jail. The only people whom we hear talking sense are in jail. Anyone
in the novel who ever had an honest thought or did a good deed is in
jail or on the way to jail. Even loyal and convinced Communists—
Rubin is a case in point—are in jail. The Lubyanka functions in the
novel as a kind of evil magnet that drew into its narrow cells in successive periods the best that the country and the Party had produced:
leaders of industry, engineers and architects, bourgeois politicians, almost all the leaders of the Revolution; revolutionaries who fought the
Bolsheviks; Bolsheviks opposed to Stalin; Bolsheviks loyal to Stalin—
all somehow found their way into the interrogation rooms of the Lubyanka. The little interrogation table at which Gerasimovich and his
wife have their meeting concentrates for a moment the long history of
the prison and of the Soviet Union itself:

> This crude little table had a story richer than many human lives.
> For many years people had sat behind it, sobbed, shuddered in
> terror, struggled with devastating sleeplessness, spoken proud,
> angry words, or signed scurrilous denunciations of those close to
> them. Ordinarily they were not given either pencils or pens—only
> for rare handwritten statements. But the prisoners had left marks
> on the warped surface of the table, strange, wavy or angular graf-
> fiti, which in a mysterious way preserved the subconscious twist-
> ings of the soul.

The French scholar Georges Nivat has pointed out that two symbolic
banquets are central to the meaning of *The First Circle*.[2] The first (chapter 53) is the prison feast organized in honor of Nerzhin's thirty-first
birthday, where the fare is scant and simple and the liquor a kind of
prison brew, but around the table made of "three night tables of vary-
ing height and covered with a piece of bright green paper," we experience a moment of pure friendship, total trust, and absolute intellectual
freedom. The second banquet celebrates (chapter 56) the Prosecutor
Makarygin's new Order of Lenin. He has gathered his family and
friends around a lavishly appointed table laden with a variety of rare

drinks and rich dishes, but the conversation is idle and silly, the guests are preoccuppied with flirtations and careers, and thought is restricted to comfortable and predictable channels. The two feasts powerfully contrast the two worlds of the novel, the pure free air of prison and the polluted ambience of "the outside." With a shock of understanding we recall the remark of Alyosha in *One Day:* "Be glad you're in prison!"

Solzhenitsyn's artistic images of a prison sub-culture morally superior in its values to the dominant culture of the outside world received powerful support from a Soviet psychiatrist, Dr. Semyon Gluzman, who was sentenced to seven years in a "strict regime labor camp" for objecting to the police use of psychiatry and stating in public that "psychiatry is a branch of medicine, not of law." In a brilliant essay, "Fear of Freedom . . ." (*American Journal of Psychiatry* 139:1, January, 1982) Dr. Gluzman reports that many prisoners he observed experienced fear and revulsion dampening their joy on the day of their release from prison. Prisoners out of tune with the cultural stereotypes of a sick society were fearful of returning to it and of leaving a social group in which their own beliefs and attitudes were the norm. Apprehension at the prospect of being forced once again into the alien mold of the world outside the prison was, according to Dr. Gluzman, a frequent experience of the prisoner about to regain his "freedom." Such fear was not pathological but perfectly normal.

Sympathy for the imprisoned, we might say, is the reader's dominant recurring emotion, and he is at last ready, almost, to agree with the prisoner, Professor Chelnov, "that only the prisoner really has an immortal soul, but the free man may be denied it for his vanity." The prisoners enjoy many advantages over the free people. They are free to think, to discuss ideas, to know at least a part of the truth. The prisoner has lost everything and therefore has nothing to fear, and the lower he sinks in the prison hierarchy the less he is afraid. But fear governs the lives of the people who live in "freedom." No matter that they've compromised themselves and discredited themselves, the free people still are not free, but live in as much of a trap as the prisoners themselves. The successful writer Galakhov must choose carefully the topics he will treat and carefully select the details to emphasize; Yakonov lives in dread of a return to prison; Roitman is afraid he'll be attacked as a Jew; we are certain that the prosecutor Makarygin and his family will be in deep trouble as the result of his son-in-law's arrest; Major Shikin is obliged to conceal his brutish inefficiency from his superiors by "redoubled vigilance" and constant interrogations; Oskolupov is afraid of Sevastyanov; Sevastyanov is afraid of Abakumov; Abakumov lives in terror of Stalin, who could shoot him without reason and even without notice;

and Stalin himself in his stuffy quarters, old and half sick, is afraid of conspirators, afraid of his doctors, afraid of his enemies, and he doesn't trust his friends. The enormous machine that he has fashioned for purposes of security functions only to produce an atmosphere of terror which he himself breathes.

Over it all presides the morose, brooding figure of that very Stalin, a "gloomy giant" who rules half the world. Solzhenitsyn's purpose in his portrait is to examine the psychic makeup of one of history's great criminals, to explore the rubbish of his mind, to follow its halting lucubrations, to invade its privacy. Solzhenitsyn likes to expose what is hidden from the normal view, to turn up the inside of the cup, to tear the veils from the cancer ward or the *sharashka;* and in his portrait of Stalin he penetrates a whited sepulcher that within was full of dead men's bones and of all uncleanness.

By introducing Stalin as he pads about in his musty little underground—his windowless cell—Solzhenitsyn provides the reader with a viscerally satisfying sense of moral superiority to the Ruler of Half the World, the Father of Western and Eastern Peoples, the Leader of All Progressive Humanity, the Wise Father and Teacher, the Caesar of all Caesars, for whom we feel scorn as for a moral idiot.

The chapter entitled "Phonoscopy" is critical for the novel's moral argument, for it is in that chapter that the prisoner Rubin, who still considers himself a member of the Communist Party, agrees with his jailers to help them run down the criminal. Rubin is one of the best examples of the "captive mind" that we meet in Solzhenitsyn's works. His natural human feelings, his instinctive sympathy for helpless victims of the terror like himself, is smothered by what he calls the "dialectic of history," whose perverse logic frustrated every clear thought, and any human impulse. Rubin hears the voice of Volodin on the tape provided by the secret police: it is a distraught and terror-stricken voice, but the voice of a man who still has the courage to do something decent, and Rubin is deeply moved as he listens to it. But the voice is effectively shut off by Rubin's dialectic, with its set of fixed formulas that are divorced from reality. *If* the Soviet Union is the most progressive nation; and *if* these dull and despicable policemen represent the Soviet Union *at this stage of history,* and *if* they are engaged in the pursuit of someone who *could* harm the Soviet Union; then it *follows* that one must give up one's human feelings and work with the abhorred policemen, which is what Rubin agrees to do. Rubin is impaled on the triple prong of a syllogism: USSR = progress; Police = USSR; therefore Police = Human Progress. But in that syllogism the major premise, the minor premise, and the conclusion all are false, and the responsibility of Rubin, as of so many others who reasoned in that way, for all the human victims, is driven home to us as the chapter ends with the names of the five human beings—the suspects—who are threatened with destruction, each an individual life with its own right to existence: Petrov, Syagovityi, Volodin, Shchevronok, Zavarzin.

The Cancer Ward also deals with the security system, with repression and rehabilitation, but it presents these matters from the viewpoint of a Soviet official who has been deeply involved with "security" during the Stalin period. The highly placed official, Rusanov, is beset by a tumor in his neck which increases in size so rapidly that it leaves him no time to utilize his good "connections" in order to get to a Moscow clinic or arrange for private treatment. He is obliged to enter a crowded cancer ward that he must share with lesser men, whose presence irritates and upsets him. Accustomed to giving orders, indeed to disposing of the lives of other men, Rusanov is suddenly bereft of authority and subjected to procedures that he doesn't understand but must accept because they offer the only hope of life.

There are explicit reminiscences of Leo Tolstoy, especially *The Death of Ivan Ilych* and the moral tales. Tolstoy's Ivan Ilych, when he faces death from cancer (his ineluctable pain), discovers that his former life with its systematized proprieties has lost all value; like him, Rusanov finds that his model Soviet family, his well-organized and useful official activities, his nicely furnished apartment, all seem remote and unreachable, somewhere beyond the great swelling that has become his intimate companion, perhaps his death. But unlike Ivan Ilych, who in the end experiences salvation through relaxing his grip on life, Rusanov holds on with obdurate desperation. A note of factitious optimism is sounded by his daughter, a budding Soviet writer, who visits him in the cancer ward and even in the face of the suffering and certain death that surround her still preaches the official Soviet literary creed of positive thinking: "All right, father, struggle for health! Carry on the struggle, get rid of that swelling . . . and *don't worry about a thing!* Everything, just everything, is going to be great!"

The most striking feature of *The Cancer Ward* is its penetrating investigation of a Soviet bureaucrat's fashion of life and especially of his mind, his interests, his tastes, his view of himself. Through the device of narrated monologue, as we have seen, Solzhenitsyn provides an imaginative re-creation of the thought process, memories, and reflections of a man who, in the interest of state security, has brought ruin to many people and is now threatened (the action takes place in 1955) by the rehabilitation and return of many of his victims. We are given the opportunity of imagining his fear, his guilt, his arrogant self-justification. We experience the dismal amalgam of platitude and prejudice that fortifies him. Oleg Kostoglotov, another cancer victim and an unwilling neighbor of Rusanov, is in every sense his antipode and enemy. Caught up in the police terror of the thirties because of some frank comments on the "Father of Peoples," Stalin, Kostoglotov has spent his whole life in physical exile and moral alienation from the society managed by Rusanov and his collegues. He values neither life nor death, and having nothing more to lose, he has nothing to fear. Kostoglotov may be taken to represent those intellectuals and others who have always stood apart from the official world.

But *The Cancer Ward* has a deeper symbolic meaning in the sense that death and its pain are the central concern of all the characters. Death as the reality that transforms all values is the abiding presence in the story, and attitudes toward it range from the advice of Aunty Stepha, an ignorant peasant woman, who simply counsels resignation before the will of God, to the thoughtful query suddenly introduced by a character who has been reading Tolstoy: "What do men live by?" Only the apparatus-man has an assured answer to this question, and his answer takes the form of an official platitude: "Man lives by his ideology and his social concerns."

Solzhenitsyn's novels form part of a genre with many famous representatives in world literature, one which might be called "the accidental assemblage." Such works feature a strange variety of characters all together in a grievously abnormal situation. They are together because of one exceptional thing held in common: in *The Canterbury Tales* they are all pilgrims, in *The Magic Mountain* they are all consumptives, in Norman Mailer's powerful first novel *The Naked and the Dead* they are ordinary soldiers drafted from a contrasting variety of American environments, in Maximov's *Quarantine* they are held in quarantine aboard a train near Moscow. In *One Day, The First Circle,* and *The Gulag Archipelago* they are all prisoners or jailers, in *The Cancer Ward* they all face death from cancer or work at curing it.

Cancer itself figures in *The Cancer Ward* as a complex many-layered symbol, and its literary function is to reveal a character's attitude not just toward death but toward life. Solzhenitsyn's novel has much in common with Thomas Mann's *The Magic Mountain,* in which the businessman Hans Castorp, an inhabitant normally of the flat German plains, is "promoted," as Susan Sontag put it, to the mountain and to the disease of poetry and sensitivity, tuberculosis. The sanitorium on the mountain is a catalyst where ideas thrive, latent thoughts surface, fixed ideological positions are shaken, and love prospers. Solzhenitsyn's disease lacks, of course, the romantic literary associations of *La Bohème*. The very word cancer is like a knell announcing painful dissolution and a wasting into death. It can have only negative modifiers: morbid, malignant, ulcerous; it has given rise only to awful metaphors. Yet the disease does figure in *The Cancer Ward* as a catalyst of truth in the lives of its many characters, whose confrontation with themselves is revealed in dialogue and narrated monologues of astonishing variety and power. The story of each life has a single overriding climax: everything is reduced to "before" and "after" the tumor. Before that reality all preconceptions are helpless. Almost all the characters are moral illiterates in the sense that they have no answer to the question "What do men live by?" but at least *here* the question is asked and considered. Like Alyosha in *One Day*, they see confinement as an opportunity to think of their immortal souls.

It remains to speak of the "original" version of *The First Circle*, the 1978 Vermont edition, and to explain why, in spite of a basic structural congruence, it is a very different book from the one published in 1968. In the Vermont edition the central character Volodin when he makes his fateful call on Christmas Eve is not inspired by feelings of humanity and pity; quite the contrary. Moved by a holy hatred of the Communist regime, he calls the American Embassy to warn them that certain American scientists are on the point of passing over "important technical details about atom bomb production" to a Soviet agent in "a radio parts store" in New York City. Lev Kopelev, the prisoner who served as model for the character Rubin in the novel, tells us in his memoirs that such indeed was the nature of the conversation overheard by the KGB. However, imitation of reality in the first version robs the novel of that deep sympathy for the pursued culprit which was an ingredient of greatness in the 1968 version. The magnificent scene we examined above in which the prisoner Rubin suffers inner torment over whether to help build the voice decoder loses in the Vermont version much of its power: the still loyal Communist Rubin would have had no problem about helping to catch a traitor to the Soviet Union. Nor has the reader a heavy emotional investment in Volodin's fate: it is part of the ethos of spying that you take certain chances and make the best of your skill or luck, and Volodin uses his high position to gather and betray information of a top-secret nature. Much of the novel's power has been lost, though Volodin's action is motivated by a long disquisition on the necessity for treason against an immoral and tyrannical regime. And there are many other alterations, not all of them happy ones. The portrait of Stalin is embellished by lengthy chapters in which art is diminished and polemic holds full sway. Stalin daydreams about how he will conquer all Europe once he has that atom bomb. And it turns out according to this version that in his early years Stalin was an informer for the Czarist Secret Police against his Bolshevik comrades. Thus an accusation for which the evidence is at best inconclusive—Trotsky flatly rejected it—receives in the Vermont edition the fictional privilege of immunity from cross-examination.

The Vermont version of *The First Circle* is clearly inferior as art to the 1968 edition, which was written with the censorship in mind. We witness here a paradoxical phenomenon not unknown in literary history, many instances of which can be found in nineteenth-century Russia. State censorship obliged a writer to ambiguity, ambivalence, Aesopian language, symbolic structure, and *skaz*, thereby often working to enhance literary quality. Solzhenitsyn's earlier version, written without reference to the censor and published in 1978, suffers from an overtly polemical structure and style and makes its points with less artistic force than does the 1968 version.

The Gulag

The Gulag Archipelago (1973–1975) has no rivals and almost no relatives in literary history. By itself it constitutes a genre, one which Solzhenitsyn called "An Essay in Literary Investigation." It is a historical document based on an immense accumulation of evidence, gathered and fashioned by an artist consciously engaged on the side of Ultimate Good and against Evil. It is one of the profound human epics. The first two volumes chronicle the descent into the nether regions of the Archipelago, the State Penal Camp System, and the third volume presages the upward struggle out of it in tales of brave resistance against impossible odds, of elaborately planned escapes and bloody uprisings in the camps—a series of powerfully written adventure stories in which the stakes are freedom or death.

As an artist Solzhenitsyn can move mountains, and as an artist it seems he was given to the world to demonstrate the classic metaphor of Pelion piled on Ossa. The piling of one mountain of evidence onto another is the structural principle of this, one of the longest books in world literature. *The Gulag* multiplies and elaborates, piles horror on horror, drives a part of the awful truth home, then reveals and elaborates more of it, then discovers still unsuspected islands of mass murder, piling perversion on brutishness on dull-witted crime. The powerful motive that drives the author is his resolve to expose what has been hidden by lies and to reveal the whole truth about the Soviet system. "Our sewage disposal system," the *Gulag* in other words, is an ironic metaphor: in *that* system the clean people were drained off into the underground and the unclean remained on the surface, and his purpose is to upset certain settled views of that process promulgated by the unclean themselves. His true history of that system reveals its origin, its function, and the enormous extent of the territory it drained. Khrushchev in 1956 spoke of Stalin's purge of the party in 1936, 1937, and 1938, and he belatedly beat his official breast over the murder of his old comrades, with perhaps a nod to the few hundred thousand victims who fell with them. But he said nothing about the millions of peasants who had been executed, deported, or done to death when the land was collectivized in the early thirties. And before that thousands had been arrested and sent away or shot in the twenties after trials of Mensheviks, Social-Revolutionaries, "bourgeois" engineers. And is it not necessary to count also the hundreds of thousands who perished in the far North building the totally useless Belomor Canal, people from every walk of life? And before that, how many hundreds of thousands were arrested and exiled during Lenin's time, when the Gulag system was founded. And if you think it's impossible that there should be more millions you are obliged to remember the deportation of whole nationalities, Chechens, Crimean Tartars, Volga Germans. Could there be more? But of course. Consider the Russian prisoners of war returning from German stockades who went directly into concentration camps. Solzhenitsyn proposes to right the balance, to reveal all the unpublished victims. Given the monstrous crimes and the necessity to expose them, Solzhenitsyn can only pile Pelion on Ossa, and woe to any shallow soul who grows weary of the dreadful evidence. Merciless accumulation of detail serves to undermine our normal notions of civilized limit and tears to shreds all comfortable stereotypes.

A device of narration is Solzhenitsyn's characteristic weapon, irony, here woven into the very texture of language. The language of *The Gulag* combines historical chronicle with narrated monologue and inspired, sustained invective. Direct quotations from the theorists and architects of the Gulag are scornfully exposed by written and oral evidence of the truth. Voluminous scholarly footnotes, probably for the first time in world literature, function as a continuing judgment upon liars and murderers who figure in the body of the narrative. It is a rich if harsh language, compact of Soviet camp slang, official opacities, literary resonances, religious intonations, and greatly moving personal statements of admiration, pity, love, and anguish. The effect is similar to that achieved in *One Day*—total immersion in the life of the Gulag, leading almost to the conviction in the reader that he has been through it himself. But here the narrator is Solzhenitsyn himself, hovering over the inferno like an adjunct of God's judgment.

And Solzhenitsyn has developed a theory which, he believes, explains the inordinate dimensions of Soviet evil. The head and source of it, he says, was "ideology," a term which he uses as though its meaning were simple and obvious, as indeed it seems to be to him: "Macbeth could justify his murders only weakly, and so his conscience bothered him. Even Iago was a lamb. The imagination and the spiritual capacity of Shakespeare's heroes was exhausted by only a dozen corpses. *Because they had no ideology.*" But Solzhenitsyn has provided no clear definition of ideology. He is apparently talking about "Marxism," but he cannot mean the thought of Marx and Engels, who are not quoted, nor of Lenin, whose leading philosophical works are seldon referred to, though he is quoted selectively and out of context, or even of Stalin in his voluminous published lucubrations. Solzhenitsyn's use of the term ideology is crudely Soviet, and refers to the complex of notions summed up under the triadic formula Marxism-Leninism-Stalinism, a set of ritual verbalizations known as "the most advanced teaching." What he really means by ideology is the vulgarized and sloganized doctrines learned by rote in the Soviet schools, and ritually repeated in public by Soviet leaders. Andrey Sakharov has argued brilliantly that these are empty phrases, a ritual hypocrisy covering up the real nature of the Soviet state. *That* ideology has as much to do with Marx as the Inquisitor Torquemada's pronouncements had to do with the gentle Jesus. As a matter of fact Solzhenitsyn has demonstrated inadvertently that the root of the evil was not ideology at all but the absence in the Soviet Union, as in Hitler's Germany, of any firmly held set of rational principles—the absence, in other words, of an ideology. This fundamental lack opened the way to systematic perversions of thought. The logic of the Gulag, as of Hitler's Germany, was a madman's logic, the basic procedure of which was the literalization of metaphors. To quote Solzhenitsyn:

> Vladimir Ilych Lenin announced as the one general purpose the purge from the Russian land of all harmful *insects*. And by "insects" he meant not only all members of alien classes, but also "workers lackadaisical about labor."

Lenin's language, apprehended by moral illiterates without ideology, lost, as Solzhenitsyn clearly demonstrates, its figurative nature and became a directive for extermination. Such directives could become fully operative only in the absence of an independent judicial process of some kind, and Lenin himself was responsible for setting up a state system in which, as Solzhenitsyn points out, a single entity operated as policeman, prosecutor, judge, jury, defense attorney, and higher instance of appeal. There was no check, therefore, on perversions of the judicial process in the interest of something called "class justice," nor on the insane syllogisms that replaced judicial logic. Absurd hierarchies of guilt also became possible: guilty, accused, suspected, open to suspicion, arrested—with appropriate sentences for each category. A single mad syllogism dominated the Stalin period: Soviet socialism is the highest form of economic organization; its catastrophic failures, therefore, can only be the result of sabotage.

All of this Solzhenitsyn's *Gulag*, "An Essay in Literary Investigation," has shown us magnificently, and of course it is the function of art to *show* rather than to *prove*. Solzhenitsyn's attempts at argument and proof, especially his attempt to demonstrate that some kind of "Marxist ideology" led inevitably to the Gulag, are largely unsuccessful, here as elsewhere. He is not deeply knowledgeable in the vast movement of thought which led from the empiricists through Kant, Schopenhauer, Fichte, and Hegel to Marx. He comes to Marx not from Hegel but from the Gulag; and that has made all the difference. Alert though he is to Soviet falsifications, he has apparently been victimized by one of their biggest lies, the claim that their repressive and inhuman system is Marxist.

The Calf and the Oak: Dichtung and Wahrheit.

Readers of *The Calf and the Oak* (1974) are fascinated and shaken by its account of a lone writer's courageous, unremitting struggle against one of the powers of darkness, with all its police, its armies and navies, and its thousands of atomic weapons; though the "oak" still stands at the end we know that our "calf," head unbowed and ready to engage the enemy again, is the real victor. David has met Goliath—the comparison is suggested by Solzhenitsyn himself—and while he has not killed him, he has planted a heavy stone in his stupid forehead and exposed the rude creature to scorn and contempt. Many consider this to be the best thing Solzhenitsyn has yet written, and indeed one is tempted to shout, with Vladimir Weidle: "An astonishing, a magnificent book. When reading it you are simply absorbed and cannot tear yourself away. I find no flaws in it. I'm ready to ring out all the bells for it." And Efim Etkind's comment draws attention to its extraordinary linguistic power: "Every new book of this author is a revelation of the Russian language." There are some who deny the historical value of *The Calf* and accuse its author of errors, distortions, and worse, but even they offer tribute to it as a work of verbal art.[3]

The Calf is much like the *Gulag* in that it provides total aesthetic satisfaction simply because it draws upon the primal eldest archetype: the struggle between good and evil, two forces once seen by Milton "in dubious battle" on the plains of heaven. We follow every turn of that dubious, unequal, and shifting battle in the calf's case from his emergence out of the underground (from the deep water, he will say) to deliver that first magnificent volley, *One Day in the Life of Ivan Denisovich*, down to the latest but not yet final maneuver, his expulsion by the minions of evil from the territory of the Soviet Union itself. And of course that territory is always the ground of contention. The story of the struggle in heaven is exactly reversed: here the forces of evil are in control of Russia, which they have turned into a regimented, infernal paradise, and they expel good angels onto foreign territory which they have designated as hell.

The genre of such a deeply archetypal work is difficult to fix. It bears the subtitle "Sketches of Literary Life," but what is there literary about the life of a writer who must hide what he writes from the police, protect every source and helper from the threat of incarceration, squirrel away a magnum opus from all eyes until "the proper time," outwit, outflank, and defeat the enemies of literature, who happen also in the Soviet Union to be its tutors and publishers? The subtitle is of course ironic.

Solzhenitsyn's novels all lie on that uncertain border between history and literature, a disputed area occupied by historians but sometimes contested by novelists. *The First Circle* and *August 1914* deal directly with historical matters and, like Tolstoy's *War and Peace*, introduce real historical characters into the artist's plotted action. *August 1914* (1971) and *Lenin in Zurich* (1975) are parts of a projected multivolume work on the historical destiny of Russia in the twentieth century. The first of these concentrates on the Russian military catastrophe at Tannenberg in 1914, the beginning of her woe, and the second offers, in a masterfully sustained narrated monologue, an acccunt of Lenin's violently dogmatic thoughts on the eve of his return to Russia. *Prussian Nights* (1974) depicts the mindless rapine and murder perpetrated by Russian soldiers in 1945 as soon as they crossed the border into Germany. Solzhenitsyn conceived the work in the camps, where nothing could be written down, so he composed it as a mnemonic device in rhyming couplets.

All of his works, in all genres, investigate, analyze, reflect, and represent the reality of Russian experience in the twentieth century and therefore are historical documents of a special kind. *The Calf* too is located in that border area of which I have spoken, but the historically real personages in it figure as agents in a fateful struggle between God and his enemies, a struggle in which Solzhenitsyn is the chosen instrument of the former. The result is that the people, some of them still living, who take part as actors in this mighty drama play out their parts in it without fully literal reference to themselves as living individuals. This led to understandable outrage on the part of some of them.

The book is aglow with a sense of mission and studded with affirmations of faith in that mission. "Many things in life I did contrary to my own principal purpose, not understanding the true path, but always something set me straight." "And I think that for the first time in my life I saw, I realized that I was making history." "From December to February, ailing though I was and obliged to tend the fire and cook for myself, I completed the first version of *The Gulag* . . . But it was not I that did it. My hand was guided!" "*The Cancer Ward* I never dispatched to the West. It was proposed that I do so and there were channels, but for some reason I refused, and without any ulterior plan. But it reached the West anyway (*sam popal*), and—well, that means it had to, God's good time had come." "God saved me from covering myself with shame." And there are of course prayerful acknowledgements of the true source of his more-than-human strength: "How wisely and strongly dost thou lead me, O Lord!"

Verbal echoes of higher intervention are frequent in *The Calf*. Could it have been an accident that the typing of *The Gulag* took place at his retreat far from Moscow, a place of peace and of tender green called Christmas (*Rozhdestvo*), or that Tvardovsky, the editor, underwent his harrowing experience of truth, the reading of *The First Circle*, during "the three days of Easter"? It is true that military metaphors and analogies are frequent in *The Calf*, but when he speaks of the onward march of those "*samizdat* battalions" there is no doubt that we have to do here with *Christian* soldiers in a holy struggle.

A leitmotif of *The Calf* is the unique human quality of the camp experience. Of Soviet literary men who had never shared this experience he says that all of them, "social novelists, solemn dramatists, and of course all the more the journalists and critics, all have agreed in concert not to tell the main truth, whatever they write about." During his years in the underground the Calf had been convinced that there were many more like himself who knew the truth and could tell it: "The truth consists not only of jails, executions, camps, and exile, but if you avoid those things entirely you cannot write the main truth." The following marvellously moving passage, difficult if not impossible to convey fully in English, reveals the gulf that separated Solzhenitsyn from Tvardovsky and the editors of *New World*, helps to explain the awkward relationship between them, and effectively answers any charge of ingratitude to his publisher:

Of course I was obliged to Tvardovsky, but only for myself. I had no right to consider just my personal interest or what the opinion of me might be on the *New World* staff, but must take as my main premise that I stand not for myself alone, that my destined career in literature is not just mine but belongs to all those millions who never scratched and clawed their way out, never told in hoarse whispers the story of their fate as prisoners or revealed the things they discovered too late in the camps. Just as Troy was not in the least obliged to Schliemann for its existence, so also our buried camp culture has left us its own legacy. And so when I returned from a world which never returned its dead I dared not swear an oath of loyalty either to *New World* or to Tvardovsky, dared not reckon on whether they would see that my head was not a bit turned by my fame and that I was simply engaged in occupying a *place d'armes* and doing it with cold calculation.

The sense of a prior debt to the unjustly dead of the labor camps permeates *The Calf* and colors every moment of the protagonist's struggle. While writing his Nobel acceptance speech he noted that it had been customary for laureates to speak of the nature of art, of beauty, and the structures of literature, but

> to discuss the nature of literature or its possibilities would be for me a difficult and boring treatment of what is of secondary importance: what I'm able to do, that I'll do and show; what I can't do I won't attempt. And if I gave such a lecture, just how would former prisoners react to it? Why was he given a voice and a platform? Was he afraid? . . . Has he betrayed the dead?

Just as in *The First Circle, The Cancer Ward* and *One Day*, the pivot of movement in *The Calf* is contrast and conflict between the *zek* world and the world of those "others" whether camp guards or free and prosperous citizens. It is important to realize, moreover, that the "others" in this work include the editorial staff of *New World*, the journal that found him and published *One Day*. The ex-prisoner from the provinces who still lives in a humble shack is repelled by their ample quarters, which one reached by way of a wide and lordly staircase "suitable for filming in a scene of a grand ball." His honest poverty is insulted by the handsome advance they can offer him: "The advance alone was equal to two years of my salary." Tvardovsky loved him "as a feudal lord loves his best vassal." The protagonist (whom I refer to as the Calf), afraid he will not find time in his life to complete his sacred mission, is always in a hurry, but Tvardovsky's tempos are different: "Now, after our great success [says Tvardovsky] why shouldn't we sit a while, sip a bit of tea with rolls, chew the fat about big things and little?" But the Calf's needs are simple: just to be let alone to do his writing in peace and free of worry about publishers, and to hell with all those unwanted and unasked-for laudatory reviews by respectable figures like Simonov, reviews which are like "the threads of a spider-web" threatening to entangle him and impede him from his true purpose, upon which no Tvardovsky could ever look with favor. Nor was he impressed by the "slavishly exaggerated" celebration of his talents that filled the sycophantic press immediately after the appearance, with Khrushchev's blessing, of *One Day*.

The former *zek* is not obliged to treat those others as equals, and to be open and honest with them could be a fatal mistake. When Tvardovsky managed to get him an interview with Demichev, the head of Agitation and Propaganda, a man whose face showed not a trace of honest human feeling and whose speech was dull and banal, the Calf managed deftly to pull the wool over his eyes: "At first he was watchful and suspicious, but in the course of our two-hour interview he warmed up to me and believed everything I said." Similarly in his informal chat with the secretaries of the Writers' Union he quite frankly lied about the writing of his famous letter to the Congress of the Writers' Union, and they believed and nodded. Not even with Tvardovsky could he be open about his plans and strategies: "I hadn't opened myself to him; the full network of my plans, moves, and calculations had been concealed from him."

Tvardovsky figures in the book as a kind of tragic hero, his fatal flaw symbolized by the red Party booklet he carried in his coat pocket ("next to his heart"), whose conscience is crippled by his commitment to the vile system that rewarded him well. The Calf tried with some success to re-educate the chief of *New World*, and if he never fully succeeded the reason probably was that Tvardovsky had never walked through the purifying fire of the camps:

> My own head had been straightened out by my first years in jail and a similar process had begun with Tvardovsky after Khrushchev's speech at the Twentieth Congress. But, just as in the Party as a whole, the process soon slowed down, then was choked off and even reversed itself. Tvardovsky, like Khrushchev, was in a trancelike (*zaklyatom*) state of lifelong captivity to the accepted ideology.

And if Tvardovsky lacked the fortitude to fight when *New World* was slowly being strangled, the reason was that for such a struggle "Tvardovsky needed that fire-resistant hardness which is cultivated only in the Archipelago of the *zeks*."

Only the camp, only isolation and suffering bestowed upon a human being the mark of authenticity. In one of many great scenes the Calf, with an uncanny sense of novelistic structure, shows the chief of *New World* in a drunken stupor in the course of which, visiting upon himself an exquisite poetic justice, he demands to be treated as a *zek* and asks the Calf to abuse him and give him a tongue-lashing as a camp officer would. It happened in Solzhenitsyn's house in Ryazan during Tvardovsky's visit to read *The First Circle*. The chief was mesmerized by the book as he read it over a three-day period, swilling the while heroic quantities of cognac and vodka. Friends of Tvardovsky have expressed understandable outrage at this scene and at Solzhenitsyn for invading the privacy of an embarrassing alcoholic episode, but he has replied that no one has a right to withhold the truth, and he might have added that in the artistic economy of the book as a whole the scene could not be spared. Tvardovsky had been joking drunkenly about the possibility of being sent to jail himself:

> He kept on joking, but the air of the prison penetrated him more and more as he read, and it infected his lungs . . . The feeling he had that maybe he himself would not escape a sentence showed itself a number of times during that visit . . . He was especially interested in life behind bars and he'd question me curiously: "But why do they shave the heads?" or "Why don't they allow any glass dishes in?" Apropos of one line in the novel he said "If you're going to the stake, then go, but it has to be for something." Several times, without any air or feeling of amusement, he reiterated his promise to take packages to me in jail, but only on condition that I bring things to him if I stayed out. And toward the evening of the second day when it became clear as he read that the jailing of Innokentii was inevitable—and also after three tumblers of well-aged vodka—he got terribly drunk and insisted that I "play" with him at being an "KGB lieutenant," in fact that I shout at him and accuse him of things while he stood at stiff attention . . .
>
> I had to help him undress and get to bed. But in a little while we were all awakened by a loud noise: A. T. was shouting and carrying on a conversation with himself, in a number of different voices, taking the part of several speakers. He'd lit all the lamps that there were in his room (in fact he liked to have all the lights on he could in a room—"it's jollier that way") and he was sitting at the table, no bottle now, in just his undershorts. He was saying pathetically: "I'll soon go away and die." Then he'd give out a roar: "Silence! On your feet!" and he'd leap up at his own command and stand at attention before himself. Then again he'd feel very grieved: "Well, no matter, I can do no other." (Meaning that he'd made up his mind to go to the stake for my fearsome novel).

Thus the chief, who claimed to have discovered Solzhenitsyn and who treated him as a vassal, who had prospered under Stalin and even given his talent to a poetic justification of collectivization, is so shattered by *The First Circle* that he catches at last a momentary glimpse of the prison truth, and is ready, even if only for an alcoholic moment, to accept the stake itself for the sake of that truth. Truly a moving and a pregnant scene, it is the product of a consummate artist who has himself suffered through to the truth and spares no one in his pursuit of it.

The portrait of Tvardovsky in *The Calf*, though it offended his friends and his family, is in fact a brilliant literary achievement. The Calf brings to life an immensely attractive and able human being, a good poet and in his deep Russian heart an honest man, who suffers from the afflictions of intellect and conscience that have resulted, as the Calf sees it, from a long compromise with evil. But Tvardovsky is not totally lost, and the account of his dealings with the Calf is also the story of his gradual evolution toward enlightenment. At first he is shown as a typical bloated Soviet bureaucrat, alien to the streets of Moscow and unable to move about in them except by chauffeured limousine—and he had to have a large limousine, his bulk was uncomfortable in a modest Moskvich. He is often absorbed in familial creature comforts, the purchase of a new *dacha*, for instance, and is a lordly *barin* who hardly spoke to his subordinate editors on the lower floor, regarding the *New World* operation as his own fief. An eminence of power, when he took a train he never had to stand in line with other people to get his ticket. A typical Soviet contradiction in terms: he was a poet decorated with a Stalin Prize. In his social position and in his style of life with all its power and privilege *that* Tvardovsky is hardly distinct from the Party bureaucrats, literary hacks, and successful writers we meet both in *The Calf* and in the novels. But Tvardovsky is radically different from all of them because he had once allowed himself, as we have seen, a breath of the prison air.

It was Tvardovsky's fatal flaw that he was devoted both to the Party and to Russian literature, and it was impossible to serve at one time those two masters. He served Russian literature well by publishing Solzhenitsyn's works, but only at the cost of persuading himself that "there was nothing in them incompatible with the idea of Communism," that, in fact, they were not anti-Soviet works. He even maintained that Solzhenitsyn "took a Party position":

> A Party position—that's my novel he was talking about! Very interesting. Nor was that the cynical formulation of an editor determined to "push the novel through." That confusion of my novel with the "Party position" was honestly and sincerely the only possible method, otherwise Tvardovsky, a poet and a Communist, could not have set himself the goal of publishing my novel.

Clearly the Calf could never open himself fully to his benefactor: "Our orbits were so far apart that we could never meet." He is aware, moreover, that Tvardovsky's false position accounted for his many weaknesses, not least the weakness for alcohol. As he himself is drawn deeper and deeper into the sickening and frustrating struggle with the literary bureaucrats he grows in understanding of Tvardovsky and even sympathizes with his alcoholic excesses:

> As I prepared to break a lance again [with the various "secretaries"] I felt weary and needed to shed that useless, sterile, and totally unnecessary nervous tension that I felt. But how? Take medicine? But there is one simple remedy: a little vodka early in the evening. Right away all edges softened, and I wasn't harassed for an answer or a snappish retort, and I slept soundly. And then I understood another thing about Tvardovsky: for thirty years what had he had except vodka to help him shed that vexing, scalding, shameful and bootless tension? Just cast a stone at him after that!

One of the chief themes of *The Calf* is Tvardovsky's suffering, hesitant movement toward resolution of the inner conflict. Gradually the Calf came to recognize that the chief possessed qualities he had not suspected and that did not fit the image of a Soviet bureaucrat. To the Calf's astonishment he warmly approved the famous letter to the Writer's Union on censorship and other things. "No, I hadn't really figured that man out" is his comment. And evidence begins to accumulate that Tvardovsky is changing. After circulating copies of a second letter of complaint to the "secretaries" the Calf, for a moment doubting and disheartened about the course he had taken, shared his doubts with Tvardovsky, but to his great surprise the chief said he'd done just the right thing: if you start something you should finish it. "Once more he astonished me. What had become of his timidity and all his weary evasions?" And a further reflection in the same context: "How long we'd known one another—and we didn't know one another at all." The deeper into the plot we go the more attractive Tvardovsky becomes. The Calf, with his perfect eye for a scene, pictures Tvardovsky as he saw his visitors off from the *dacha* on a snowy evening:

> A. T. thought he'd like to take a walk and he put on a kind of rough half-length jacket and a cap, took a stick for support—not a very thick one—and in the quiet snow he walked with us to the gate. He looked like a peasant, maybe a just barely literate one. He took off his cap and snow fell on his bright, huge, balding head, the head of a peasant. But his face was pale and haggard. He was heartsick. I gave him a farewell kiss . . . The car moved off and he just stood there in the snow, a peasant leaning on a staff.

As Tvardovsky's evolution proceeds and he moves closer to his downfall and death he not only excites our sympathy as a human being but we see him more and more in his true native context as a peasant from Smolensk, out of place in the lordly quarters of *New World* among his sycophantic staff, one whose Party booklet had been an honest aberration.

Throughout the year 1968 his evolution proceeded apace and we hear of the rapid "broadening and deepening" of views and principles that had seemed fixed forever: "And he was going on fifty-eight! Neither straight nor easy was the path of his growth, but he was moving!" He even got to be interested in Western broadcasts: "And what do you know! We were sitting and chatting and suddenly he jumped up, very gracefully considering his bulk, and caught himself up, quite openly: 'Why we've missed three minutes of it. Come on and listen to the BBC!' Him?! The BBC?!" Soon we find Tvardovsky being called by his patronymic alone, Trifonych, a measure of rapid progress toward enlightenment, the simple life, and intimacy with the Calf. That "Trifonych" has come a long way from the power-conscious literary bureaucrat we met in the early pages of *The Calf.* I would suggest without any attempt at irony that modern literature offers few examples of "character development" more poignant than this account of Tvardovsky during the last years of his life, and the poignance is sharpened unbearably by the fact that the events of the story are intimately involved with our own history and heavy with our hopes and fears. With overtones of agony and grief the Calf unfolds the story of Trifonych's gradual reduction to impotence as editor of *New World,* his forced resignation, and his death. In a scene which Solzhenitsyn, in a footnote, tells us is reminiscent of the defeated and hopeless General Samsonov's farewell to his troops in the novel *August 1914,* we witness Tvardovsky's last words to his editorial staff, even including those on the lower floors who had worked faithfully but with little recognition from Tvardovsky or anyone else. After the chief's departure,

> The members of the editorial board had some drinks in Lakshin's capacious office, sat together for a while, then left. But the small fry couldn't bring themselves to break up on that last day. They anted up a ruble apiece—even some of the authors, the more modest ones, contributed—got some wine and refreshments, and it occurred to them: why not go up to Tvardovsky's office! It was already dark but they lit the lights, set the plates and glasses around and sat down in quarters to which they'd seldom been admitted and never all together. "We're abandoned now!"
>
> No one sat at Tvardovsky's desk but they poured a glass for him and set it down there: "Let's forgive him his unjust persecutions."

The line spoken in that passage is from a celebratory poem on Push-kin's alma mater, the *Lycee,* in which the poet celebrates among others Alexander I, who founded the school and later sent Pushkin himself into exile. The next line, not quoted in the passage, is a profound trib-ute to the Czar, who, whatever else he had done, "captured Paris and founded the *Lycee."* Clearly the minor employee who said that was of-fering honest tribute to Tvardovsky as a man who, with all his faults, arrogant and dictatorial as he was at times, had accomplished won-derful things.

Tvardovsky is a tragic figure, but his associates on the editorial board seem a company of evil grotesques. And it is precisely as a *company,* a band of weaklings and compromisers, that they appear in *The Calf.* Sev-eral pages are devoted to Lakshin, the chief critic, but as a rule he is coupled with the others, and we are invited to feel distaste for the spinelessness or dishonesty of Lakshin-Kondratovich, or Lakshin-Khi-trov-Kondratovich, or Sats-Kondratovich. (Three others, members of board at that time, Maryamov, Dorosh, and Vinogradov, are mentioned only occasionally, and with no particular venom.) The Calf blames them for the failure to capitalize on that golden moment right after the Twenty-second Congress when Khrushchev's campaign against Stalin reached its apogee and radical departures on the part of *New World* might have succeeded. And why weren't any undertaken? "Only be-cause the vital forces on the journal were crushed and the camouflaged puppet show at the top (Sats-Kondratovich) were quick to sacrifice any-thing you like just as long as nobody made any waves or rocked their comfortable boats."

Solzhenitsyn has contrived an aesthetically satisfying structure for the editorial operations of *New World,* one that fits well the overall de-sign of the book. Presiding on the very top floor is a heroic but flawed figure who has been granted a glimpse of the truth but still serves the devil and lies. On the lower floors the work of producing the journal proceeds under the guidance of honest people like Berzer, head of the prose section, and others devoted to literature and to the truth. It is they who welcome the *zek* when he brings them a manuscript and through their crafty intercession succeed in bypassing the editorial board to bring *One Day* directly to the chief, who immediately understands its virtues and knows he must publish it. Between the people on the lower floor with whom the *zek* identifies and the chief sits the editorial board, Lakshin-Sats-Kondratovich-Dementiev-Khitrov, whose function it is to maintain the journal's comfortable compromise and see to it that the chief does nothing "foolish." The pattern faintly suggests an old Rus-sian political archetype: the Little Father Czar is a benevolent force if you can just get to him, but his officials are deceivers and oppressors.

Lakshin in his answer to *The Calf* contended that this picture is a primitive distortion of the facts, then promptly wrecks his case by ascribing Solzhenitsyn's "mistaken" picture to the lies and gossip of Berzer, the prose editor; a curious lapse on the part of a frequently perceptive literary critic.

The Calf is a structure of basic archetypal themes, but the artistic power of the book is an effect also of its carefully fashioned language, a style that perfectly suits the theme of truth in conflict with lies and evil. In this too *The Calf* invites comparison with Solzhenitsyn's work as a whole. What stunned and delighted readers of *New World* when they found *One Day* in 1962 was precisely its language, and Tvardovsky in his Introduction was at pains to explain and justify such a radical departure from normal publishing practice. Read against a background of Soviet socialist realism, the uninhibited conversational style of *The Calf* is a sudden free torrent of truth, a speech full of honest scorn at the faces of evil the ex-prisoner sees all around him. In a wonderfully revealing passage the Calf tells us how he "dreamed of a photo album":

> Some photographer should do an album to be entitled: "Dictatorship of the Proletariat." No commentary, no text at all, just *faces*, two or three hundred self-important, overfed, sleepy but also violent mugs—getting into their limousines, mounting the speakers' platform, looming over their desks—and no commentary at all, just "Dictatorship of the Proletariat."

That passage is a key to *The Calf*, which invites us to contemplate just such a collection of faces, caught at ugly work of various kinds. These pictures are of course created out of language and supplied with a commentary where the dominant linguistic figure is the epithet, in the use of which the Calf exhibits impressive range and resources. I. A. Sats of the editorial board seldom appears without an epithet: "sterile, somewhat boring," "cowardly," "the circumspect Sats." Adzhubey, the editor of *Izvestia*, is "red-faced and supercilious," and Satyukov, the editor of *Pravda*, is "worthless and insinuating." The Calf meets with three secretaries of the Writers' Union to discuss his famous letter: "K. Voronkov (a jawbone!), G. Markov (a fox fresh from a meal), S. Sartakov (an ugly mug but kind of funny)." When the Calf entered the room "Voronkov deferentially swung himself out of his armchair—he had the build of a heavyset bouncer—and draped a smile over the jawbone. For all you knew it could have been one of his happiest days." When all the secretaries and their companion lackeys gather at a meeting to discuss your latest novel they are like an assemblage of dogs, and they bite at your heels. There is the "poisonous" Chakovsky, editor of the *Literary Gazette*, and the "fierce" Gribachev, a poet who writes lyrics about the unity of Party and people. They are "cheats and swindlers", all of them. The repugnant gallery of grotesques includes the face of the venerable and long-established novelist, Fedin, member of the editorial board of *New World* and Chairman, no less, of the Union of Writers. His long life has left the ugly marks of all his baseness and many betrayals (Sinyavsky and Daniel, Pasternak): "In the case of Dorian Gray all of it accumulated on the picture, but Fedin managed to show it all on his face." Pozdnyaev, editor of *Literary Russia*, is "bald, shameless, slippery, and cautious." Not only their faces, but their names also, by some happy poetic accident, are grotesque. At the Sheremetevo customs office the Calf meets one "Zhizhin" and asks himself: "But what has become of the Russian people? We know where they went—they were sucked down into the Gulag. And look what's come to the surface: these Zhizhins, Chechevs, Shkaevs." The name of Ovcharenko apparently suggests a police dog. And the whole crew collectively are nothing but *"plyugavtsy,"* a vulgar epithet of contempt—palely translated by some such English paraphrase as "scummy bastards."

The Calf is loaded with such epithets, studded with popular proverbs and sayings (in fact the Calf refers explicitly to the proverbial riches upon which he draws), and colloquial in its syntax and sentence structure. Its sentences, though not short, tend to be loosely structured. Syntactic inversion, occasional anacoluthon, and casual ellipsis are elements in the structure of an oral discourse so charged with emotion that sometimes it forgets the rules of syntactic clarity. A better vehicle could hardly have been contrived for conveying the Calf's high anger at the very sight of the moral lepers, who, he maintains, dominate Soviet society.

A formidable set of essays sharply challenged the historical value of *The Calf* and even called in question the honesty and humanity of its author. Nor is it surprising that some of the living people who figure among the gargoyles displayed in it have spoken up in their own defense. The historian Roy Medvedev, who receives brief but harsh treatment for his mistaken views, has answered with an essay in defense of Tvardovsky accusing Solzhenitsyn of ingratitude to a number of people who in fact contributed a great deal to his literary career. Medvedev enters a number of corrections into the picture of Tvardovsky and presents convincing evidence both of character and courage in the editor of *New World*. He touches the nub of the matter in trying to make a distinction between Tvardovsky and other card-carrying characters such as Sofronov and Kochetov: "Yes, Tvardovsky was a member of the

Party. But the main lines in the struggle of the 1960s ran precisely between various currents of socialist thought and between different tendencies within the Party."[4] *Da ist der Hund begraben!* As suggested above, the Calf viewed all those card carriers from a galactic distance; in his perspective they merge into a single mass whose disputes over the correct "socialist" path are pointless quibbling far astray from the principal business of humanity. He singles out Tvardovsky alone and presents him as a beautiful human being torn by a tragic contradiction between "ideology" and his best impulses. Solzhenitsyn in that portrait does not break faith with essential historical truth. The friends of Tvardovsky who objected to the dark colors in the portrait betray an expectation that someone they admired and revered will be presented to history as a kind of saint, an icon worthy to hang on the wall beside Belinsky, Tolstoy, the sainted Pushkin, and even, perhaps, Lenin. In other words, the shape taken by this dispute betrays its Soviet provenance.

Tvardovsky's daughter, Valentina Aleksandrovna, sent an outraged open letter to Solzhenitsyn which bitterly accuses him of injustice to the memory of her father, who was responsible for Solzhenitsyn's literary career.[5] She makes in a briefer compass some of the same points made by others: (1) that Tvardovsky did indeed discover and push Solzhenitsyn's works through to publication against heavy odds, and that the treatment of him in *The Calf* is evidence of base ingratitude; (2) that Solzhenitsyn arrogates to himself a special, privileged knowledge of what is true and right; (3) that he rejects absolutely Soviet life and any democratic organization in favor of a return to some earlier patriarchal form of social organization. The last two charges are undoubtedly just, as Solzhenitsyn's later writings make perfectly clear, but what about the Calf's ingratitude? Lakshin and Valentina Aleksandrovna insist on standards of gratitude more suitable to a feudal society or a modern analogue of feudalism than to a society based on intercourse between free and equal men. Solzhenitsyn acknowledges no fealty to Tvardovsky as his lord, master and protector, and why should he? He was obligated only to give Tvardovsky works of high literary quality and to treat him with respect; having done that his debt is fully discharged. Nor did fealty oblige him to soften the contours or touch up the rough spots (of which there are many) in his portrait of Tvardovsky. As a matter of fact the reactions to *The Calf* of Lakshin, Medvedev, V. A. Tvardovsky, and many others betray in the most innocent and unsuspecting manner the effect of Soviet conditioning, of the attitude that the lone individual, having no assured rights in law or custom, has a special need for and owes a sacred debt to his patron and benefactor.

It is an attitude not unknown outside the Soviet Union, in the Mafia for instance, or in certain modern American political or business organizations where the one thing you must have is loyalty to the man who put you in your job. But obviously the accusation of ingratitude contributes nothing to an understanding of *The Calf*, or of Tvardovsky, though one must sympathize with Valentina's indignant feeling that her father has not been presented in the most favorable light, and with Lakshin's urge to defend the staff of *New World*; that journal published, after all, some of the most important contemporary writers: Vladimov, Nekrasov, Sinyavsky, Belov, Bondaryev, Ehrenburg (his memoirs), and of course Solzhenitsyn.

There is one important piece of evidence suggesting that the Calf does less than justice to Lakshin. We recall the many pages given to Tvardovsky's alcoholic episodes and the Calf's final judgment that the strain of his false position in dealing every day with brutish *apparatchiks* was responsible for his excesses and "Just cast a stone at him after that!" But there is no suggestion anywhere that Lakshin or other members of the staff ever felt disgust or strain or sought relief from them in vodka, an omission which I think falsifies history in the interest of literary effect. In the structure of *The Calf* there could be only one tragic hero, Tvardovsky, supported by humble editors on the lower floor— and one lone *zek*.

Whatever the eventual judgment of history as to Solzhenitsyn's greatness, he does bear comparison with the giants of nineteenth-century literature. Like Gogol and Tolstoy he held in his hands the thaumaturgic fire of art, yet he was torn by an inner need to abandon his magic in favor of preachment and prophecy. As an artist Solzhenitsyn can move mountains. But when he abandons art, as in the *Letter to the Soviet Leaders* (Paris, 1974), parts of *The Gulag*, or the Harvard Commencement Speech of 1978, he cannot move a single grain. Like Dostoevsky he felt an obligation to use his power in a high moral enterprise: "Beauty will save the world." And it is clear that his art has served that enterprise.

Other Contributions to the Epic

A powerful contribution to the literature of persecution, denunciation, and imprisonment is V. S. Grossman's *Everything Flows* (1972). Grossman is the author of a number of novels, one of them, *The People Immortal* (1942), a deeply human treatment of the German invasion as it affected ordinary provincial Russians. *Everything Flows* is a mixture of story and commentary on life in the Soviet Union, the system of informers, the crushing of the peasantry, and the debasing of human beings, especially women, in the camps. Grossman is in full agreement with Solzhenitsyn that the source of the evil was Lenin himself. The novel *Life and Destiny* (1981), the second part of *For a Just Cause* (1952), is a stunning treatment of life in the camps and elsewhere.

Lydia Chukovskaya's *Deserted House* (1965) is a poignant account of the terrible effect on the life of a Soviet intellectual of the sudden, unexpected, and unexplained arrest of one near to her. Her *Going Under* (1972) reveals the effect on the writers' community of the Stalinist terror.

A literary treatment of the camp system very different from that of Solzhenitsyn is Varlaam Shalamov's *Tales of Kolyma* (1966–1975). Shalamov is a poet, highly regarded by Solzhenitsyn among others, who survived seventeen years of hard labor in the notorious Kolyma gold fields, a longer and far more terrible experience than that of Solzhenitsyn. Shalamov in his *Tales* is less interested in a general indictment of the system than in registering brief, particular fragments of physical and mental misery, refractions of the world through a mind *in extremis*. The psychological state of a man laboring long hours in the bitter cold is caught in a few lines:

> And I noticed a remarkable thing. Only the first six or seven hours of a long stretch of work were sorely, agonizingly hard. After that you lose your sense of time, subconsciously you attend only to one thing: not to freeze to death. You stamp your feet and swing your shovel and you don't think about anything, you don't hope for anything.
>
> The end of such work is always a surprise, a sudden happiness you never dared to count on. Everybody is quite gay and noisy and for a time it's as though there were no hunger, no mortal weariness.

And since Shalamov is a poet his mind generates a rich series of images. These lines about a river, for instance, express the never-dying hope for life:

> The river was not only the incarnation of life, not just a symbol of life, but life itself. It possessed eternal movement, calm, a silent and secret language of its own, its own business that forced it to run downhill against the wind, beating its way through rocks, crossing the steppes, the meadows. The river left its channel when it was dried out and laid bare by the sun, and in a barely visible watery thread made its way as a thin brook among the rocks, obedient to its age-old duty, but without hope for help from heaven in a saving rain. But with the first thunderstorm, the first heavy

downpour, the river changed its banks again, smashed rocks, cast trees in the air, and madly rushed down that same eternal path.[6]

One of the finest products of the Soviet forced labor system is a novel by Georgii Vladimov (b. 1931), *Faithful Ruslan* (1963–1975), which he began writing in 1963, shortly after the appearance of *One Day*, in the belief that the full story might finally be told. He offered the manuscript to Tvardovsky, who liked it but suggested some revisions. By the time it was finished in 1965 Khrushchev had been overthrown and the word had come down to "cool it on the camp theme." But by that time the novel was widely circulating in *samizdat*, and it was finally published abroad in 1975. The novel's central character is a labor camp guard dog, good at his job, loyal to the "service" and to his masters, capable of high courage and abject love. Somewhat like Tolstoy's *Kholstomer*, where the viewpoint is that of a horse, *Faithful Ruslan* estranges and illuminates camp life by showing it all from the narrowly trained viewpoint of a camp dog. And Ruslan is a noble dog who has acquired sharp expertise in an ignoble profession and who thinks nothing of tearing a prisoner's body to tatters. Man's worst enemy, to reverse the cliché, is here a noble dog trained to do evil. Khrushchev's release of the convict laborers and their replacement by free labor is the great tragedy of Ruslan's life, and he cannot adjust to it.

Everyday and obvious things in the environment are effectively estranged, for instance the statues of the pair, Lenin and Stalin:

> In the middle of the square there was something which Ruslan had also seen at the training school: two men, who were the color of an aluminum feeding bowl and did not move, had for some reason climbed up onto a pedestal and were acting: one, without a hat, had stretched out his arm and opened his mouth, as though he had just thrown a stick and was saying, "Fetch!" while the other, in a peaked cap, was not pointing anywhere but had thrust his hand inside his uniform jacket; his whole look made it clear that whatever was being fetched should be brought to him.

And the behavior of the first group of male and female workers who replaced the convicts is given sharp relief in Ruslan's interpretation of what he sees:

> They were unloading bricks from trucks and stacking them in piles, although they seemed to be doing it very casually and in between other activities, on which they preferred to spend more time, such as wrestling in the snow, lounging around and smoking for an hour at a time, or singing in chorus while seated on logs . . . They took special pleasure in doing body searches on the women,

slapping them on the seat of the pants or the chest, and while they were being frisked, the women roared with laughter or squealed like stuck pigs.

The story is built around Ruslan's suspenseful expectation of the train that will surely bring back the prisoners. An arriving trainload of free workers, whom he takes to be prisoners, is the answer to his hope and dream; he proceeds to guard them, keeping them in straight lines and viciously attacking any who break ranks. And that is the end of him.

The novel not only produces a vivid experience of camp life and provides a commentary on the brutalized conformity of the Soviet system, but it is also a tender dog story. The dog characters we meet—opportunitists, pragmatists, timeservers, cowards, reliable friends, and the noble Ruslan himself, are symbolically human but realistically quite canine.

Eugenia Ginzburg's *Journey into the Whirlwind* and *Within the Whirlwind* (*Krutoy marshrut*, I and II, 1967, 1978) are beautiful and moving accounts of arrests, courts, trials, jails, and labor camps written by a highly intelligent and sensitive woman who is also a literary artist. Near the end of the second volume, when the author/narrator has served out her term and has been released but is threatened again with arrest, she addresses a kind of apology to the reader: "I feel guilty vis-à-vis the reader. This is so monotonous. Here we are again awaiting arrest! Not another round of these nightmares!" She then assures us that though her readers may be bored at the endless iteration of horror, she herself was not: "The second arrest is far more terrifying than the first, and the third is worse than the second. Yes, by the time you have tottered as far as the seventh circle of hell, the first seems utter paradise." But of course we are not bored for a moment, even though we know the essentials of the grim labor camp story from Solzhenitsyn's voluminous *Gulag* and Shalamov's *Kolyma Tales*. Her first volume tells of her arrest in 1937 and sentence to ten years imprisonment on a charge of "participation in a Trotskyist terrorist" counterrevolutionary group. Thanks to her own tough vitality and, paradoxically, to sheer amazement and curiosity about the hideous world in which she, a loyal member of the Party, found herself, she survived these years and set down her observations. The second volume tells of the remaining years of her sentence, her tender love for the prisoner Anton Walter, who became her second husband, her own release while he still had more years to serve, and her efforts to build a home near Anton's prison camp, an island of family intimacy always threatened by arbitrary rearrest and the renewal of misery.

The two books taken together place Ginzburg securely in the Russian company of superb creators of autobiographical literature, writers who are able to transform the rude facts of history into artistic structures. Ginzburg's work possesses, moreover, a dimension of personal tragedy absent from most members of the genre, in that she experienced her eighteen years in hell as an expiation of guilt, though not for the crimes the state charged her with. She tells us in her first volume that at the time of her first arrest in 1937 she had "never had the slightest doubt as to the rightness of the Party line"; she would have "died" for the Party; she supported fervently "the programs of industrialization and collectivization"; and on the eve of her own arrest she was dutifully repeating, as a Party activist and educator, the fabricated official account of Kirov's assassination. The sadistic interrogators and brutish jailers who surprised and horrified her in 1937 already by that time had long practice in tormenting and murdering people: peasants uprooted from the land and charged as kulaks, suspected Mensheviks and "wreckers," Trotskyites, not to speak of suspected "speculators," "diversionists," "bourgeois nationalists," and many other enemies. As a loyal supporter of the Party she and others like her bore a heavy share of blame for all the innocent victims, and in the chapter of the latest volume entitled "Mea Culpa" the author acknowledges the operation in her life of a mysterious justice:

> These two words are easy to hear during sleepless periods, when you look back on your life with loathing, when you tremble and curse. When you can't sleep, the knowledge that you did not directly take part in the murders and betrayals is no consolation. After all, the assassin is not only he who struck the blow, but whoever supported evil, no matter how: by thoughtless repetition of dangerous political theories; by silently raising their right hands; by faint-heartedly writing half-truths. *Mea Culpa* . . . and it occurs to me more and more frequently that even eighteen years of hell on earth is insufficient expiation of the guilt.

The vivid portraits of prisoners she met fill in many details of the tragedy. The choice of victims and allotment of sentences seemed random and irrational, and attempts to figure out the Gulag system she compares to "playing at chess with an orangutan." Yet a kind of rough-hewn pattern does emerge from the evidence she gives. The political prisoners accused of the most heinous crimes against the state and the Russian people tended to come from the Soviet intellectual establishment of the twenties and thirties: a famous Sinologist, who hanged herself in the camp; a highly placed German Communist from Berlin; a former professor of language and literature; a former civil engineer from Leningrad; a student from Kiev; the *daughter* of the once famous critic and publisher Voronsky; an engineer with a talent for literature; an authority on Mandelshtam, Elena Mikhailovna Tager; many former Soviet officials or their wives; the artist Vera Shukhaeva, who knew Modigliani and Léger; and many others. The prisoners tended to be intellectuals and members of the Soviet privileged class (we note that when Ginzburg went to Moscow to be interrogated concerning possible criminal Trotskyist connections she was quartered in a downtown luxury hotel and was taken to her sessions in a chauffeured limousine); their jailers were almost all recently and barely educated peasants or workers, moral illiterates full of hatred for these alien types who had once "eaten caviar by the spoonful" in hungry and miserable Russia.

Ginzburg is a superb observer and narrator, and the method of her art is to fashion scenes and characters charged with symbolic meaning. The slave-labor system violated the spirit of law and justice, but its administrators were fanatical sticklers for the letter. This book contains many examples of fixation on the external form, and their meaning reaches well beyond the camp system itself. Floors must be kept shiny and clean in the filthy and suffocating barracks housing the children of the convicts: "the whiteness of the floor was the one criterion of hygiene." A peasant woman who became a doctor in the era of women's liberation and proletarian advancement is very proud of her "permanent wave and her magical ability to write prescriptions in Latin." For every death in the hospital where she worked the documentation must be in order. At the top of each page instead of "History of the Illness" one should have written "History of a Murder," but no one had the courage for that. On one occasion eighteen women were kept sitting in an open truck "frozen into virtual unconsciousness" because someone was late in processing their documents. (As a character in Bulgakov's *The Master and Margarita* remarked: "Lose the document and you lose the man.") The director of the Elgen State Farm had been semieducated as a Soviet philosopher, and his lectures on theoretical questions were letter-perfect: " 'Pride' was always qualified by 'legitimate'; 'glory' had to be 'unfading'; 'patriotism' 'life-giving.' " He knew his way around the philosophical categories. " 'Theorizing' always went with the damning epithet 'naked.' 'Rhetoric' was 'bombastic,' and 'empiricism' had inevitably to be 'creeping.' The ultimate symbol of *literal* reliance on the letter is the camp commandant Timoshkin stubbornly teaching himself to write so he can compose official documents: "When it came to doing the written work in his correspondence course he used to drive me crazy with questions as to how to write this or that letter."

The camp system was beyond the law but it set great store by mimicry of legal procedures, and these instances of careful adherence to the letter by illiterates tell us much about the Soviet system itself. Ginzburg would not agree with Solzhenitsyn that Marxist ideology is responsible for the excesses of inhumanity she records. Nothing in the heads of the policemen, interrogators, commandants, jailers, and guards can possibly be dignified by the word ideology. Ginzburg exposes for us a set of minds whose philistine prejudice and narrow hatred were supported by "the inertia of set phrases," most of which had no relationship whatever to Marxism.

The minutiae of death and suffering that the author selects for emphasis are often metonymies containing in themselves the whole experience of camp life. The milk provided by the camp mothers lacked nutritive value because it was "acidulous from their grief." When the author is assigned to a poultry farm (a heavenly assignment) she finds that the traditionally harmless fowl have been transformed by hunger into violent thugs: "One enormous feathered monster, resembling a Tsarist general, perched on my shoulder, whence he subjected me to insufferable insults." In this country of death an agreeable job was the gravedigger's. It even carried certain privileges, and of course there were tricks to the trade: when the corpses were too many one simply buried them in the snow, and in the spring they would be "borne away with the freshets." We are reminded here of Shalamov's story about American lend-lease bulldozers used in the Kolyma fields to scrape up unburied corpses into a mass grave. Once a hospitalized prisoner, thought to be dead, was taken to the morgue. The mistake was discovered when he was heard groaning under a pile of corpses, and the prisoner was severely reprimanded for being where he had no right to be: a trivial episode which contains the whole—inhumanity, irrationality, crowded quarters, the thin line between the living and the dead, inefficiency, and brutish stupidity.

An underlying motif of this work, and here it reminds us of *The First Circle*, is the persistence of human love and its toughness even in the most unfriendly environment. Wherever men and women are together in the camps tender relationships appear in spite of awful inconvenience and the danger of lethal punishment if one is caught: "You might end up paying for the date with your life." One such liaison was discovered when an informer observed a horse tethered during working hours, and the lovers were punished by solitary confinement for "relations between a male and a female convict involving a horse standing idle for two hours." The author herself falls in love with Anton Walter, a doctor of German ancestry sent to prison because he had talked to a foreign scholar who had also talked to someone accused as a Trotskyite terrorist; and the history of their affair is love poetry of the first order. When she was released and given the opportunity to leave the area of the gold fields for a relatively civilized place of exile, Ginzburg elected to live near the camp in Magadan, where Walter was imprisoned, and to bring her teenage son Vasya (the novelist Vasily Aksyonov, now living in the United States) from central Russia to live with them there. Their "house of cards" in the shadow of Kolyma, threatened though it was by informers and the unpredictable actions of the secret police (chess moves of the orangutan) provided them with a haven and even a measure of family happiness.

With this second volume of her memoirs Eugenia Ginzburg records the completion of a former Communist's spiritual education. Her first volume ended with a pious hymn to the Party. In spite of her own suffering she felt the conviction that after the disgrace of Stalin "the great Leninist truths have again come into their own in our country and Party." *Within the Whirlwind* ends on a humbler and soberer note:

> I want to reveal to the reader the heroine's spiritual evolution, the gradual transformation of a naive young Communist idealist into someone who had tasted unforgettably the fruits of the tree of the knowledge of good and evil, a human being who amid all her setbacks and sufferings also had moments (however brief) of fresh insight in her search for truth. It is this cruel journey of the soul and not just the chronology of my sufferings that I want to bring home to the reader.[7]

14 The Surface Channel, I: The Village

The relationship between clandestine and exile literature on the one hand and that published in the Soviet Union on the other is a complex and fascinating question. It would be a mistake to dismiss official literature as beneath our attention just because it is published under censorship and careful guidance. Solzhenitsyn in *The Calf and the Oak* tells us that he had once thought all authentic Russian literature was underground and free of control, and that he seldom read the censored pages of the Soviet literary journals. He later modified that opinion and ruefully admitted that genuine literature—not much, it is true, but some— was still being published above ground. And he came to regard the authors of "village prose" as on a level with if not surpassing Turgenev and Tolstoy in their portrayal of the peasantry and in the native richness of their language.

Sinyavsky has pointed out that it is a gross oversimplification to treat uncensored and censored Russian literature as distinct entities, one free to tell the truth, the other not, or, as Yury Maltsev puts it, free to tell only a "permitted" truth, a lie in other words. The situation in Russian literature is actually much more interesting than that. The very existence of uncensored literature has, Sinyavsky believes, obliged the government from time to time to make concessions, to allow certain talented writers a measure of autonomy. And uncensored literature, widely read in the Soviet literary community, has had a measurable influence on certain authors, encouraging them to undertake risky and even heretofore forbidden themes. This practice may partially explain the publication and wide readership of Rasputin, Trifonov, Shukshin, the novels of Okudzhava, and many other things. With his usual clarity, Sinyavsky was able to cut through the simplistic nonsense we have sometimes been offered on this subject:

> So it turns out that the literary scene has become more varied and more complex, and all of these complications, these shadings and transitions oblige us, here in the emigration, to regard with the greatest possible attention whatever is happening in literature there, in the homeland. For it is precisely there, and not here, as I believe, you will find the source of that future renewal of literature which we must aid and encourage in every way possible.[1]

Solzhenitsyn put it more sharply and provocatively when he said in an interview with the BBC: "Not in the emigration, with its luxury of so-called free expression, has literature been successful, but in our homeland, stretched on the rack."

Beginning in the late 1950s the Russian village and rural themes entered the main stream of literature and inspired some of the best writing of the twentieth century. The resurgence of this theme was not surprising since the peasant as an object of literary treatment had once been a staple of Russian literature, beginning, in the late eighteenth century, with Radischev's idealized toilers bent under the yoke of serfdom. The nineteenth century opened with Karamzin's famous sentimental story of "poor Liza" whose master betrayed her honest love, and the peasant was a major concern of Turgenev, Dostoevsky, Tolstoy, Chekhov, Bunin, and Gorky. Yet the nineteenth century, the great age of the novel, as Donald Fanger has pointed out, "shows us not a single significant novel of peasant life";[2] the twentieth century, in contrast, offers a series of highly significant works, both in prose and in verse, some of which I shall examine in detail. Obviously the difference between the two centuries is connected with the revolutionary upheaval and increased interest in "the people," but the chief reason for the difference would seem to be that in the second half of this century a number of writers, some of them close to peasant life, attempted to give us an account of that life from the inside. Nineteenth-century studies of the peasant, in contrast, were written for the most part by intellectuals who observed them from an aesthetic distance. The narrator of Turgenev's *Hunter's Sketches*, for instance, is an educated gentleman with a poetic nature and a romantic outlook whose preconceptions tend to filter out negative or unpleasant features in the life he observes.

An exactly opposite system of selection and emphasis guided Chekhov near the end of the century in writing his story "Peasants," in which the picture of peasant life after emancipation is unrelievedly dark and violent. Chekhov's work represents a later stage in the evolution of the intelligentsia's attitude toward the peasant; both he and Gorky are symptomatic of the incursion into Russian intellectual life of Marxist ideas concerning the superiority of the urban proletariat and the primacy of industrialized centers, and both writers tend to offer evidence in support of Marx's famous obiter dictum as to "the idiocy of rural life." In any case we still have to do with a literary attitude toward the peasantry, their image as cultivated by educated Russians.

Treatment of the village in Russian literature of the Soviet period, especially in the thirties and forties, told us little about peasant life but much about the concern of the Party and the regime with the "peasant question." At that time the overriding mission of literature was to justify collectivization and celebrate its triumphs. A classic of its kind was Sholokhov's *Virgin Soil Upturned* (*Podnyataya tselina*, 1933–1959), which does present a part of the truth in harrowing scenes of peasants brutally uprooted from their land, but in the end blames the trouble not on the policy of the regime but on local "deviationists" and infiltrating bourgeois agents. Tvardovsky's *Muravia Land* (1936) is a verse epic in which the peasant in search of the promised land of happiness and plenty finds it only when he gives up his old ways and joins the collective; the poem won a Stalin Prize in 1941. Typical of roseate novelistic depictions of collective farm life were Semyon Babayevsky's *Knight of the Red Star* (1948) and its sequel *Light over the Earth* (1949), upon which Stalin Prizes and other honors were lavished, only to be withdrawn some years later when it was discovered that both works crudely distorted the harsh reality of rural life. The disgrace of Babayevsky was a symptom of radical change in the policy of the Party toward the rural sector. No impediment was offered to the publication in the late fifties of Valentin Ovechkin's sharply critical sketches of Party mismanagement on the collective farms, and Yefim Dorosh's *Village Diary* (1958–1963) introduced some of the basic themes of "village literature": reverence for traditional peasant culture, respect for peasants as individual human beings, and merciless exposure of oppressive bureaucratic managers. It is important to realize that the thematic emphasis, not only of Ovechkin and Dorosh but of Zalygin, Abramov, Rasputin, and Belov, writers of major stature, were never at odds with the announced program of the Party to decentralize authority on the farms, end bureaucratic management from distant urban centers, encourage local initiative, increase investment in agriculture, and improve the quality of rural life. Even the modern enserfment of the peasants was ended when in 1976 the internal passport, in however modified a form, was restored, giving them limited mobility within the Soviet Union. Village prose when it raised all such issues was in no sense a protest literature, and it would be a mistake to suppose, as some have, that its publication in *gosizdat* was ever the result of misunderstanding or negligence on the part of the censorship.

The village writers were important also as evidence of an evolution in Soviet ideology itself. They represent a departure from the traditional Soviet Marxist view of the peasant as a cultural and economic inferior to be forcibly drawn into socialism by the urban proletariat. That doctrine provided the ideological justification for the collectivization program, which was instituted by directive and largely implemented by proletarian agitators from the city. All such Marxist and pseudo-Marxist ideology is either refuted or ignored in village writing of the sixties and seventies, a fact which has been taken as evidence of the "weakened hold of Marxism-Leninism since World War II."[3] The point should not be missed that the unopposed publication of such writing in *gosizdat* argues that, at the time, ideology had lost its hold even at the highest level.

The earliest practitioner of village prose, Solzhenitsyn, treated peasant characters and traditional Russian values in both *gosizdat* and *samizdat*. His *One Day*, published in 1962, with the support of Khrushchev and as a matter of high policy, features a prisoner with a characteristically peasant name, Ivan Denisovich, one whose speech is studded with popular proverbs and peasant locutions, a man from the Russian village who is above all a skillful and devoted worker. Clearly Solzhenitsyn's first officially published novel raised issues that would be pursued in village prose, and it is reasonable to credit that explosive piece of writing with a measure of influence on a number of writers.

Matryona's House, also published in *gosizdat*, expanded and deepened the treatment of the village. The narrator of *Matryona's House* had been obliged to spend many years "beyond the Urals," and as the story opens he is trying to find his way back to his roots in the central Russian forests and fields. The ex-prisoner is especially sensitive to language, and after his long exile among aliens he yearns for the unspoiled idiom and intonation of Russian speech. Assigned at his own request to a settlement in the interior, he finds that the forest has been cut down and the land dug up for peat, and that Soviet industrial development has polluted the environment and nearly obliterated the old village. A kind of industrial gloom hangs over the area. Even the language has been violated by foreign-sounding monstrosities like the typically Soviet new name of the settlement: *Torfo-produkt* (Peat-product). "Turgenev never knew it was possible to put together something like that in

Russian," the narrator reflects. New-fangled acronyms, jargon, and propaganda are spoiling natural speech rhythms.

But not entirely. The railway line is the source of evil in the story, the purveyor of modernization, and the scene of a tragic accident, but if one moves far away from the line deep into the interior one escapes the peat works and finds that "first there is a hill, and beyond it the village of Talnovo that's stood there for ages ... And beyond that a whole realm of villages: Chaslitsy, Ovintsy, Spudni, Shevertni, Shesti-mirovo—more and more remote, far from the railway, way off toward the lake." The narrator is calmed and soothed by their very names. He finds Matryona in Talnovo, and the suggestion has been made that she symbolizes Mother Russia, since the root of her name is the Russian word for mother. Her cottage is the negation of modernity and proper philistine taste, and she herself is a kind of saintly icon. A horned goat lives with them, mice and cockroaches inhabit the walls, and the structure is alive with the noise of these harmless natural beings who "do not lie." The cottage is not only close to nature, in fact it is in a state of dissolution on its way back to nature. Matryona speaks a pure Russian without modernisms, and her intonation suggests the teller of fairy tales. But Matryona, who never wanted to own anything, is destroyed by the savage urge of her relatives to acquire property. The central episode in the story is the dismantling of her cottage and the destruction of Matryona herself in a railway accident. The narrator's refuge from the encompassing gloom has literally been torn asunder.

In his *Studies and Brief Stories*, published abroad in 1964, Solzhenitsyn develops many of the basic concerns of village prose. Those *Studies* are a series of lyrics in prose which convey with great felicity of language Solzhenitsyn's feeling for nature, for Russia, and for some undefined existence, a being of some kind, immanent in the universe. These prose poems deal with the beauty and mystery of nature ("Lake Segden," "The Duckling"); they suggest the wonder of creation itself ("A Storm in the Mountains"); they express a personal loss in the death and disappearance of great poets—Sergey Yesenin, a poet of the Russian village, "who looked around amazed and found so much raw beauty" ("Ye-senin's Birthplace"); they speak awesomely of the beauty created in the past by human beings and plead earnestly for its preservation ("The City on the Neva"); and one of them ("A Journey down the Oka") conveys a sense of the historical and architectural ambience of central Russia, a beauty defined by churches: "Our ancestors put their best into these stones and these belfries," says Solzhenitsyn, "all their knowledge and all their faith," but now this precious Russian heritage has been desecrated. Some of the churches have been locked up, others turned into clubs where propaganda meetings are held: "We will achieve high yields of milk!" Concern for preservation of the Russian cultural heritage is, as we shall see, a basic theme of village prose.

Finally, the novel *The First Circle* contains in the autobiography of the prisoner Spiridon a long narrative reminiscent in both style and substance of the best officially published rural prose. In a masterful example of quasi-direct discourse, or narrated monologue—Spiridon's own idiom embedded in the author's third-person narrative—the tragic experience of a peasant in the Soviet period is given to us from his own often uncomprehending viewpoint. The narrator's voice seems to merge with that of Spiridon, while at the same time maintaining a distance for wonder and pity at the trials he has suffered. Some of the most effective rural prose, as we shall see, is cast in the form of narrated monologue. Translation of such passages is often impossible and always precarious, but it is worthwhile to attempt an English version of Spiridon's story which, in beautifully nuanced narrated monologue, curiously distances and estranges the mighty events of recent Russian history.

> Night after night the life story of a single grain of sand—a Russian peasant—unfolded before Nerzhin, a peasant who was seventeen the year of the revolution and already past forty when the war with Hitler began. What niagaras had dropped on him, what immense surges had ground away at the ruddy head of Spiridon . . .
>
> When [in 1918] they announced the land was the peasants' he rushed back to the village, took a section for himself. That year he and his mother and his little brothers and sisters, they all really bent their backs and by Annunciation they had their bread. But after Christmas the city began drawing down on that bread a lot— give us more, more! And after Easter Spiridon was going on nineteen and they tried to grab him up for the Red Army. But he had no intention of going into the army and leaving his bit of land, so he and some other lads went off into the forest and there they were "The Greens" ("don't bother us, we won't bother you"). But then it got hot for them even in the forest and they went over to the Whites (the Whites turned up there but not for long) . . . But as a rule the Whites stuck to the old ways, like under the Czar. He fought a bit for the Whites, captured Red prisoners (they didn't resist much, gave themselves up). Then the Reds shot their White officers and ordered the soldiers to take the white cockade off their hats and put on red ribbons. And Spiridon stayed with the Reds until the end of the Civil War . . . Once on Shrovetide they shipped him to Peter [St. Petersburg] and on the first week of Lent they marched right over the sea on the ice and took some fort there. And after that Spiridon managed to get home.

Clearly Solzhenitsyn belongs to rural prose in his frequent cultivation of Russian peasant themes and often in the manner of his prose, and it is therefore not surprising that in answer to a query by correspondents for the Associated Press and *Le Monde* as to the character and quality of *gosizdat* literature the list he give of the fifteen writers he considered "the nucleus of contemporary Russian prose" included ten of the ruralists.[4]

Since it is obviously out of the question to present a detailed analysis of more than a few of the ruralists, I have selected for special attention three writers, Abramov, Belov, and Rasputin, whose work is not only typical of the genre but offers human context and literary value far above the temporary or topical. Probably not all readers will agree with this selection, and for the sake of completeness I shall mention and place in perspective other members of Solzhenitsyn's list. One of the most important is Vladimir Soloukhin (b. 1924), a writer of peasant origin whose poetry has received high praise, and who was one of the first writers to turn to the Russian provinces for character and situation. *"Back Roads of Vladimir District"* (1957) is a lyrical account of a returning native's journey on foot into the deep interior of central Russia, and of the natural beauty and peasant life he found there. Soloukhin is an enthusiast of old Russian icons and of ancient churches, the wanton destruction of which he deplored. He is himself a collector of icons and the author of *Letters from the Russian Museum* (1966), a book concerned with the art of the icon which contains also an impassioned plea for the preservation of religious architecture and gives a searing, desolating account of the many churches torn down to make way for ice cream stands or movie houses or worse: "The Church of the Savior was the tallest and the most majestic building in Moscow. It was visible from any part of the city . . . It formed, together with the Kremlin ensemble, the architectural center of the city. But they tore it down. Built a swimming pool. In Budapest alone I think there are at least five hundred such pools, but not a single architectural monument has been damaged." Soloukhin is perhaps the most respected and certainly the most eloquent spokesman for a nationalist viewpoint; among irreplaceable Russian values he sometimes seems to include the Russian religious heritage.

Sergey Pavlovich Zalygin (b. 1913) has received a State Prize for literature, as well as high praise from Solzhenitsyn, who said that his novel *On the Irtysh* (1964) is "one of the best things to appear in the fifty years of Soviet literature." That novel deals with the forced drive for collectivization in a Siberian farming village in 1931, and exposes, in the story of a peasant who is loyal to the regime and is a leader in his community, the basic inhumanity and the ghastly stupidity involved in the process. Chausov, the peasant, earns the lethal enmity of the authorities by his energy and independence, and in the end they take his farm away from him and send him into exile. The injustice and wasteful cruelty of collectivization is a recurrent theme in the works of village writers, as we shall see. Boris Andreevich Mozhaev (b. 1923) published his novel *From the Life of Fyodor Kuzkin* (1966) in Tvardovsky's *New World*, and it received a share of unfavorable notice. In telling of Kuzkin's suffering as a collective farm worker, Mozhaev manages to draw a harrowing picture of everyday village life. Victor Petrovich Astafev (b. 1924) primarily works in short prose forms, and his principal theme is the difficult process of growing up in the harsh circumstances of village life.

A powerful impetus to the literary cultivation of the village theme was Fyodor Abramov's essay entitled "People of the Collective Farm Village in Postwar Prose," published in *New World* (no. 4, 1954). That essay, a kind of companion piece to Pomerantsev's earlier (*New World*, no. 12, 1953) diagnosis of "insincerity" as the deep malaise of Soviet literature, extends that diagnosis specifically to the treatment in prose of the collectivized village. Roseate literary pictures of happy rustics collectively transforming the backward village into a mechanized land of milk and honey Abramov deplored as a cowardly deception, and he indicted such novelists as Babayevsky, the recent recipient of a Stalin Prize, for "varnishing" the reality of collective farm life, and avoiding its real problems. Although he was taken to task severely for that essay by the governing board of the Union of Writers, who in their turn officially deplored his "pessimism" and his "mockery of writers who . . . emphasize progressive phenomena in the life of Soviet peasants," Abramov's career was not adversely affected, and he occupied the Chair of Russian Literature at Leningrad University from 1956 to 1960, when he resigned to devote full time to writing. It should be pointed out, however, that Tvardovsky was later removed as editor of *New World* for publishing Abramov's essay, and for other "mistakes."

Abramov's powerful story *Beating About the Bush* (1963), which actually hovers on the genre boundary between the sketch and fictional narrative, raises in a short space the persistent problems of life on the collective farms. The story is told in the reflections of the chairman of a collective farm in a northern village as he makes the rounds of his poverty-stricken neighbors in an effort to enlist volunteers to bring in the hay. The collective farm chairman, Mysovsky, is a devoted Communist with a history of activity as an agricultural leader going back to the early days of collectivization. As in many other works of village prose the implication is present that forced collectivization in the thirties was the origin of present trouble. This thought becomes explicit in the chairman's memories of himself as a young man just demobilized from the Red Army and assigned to collectivize one of the northern villages. He remembers how he "descended on the village council like an eagle, in a long cavalry cloak and a red-starred helmet." They "turned the whole village around," just he himself, and the village chairman, a half-literate "Red partisan," in forty-eight hours. And they had to: the rule in the regional committee was "complete collectivization in forty-eight hours or give us back your Party membership card." So they did it. If a peasant did not want to sign up they terrorized him. "So you don't like the Soviet power. You're in cahoots with the class enemy." That is how they enlisted the peasants. "And suddenly the thought entered his head, maybe that's why it's so hard now, because it was so easy then."

The collective farm in Mysovsky's charge is in a state of deep trouble, the concrete details of which appear in the chairman's visit to a number of households. He meets an old widow whose only son had "disappeared for talking too much" (*propal za slovo*) and who gains her daily bread by begging. Alcohol has disabled some of the best workers. Stealing from the common fields is a regular thing and he can do nothing about it. Malingering is widespread, but "how can you prove it?" The best and most prosperous peasant is one who produces for the market on his private plot and pays little attention to the *kolkhoz*. And yet any chairman who rewarded private effort would be accused of "antistate practices! Encouraging the private sector!" One of the peasants he asks for help with the haying wants to know why the collective farm workers are not given passports and therefore are not free to leave. (It was many years later that the government ended the near enserfment of the peasants by issuing them passports.) As it turns out, the chairman's long day of explanation and persuasion among the peasants had been an exercise in "beating about the bush," but at the end of it in a moment of drunken euphoria he promises them a share of the hay that will enable each family to keep a private cow. That was the real point: on mowing day they turn out in force and take in the abundant harvest in record time. Mysovsky can expect a severe reprimand from regional headquarters, but he did get the hay. The story can only be read—and indeed it was read—as a powerful plea to encourage private motivation on the collective, and to eliminate dictatorial interference by higher authority not in touch with the realities of peasant life—in other words, to undo in some measure the damage done in the thirties.

Abramov is the author also of a multivolume novel which traces the fortunes of a peasant family during World War II and the period after the war up to the death of Stalin. That novel, *The Pryaslins* (1975), is a powerful depiction of peasant character and customs, and in a number of effective portraits emphasizes the resourcefulness and strength of individual peasants in dealing with calamitous events of various kinds.

Vasilii Ivanovich Belov (b. 1932) was, like Abramov, a native of the Vologda region, which is the setting of his novels and stories.[5] His short novel *The Usual Thing* (1966) revealed extraordinary power in the sympathetic treatment of nature as the setting for the toilsome and often tragic lives of highly resourceful Russian peasants. Without skill and toughness no human could have survived in the harsh winters and short summers of northern Russia, and Belov communicates in this novel, and in other stories and essays, a deep respect for the farmers and workers who carved a life out of that cruel northern forest, and, armed only with axes, fashioned beautiful wooden structures of every kind. The hero of *The Usual Thing* is offered as a "typical" peasant: he is an ordinary collective farmer, somewhat undisciplined, prone to vodka and foolish drunken scenes, but a solid and loyal worker who is dependable in the pinches. Ivan Afrikanovich was a refreshing contrast to the crudely idealized peasant types of Stalinist rural novels, but it would probably be a mistake to understand Belov's starkly realistic scenes as evidence of a dissident posture. The social message here concerns the evil effects of arbitrary and illegal methods when employed in government dealings with the peasant, a message not at odds with innumerable contemporary official directives. Ivan suffers because he "is not his own master" because his own initiatives to increase production are rejected by central bodies out of touch with the land. Yefim Dorosh wrote a perceptive and favorable review of the novel in which he pointed out that, in fact, "under the recent reforms ... the collective farm must treat Ivan Afrikanovich with as much interest and respect ... as does the author, Belov."[6] That message is reiterated with great artistic power in everything Belov (who was a member of the Party) has written.

His *Carpenters' Stories* (1968) touches the sorest spots in the life of the peasants, especially their relationship to the city in the form of forced collectivization with its blind cruelties and devastating effect on the peasants' community. The narrator and observer of the village malaise is a native who has left the country for the city and now returns for a brief vacation at his old homestead. He has "twenty-four days not counting Sundays," and he hopes in so brief a period to recover something precious that had dropped out of his life. The deep affinity he feels with country scenes and country life is in his case, and perhaps in that of most returnees in village prose, only an aching nostalgia for the time of his own boyhood, when just to be alive was rapture. It is his youth he remembers rather than village life itself: "We were constantly hungry, even when we slept, but life still seemed fine and joyful. And our life in the future seemed even more wonderful and joyful."

The future as he finds it is nothing like that. The story of the village is developed in a series of conversations with two old men who are polar opposites and have been enemies all their lives. As he develops a sharp contrast between these two characters the narrator touches the still festering wound of forced collectivization. Olyosha is a generous, warm, and hard-working peasant, a good farmer and a fine carpenter. He is direct, honest, at times even naïve, and he has no skill at self-promotion. His enemy Aviner had always been a trickster and a schemer and was never on close terms with hard work. During collectivization he became a favorite of the local Party boss, took an eager part in desecrating churches, urinating once from a steeple after throwing down the cross, and as a village activist fastened on each of his neighbors one of the vicious trio of epithets "poor, middle, or kulak," and lent a busy hand in uprooting those labelled as "kulaks" from the land they had worked. The deepest tragedy of Olyosha's life is bound up with collectivization: his great love, Tanya, was the daughter of a local "kulak," and he had lost her forever when the family was loaded on a boxcar for the long exile.

Belov brings great artistry to bear in contrasting the two old and apparently irreconcilable enemies. Olyosha speaks in an unspoiled peasant idiom studded with poetic figures and rhyming proverbs; Aviner's speech has been contaminated by degraded bureaucratic jargon: "personal pension," "readership cadres," "MTS chief," "passed a resholaoshun," "sploitator and burzhui," and many others. Aviner considers only personal advantage and narrow material gain; Olyosha is a rustic philosopher concerned with the ultimate questions of human life: "You take a man, he's living, and all of a sudden he up and dies. How, I ask you, can you explain that? . . . There was a man and now he isn't. What became of him?" By far the most important item in the inventory of contrasts is Olyosha's skill as a builder and his devotion to making a structure out of wood and stone that will stand straight and endure. There are passages that describe with loving detail the joint labor of Olyosha and the narrator on the rebuilding of a bathhouse. Belov's persistent theme is the value and dignity of peasant labor, which he sees frustrated and insulted by alien organizers and collectivizers whose version of progress threatens to obliterate priceless cultural values.

The action of Belov's *On the Eve* (1976) is set in that same northern agricultural area in the year 1928, when the Stalinist collectivization program was being introduced. The novel shares with *Carpenters' Stories* essential thematic and structural features. The contrast between Olyosha and Aviner is repeated here in the enmity between Danilo Pachin, and indeed nearly all of the working peasants in the village on one side, and a Party member and activist, Ignakha Sopronov, a weak, worthless, and evil character.

Sopronov is a misfit, a poor creature held in contempt by his neighbors and not esteemed even by his comrades of the local Party cell. His days and nights are busy not with productive labor but with hatching plots and writing denunciations, the latter couched in the pseudo-Marxist set phrases of the period: class enemy, kulak, vigilance, proletarian cause, and the like. He hates the whole community but the special object of his venom is Danilo Pachin, a substantial peasant who owns all of three cows, and Danilo's son Pavel, who is engaged at the time in building a mill much needed in the village. Sopronov engineers the denial of voting rights to Danilo after labelling him a "kulak," and those rights are restored on the order of President Kalinin himself, to whom Danilo complained in Moscow—an implausible intervention *ex machina* out of tune with the sense of the novel as a whole. In a grotesque scene Sopronov materializes in the church near the altar at the wedding of Pavel, announcing that he has been sent there by the local executive committee. "You're sent by the devil" one of the peasants answers, an opinion shared by the peasant community, and one which fully infects the reader. Unsuccessful in his effort to disrupt the wedding, Sopronov declares a "general meeting" to discuss, among other things, "Aid to the Chinese Revolution," and he reads to the assembled wedding guests a resonant declaration on the subject of international proletarian solidarity, a typical document of the period here reduced to absurdity.

In several narrated monologues Sopronov reveals the psychology of the abused outcast who can never forgive his humiliations, and who has found in Party work a means of vengeance on his abusers:

> He didn't forget . . . that they all, taking turns, used to beat him, Ignakha. All of them, beginning with his father and ending with his drunken comrade Mitka. And he could never even forget all the other injuries: how he worked as a barge hauler and not even the local girls would give him a tumble. It was then he swore he'd never go back to the village. But he came back all right. He'd showed them all what he was really like, and he'd show them again a thousand times. He was ready to die for the proletarian cause. They'd find out who Ignakha Sopronov was. He'd found himself a career. He'd go anywhere the Party sent him, he'd do anything for the Party . . . We'll see who'll get the upper hand. They know Sopronov even outside this district. Because Sopronov is harder than

all these phony local Communists. They're the ones, they're the ones who've betrayed the Revolution. They'd get to know Ignakha all right, every one of those bourgeois toadies and sneaks.

Sopronov is moved by sheer hatred to destroy the Pachins and a long list of others whom he labels as kulaks, anti-Soviet agitators, or traitors, and his frequent denunciations addressed to higher authorities are a startling revelation of how the Soviet purge actually worked. Belov has provided important literary documentation of that process in the depiction of a convinced informer.

Pavel Pachin, the diametrical opposite of Sopronov, is immersed in the life of the village, an eager participant in traditional village entertainments and games, and above all a peasant for whom work is both a delight and an object of devotion. The mill he is building is a sweet dream and felling the tree for it involves the whole community as an instance of spontaneous collective labor, a form of assistance rewarded by a communal feast complete with drinking and traditional singing provided by the builder. Felling the majestic pine tree which will provide the lumber is one of the high pleasures of Pavel's life; every skilled movement in the process of cutting, notching, and sawing the leafy giant is dwelt upon in loving detail. Labor is poetry, love, and even religion; fashioning a solid structure is in itself a rich reward for the peasant. But Sopronov manages to poison the joy of labor when he announces that as a mill owner Pavel will have his taxes trebled.

The affliction visited upon the village appears in this novel as the work of outsiders employing for their purpose village ne'er-do-wells. As the novel opens the chairman of the Shibanov village Soviet, Mikulin, an easygoing chap more interested in vodka and love than in civil matters, receives from district headquarters a sternly worded order on the implementation of Party policy. The directive is signed by one Meierson, a person alien to the peasant ambience. The members of the local Party cell participate neither in village labor nor in the traditional life of the community; they too are outsiders, and one (Luzin) is a "former worker" who represents the authority of the proletariat and the city. Through such an agency and guided by Sopronov's denunciations the secret police carry out their terror in the village, arresting Prozorov, a radical since his college days and a philosopher whose crime is that he is a "former nobleman," along with the local priest, even though he is bedridden and harmless, and others accused as enemies. Once again, Belov expresses pain and sorrow at the destruction of Russian village life by an alien force.

On the Eve is a tragic and terrible book, but, as in all of Belov's writing, the dominant note is lyrical, especially in the treatment of nature, the animal world, and the peasant community. Nature descriptions are frequent and have reminded some of Turgenev, but Belov's evocation of a rural scene is always linked, either directly or by association, with peasant life, and especially with labor. Belov is a marked contrast to Turgenev also in that the latter figures in his own narration as an observer distinct both in attitude and language from his peasant characters; Belov's narrator is himself immersed in peasant life, in rapport with peasant culture, and through the device of narrated monologue he embodies even in his own narrative passages the rhythms of peasant idiom.

Valentin Grigorievich Rasputin was born (1937) in eastern Siberia in the region of Irkutsk, a locale which is the setting of all his important work. That work, perhaps the most powerful exploration of the peasant experience ever published in *gosizdat*, draws upon and develops the tragic life experience of individual human beings and gives us in their own simple thought patterns and their own peasant idioms the reality of a hard life and sometimes harder death. In fact death is a constant concern of Rasputin, the death of a single peasant, as in *The Last Days* (1970) or *Live and Remember* (1975), or even the death of a whole peasant community, as in *Farewell to Matyora* (1976).

One of his first successes, *Money for Maria* (1968), is a terribly poignant story of a peasant woman, uneducated, inexperienced in trade, and barely able to read, who is prevailed upon to take over the management of a collective farm supply store after several former managers, accused of misfeasance or embezzlement, had experienced the full ferocity of Soviet law. Weak in arithmetic, Maria kept her accounts quite casually, and turned up at inventory time with a shortage of 1000 rubles. Draconian Soviet law and its brutal administrators make it certain that she will be taken away to prison unless the money is found. There is never any doubt of that; the idea of "extenuating circumstances" is never once raised. The plot is built around her husband's efforts to collect enough money to cover the shortage and save Maria from a jail sentence. There is a kind of dim nostalgia in this story, as in so much of village prose, for the lost community life of the village, and regret over the invasion of the country by the city and the money culture. Neither Kuzma nor his Maria readily grasp the reality of "one thousand rubles." "Old rubles or new rubles?" they ask, and such a sum in new rubles is beyond comprehension. A related theme is the absence of contact and understanding between city and village. Unable to raise enough in small loans from his neighbors, Kuzma at last takes the train for Moscow to seek help from a brother who left the village for a prestigious and lucrative job in the city. The brother has more than enough to help, but Kuzma and he have been estranged for years, and it's not certain that he will welcome the country relative. Since there are only first-class tickets available on the train, Kuzma makes his way to that compartment, where his appearance causes consternation among the well-dressed urban clientele of the best accommodation. Kuzma is eminently recognizable not only by his clothing and gait but by the "country aroma" he carries with him, and the conversation of the urban passengers betrays distance, alienation, even hostility toward the village as a "backward element," even though one of them does acknowledge that "we all eat their bread." Kuzma regards his rich city brother and the first-class passengers, themselves the sons and grandsons of peasants, as "slices severed from the loaf." The story ends when he is about to knock on his brother's door, and we never know whether his brother saved Maria from prison or not.

The Last Days tells of a very old peasant woman who is on the point of death. When her children arrive to say their farewells she comes to life again, even tries to get up and go out with them, as though given a new hold on life. The children feel cheated: here they have come all this way, left their jobs and their businesses, and now look at her—not dying at all. They leave her abruptly, and on that same night she dies, crushed by the cruel indifference of her own brood. Not only have they consigned her to the grave, but they have trampled upon the old traditions of household and family, which are also dying.

Live and Remember is the story of a peasant woman, Nastyona, whose husband Andrey deserts from his unit at the front and makes his way back to the village. Caught in a trap from which there is no exit for either of them, Nastyona hides him, feeds him, loves and cares for him, and is soon pregnant with his child. Her pregnancy at such a time is a cruel irony, since they had been childless for the four years of their marriage.

Nastyona is the central character in the novel and it is largely in her thoughts and in the narrative of her vicissitudes as an orphan that we experience the Siberian countryside, life on the collective farm, the privations of the war years, and her final agony of love and deception with Andrey. Memories of collectivization, while not organic to this novel as they are to Belov's *Carpenters' Stories*, or Abramov's *Beating About the Bush*, are still in the near background and ready to appear at any moment. Nastyona had wandered homeless after the "hunger year" of 1933, when her father had been killed. "He was killed accidentally. They were shooting at somebody else, but they never found the one that did the shooting." Events long enshrined in official Soviet histories are related objectively as items of misfortune still alive in the peasant memory: the campaign against the White general Kolchak, for instance, during which some "strange bearded men," called "Partisans," came to drag out of his hiding place in the cellar a relative who had fought on the wrong side.

Nastyona met Andrey during her wanderings and he took her home with him to his small village as his wife. They were happy at first, but her failure to conceive clouded his life, especially since Andrey held her solely responsible for it. As a woman she suffers from the coldness and unconscious contempt revealed in Andrey's treatment of her, but she is an exemplary wife and worker, accepted as such by Andrey's ailing mother and aging father, and she loves her husband. The war came, Andrey was called up, and the burden of all the household and collective farm labor fell upon the women and the old men. When Andrey returned as a deserter Nastyona's full devotion as a wife and worker was given to him, in a situation that could only result in death for him and death or unbearable disgrace for her.

The two chief characters in the novel are a deserter and a wife who aids and hides him, both outlaws of the worst kind, but the story is told exclusively from their point of view and with deep sympathy for the mortal bind in which they are caught. Desertion was a major problem during the war, and Andrey reflects that there were "thousands like me" roaming the deep countryside; Rasputin's novel is a striking departure in that it enters sympathetically into the experience of one of them. Andrey, wounded three times, is certain that after his final, severe wounds he will be sent home, but after three months in the hospital he is ordered back to the front. Rasputin has an uncommon gift for realizing the soldier's viewpoint and his totally unheroic experience of war.

The soldier who had once accepted his lot, who like every other soldier had considered himself a "hopeless goner" (*chelovek konchenyi*), now cannot accept the dashing of the sudden hope offered him for survival and return home. His desertion is unintentional, almost involuntary: he would just go home for a while, then go back, but the trip home took too long and by the time he reached his village no return was possible. He was a deserter.

Nastyona first suspects his presence when an especially valuable, well-made axe disappears from a hiding place in the bathhouse known only to the family, and it is in the bathhouse, traditionally the place of mystery, magic, and meetings with the devil, that she finds her own outlaw, Andrey, and arranges to conceal him from the good people of the village. Banished from intercourse with human beings, Andrey in his lonely animal life comes to behave like one himself, howls like a wolf, kills a calf in full view of its mother then covers the evidence with leaves "like a bear," visits a mill that once had many pleasant associations for him, then suddenly feels an urge, which he resists, to burn it down. Andrey's experience is that of a man really lost to the community but still irresistibly drawn to it, unable to believe in his own fate, sometimes hoping against hope, then utterly despairing and destructive when the truth comes home to him. The psychological impasse is skillfully analyzed and presented in his case as in that of Nastyona.

One Soviet critic naïvely points out that in Rasputin's narration the "author's voice" is never sharply separated from that of the characters but seems to merge with each of them, and the critic complained that the author's own position on the issues agitating his people is therefore unclear. That observation is certainly valid, and it focusses on the principal source of Rasputin's artistic power. The dominant in his style is quasi-direct discourse, where the narration is carried out from the viewpoint of a character. The result is a striking and powerful refraction of the third-person narrative through the psychological and at times linguistic idiom of another human being. The effect of this narrative method as used by some authors, Solzhenitsyn for instance, is ironic, but in Rasputin's case quasi-direct discourse has the effect of immersing both the author and the reader in the life and thought of a given character. Near the end of the story Nastyona, who knows that her criminal deception of both her neighbors and the state will soon be discovered, rows out on the Angara for what may be her last meeting with Andrey:

> She rowed slowly, the oars taking their toll after a day's use: her arms ached and her back was stiff and prickly from the same repeated movements. The murmur of the smooth surface broken by the boat was pleasing to her ears—it was soft and melodic, like tiny drowning bells. The second sound, the heavy squeakiness of the oars breaking the water, came from her labor. From the middle of the river she could see far and wide, and everything rocked and blended into one—the cottages, forest, sky, the sowing up on the hill, the shore, everything seemed unsteady, and under everything, there was only a washout and emptiness. High in the sky above the Angara, a black dot, a hawk, soared, setting its sights on something—and for the first time in her life Nastyona pitied the predator: it didn't get its daily bread the easy way, either. Lately, Nastyona felt that she had no right to criticize anyone at all—no man, no animal, no bird, because each lived his own life, which was not in his control and which he could not change.

If there is a clear message in *Live and Remember* it is given in Nastyona's experience of sympathy for all sentient beings, each caught in a world he never made. For her the predatory hawk is her own deserter husband, Andrey, whom she loves to the end.

Farewell to Matyora (1976) deals masterfully with Rasputin's persistent theme, the tragic impact of industrial progress and unbridled urbanization on a peasant community still rooted in the past and fatally attached to ancient and decaying buildings, old artifacts, animals, and fields, and to the old methods for securing and continuing life. The village of Matyora, situated on an island in the upper Angara River, will be flooded and disappear forever when the river waters back up behind the huge Bratsk Hydroelectric Dam, one of the most massive water-power projects ever undertaken anywhere. The action of the novel is set during the last days of Matyora; the inhabitants know their fate, and preparations are already afoot to destroy all structures and move the remaining peasants to a new, urbanized settlement on the mainland: "So it turned out you didn't need to go to town any more. The town has come here itself." Read in the context of journalistic and even literary celebrations of the Bratsk engineering triumph—Yevtushenko's famous poem "The Bratsk Station," for instance—Rasputin's novel has the effect of shifting the focus of attention to the project's real cost in the dislocation of human beings and displacement of cultural values. Whether he intended it or not, Rasputin's Matyora might be understood as a microcosm of Russia itself undergoing the experience of forced industrialization.

The several characters represent three generations and at least as many distinct experiences of the approaching catastrophe. Andrey, the eighteen-year-old grandson in the family which is the narrative center, tries to understand the feelings of his elders, but is glad to be leaving the old farm and is straining "like all the young ones" for the "front line" of industrial construction and a job on the very hydroelectric project which will inundate Matyora. Andrey is full of Soviet wisdom on the broad horizons and unlimited possibilities of "Man," and somewhat haltingly intones prose poems to the radiant future. There are several modulations on the theme of the young ones who go along cheerfully with the decision to "liquidate" Matyora. Petrukha, so called because he is ridiculous and worthless, sets fire to his own house in order to speed his compensation payment, leaving his old mother without a place to live. His remarks about the need for change (he "spits on the old ways") and his oratorically lengthened intonation of the word "life," suggest a budding Soviet bureaucrat, and as a matter of fact the higher authorities do single him out for special commissions.

A tragic contrast to the young ones are the old women of the village whose viewpoint dominates the novel. Those old and near death refuse to accept the passing of their native and habitual haunt, an event they dimly understand as a figure of their own deaths. As a matter of fact death is the underlying theme of the novel; concern with the ultimate and universal experience raises it well above the temporary and topical. The pathetic relics of the village are like the unwelcome and sickly old people whose departure from the scene everyone secretly hopes for: "You can't let old age drag on. No one needs it." The narrative is so devised that a reader experiences the ancient Darya's thoughts and reflections as his own, and sympathizes totally with her attachment to the fields she has mowed, the weathered house she has lived in, and even to the cemetery where she had hoped to join her forebears for a final rest. Not even that place is sacred to the alien builders who invade Matyora. Before the waters rise the grave markers and the crosses must be leveled and disposed of, and one of the most moving scenes in the novel is a confrontation between the village old people and a crew sent in to perform that desecration upon the only place left that links them to the past, and to religion. The official in charge of the operation explains that they are acting according to a "special resolution on the sanitary cleaning of the entire floor of the reservoir," but the villagers see only the fallen crosses over the graves of their fathers and grandfathers.

Darya questions her grandson Andrey's belief in the omnipotence of Man and his vast horizons, and the debates between them offer a touching contract between youth and age. Andrey doesn't understand why she "feels sorry for Man," and she answers that "people have forgotten their place under God." And again:

> Man thinks he's master of life but he lost that mastery long ago
> . . . He ought to take the time to turn around, hold her back, slow
> down a bit and take stock of what's still there and what's been car-
> ried away by the wind. But no, he makes it worse, he tries to drive
> her on and on! That way he'll overstrain himself. He's overstrained
> himself already.

Rasputin's novels are published in *gosizdat*, and we must assume, given all the evidence we have as to officially induced inhibition in writers, editors, and publishers, that many things it might have said are either not explicit or not said at all. A much earlier disruption of peasant life, collectivization during the thirties, is seemingly taken for granted, in fact the *kolkhoz* figures here as a kind of idyllic entity soon to be displaced by the state farm. Violation of the peasants' religious feelings is a regular feature of Soviet life, and though Darya is clearly a religious woman, she never mentions a church, so we must assume that churches have either been destroyed or converted to secular uses, a matter that Rasputin would surely have commented on had he not been writing for *gosizdat*. The drunken and crooked Petrukha is clearly carving a career for himself and may go far in the regime, but that is only hinted at here. Rasputin has produced a beautiful and moving story about the human cost of industrial progress, and as such it is a vital work; the characteristic Soviet features at work in Matyora are not ignored but muted.

Vasilii Makarovich Shukshin (1929–1974) was a man of varied and brilliant talent whose prose writing should be included with the village writers, though he is very different from them in his thematic range and versatility. He was a film director, the author of film scripts, and an accomplished actor as well as a writer of prose. His collected works are published in enormous editions and the film made from his novella *Snowball Berry Red* (*Kalina krasnaya*, 1973) was awarded the highest state prize. He is that rare phenomenon, an original and powerful writer with a broad popular following and the complete support of the regime.

Shukshin's stories deal with a variety of experiences in Soviet life and they are peopled by characters that never fail to amuse us whatever the danger, extremity, or hopelessness of the situation in which they find themselves. Even in the presence of relentlessly approaching death his characters manage to be innocently absurd. Comedy in his work cohabits intimately with tragedy, as in the story "How the Old Man Died" where the dying man refuses chicken soup, which is good for him, but asks for half a glass of vodka, "the best medicine." "It might make you worse." "Don't matter, as long as it quickens my blood some." Or in the story "Bird of Passage" where a very old man with every imaginable ailment, ulcers, cirrhosis, heart disease, kidney failure, and the like, continues to drink vodka, enjoy the sunsets and the coming of spring, and still wants a little more life: " 'I'm not afraid,' whispered Sanya, hurrying because his strength was leaving him. 'I can face it . . . But just another year . . . then I'll face it. After all you must accept it. But it can't just happen like this. This isn't an execution. So why now?' "

Shukshin's typical protagonist is a peasant in deep trouble, usually as the result of an effort to assert himself against the constraints of a safe and settled way of life. As Michel Heller puts it: "His hero is a Russian *muzhik* in search of freedom." That hero is often also an illiterate philosopher, concerned about questions of life and death and the meaning of both. In a number of embodiments he is a criminal, a convict escaped from the camps, as in the story "Stepka," or a talented thief just released after a long term, as is Yegor in the famous story and movie *Snowball Berry Red*. Shukshin offers us an account of what might be called the criminal personality: a young man, for instance, who rejects his village, his job, his mother, even his old and faithful dog to go off restlessly in search for *something else* ("Front View and Profile"); another with a handsome face and a penchant for unpredictable stunts, both good and bad, who "never wanted to have a wife and family like I'm supposed to" ("The Bastard"). The hero of *Snowball Berry Red*, Yegor Prokudin, tries after his release from the camp to go straight. He seeks out a simple, charming peasant girl who had corresponded with him while he was a prisoner, but he is so entangled with the city gang that it does not work. "Once in, there's no out," would seem to be the dismal message. Yegor's story offers a tragic complication in that he had once sought freedom from the land in the lawless city gang, then realized the emptiness and the constraints of that life but was unable to break free of it. And the story ends with Yegor's death: "There he lay, a Russian peasant on his native steppe . . . Not far from home . . . He lay with his cheek to the ground, as though listening to something only he could hear."

**The Surface Channel, II:
Variety of Theme and Style**

The City: Intelligentsia, Women, Workers

Yury Trifonov (1925–1981) has written a number of works which deal with the Soviet way of life in what might be called the urban upper middle class. He encompasses an astonishing variety of characters and situations and he is a faithful recorder of Soviet speech as well as a master of novelistic structure. *The House on the Embankment* (1976) lays bare with a subtle and pitiless irony the emptiness of life among the middle and upper intelligentsia, a people without inspiration, ideals, or firm principles. The central character is one Vadim Glebov, whose first steps in a successful career as a Soviet critic and essayist are described from his own viewpoint, and in his own self-serving but transparent idiom. Trifonov has such mastery in the presentation of the thoughts and words of the "other" that we are led, not to sympathize with Glebov, who repels us at every turn, but to understand perfectly his inner "struggle" over a terrible choice that confronts him very early in his career and torments his "conscience." It is an impossible dilemma, and it seems to him there is "no way out." Should he join in a scurrilous campaign against the professor whose protégé he had once been and by so doing guarantee his own advancement? Or should he refuse to take part in the official fabrication, expose the charges as absurd, and thus lose all possibility of a lucrative career? The choice is unbearably complicated by the fact that he is engaged to the professor's daughter, Sonya, through whom he had hoped to become a participant in Professor Ganchuk's rich life with all its perquisites. And Sonya really loves him.

Through every page of inner lucubration, careful weighing of complex arguments and trying out of various scenarios, Glebov finds no firm ground for a clear choice. Finally he gives a mild assent under pressure to the charges against Ganchuk of "Menshevism," "kowtowing to the West," "undervaluing materialist philosophy" and the like; "of course Academician Ganchuk, with all his good qualities ... but there were, as a matter of fact ... some negative things ... As Ganchuk's student he had of course not attached great significance to them," and so on. He never remembered exactly what he had said. As for Sonya, he was convinced that she would understand the nature of his "terrible dilemma." "That was the best thing about her. She had always been understanding."

Glebov did receive a coveted fellowship, and his career prospered. We meet him late in life as an aging but comfortable, even honored, intellectual figure, the Soviet representative to an "International Conference of Literary Specialists and Essayists" in Paris. He had made a systematic effort to root from his memory all images of those difficult early days and had largely succeeded, though a few scenes remained ineradicable, one especially: Ganchuk calmly eating a chocolate eclair in a pastry shop on Gorky Street right after the meeting at which his reputation had been destroyed: "But just half an hour ago they'd been trying to murder that man. Yes. There were a lot of things he could tell ... one thing and another, this and that, things better not remembered. Yet Ganchuk stood there and ate an eclair with great relish."

The moral and artistic issues would have been simple and the lineaments of injustice clear had Trifonov represented Ganchuk and his party as noble and guiltless victims, but here Trifonov introduces a profoundly human and genuinely tragic complication, the nature of which is adumbrated in the title of the novel. *The House on the Embankment* carries a symbolism that would not be lost on a Muscovite. That enormous, luxurious apartment building on the Embankment, near one of the bridges over the Moscow River, towers over that section of the city like a great granite metropolis sufficient unto itself. Since the early thirties it has housed the cream of the Soviet elite: officials of the NKVD, ministers of various commissariats, honored writers and members of the Academy, the Secretary of the Moscow Party Committee and others of like dignity. Its walls carry more than one plaque dedicated to the memory of favored one-time residents, provided they have not been purged as enemies. In that house the Academician Ganchuk occupied a spacious and richly appointed apartment on a high floor, one coveted by his student Glebov, among others. While there is no explicit mention of the fact, tenure in that building had always been precarious, as one wave of honored occupants moved out into the shadows to be replaced by others. Ganchuk himself had a history of eager participation, not only in the Revolution and the Civil War, but in the lethal ideological battles of the twenties and early thirties. Something of a bore on the subject, he constantly regaled Glebov with stories of mortal struggles against deviant figures in the intellectual life of those days. He himself had been merciless against the Bogdanovists, Pereverzevites, Bespalovists, and the followers of other fallen and forgotten figures of the twenties. Speaking of one of the repellent philistines now attacking him, Ganchuk explained him as a kind of nemesis: "He should be thankful he didn't fall into my hands in 1920, I would have taken him apart like a counterrevolutionary! That was the cardinal error. The petit-bourgeois element was scotched but not killed . . . And now . . . they're coming out of their holes."

Ganchuk, and Trifonov through him, no doubt provides here a partially accurate capsule analysis of Soviet intellectual and social history, and the novel includes a number of scenes in which illiterate but profoundly Russian students express their contempt for learned and bespectacled professors adept in various non-native terminologies. But Ganchuk, now suffering at their hands, is himself a compromised figure. He has been, in 1949, the victim of just such polemics as he had earlier used against others, though the intellectual and moral level of the discussion has fallen catastrophically, and now the consequences could be fatal. The result of this essential irony in the structure of the story is that while we find Glebov utterly repellent as a human being, we see him as part of an intellectual environment in which clear and objective moral standards have given way to an almost universal opportunism, an early stage of which was the repetitive use against opponents, by Ganchuk himself, of politically opprobrious but meaningless labels.

Trifonov's social message and his deep moral concerns are conveyed with great and sustained artistry. Chronological narration is abandoned for a system of flashbacks and anticipations in which the behavior of a character at any given moment is given perspective by reference, for example, to boyhood escapades in which his quality of cautious opportunism appears unmasked. Once Glebov had agreed with some comrades to attack and humiliate a contemporary but at the last minute decided not to take part but watch from a safe distance. Later, under extreme pressure it is true, he gave the victim's father, an NKVD officer, the names of the attackers. The account of Glebov's rise to eminence in the academic world is framed, so to speak, by opening and concluding scenes set in 1974. The first presents a chance meeting with an old comrade fallen on evil days who refuses to speak to him; the second, the penultimate scene in the novel, shows Glebov settling into a hotel room in Paris in preparation for learned meetings at which he will represent Soviet scholarship. In the novel's final scene the author himself, writing a book about the twenties, seeks out Ganchuk to interview him on matters the professor had been deeply involved in. Someone had said the old man was still alive. But Ganchuk, now eighty-six, has lost all interest in that period of his life, reads only the latest things, and watches television. The novel ends with the expression of a historian's melancholy over the almost total disappearance of all witnesses to those "semilegendary days."

Trifonov's novel *The Old Man* (1978) takes up again the moral problems confronted in *The House on the Embankment* and in some earlier pieces. In the later novel Pavel, an old revolutionary in his seventies and in rapidly failing health, makes a last effort to discover the truth about an episode of his youth in which a Cossack officer in the Red Army, Migulin, had been tried and shot as a traitor. The novel opens with news of Migulin's rehabilitation, and the old man has an imperative need to discuss the disturbing case with someone who might share his concern and his urge to get at the truth. But there are no such people left.

As in *The House on the Embankment* the story here is told mainly through the mind of a character, the old revolutionary, and it is more the story of that mind itself than of clearly verifiable historical facts. Trifonov, with his accustomed deft control of idiom and viewpoint, succeeds in entering that mind and experiencing in its memory the stirring and confusing days of the Revolution and Civil War, when the old man was a young man full of energy and faith. He remembers his aching love for nineteen-year-old Asya, who became Migulin's wife, and recalls his own much-loved wife, recently deceased; he contrasts those memories with his present sad revulsion at the crass philistine tastes and ambitions of his offspring and their mates. George Gibian has suggested an affinity with Henry James in Trifonov's portrayal of a mind at work on reality, and it should be pointed out that James believed the most interesting subject was a fine but "bewildered" mind dealing with life. The mind here presented is precisely such a mind, one without dogmatic patterns, confused amid uncharted memories, released by the sense of approaching death from habitual fealty to established pieties. Working on memories of the past that may be selective or slanted and are surely colored by later knowledge and present impressions, Pavel's mind finds that the truth he seeks is elusive. He cannot abide those who remember everything as either black or white with nothing "in the middle." For him nothing can be stated with absolute certainty:

I can't understand these blacks or whites, either devils of darkness or angels. And nothing else, nothing in between. But everything is in between. Everyone has something in him of darkness and the devil and something of the angels. What was I in the autumn of 1917? Now, when I try to remember, I can't understand or imagine myself at all.

And the shifting, uncertain focus of memory provides the following pictures of the revolutionary days in Petrograd:

We kept walking as long as our legs would support us. On the streets there was the same turmoil, the frightful swaying of the crowds, meetings, fistfights, shouting. I see more armed workers marching down the Nevsky. They're carrying a banner: "Down with the Provisional Government." A demonstration of students, officers, and some well-dressed women meets up with them. They have a banner: "Three Cheers for the Provisional Government." Somebody is throwing rocks from the roofs. You can't tell who they're throwing them at. The two demonstrations mix it up. The women are screaming, people fall, run away, tear up the banners, break the poles!

Past events are dim and blurred in the mind of Pavel, and as he researches the history of Migulin's trial he finds the pertinent documents not totally relevant. In their stark black and white statement they allow no account of human complexities. Out of those documents there does emerge, however, a fascinating picture of the Revolution and its "heroes" and a rich harvest of human character and experience, but no incontrovertible truths. The old man's tentative, groping treatment of the "glorious days" and his ironic neglect of established Soviet certitude was a radical departure in Soviet literature, and some readers believed the censors must have blundered in passing the novel. Yet it appeared unchanged in book form two years after its first publication in the journal *Friendship of Peoples* in 1978.

Trifonov possesses a miraculous (I have chosen my words carefully) gift of characterization, and his novels exuberate with Russian—and non-Russian—types in great variety, each realized with parsimonious selection of effective detail. The Red Cossack Migulin is one of his most impressive portraits. The popular Civil War hero is a charismatic leader whose presence on a platform could electrify an audience and inspire an army, but he is headstrong, choleric, and anarchic, a leader constitutionally unable to "fit into the command structure." As an officer in the Czar's army and in the Red Army after the Revolution he was in trouble for his outspoken attacks on higher authority. In his speech defending himself at the trial he said:

"And I told the [czarist] commander publicly . . . that it was impossible to endure the vileness perpetrated by our army . . . And for that I was sent to a hospital for the mentally ill. For my honesty they wanted me declared insane . . . I won't tell you what happened between me and General Shirokov, as a result of which they sent me to a settlement . . . And when I was assigned to the First Cossack Division under Generals Samsonov and Vershinin I had some very rough times, nobody understood me, and after one of my conflicts with my superior officer, I told him he was not a man but an animal. And so, wherever I was I always undertook revolutionary actions, so as to discredit the authorities."

One thing emerges quite clearly: the charge of anti-Soviet activity, of traitorously "opening the front" to the enemy, was a fabrication by Migulin's enemies. Those enemies included: (1) doctrinaire comrades with exotic names, Naum Orlik, and Yanson, who distrusted him as a representative of the Russian Cossack mass; (2) Trotsky, who destroyed Migulin with a meaningless label, "S-R-ish"; (3) military commanders who ordered a hard line against the local Cossack communities, a line which Migulin would not carry out; (4) and, yes, Lenin himself with his telegram on the *"criminally* slow pace in the organization of resistance on the southern front."

Saddest of all is the record of the old man Pavel's own contribution to the conviction and execution of Migulin. He had been asked as a witness whether he admitted the *possibility* that Migulin had been part of a conspiracy, and he had answered that, yes, he did admit that possibility. An innocent, almost inevitable answer, but lethal in the context of that trial. And Pavel would never know to what extent his answer had been prompted by jealousy of the man who had taken from him the great love of his early life, Asya.

Perhaps the most persistent message in Trifonov's novel is the idea that the infringements of legality and simple justice that began during the revolutionary period and are usually explained by the exigencies and the atmosphere of that time have persisted into Pavel's own day. It follows that the "aliens" and "Trotskyites" who destroyed a fine Russian chap, Migulin, could do their evil only because the judicial process had already been poisoned. And Pavel's own answer at the trial that "it was possible" could damage Migulin only because standards of evidence and of guilt had already been perverted by "revolutionary justice," whatever that might be.

The alternate focus in the novel on past and present powerfully develops another persistent theme in Trifonov's work as a whole: the decay of civic ideals and the dominance in Soviet life of the philistine (*meshchanin*). In contrast to the high ideals of his past the old man finds the present shoddily materialistic. His son and daughter-in-law are totally absorbed in a campaign to get themselves a new house on which they have only a tenuous claim, and insist on using their father's long record of service to the Revolution and his Party reputation to advance their ambition. His son, moreover, is an alcoholic, an infantile nonentity. The brave phrases and self-sacrificing deeds of the old man as a young man have added up to infirmity and approaching death, and issued in a society where the old fervor has disappeared without a trace. The action takes place in the seventies during a summer of heat and drought when there were vast fires in the peat fields and forests around Moscow, a summer the residents will never forget. The whole world of the story is enveloped in an acrid mist of smoke and heat from the burning peat and trees. That realistic historical detail, the seemingly universal fog over the world, stands as a symbol of the old man's quietly bewildered uncertainty over the meaning of his life and the validity of his own memories.

Trifonov's work, especially the two novels we have examined, is one of the most important achievements of Russian literature in the twentieth century. Not only has he mastered the contemporary idiom and characteristic viewpoint of the milieu in which he specializes, but, as George Gibian puts it, "he has an intimate knowledge of the small superficial details, the ways of doing and living of Soviet people today, and of the central moral issues . . . which daily confront Soviet people in the middle and upper reaches of the urban social pyramid."

Natalya Baranskaya (b. 1908), a writer who first gained fame in her late sixties, has given us in her story *A Week Like Any Other* (*Nedelya kak nedelya*, 1969) a beautifully conceived and powerfully written statement on the degraded state of women in Soviet urban society. Her story is also a literary revelation of the harried way of life both sexes follow in Russia's enormous, overgrown cities. The narrator in this day-by-day account of a hectic week of her life—a perfectly normal week—is a research assistant in a Moscow institute concerned with the development of plastics. She has a decent husband—not an alcoholic, that is—and a good apartment, and they have an adequate double salary. But she lives under constant pressure to fit all her duties into the scant twenty-four hours of each day. Three hours a day she commutes, that is to say she runs quite a way to a bus stop where she fights the queue, pushes and shoves her way onto the bus and sometimes hangs on the step; after the bus she has a long ride on the subway where she is held erect by the crush of fellow passengers around her and is even able to read Aksyonov. Since there is not enough time she is always late. She gets the meals, washes and dresses the kids, cleans the house, does the shopping, worries about the children's sicknesses, irons and sews, all of this, it's true, with occasional minor help from her husband. And of course she also carries a full time load at the institute. Sundays, though, are a blessed release from the daily routine: on Sundays she can wash the clothes and ventilate the rooms, always working under forced draft so there will still be time to fix the family a good Sunday dinner. This woman's work is really never done.

The documentary value of this account of urban life in the seventies will be obvious to anyone who has lived in the Soviet Union, yet in style and structure the work is a negation of documentary prose. Nor is anything ever recollected in tranquility. Everything is told in a frantic present tense dominated by the verbs for hurrying, worrying, and scurrying. The first person narration is a staccato mimicry of the heroine's life: quick short sentences, incomplete snatches of dialogue, remarks thrown back over the shoulder as one rushes downstairs, anecdotes and one-liners dropped in passing. The story is a magnificent tour de force in the direct embodiment in language of a particular kind of life experience.

The story's message on the exploitation of women is given in the ironic juxtaposition of an official demographer's questionnaire on the "time distribution" in a Soviet woman's life with the exposition of actual events, and here too the irony is carried by language itself. The dead bureaucratic phrases of a document which expresses concern about the "inadequate tempos in the increase in the population," and seeks to discover "why women don't want to give birth" are in stark contrast to the uninhibited language of the narrator and her female compeers which characteristically mocks official jargon. This is exemplified when the narrator reaches a state of near hysteria, a disease, it is pointed out "no longer fashionable among Soviet women," or when her friend's normal human speech is unaccountably poisoned by specialized official cant, for instance: "We have performed a colossal labor in liberating women from oppression, and there is no foundation for a failure to believe in our efforts to do even more."

The heroine's experience is that both at home and at work women have much less status than men, though their tender shoulders bear heavier burdens. At the institute the higher positions are filled by men, while the women, condescendingly referred to as "the mamas," struggle with experiments and at times make discoveries for which a male receives credit. In the family the "men-folks" go out sledding while mother and daughter stay home and do the work, then papa complains that "Galka isn't getting enough exercise." A leitmotif of Olga's hectic week is a missing hook on her own intimate girdle, which she never finds time the whole week long to repair.

Natalya Baranskaya's story received attention in the official press, some of it quite unfavorable, as might have been expected. She could easily have produced herself, in a few paragraphs of ironic quasi-direct discourse, the negative official description of her work. However she continued to write and a collection of her stories including the short novel *A Week Like Any Other* was published in 1981.

Another accomplished writer who made her debut late in life was Elena Sergeevna Ventzel (b. 1907), who wrote under the pseudonym I. Grekova, a name which in rapid speech suggests the Russian word for an unknown quantity in mathematics, as also for an unknown or unnamed person: "Ms. X." She was a mathematician, a professor, and an honored figure in Soviet science when her first story, "Beyond the Entryway," was published in *New World* (1962). The setting is a scientific research laboratory and the story is narrated by a mature woman on the research team who shrewdly and humorously observes her colleagues and reproduces the special idiom and vocal register of each one, constructing an intriguing picture of the human makeup of a research institute. Grekova exhibits great expertise in the control of casual dialogue and unpretentious colloquial narrative. Though chronologically not young, she was an inseparable part of what was called the "youth movement" in Russian prose in the sixties.

Probably her best story is "Ladies' Hairdresser" (1963), in which the narrator is a widow of a certain age who works in a research institute, and who is interested in maintaining a viable female appearance. The central character is the ladies' hairdresser himself, Vitaly, whose portrait is one of the most vivid and economically sketched in contemporary literature. The meeting of this interesting woman, of an age "deserving reverence," as she ironically puts it, with an accomplished hairdresser who is a master of his trade—his "art," he would say—introduces us to the mysterious world of permanents, shampoos, bleaches, tints, upsweeps, teasing, and styling, and to the practitioners in the proletarian state of so bourgeois an art. In this story, too, Grekova gives us an intimate feeling of Soviet urban setting and character. The hairdresser, Vitaly, is an exemplary young man very serious about his career and intent on self-improvement. He has had no proper formal education, having been raised in an orphan's home. The narrator does not say so, but the circumstances of Vitaly's life suggest that he is one of the numerous company of Soviet citizens whose parents and homes were lost in the purges or the war, intelligent people who turn out not to have a proper education. But Vitaly is a conscientious autodidact. He is learning to speak properly, with good accent and grammar, and he is educating himself in literature by reading the works of

Belinsky from cover to cover. His efforts at self-improvement lend a curious stilted note to his speech. He would like to become an expert in what he understands is the most important science, "dialectical materialism," though he knows nothing about it. But he is serious chiefly about the hairdressing art, at which he is an acknowledged master in great demand, and an independent, even creative talent. He is interested in innovative experiment and works free of charge on female heads that offer special possibilities.

Precisely because he is a "great" artist, a free spirit seeking new forms, Vitaly falls afoul of the official standards and procedures of the Soviet hairdressing establishment, who insist on their own "plan of work" and on disciplined behavior as part of the collective. Discouraged with hairdressing Vitaly abandons his art to become an apprentice in a factory. The hostile reaction of certain critics to the story would seem to indicate that they were not impervious to its Aesopian language.

Grekova's short novel *Hotel Manager* (1976) brings to life another urban type not normally considered good material for literature: one of the multitude of women whose iron hands administer Soviet hotels. Verochka, the heroine of this story, resembles Vitaly in that she too is devoted to her work and gives it her honest best both physically and spiritually. She too has trouble with dense superiors, who in her case happen to be men. The point of the story is that Verochka, whatever her profession, will always have the generous capacity for work that makes life somewhat better for her clientele, her customers, and of course for her family.

Vitaly Nikolaevich Syomin (b. 1927) has produced in the novel *Seven in a Single House* (1965) one of the relatively rare literary treatments of the actual life and working conditions of the urban working class. Syomin's objectivity and honesty in the depiction of morally and physically drab and brutally impoverished workers living in one of the suburbs of a medium-sized industrial city, provoked a prolonged and bitter discussion in the course of which hostile critics insisted the situation was atypical. Actually, the central character Mulya, from whose viewpoint the story is told, is a simple Russian woman capable of withstanding great hardship and dealing with severe problems: a shiftless son, the curse of vodka among her men, inadequate living space, shortages of everything. Perhaps the most striking feature of the workers portrayed here is their laziness and their indifference to all but narrow personal considerations. The novel contains an absolutely devastating picture of civic morale among the supposed beneficiaries of the proletarian revolution.

The Backwoods: Ethical Problems

A writer of considerable talent is Vladimir Tendryakov (b. 1923) whose work began appearing during the so-called thaw and attracted the attention of critics in the Soviet Union and outside. Like Trifonov he is principally concerned with the problem of moral choices, but in some of his novels he deals also, through the thoughts and experiences of his characters, with philosophical and religious questions not as a rule covered in orthodox Soviet texts. His work deals for the most part with life in the remote countryside and in the *kolkhozes*, and he treats problems of personal morality, giving much attention to individual differences of character and personality. Stagnant habits of the old way of life—attachment to selfish interests and to creature comforts, hatred and violence—he exposes in Soviet men with reticent scorn. Two of his stories are especially interesting in that respect. "Three, Seven, Ace" (*New World* no. 3, 1960) is a story set on the banks of a wide river in a logging settlement in the interior. A man who has been saved from drowning in the river and has become a member of the colony turns out to be an ex-convict and professional gambler. Having infected the laborers with gambling fever, he cleans them out thoroughly, hides the money in the bunk of Leshka, one of the laborers, then is killed when he attacks their chief, Dubinin. The chief is suspected of having killed him in a quarrel over money, and suspicion is strengthened by the circumstance that the money cannot be found. Leshka, though he idolizes the chief, is in such panic at the thought of being suspected himself that he throws the money into the river. Dubinin is taken away, and as the story ends Leshka, like Peter, sobs disconsolately.

The laborers in the story are not bad men, but they are low on the human scale. They lack not only education and intelligence, but also the barest minimum of moral responsibility. They live on the fringe of civilization. News of the launching of a sputnik weighing a ton stirs them less than gossip about a bear in the neighborhood. The story is a simple one of primitive passion and violence, and, as the author reflects, could have been told in much the same way a thousand years ago. The men who figure in it are in no way positive characters, and no idea is developed in their story. Tendryakov, like Trifonov, avoids socialist-realist clichés.

"The Trial" (*New World*, no. 3, 1961) is a brief excursion into the remote Russian forest where life is as yet not fully under the control of civilized legal formalities. A hunter who belongs to the primeval woods makes the acquaintance on a bear hunt of a Soviet construction director whose enterprise is slowly destroying the habitat of both the bear and the hunter. They are joined on the hunt by Mityagin, a village simpleton who has never before handled a gun. The description of the hunt is one of the most exciting passages in Soviet writing. It is a mosaic of human experience: the hunter's courage in the face of danger as he tracks the great beast, suspense and fear as the dogs corner the animal, and the moment of finality when two men fire at the enraged and advancing monster. Then suddenly tragedy strikes, for one of the two misses the bear and kills a man who happened to be walking in the woods. The police and the prosecutor are called in, and the dry formalism of legal procedure invades the forest. Apparently trivial matters, not even noticed at the moment of danger, now become very important—the determination, for instance, of the exact position of each man when the shots were fired. The question to be answered is, who killed the man, the construction director or the village simpleton. The hunter, who has cut out of the bear's skull the bullet that killed him, knows that it came from the simpleton's gun. But no one wants to believe that the director, not the simpleton, had missed the bear and killed a man. The hunter, certain that the evidential bullet would only cause trouble for him, throws it away in a swamp and denies in court that he ever found it. The truth could only cause him trouble. The author reflects on the long and painful road still to be traveled:

> People change more slowly than life itself . . . A metallurgical combine can be built in two or three years, but human character changes only after decades. It's not enough to build factories, lay down roads into the wilderness, move people into well-built houses. That's necessary, but it's not everything. People must also be taught how to live.

One of Tendryakov's best things is *A Topsy-Turvy Spring* (*Perevertyshi*, 1973). It is a short novel about adolescence and first love and about the spring freshets that sometimes nourish imagination and defamiliarize fixed habits of seeing and thinking. The hero thought he knew how the world was organized and what was good and what was evil "because he'd lived for thirteen years. But then something odd happened, just like that. And the bright stable world began to go all topsy-turvy." Strange things happen. He notices that his young neighbor and schoolmate, Rimka, who had never before seemed remarkable for anything, is, as Pushkin said of his wife Natalya, "the purest pattern of pure delight." Just her presence on the stairway or chattering on the street causes him an agreeable ache. And she looks like pictures of that Natalya, Pushkin's wife—hair and everything. The action that develops leads to serious questioning of the conventional wisdom. Maybe Rimka is Natalya reincarnated. Mathematical cerebration and a new sense of continuous time lead him (with the help of an older comrade) to rediscover the doctrine of eternal return, according to which, in his version, "if our universe does not end anywhere, or at any time, then some place, some time, early or late, but absolutely for sure . . . Do you get that, *for sure!* . . . the incredible will happen. The atoms, by pure chance, will reform again exactly as they are in me now." Thus the pain of death is softened by scientific argument, and the idea of immortality, even if only a poor substitute therefor, is introduced and contemplated. The excellent young man from whose adolescent viewpoint the story is told is pleasantly surprised by his discovery of the mysterious universe: "Face to face with one another were his frail intellect and the inexhaustible mystery of being." And why should Rimka and Natalya not be the same person, then? Random interactions produce unpredictable results.

The spring madness overturns other firmly held beliefs. The young man's father is an efficient manager of a lumber operation, immersed in his work and indifferent to feelings. Once, many years ago, he had brought his wife some flowers, but only once in his whole life. Before this story ends, however, he too is touched by spring and sends away for some narcissi as a present for her. Love and gentleness are important, it turns out. And the town's outstanding failure, who commands little respect, reveals himself as a loving husband and father and a frustrated poet who quotes both Pushkin and Pasternak. How can you feel proper contempt for such a person?

The story is not marked by any originality, either in plot development or in the use of language, but in the hero, Dyushka, Tendryakov has given us a touching portrait of an intelligent, sensitive adolescent on the verge of discovering the world. Major notes dominate: the father rediscovers feeling; the town failure gets a good job; and the town bully, Dyushka's enemy, is exposed as a criminal and sent away. Yet the bully Sanka's presence is an ominous and not fully mastered threat to the humanity present in Dyushka and growing in others. The Sankas of the world are ugly, vicious, and cruel: "People like that make life not worth living. It's people like that who start wars . . ." Who are they, one asks, and how many? The exigencies of Soviet literary life necessitate that they be defeated in the fictional world, but the defeat is much too easy.

Other New Voices of the Sixties and Seventies

The poet Bulat Okudzhava is the author of a short novel entitled *Good Luck, Boy!* (1961), which is an authentic tour de force in the unheroic treatment of war. It sets forth, from the viewpoint of a young volunteer who entered the army before he had finished school, the ugly, monotonous, and dangerous workdays of a front-line soldier. The focus is narrowed to the frame of a single mind, and a rather simple one. The boy's needs are modest and very basic. He does not want to be killed and he is afraid he will be killed. He needs sleep and wants to be warm, to eat something, to be liked by a girl. The problem of his spoon figures as an ironic symbol of a soldier's real life and real concerns. The hero has no spoon and must use a piece of wood to feed himself. In the end, when a comrade dies in action, the boy inherits a spoon and has his heart's desire. The story is a continuous inner monologue interrupted by thoughts of the past and repellent events of the present. The movement of the boy's thought and the recorded conversations reflect the state of near mental collapse that is the everyday experience of a soldier in combat. He lives in a kind of trance induced by frequent death, noise, and insuperable fatigue. He never knows what he is doing, where he is going, or what the war is all about.

Good Luck, Boy! appeared in the collection *Pages from Tarusa* (1961), which was edited by Paustovsky and included a number of poets and prose writers representative of a new and independent accent in literature. That collection soon became a bibliographical rarity and has never been reprinted; nor has Okudzhava's pacifistic novel about war ever been republished in book form in the Soviet Union. His next effort in prose was a novel dealing with the aftermath of the Decembrist uprising in 1825 and focussed on the official interrogation of the leading figure in that rebellion, Pavel Pestel. Pestel is the novel's central historical figure, but the narrative viewpoint is that of a young man from the country, naïve, romantic, and prone to fantasy, who has quite accidentally been appointed as a stenographer to keep the written record of Pestel's interrogation. The novel in its first serial publication was named for that rather humble young man: *Poor Avrosimov* (1969). But its title when published as a book emphasized the high significance of the historical subject: *The Taste of Freedom; A Story About Pavel Pestel* (*Glotok svobody; povest' o Pavle Pestele*, 1971). The source of the novel's peculiar originality and power, however, lies precisely in the fact that it is not the story of the brilliant theoretician and political leader of the Decembrists, Pestel, but of poor Avrosimov, who lacks even an elementary education in the great social issues that hang in the balance, but who does have an honest heart and who can feel the difference between nobility of character and baseness. And the historical subject is estranged and distanced yet another remove by the fact that Avrosimov's own story is told by a somewhat older and garrulous narrator full of wise saws and modern instances and having his own special notions about Pestel, about human character, and about the storytelling art; thus the author himself speaks to us through a double mask.

Avrosimov is young and naïve, but in his psychic makeup rather complex, as the narrator often points out for us. He thinks he believes that Pestel and his band were scoundrels not even deserving the formality of a trial; then he finds himself horrified and incredulous at the thought that a subject could even think of raising his hand against an anointed Czar, but if a subject *could think of it*, "then is the Czar really so great?" Of course the narrator adds in parentheses, "You know, good sir, you could be executed for having such doubts." Pestel, even in chains and under guard, attracts Avrosimov, while the members of the Czar's Commission of Inquiry appear to him as masked marionettes "walking past in single file" to go through a cruel charade. The copyist commits certain significant "Freudian slips" in taking down the testimony, leaving out inadvertently the prejudicial epithets regularly used by the judges to characterize Pestel and his enterprise: "the vile and malicious secret society" appears in Avrosimov's records as, simply, "the secret society," a matter which caused his immediate superior great concern. Predisposed by his own idealistic nature to sympathize with a man who had sacrificed everything for an ideal, Avrosimov is at great pains to penetrate the tangle of lies and slander that obscured Pestel and his purpose. Especially repugnant are the informers who, to save their own skins, accuse Pestel of intending to commit various crimes but say nothing of his ideas about "Russian Justice." The narrator, as well as Avrosimov, reveals a sympathetic interest for the prisoner in the dock:

> Just take the news reports of those years, my dear sir, just read them (I've read them, a lot of them), and you won't find in them any idea except that of crime. Nothing about how Pestel had drawn up a plan to free the serfs, nor about how he proposed to end official corruption, to improve the lot of soldiers, and many other similar things. You read just one thing: he was a thief, a pirate, a regicide.

The novel is a case study in the immense difficulty involved in delivering a few morsels of historical meaning out of the complex and stormy events of a particular moment in the past. The real facts are filtered to us through the unversed intelligence of poor Avrosimov, as understood and interpreted by an honest but quirky narrator writing forty years after the events which themselves take place in the misty, fantastic, and dreamlike atmosphere of St. Petersburg. Through all the mystification it is possible to believe that a Soviet reader would find in the novel allegories of actual Soviet conditions: police surveillance, spies and informers, official vilification of proscribed ideas.

The Adventures of Shipov, or, An Old-Time Vaudeville (1971), Okudzhava's second "historical" novel, also dealt with a "true and documented event," the police surveillance of the novelist Leo Tolstoy and their raid upon his quarters in 1865. Real historical personages appear here as characters in what Okudzhava calls a vaudeville, a dramatic form featuring grotesque and ridiculous characters, absurd situations, and farcical actions. The grotesque characters (for instance the police chief who has mastered every imaginable disguise, male or female), tend to merge with dreams and the supernatural, yet at the same time every scene is a nicely calculated and developed farce. The two detectives shadowing Tolstoy, for instance, end up hanging from trees in a wintry landscape, themselves pursued by wolves. And in the widow Dasya's house there is a Feydeau-like comedy situation when the widow herself is pursued from one room to another by the detectives, who are in turn pursued by the police chief dressed as a female religious pilgrim, with nicely timed elusive entrances and exits from the rooms of her house. The whole is offered as a complicated farce in which real documents from the police files, with their heavy-footed official language, become solemn items in a concatenation of absurdities.

This novel too offers some easily developed modern allegories. The action against Tolstoy was initiated as the result of a denunciation (*donos*) lodged against him by an anonymous character who had heard rumors about his "school for peasants" and other suspicious matters. The informer knows him only as a "retired artillery officer, with a good education." Once started the rumor feeds on itself, and the reports of agents in the field to their supervisors create an enclosed reality of their own having nothing to do with the actual world of Leo Tolstoy, who goes on writing to his friends, dealing with his publisher, suffering from his gambling fever, and so on. Two levels are created in the material Okudzhava uses: the real world of Tolstoy and the world of doltish fantasy in the police documents. And the police conspiracy has a momentum of its own: once they have placed their confidence in the drunken and incompetent detective Shipov his supervisors have to find or invent reasons for trusting him. In the end even his crazy project to set up an illegal printing press as a bait for Tolstoy is used as evidence in his favor: "—still, that rascal . . . has been working, he did set up a press. The fact that he's a drunk and a scoundrel means nothing . . . Results are important, isn't that so?"

The vaudeville form easily accommodates in the account of Shipov's life a parody of the "lives of Holy Men" genre. The disoriented and suffering detective is at times decked out with a halo, and in the end manages an ascent into heaven which clearly violates a fundamental rule of the historical novel. And as a matter of fact Okudzhava's historical novels are a continuation of his poetry by other means. Each one of them scrupulously adheres to historical fact and archival documents, but uses these materials to develop a multileveled and highly personal message. The third "historical" novel, *Dilettantes' Journey* (*Puteshestvie diletantov*, 1979), is especially notable in this respect. Just as Pestel and the scrivener Avrosimov are granted no more than a "taste of freedom," so Prince Myatlev and his love have only two brief moments of rapture, before and after his long martyrdom at the hands of the Czar, in the course of which he suffers separation, sudden interrogatories, humiliation, and imprisonment. And yet Myatlev was neither a Decembrist nor a liberal democrat nor a nihilist, though he was a contemporary of them all. His problem was just that he was a dilettante, an apolitical man, withdrawn from affairs, ambitious only to be a cultivated individual to some extent free of the society in which he lived. That was not enough for the philistines in power and their representative and chief, Nicholas I.

At the time his first stories appeared in the fifties Yury Kazakov (b. 1927) seemed one of the most original and promising of the new voices in Soviet literature, and it is probably fair to say that more was expected of him than he was able to give. The stories he produced bear his own original stamp but were at the same time an inseparable part of the new currents moving in Soviet literature at the time. He might be discussed as part of the youth movement in prose (see chapter 16), and some have suggested that he introduced certain themes that became a staple in village prose. His most characteristic story, "Blue and Green," written in 1956, is told in the words and thoughts of the central character. That character relates in direct, naïve terms his love for a girl whom he met accidentally, the irreplaceable happiness it gave him, and his grief at losing her. The young man's story, somewhat reminiscent of Yury Olesha, relates entirely to his own consciousness, and the author, scrupulously inarticulate, offers no wise comment on his character's experience.

"The Deer's Antlers" (1958) is another exploration of a single mind, in this case the mind of a young girl recovering from disease and separated in thought from her comrades. She experiences a fantastic fairytale hallucination, sees trolls and other wonders, and has a purely subjective vision of someone she might love. Again, the story is constructed out of the thoughts and impressions of a particular consciousness, and the atmosphere of wonder is related to the young girl's clinical condition. The story has no discoverable moral but only imaginative interest.

In *Pages from Tarusa* (1961) Kazakov published three new stories, one of which, "The Smell of Bread," is characteristic of his sensitive recording of fleeting mental states so intimately personal that they elude verbalization. It is the story of a Moscow woman who hears that her mother, whom she had not seen for fifteen years, has died in her far-off native village. At first she seems to feel nothing, but when she returns to the village in the spring to sell her mother's property, sensory memories of childhood—the smell of bread and of her mother's old clothing—gradually invade her consciousness, and when, as a kind of afterthought, she visits her mother's grave, a deep source of grief suddenly wells up in her, and she keens over the grave like any peasant woman. The spell of grief passes quickly, however, and she returns to Moscow the next day in a contented frame of mind. In this story as in many others Kazakov subtly traces apparently erratic emotional shifts, showing their connection with accidental sensory impressions of sight or smell.

Fazil Abdulovich Iskander (b. 1929) is a native of Abkhazia, an autonomous area in the northwest section of the Georgian Republic. He writes in Russian, though the locale of most of his stories is his native province. The mountains of Abkhazia, its forests and clear streams, figure in his work as a refreshing contrast to the urban or village settings of most Russian writing, and the characters whose adventures and misadventures he relates with such great skill and humor are native Abkhazians or inhabitants of neighboring Georgia. His *Sandro from Chegem* (1973–1981) is a kind of picaresque novel, a series of episodes in the life of one Uncle Sandro, a humorous and absurd character expert in manipulating the life around him. The customs, traditions, and folklore of his native Caucasus region figure in *Sandro*, as in many of Iskander's other things.

Iskander, like Kazakov and Aksyonov, was one of the authentic new voices of the early sixties and he too might be considered a part of the young prose movement. However, his development has been different from that of the writers usually associated with that phenomenon, though he did publish an excellent piece in the illegal collection *Metropol*, in which he collaborated along with Aksyonov, Bitov, Erofeev, and Evgenii Popov. A complete text of his *Sandro* has been published only in the West, by Ardis Publishers.

Iskander provides an exhilarating bit of evidence that good satire is not dead in the Soviet Union and that it may even get published. He is a specialist in humorous, innocent-seeming satire that hits squarely upon its social target without arousing offense or anger. Each of his stories delivers a sharp point, but delivers it with a smile. He manages this by presenting situations—and we have seen that in general this device is very common in contemporary fiction—from the viewpoint of simple-minded, faintly ridiculous characters or of children. He has been published in various journals and in the *Literary Gazette*, and collections of his stories have been published in book form. A story that demonstrates his method in its purest form is one called "My Uncle Had the Highest Principles," in which an absurd little boy of approximately cub-scout age, his patriotic head full of journalistic warnings about the need for vigilance against spies, is suddenly visited by the idea that his crazy uncle is neither crazy nor an uncle but a foreign spy. Once the idea has taken firm root, uncle's innocent but daft actions all take on an aura of suspicion. So much evidence accumulates that the boy is soon ready to make a formal accusation, which he does in an exquisitely amusing scene. Iskander, in this story about an unhinged old man and his silly nephew, thus treats very lightly a situation that contains essential ingredients of the terror and the purge.

Perhaps Iskander's best story is one entitled "The Constellation of the Goat-Buffalo." It relates the misadventures of a dogmatic bureaucrat who devises a project to cross goats with buffalo in order to produce a new animal that will give more milk, be more lively, and grow a new kind of wool. With Party support this weird project is adopted, in spite of the serious doubts raised by qualified geneticists and agrobiologists. Iskander's style in the story is freshly ironical, and at times it is a parody of the somber and solemn cant to be found in much Soviet journalism and other writing. He pointedly mimics the elaborately vacuous Byzantine statement, the worn political cliché, the empty phrase. Both satire and parody are specifically aimed at the so-called Michurinist school of agrobiology, the group led by Trofim Lysenko, whose theories did great harm to Russian science.

Iskander has mastered, no doubt by taking great pains, a very casual narrative style. Ordinary joys and frustrations—the loss of a watch, a momentary glimpse of an attractive girl, a conversation in a café, an effort to catch a bus—are all presented as at least on an equal level of importance with such world-shaking projects as the discovery of the goat-buffalo. What happens to ordinary people in the struggle to live decently is in the forefront of Iskander's attention.

Another non-Russian who writes for the most part in Russian is Chingiz Aitmatov (b. 1928). Born in Kirghizia into a family that had only recently developed beyond the native nomadic culture of the area, Aitmatov is bilingual in Russian and Tartar, and an old unbroken attachment to the land of his birth appears persistently in his fiction. As a matter of fact some of the concerns of the Russian ruralists appear in

Aitmatov's work in a Kirghiz setting: nostalgia for old values, resistance to urbanization, and loving attention to native myths. His *Farewell Gulsary* (1966), which was awarded a Lenin Prize, develops themes quite common in Russian rural prose: the arbitrary violation of rural life by a Party bureaucracy, mistaken but strictly enforced decisions made at a distance from the land itself, and the persecution of hard-working independent peasants.

His best work is *The White Steamship* (1970), the story of a young orphan boy growing up in Kirghizia who turns away from the materialistic evil that has invaded his native land and chooses to live a kind of fairy-tale dream life in which a mythical white steamship—plying a distant lake—figures as a refuge and escape from the real world. Whatever happens in that world, the boy always has the hope that one day he will reach the white steamship. He is certain that on that steamer he will find his own father, who was once a sailor. He dreams that one day he will change into a fish and swim down the river to the lake and his white steamship.

That is his first fairy tale, and it is personal, his invention. His grandfather Momun hands on to him the story of their people and of the special debt they owe to the Horned Deer, who in the old days preserved and fostered their clan and were plentiful in the forest. In gratitude the tribe was obliged to protect the Horned Deer, but they were remiss in their duty, so the animals went away. But they will come back. Momun and the boy live for their return. Such is the second tale.

The book conveys a tragic sense of the disappearance of myths and folk tales, as the city with its pragmatic machines penetrates the countryside. The repository and preserver of myths is the boy's grandfather Momun, a luckless old man whom no adult respects. The only eager listener he has is his grandson, who disappears in the end in search of the white steamship: "The boy had two fairy tales. One was his own. The other one his grandfather told him. Then there weren't any fairy tales at all. That's what our story is about."

Yury Nagibin, whose stories "The Khazar Ornament" and "Light in the Window," both attacks on the Stalinist bureaucracy, were published in *Literary Moscow* (1956), has written since that time about simple, unpretentious people who feel emotions of pity, love or sympathy in basic human terms. His story "Love" is typical. It portrays the constancy of a nice boy's love for a girl in spite of her cheap and vulgar cynicism. The story explores the working of a mysterious emotional process, but Nagibin eschews any effort to explain or pass judgment on it. The author, like his youthful characters, is reverent but tongue-tied.

His story "Echoes" (1960) is a reminiscence of a childhood encounter with a little girl named Vitka, who collects echoes as other people collect stamps or coins. Somewhat strange in appearance and original in manner, the girl, as she scrambles over rocks looking for the best places to produce echoes, seems a bit crazy, but she has imagination and goodness, and she is a real friend. Yet the narrator recalls that when his properly stodgy contemporaries made fun of her he did not have the courage to take her part. His story is a melancholy rumination of regret at his failure to recognize the beauty of this little offbeat sprite. There is a deep human sadness in it.

Andrey Bitov (b. 1937) published a number of original short narratives in the Soviet Union, most of them focussed on the psychological experience of a character at a moment of intense inner agitation. Such moments are not as a rule occasioned by obviously important events in either private or public life, but by minor, deeply personal crises. Bitov conveys the texture of such moments with great skill. He was part of the "youth movement" in fiction in the early sixties (see chapter 16) and like many of his contemporaries he contributed to the development of a free, natural idiom and new narrative forms. What is probably his most important work, *Pushkin House* (1965–1978), has never been published in the Soviet Union but circulated widely in *samizdat* before publication abroad. That novel, which has an explicitly autobiographical component, deals with the ethical morass in which intellectuals, even those among them who were descended from noble forbears, often lost their bearings and compromised with contemptible inferiors. In the long alcoholic monologue of the hero's grandfather, a linguist who had been arrested and held in jail for many years, Bitov has given us a magnificent portrait of a free mind incapable of compromise.

Another interesting practitioner of the short story and short novel form is Nikolai Dubov, whose story "The Escapee" appeared in *New World* (no. 4, 1966). This is an entertaining, instructive, and very well made story. Once again the narrative viewpoint is an innocent one: the story is told by an intelligent, sensitive, and awkwardly adolescent boy named Yurka. A man and a woman from the city turn up in the southern community where he lives and rent a plot of ground on which to pitch their tent. Yurka promptly falls in love with Vitaly and Yulivanna. Unlike his own family, they are cultivated, gentle, kind. At first their identity and purposes are a mystery, but gradually and deftly the author reveals that Vitaly is an architect who abandoned his work to escape the philistines in the profession who regularly canceled out anything original and creative in his projects. When tragedy strikes with Vitaly's death by drowning, it turns out that Yulivanna is his mistress, that indeed he had abandoned a living and legal wife. Immediately the attitude of Yurka's family toward Yulivanna changes, and he is honestly repelled when they abuse her, cheat her, and drive her away. There are good and bad people in the story. The good people are unconventional in taste and behavior. They are runaways from respectable family life, from the ponderous art world of socialist-realist canvases and monumental structures, from established social values. The bad ones are legal wives, demanding mothers, and honored artists of the republic. Dubov attempts in this story to examine the experience of growing up in a given milieu and to realize as moral problems the difficulties an adolescent faces.

A number of writers not as well known as those so far discussed have published short stories and novellas that contain original traits of both style and theme. One of them is Lev Slavin, whose story "A Presage of Truth" (*New World*, no. 5, 1966) is, like so much of contemporary fiction, told from the narrative viewpoint of a very young mind. In this case it is a Jewish boy; through his eyes we see the life of his Jewish family and come to know the character of his grandfather Simon—a pillar, very nearly a saint, in the local Hassidic community. The story is told with gentle humor and is remarkable for the naïve and at the same time sympathetic view of this Jewish community before the Revolution. The young boy who narrates the story expresses wide-eyed wonder at everything that happens. A number of original characters are brought to life: for instance, the grandfather, a Talmudic scholar who can cite a learned instance in every crisis of faith or judgment, and the great-grandmother with her memories of the family's deep past, as well as many uncles and aunts who play a variety of roles in the community. The incongruous juxtaposition of the child's real concerns with those of the adult world is the thread of humor which holds the story together. The young boy experiences a growing sense of the presence of God, and we are made to feel the boy's awe at the interest God takes in every action of his. The story seems at first to promise a kind of autobiography of religious feeling, but a contrived ending—one might almost say a *deus ex machina*—converts the boy at an early age to atheism. In spite of the contrivance, the story is an excellent piece of work—restrained, humorous, full of sympathy.

World War II

A persistent and deep concern of Soviet literature since 1945 has been the Second World War and Russia's part in it, a fact which is not surprising in view of Russia's terrible human losses in that war. Much of what has been written on the subject has fallen obediently into the well-worn ruts of the patriotic cliché, but after 1956 a number of works appeared whose conscious purpose was to provide a frank and, as the Soviet critics put it, truthful literary treatment of that catastrophic experience. I have already mentioned Okudzhava's *Good Luck, Boy!* This development, like the current popularity of memoir literature, reveals the passionate interest of the Soviet reader in books that purport to correct particular items in the general falsehood that enveloped the years of Stalin. Some excellent and important novels about World War II have just this purpose. Grigory Baklanov's *July 1941* relates the experiences of a front-line commander who is in charge of a unit at the border in the early stages of the war. The novel is written in a lean and vigorous prose, and in one dramatic scene after another it depicts the military collapse in the summer of 1941 and the deep retreats that took place. The central concern of the novel is a subject until recently taboo: the dreadful defeats of the first months of the war.

Vasily Bykov's *The Dead Feel No Pain* (1966) describes the Stalinist methods used at the front lines during the war and their survival into the present. Sakhno is a Stalinist commissar who was responsible for the execution of many soldiers; his double, Gorbiotok, survived the war and the de-Stalinization period and still stands ready to apply brutal measures if given a chance. Bykov's novel opens questions that were closed but never answered by the official formulas—"cult of personality," for instance—offered to explain the purges. Who were the police officials who actually carried out the thousands of illegal sentences, and where are the ones who provided them with the denunciations upon which to act? How do they explain what they did? What deep sources of fear, suspicion, racial hatred, paranoia, or sheer brutality fed the purges? These questions take dramatic form in Bykov's novel.

Anatoly Kuznetsov's *Babi Yar* (1966–1969), in some ways one of the best of the Soviet war novels, graphically brings to light the Russian retreat in the Ukraine and the German capture of Kiev as seen through the eyes of a young boy. The novel has an explicit documentary flavor: together with eyewitness accounts by the youthful observer, it presents the brutal communiqués and proclamations of the Germans. From direct and incredibly detailed accounts we learn of the mass murders of Jews and gypsies. Very quietly and without emphasis the book reveals widespread anti-Soviet attitudes among the local populace. After defecting to England in 1966 Kuznetsov published, under the pen name A. Anatolii, a new version of the novel in which all passages removed by the censors from the first edition, and others not even written, in deference to the censorship, have been included.

Another important novelist whose subject is World War II is Yury Bondarev, who wrote *Battalions Ask for Fire* and *The Last Command*. His novel *Quietude* (1962) deals with the aftermath of war and the search for civilian readjustment of two demobilized officers who find the peaceful life of postwar Moscow beset with difficulties, many of which stem from government policies. That novel also contains harrowing accounts of the arrests and murders of the Stalin period. *Burning Snow* (1970) is set in Stalingrad at the critical moment of the battle. *The Shore* (1975), one of his best and most popular novels, has a double temporal frame—the time of the war's end in 1945 and a much later date, when the central character makes a journey to Hamburg. Bondarev as a writer is more than equal to the formidable themes he has set himself.

Published Poets

Curiously enough, in the sixties poets created a great stir and received wide acclaim both at home and abroad. Public poetry readings attracted enormous and enthusiastic crowds—large enough even to fill the giant Luzhniki Sports Stadium in Moscow. Certain poets, Yevtushenko and Voznesensky, for instance, had a devoted following among the young and obviously regarded themselves as tribunes of the people. They spoke out on issues with a certain frankness, and the political regime found it expedient to tolerate them—within limits—and even to use them.

The name of Yevgeny Yevtushenko is perhaps associated most vividly in the minds of foreigners with the struggle for liberalization in the Soviet Union, and his own exuberance in taking intellectually honest positions has caused him some trouble. The main tendency of his life and his writing is an effort to escape from chauvinistic isolation. He has frequently traveled abroad. He was severely called to task in 1963 for the publication in Paris without authorization of *A Precocious Autobiography,* and a projected visit to the United States was canceled at that time. His work began appearing again in 1964, and he visited the United States several times and toured the country, giving a number of poetry readings.

Most readers will recall his two famous poems, "Babi Yar" (1961) and "Stantsia Zima" (1955). His poetry is characteristically topical, as is the prose of his *Precocious Autobiography.* That work is naïve, but like so much of Yevtushenko, beautifully so. Consider this quotation, the innocence of which is not lost in translation: "Gradually I came to understand that some people who called themselves Communists and were fond of quoting Lenin and Stalin were not genuine Communists at all." The story of his own literary education is significant. His mentor,

Barlas, he says, "revealed to me that Hemingway existed." He also revealed to him writers who were at that time "bibliographical rarities" in the Soviet Union: Hamsun, Joyce, Freud, Proust, Steinbeck, Faulkner, Remarque, Saint-Exupéry. He goes on: "I drank in the might of Whitman, the violence of Rimbaud . . . the tragic in Baudelaire, the magic in Verlaine, the subtlety of Rilke, the sensitive visions of T. S. Eliot, and the healthy, peasant wisdom of Robert Frost." Frost specialists will of course question the terms "healthy" and "peasant" as applied to him, but what Yevtushenko means is that he managed to make the acquaintance of European and American literature and found it a revelation. At another point he writes:

> I don't want borders.
> It's awkward
>   not to know Buenos Aires
>   and New York.
> I want to wander
> As much as I like
> Around London
> And talk to everybody, even if only in broken English,
> And hanging on the back of a bus like a little boy,
> I want to ride around Paris in the morning.

Yevtushenko dedicated one of his best poems, "An Encounter," to Hemingway, and this is symptomatic both for him and for many of his contemporaries, who prized Hemingway and tried to learn the craft of writing from him. Hemingway has offered them, perhaps, an example of how to use words sparingly and with direct reference to experience. He is a reproachful contrast to Soviet writing of the Stalin period, specifically to its hagiographic and homiletic varieties, and that is why he is so inordinately popular in the Soviet Union.

Yevtushenko's image of himself as a poet is, nevertheless, deeply in the Russian tradition and, in fact, rather old-fashioned. He is a civic poet, one with a mission and messages. His poetry is declamatory and can be eloquent. Its surface meaning is usually the essence of the matter. He tends to shy away from verbal experiment or formal play, and it is difficult to see that he has learned much from the modern poets he claims to revere. Occasionally a sudden cadence or a striking rhyme recalls Mayakovsky, but by comparison with Mayakovsky he is a timid poet. He published in the magazine *Youth* (1965) a lengthy poem entitled, "The Bratsk Hydroelectric Station," in which he contemplates the enormous dam and installations on the Angara river, one of the most powerful sources of electricity in the world, the project which also figures in Rasputin's *Farewell to Matyora*. The poem itself is set in monumental proportions and delivers an important didactic message. The pyramids, the deep past of Russia and her history, man's fate in general, his struggle and labor—all this and much more enter into the poet's lines about a major industrial project. The unifying theme of the poem is the opposition of cynical disbelief, expressed in the monologue of the Egyptian pyramids, to that faith in mankind and in the future which the Bratsk station sets forth. It is an ambitious, even a pretentious poem, and it is not devoid of interesting thoughts and new turns of phrase. In the Prologue Yevtushenko appeals to Mayakovsky as his muse, but the poem lacks completely the latter's boldness, creativity, and verve. Set beside Mayakovsky and other poets of the early part of the century, Yevtushenko seems nothing if not "square."

Andrey Voznesensky is more original and more enterprising as a poet than Yevtushenko. He came to poetry from architecture, having graduated from the Moscow Architectural Institute, and his work was first published only in 1958. He has published a number of collections of poems, *Mosaic* (1960), *Parabola* (1961), *The Triangular Pear* (1962), *Antiworlds* (1964), *The Achilles Heart* (1966), and *Shadow of a Sound* (1970). The poem he himself considers his most characteristic is one entitled "Parabolic Ballad," which offers the idea that in poetry the shortest distance between two points is never the straight line of direct statement, but a curve. The poem takes as a case in point the painter Gauguin, who,

> To reach the royal Louvre,
> Set his course
> On a detour via Java and Sumatra.

In Voznesensky's poetry the meaning of a poem is often incidental to its texture of imagery and language, and can be arrived at only after a more or less lengthy detour which takes in the scenery of the poet's lyrical personality, and only after many a subtle linguistic twist and turn. Situations, statements, sights, and sounds often enough seem to exist in his poetry for their own sake—sometimes only for the sake of rhyme, assonance, or alliteration. In translation his work is usually distorted and can be destroyed, since translation must be concerned with *what* is said. Each Voznesensky poem is a tightly woven unity of verbal image, metaphor, and symbol, and in each one an item of reality is refracted in such a way that its shape and body become matters of speculation. A case in point is the nearly untranslatable "New York Airport at Night," which begins

> My own self-portrait, a neon retort,
> Apostle of the heavenly gates—
> An airport.

The long poem "Oza" (1964) is the poet's intellectually most ambitious piece of work. It explores philosophy and history, touches on the poet's intimate life, and deals with the confrontation of human values by the soulless world of machines and practicality. Its texture is constantly variegated by echoes from the work of many poets: Poe, Mayakovsky, Goethe, and others. Voznesensky is indeed a poet of the parabola. He seldom matches the straight, demonstrative rhetoric of Yevtushenko, but perhaps for that very reason his work is stronger. In the words of Robert Lowell, "He is full of invention, fireworks, and humor . . . a first-rate craftsman who has had the heroic patience and imagination to be himself."

Bella Akhmadulina, who was once married to Yevtushenko, has enjoyed much less notoriety than he but is held in higher esteem as a poet among Soviet intellectuals. Akhmadulina's work is interesting and original for the use she makes of concrete things: a thermometer, aspirin, icicles, a gramophone, the rain, a shiny parquet floor, a motorcycle—each of which plays in her poetry a special, personal, and paradoxical role. Nature is a favorite theme, but so are sickness (as a symbol)—even the "coming on of a cold"—and neurotic states of mind. Her "Fairy Tale about the Rain" (1963) is an allegory of the poet, whose inspiration (the rain) follows her wherever she goes, and embarrasses her by splashing the floors in fine philistine houses. The poem has been interpreted as an attack on the literary philistines, and specifically on Khrushchev's entertainment and instruction of writers. It does lend itself to such an interpretation, but its wonderfully original imagery and deep-felt disdain for the safe, the comfortable, and the obvious cannot be narrowed to the purely local and topical. The following translation of one section may give some notion of the poem's power:

> The hostess said:
> "I must scold you.
> For heaven's sake,
> What talent!
> And you walked through the rain!
> So far."
> And all the guests shouted, "Over to the fire with her!
>   To the fire!"
> But on another day and in another time,
> On a public square,
> To the sound of curses and of music,
> We might have met together, you and I, as the drums rolled,
> And you would all have shouted: "Into the fire with her!
>   Into the fire!"

Akhmadulina has a strong sense of both language and form, and it is her purpose, in part achieved, that every line be an unobtrusive *bon mot*. She delights in intricately unusual end rhymes, some of which have the effect of neat puns.

Boris Slutsky (b. 1919) began to write and to publish before the war, but his most important work appeared after 1953. His published collections—*Memory* (1957), *Time* (1959), *Today and Yesterday* (1961), *Extended Noon* (1973)—contain his most characteristic work. A selection of his poems was published in the collection *Pages from Tarusa* (1961). His thematic range is wide. He has written many lyrics that present scenes of war simply and vividly. He writes of construction work in Moscow, of schools, of how he came to write poetry, and of how poetry ought to be written. His vision is childlike at times in his clear enjoyment of the world. Both in his language and in his images he seems to aim at the obvious, almost at the banal, then deliberately to miss banality and arrive instead at something simple but slightly offbeat and surprisingly interesting, as in his short poem about the war, which beautifully concludes: "Lasted a long time, the war. Four years."

There are many other poets who might be mentioned and whose work does represent an effort to create out of verse, as Slutsky would say, "the truth and happiness." Among them are Evgeny Vinokurov and a young lyric poet whose first work appeared only in the sixties, Novella Matveeva. She is a highly gifted and disciplined poet whose themes cover a wide range of interest and experience: art, architecture, world history, literature, and other things. Matveeva deals in her work with what might be called a "lyrical problem": the relationship of the poet to the welter of experience, to "Mars, Athens, and an old shoe, a squall, a basket, and building lime, the day of judgment and mud on the road." In each of her poems there are rich layers of symbolic meaning.

The revival of poetry in the sixties featured a number of older poets as well as young ones. Alexander Tvardovsky, the editor of *New World*, published in that journal his "Tyorkin in the Other World," which follows the hero of his earlier poem "Vasily Tyorkin" into the nether regions, where he finds an inferno organized along the lines of a Stalinist bureaucracy. Bulat Okudzhava is enormously popular as a singer of his own simple, nondidactic songs about intimate and personal things. Leonid Martynov and some others have published interesting and unhackneyed lyrics.

Iosif Brodsky is an especially interesting case. Because he had no regular employment and worked only at the poet's trade, he was tried and convicted in Leningrad in 1964 on the charge that he was a parasite.

Only a scattering of his work has appeared in the Soviet press. Contemporary Soviet poets regard his talent highly, and Anna Akhmatova considered him the outstanding poet of the younger generation. He stands apart both from his contemporaries and from his predecessors, although his work is clearly related, not only to earlier Russian poets, but also to Dante, John Donne, and T. S. Eliot, all of whose work he knew. There is a deep and serious religious strain in his work, and he has clearly been affected by a study of the Bible. Gravely conceived and solemnly executed long poems such as "Isaac and Abraham," and the poem "Procession," resemble nothing that is being done in the Soviet Union today. Brodsky emigrated in 1973, and has been prolific as an exile poet. I will deal with that aspect of his work in a later chapter.

A Final Word on Socialist Realism

The writing we have examined is interesting, skillfully done, and probably honest, and it offers some measure of formal or thematic excitement. But by comparison with the experimentation that dominates literary life in the West, Soviet prose of the surface channel during the sixties and seventies was conventional in form and thematically tame. Yet there is good reason to believe that should the Party loosen its hold, there would be an immediate search for a new kind of fiction and for a new accent in poetry. New themes, hitherto taboo in the puritanical pages of the Soviet press, would suddenly blossom forth, and Soviet Russian literature might begin to resemble somewhat the literature of the West. Many writers would eagerly take up the search for the fantastic and the exaggerated, and would explore the offbeat and the unusual. Some would abandon traditional realistic narrative, the traditional story form, and the traditional novel in favor of experimenting with the perception and presentation of time, objects, or states of mind. The work of Sinyavsky is an indication that some writers would like to embark on ventures into the grotesque or to examine perversion, impotence, and paranoid states of mind. For instance, in Katayev's "The Holy Well," published in 1966, we find a conscious effort to abandon realistic narration and recover the experience of the author's long lifetime in the form of fantastic dream images framed in a dimension that has nothing to do with common-sense notions of time sequence. The work is quite frankly an experiment, and with its appearance the rebels against traditional art forms now include in their number not just a few young people who will some day grow up and be sensible, as Sholokhov would have it, but one of the oldest and most respected writers in the Soviet Union, Valentin Katayev.

Katayev's "The Grass of Oblivion" (*New World*, no. 3, 1967) is another effort to recover the past, one that uses arrangements and contrivances usually considered the property of fiction. Katayev makes no claim that his reminiscences are documentary; rather, they are an imaginative re-creation of an intricate set of relationships with certain people and events: with Bunin and Mayakovsky; with "Klavdia Zaremba," an invented character who symbolizes the women he knew who gave everything for Communism; with "Riurik Pchelkin," another invented character, who is the author's own shadow—a young man who wrote agitational articles for the Bolshevik press. The Revolution itself figures as a mysterious and overwhelming event whose complex and unpredictable effects shaped all of their lives.

"The Grass of Oblivion" is an extraordinarily subtle experiment in the creation of a literature somewhere on the border between fact and fiction. It bestows upon certain real people a vividness of character and presence that history has so far denied them. The poets Bunin and Mayakovsky are presented from the viewpoint of a young man for whom poetry is a kind of faith. We are given significant but sparse details of their appearance, manner, and effect, but they are fully characterized by remembered lines of their poetry. It may very well be that Katayev is making an important point in his juxtaposition of Bunin and Mayakovsky—two mutually exclusive human beings who hated one another—as the most important influences in his own life. His work suggests that the grass of time may at last make possible a reconciliation between the two segments of modern Russian literature, Soviet and *émigré*, which have anathematized each other. The work also contains an implicit reflection on the irreality of time and the insubstantial quality of memory. Did the young Katayev, who figures as "Riurik Pchelkin," really exist, or is he just an episodic actor temporarily incarnated in the shifting forms of memory?

Evidence as to the kind of thing that might surface should controls be lifted is contained in the collection of poetry and prose entitled *Metropol*, which has already been mentioned. That enterprise was a deliberate effort by a group of writers, some of them now in the emigration, to publish their writing in the Soviet Union without benefit of censorship. The experiment failed, and the volume has appeared only in the West, though it apparently circulates freely in *samizdat*. Sexual themes are prominent in the volume. Even "gay" sex is treated in Yuz Aleshkovsky's "Lesbian Song" which celebrates a Lesbian marriage in a labor camp for women. The song is impressive only as the first frank treatment of a common situation in the women's camps, where girls cultivated close attachments to older and stronger women, who could provide not only warmth but some protection against inmate brutality. Boris Vakhtin provides a devastating sketch of a ridiculous little man who happens to be a censor. Iskander contributed a sketch describing the corruption surrounding the executed KGB chief Beria, including his rather baroque love life. The satirical singer Vysotsky wrote a verse parody of Pushkin's *Ruslan and Lyudmila* on a theme quite common in village prose, the disappearance not only of wood nymphs and sprites but of the very woods themselves. The poets Akhmadulina and Voznesensky both contributed brief supporting pieces. The collection as a whole was noteworthy as a symptom.

Literature published in the Soviet Union roughly since the emergence of Solzhenitsyn in 1962 seldom fitted the precepts of socialist realism laid down in the Stalinist period and always honored in the letter. Nor do the novels we have examined ever follow the established pattern or, as Katerina Clark puts it,[1] the "master plot" of socialist realism as exemplified in Gladkov's *Cement*, Katayev's *Time Forward*, Ostrovsky's *How the Steel Was Tempered* or Polevoy's *Story About a Real Man*. Hosking in his study *Beyond Socialist Realism* demonstrates that writers composing a broad spectrum of modern Russian literature, whether published in *gosizdat, samizdat,* or in exile, have in effect freed themselves from the narrow confines of the old canon. Even that stalwart of socialist realism Valentin Katayev broke with realism itself, as I noted earlier, in his series of experiments with the time dimension. And the published work of Okudzhava, Iskander, Kazakov, and others we have seen has never fitted any official mold. Socialist realism by the late seventies and even earlier was a concept irrelevant to the facts of Russian literature.

A literary process was at work that involved all of Russian literature; *samizdat* has had its effect on *gosizdat,* and both are intricately involved with Russian literature in exile. Solzhenitsyn when he praised certain rural writers emphasized that "they and I have different conceptions of the ways in which our contemporary literature can serve today's society," yet he considered those writers to be "the core of contemporary Russian prose."[2] What we observe is a process with profound cultural significance, the essence of which was probably caught by Sinyavsky when he spoke of an "invitation to the dance." The two segments of Russian literature have not performed their intricate movements in total isolation from each other but as part of a loose ritual pattern in which the steps of one partner may influence or be conditioned by the movements of the others. The experiments of Valentin Katayev are part of a whole in which Sinyavsky's much bolder play with narrative time invited a response. And Trifonov in his relentless exposure of the moral desert inhabited by Soviet intellectuals is, though less obviously polemical than Solzhenitsyn, in symmetrical rapport with the famous exile's angry demand that they stop "living by the lie."

In this sense there is indeed only *one* Russian literature and not two.

16 Exiles, Early and Late

Modern Russian literature includes a variegated and substantial body of writing published outside the Soviet Union. The stream of Russian literature bifurcated in 1917 into two currents; *émigré* literature, or what the *émigrés* call "Russian literature abroad," and the domestic—and in some periods safely domiciled—literature produced in the Russian homeland. If they are eventually to place modern Russian literature in proper perspective, future historians will have to trace and follow the two currents as part of a single stream. As time moves on and the embittered political issues of the century fade into the past, *émigré* writers will eventually take their place as a component of Russian literature, just as Alexander Herzen, who wrote most of his work in exile, is now firmly established in the history of nineteenth-century Russian literature.

We have noted a kind of antiphonal response pattern between the two separated branches of Russian literature during the seventies. The interrelationship of the *émigré* and Soviet streams in the early twenties was even more striking. Efim Etkind has pointed out the response of Tsvetayeva in the emigration to both Mayakovsky and Pasternak who had remained in Russia, and Lazar Fleishman performed a subtle analysis of the complex interaction and interplay of early *émigré* literature with literature of the metropolis on the one hand, and with West-European literature on the other.[1] Obviously, there are not two Russian literature, *émigré* and Soviet, but only one.

It is very important, nevertheless, to locate clearly the distinctive features of the exile branch. Those features are the consequence of a complex set of conditioning factors: (1) the exile writer's necessary self-definition as a protester; (2) freedom from censorship; (3) physical separation from the Russian reader and the literary conventions of the homeland; (4) direct contact with non-Soviet social and literary habits and standards. And a fifth conditioning factor, more difficult to define but the most important one, is the exile experience itself. The overwhelming reality of that experience is borne out in the work of almost all writers of the early emigration. Among them the poet Vladislav Khodasevich and the novelist Vladimir Nabokov provided especially effective images of dislocation and estrangement. Of the later *émigrés*, those of the so-called third wave, the poet and novelist Eduard Limonov and the poet Iosif Brodsky both offer brilliant examples of the same phenomenon. These four *émigrés* have given particularly powerful artistic witness on the human predicament of exile.

The Exile Experience

A beautifully moving statement of the exile experience is made by Vladislav Khodasevich in his collection of poems entitled *European Night* (1927).[2] The exile's bitterness in those dark lyrics is tempered only by consummate poetic mastery: no easy effort at adjustment or optimism dilutes his poetic formulation of anger and loss. But the collection as a whole belies the poet's despairing statement, reported by Nina Berberova, that "I cannot write there, I cannot write here." As a matter of fact he could write here; and he wrote about us, in part.

In that same collection Khodasevich's long poem "Sorrento Photographs" develops a striking metaphor for the divided and confused consciousness of the exile, whose mixed images of home and abroad have the effect of defamiliarizing—of making strange in Shklovsky's sense—both the experience of exile life and memories of home. Khodasevich compares the fantastic results of this process to the double exposure of a film by an absent-minded photographer:

> Sometimes an absent-minded photographer
> will lose count of his shots on a film
> and snap a pair of friends
> on Capri, beside a little white goat—
> and on the spot, not moving the film,
> he will print over them the bay
> beyond the steamer's stern
> and the sooty stack
> with a shock of smoke on its forehead.
> This winter one of my friends

did just that. Before him
water, people, and smoke intermingled
on the muddied negative.
His friend half-transparent
with his airy body
blocked the contours of rocky giants
while the little goat, its legs flung skyward
butted Vesuvius with its tiny horns . . .
That imprint of two worlds
telescoped appealed to me:
hiding in itself a vision,
that's how my life flows by.

As the poet travels in and around Sorrento on a motorcycle he has
two memories of Russia which are superimposed, respectively, on a
view of Amalfi and on Vesuvius and the Bay of Naples. The first Russian memory is of a low and miserable house in Moscow from the base-
ment of which the body of a floor polisher in his coffin is being carried
to his grave; the funeral procession seems to move through prickly
agaves, and the dead man's head "swims in the azure air of Italy." And
in the second telescoping of memories the angel guardian which
crowns the Cathedral of Peter and Paul in St. Petersburg is

reflected in the greenish waves
of the Gulf of Castellamare,
the mighty guardian of Tsarist Russia
toppled headfirst.
Ominous, fiery, brooding,
so the Neva once reflected him
and so he appeared to me—
an error on the hapless film.

And Khodasevich, expectant of the further tricks memory may play,
ends his poem with a question concerning her caprices:

Amid what losses and troubles
after how many epitaphs,
will she surface, airy,
and what else, in turn
will the shadow of Sorrento photographs
cover, without covering.

So in Khodasevich's poems on exile dark images of a European night
give way to the bright paradox of Sorrento double exposures, suggesting that something in the exile experience balances loss and disappointment.

This paradox, however, in no way lessens the magnitude of the

exile's loss, especially that particular loss suffered by one who has participated in the artistic or literary life of his native metropolis. "No one
can prize his health fully until he has lost it; and thus it is with one's
native land," says the exiled poet of Mickiewicz's *Pan Tadeusz,* and most
exiled poets know exactly what he meant. Pushkin in exile compares
himself to the Roman poet Ovid, who, banished to the culturally barren
north coast of the Black Sea and condemned to live among Scythians,
as he called the barbarians, in most of his poetry mourned the loss of
his homeland, too far from his Italy. And yet with all his bitter complaints as to his lot Ovid was actually rather productive during his
Scythian exile. His "sad elegies" (*Tristia*) complain a lot, but also tell
about the Scythian land, its climate, and the barbarous features of its
inhabitants. Josef Skvorecky, the exiled Czech novelist, has suggested
that Conrad rather than Ovid should be the model for the *émigré.* Joseph
Conrad, though the loss of Poland lay heavily on him, learned to speak
and write the Scythian tongue in its English variant, and he loved it.

It is possible to imagine on the basis of recent records, both autobiographical and fictional, the nature of the loss experienced by the exile,
especially the exile who is a Russian writer. The disappearance of the
Russian language from everyday life—unless one chooses to isolate
oneself in a narrow circle of *émigrés*—is quite possibly the most serious
deprivation. After writing nine novels in Russian, up to 1937, Nabokov
mastered English, but felt the loss of his language as of a vital organ: "I
had to abandon my natural idiom, my untrammeled, rich, and infinitely
docile Russian tongue for a second-rate brand of English." Consider
what loss of the language means to a writer. It means the loss of an environment, the only one, where verbal nuance works. Loss of immersion in the speech community in which the language, for good or ill, is
evolving. Loss of the ears that can catch immediately a verbal invention.
A bitter thing also is the acquisition of a new circle of non-native friends
who speak Russian, as some tell them, *comme des anges,* or at least "remarkably well," but who also sound like the deaf-mute Pogorevshikh
in *Doctor Zhivago,* who could not hear language at all but had carefully
learned, by artificial contrivance, to articulate intelligible sentences in
Russian—but only when the *lights* were on. Let me draw on Limonov
for an illustration of the moral devastation this contrived language can
wreak in the life of an *émigré.* I refer to one of the cleaner passages in his
novel *This is Me, Eddie;* the hero is performing a normal act with an
American adult of the opposite sex who at the moment of climax asks
him the question *"ty konchíl?"* ("have you finished?"), putting the accent
on the last syllable. The moment is destroyed for him, not by the inept
question, but by a misplaced accent.

Received wisdom suggests that separation from the native language is indeed a grievous blow for a writer. As Dostoevsky put it, "I need Russia for my life, for my work," and Pasternak echoed him, "A departure beyond the borders of my country is for me equivalent to death." But there is evidence that this may not necessarily be so for all writers. The Polish writer Gombrowicz wrote his most innovative work while an exile in Buenos Aires, as Ewa Thompson has pointed out, and Czeslav Milosz suggests that absence of the native milieu may help a writer to "sense his native tongue in a new manner." In other words there may in many cases be a kind of Sorrento photograph effect in the exile's language experience also: one's own native tongue may be defamiliarized in the new linguistic environment, and "new aspects and tonalities of the native tongue may be discovered." But if this is to happen there must first be a true double exposure of the film, and the writer must live in two worlds at once. Very few have succeeded in that.

And it should be remarked that loss of the language and of Russian literary culture can be acutely felt even by *émigrés* who have suffered discrimination in the homeland and have no traditional ties to the Russian soil. Such writers are, paradoxically, sometimes more devoted to the language than the Russians themselves.

The second great loss, after the language—and this is true especially of the more recent *émigrés*—is to be deprived of the intellectual struggle itself and the intense supporting intimacy of the small circles that carried on that struggle at home. Alexander Herzen in *My Past and Thoughts* reflects many times on his lost comrades of the university and the philosophical freethinking circles, and as he recalls them many years later he insists that he has found nothing in Europe—except perhaps in Italy, another backward country—to compare with them.

One of the bitterest complaints of *émigrés* I have known is that they can find nothing here remotely comparable to the intense intellectual life they had shared with intimates at home. Once again I turn to the writings of Limonov for a text. Can we forget his merciless satire of well-heeled American academic intellectuals whose conversation consists of anecdotes, smart small talk, and gossip, which he bitterly contrasts to the endless discussions, always on high and serious matters, remembered from home in Moscow. I offer no opinion as to the quality of those midnight debates, but the point is that in *that* kind of a society such free inquiry could take place nowhere else. Imagine the dislocation felt by a modern exile who suddenly finds himself in a society where free inquiry and unhampered talk are a matter of course and can take place anywhere, and imagine his desolation at finding that the intimate circle of friends devoted to learning and the truth is now beside the point.

A third great loss, especially for a contemporary Russian writer, is the loss of his special position as a writer. Perhaps the initial behavior of Solzhenitsyn in our midst, his urge to lecture us on topics of which he is profoundly ignorant, was just a symptom of disorientation in an environment where the writer is neither honored as a prophet nor persecuted as an enemy of the state, two things which in the Soviet Union could be the same thing. In his own country this prophet, Solzhenitsyn, was not without honor. The whole inhuman apparatus of a powerful state, which has thousands of nuclear warheads, concentrated, as *The Calf and the Oak* shows us, on frustrating the work of one lone writer working in the underground, like a folk hero immersed in deep waters but sure of emerging victorious, engaged all the time in a deadly struggle with the powers of darkness. There is nothing comparable to that experience in the pragmatic pluralistic societies of the West. The reason writers are both honored and persecuted in the Soviet Union is that there they are important, because they are regarded as dangerous. Again Limonov: "What's a poet here? Nothing. That's what. But there, even the powers that be are afraid of poets." Even in the underground, even in a camp, a Russian writer may be more alive than in the cultural hinterland of Vermont, among Scythians. What is a calf to do when he has no oak to butt his head against? Yet there is much he *can* do if, in the words of Czeslaw Milosz, he is not like those recent immigrants who "stay in their shell and are mistrustful of the West." As the Czech novelist Josef Skvorecky has said in different words, the wrench and dislocation an exile writer suffers is richly compensated by the double exposure to which chance or fate or maybe some "Old Nobodaddy" just as absent-minded as chance or fate, has subjected the film of his memory.

Memory with its tricks of juxtaposition and interference has always opened the possibility for an exile of seeing his new land in ways the natives never see it. There are many cases that illustrate this, but probably the greatest is Vladimir Nabokov, whose novel *Lolita* produces an estrangement of commonplace American scenes that no native could possibly have contrived, just as Nabokov's richly inventive English style could only have been contrived by a foreigner—and, as I believe, by a Russian. Only a distraught Humbert Humbert, his mind full of memories of the Riviera, and Paris and Berlin, as well as of that tasteful mansion on Morskaya Street in St. Petersburg (now Herzen Street), could have revealed to us so utterly the affluent emptiness of an upper-middle bourgeois American suburb. Note that Charlotte Haze, the mother of his great love, the twelve-year-old Lolita, lived at 324 Lawn Street, the address a perfect symbol of the ample greenswards and neatly tailored hedges that ensconce vulgar American philistinism. Mrs. Haze is an expectant widow with features of a type that "are to be defined as a weak solution of Marlene Dietrich," and when she shows her prospective lodger and lover the toilet, he cannot help noticing a "pinkish cozy, coyly covering the toilet lid." So deeply is the novel *Lolita* involved with America and the American language that Nabokov, with all his ingenuity, was unable to translate that last phrase adequately into Russian. Everything is lost, the intimate cozy, the philistine coyness, the lid itself, not to speak of alliteration and rhythm. *Lolita* is an American book, which can fully exist only in English, and could have been written only by a Russian.

Defamiliarized in the context of allusions to Flaubert and numerous others, we come to know the American motel civilization, all those Sunset Motels, U-Beam Cottages, Hillcrest Courts, Pine View Courts, Mountain View Courts, Skyline Courts, and many more. And the American landscape looks stranger and stranger to the eye of a Russian who knew it only from picture-book drawings, or the painted oilcloths imported from America to be hung above washstands. The American road itself: "at night, tall trucks studded with colored lights, like dreadful giant Christmas trees." "Distant mountains. Near mountains. More mountains." "Heart- and sky-piercing snow-veined gray colossi of stone, relentless peaks appearing from nowhere at a turn of the highway; timbered enormities; butter of black lava. Hundreds of Scenic Drives, Soda Springs, Painted Canyons . . ." Nabokov's is probably the finest appreciation of the American road ever written.

Given by a narrator whose double and triple exposures include childhood memories of the spacious Rukavishnikov estate not far from St. Petersburg, which he inherited then immediately lost to the people in 1917—as he tells us in *Speak Memory*—Nabokov's American scenes are easily defamiliarized because in America even the most ordinary and obvious things are really strange to him. What a priceless gift that is for any writer, and with it life has compensated the exile writer for all of his losses.

Lolita as exile literature has special interest because it defamiliarizes the most familiar American scenes, but Nabokov's work as a whole carries out the same process. He emigrated in 1919, and all his important work was written in exile. *Camera Obscura* (1932), translated as *Laughter in the Dark*, defamiliarizes the German world of dull businessmen and sharp, ruthless operators, and exposes the nothingness of a "great love." *The Defense* (1930) focusses in a single point the dislocation of a mind absorbed in the art of chess and alienated from normal life. The melancholy ironies in the life of the *émigré* teacher of literature,

Pnin, in the novel of that name (1957), illuminate American students and American academia from a delightfully naïve foreign viewpoint. The autobiographical work *Speak Memory* (1960, 1966) is a truly beautiful evocation of past events and scenes figured against the backdrop of a present reality. The main character in *Pale Fire* (1962) is an exile from a place called Zembla for whom any piece of literature in any language must necessarily be a distorted reflection of his own native land.

The Gift (1937) is probably his greatest novel, and it is the last one he wrote in Russian. That novel is permeated with the experience of exile and a brooding sense of organic, unbreakable attachment to a literary culture that no longer existed, except in the minds of scattered exiles. The novel is a great achievement as an imaginative evocation of that culture through literary allusion and nostalgic reminiscence. The central character is a poet, Godunov-Cherdyntsev, who has an umbilical attachment to Pushkin as the head and source of Russian literature. Much of the novel consists of discussion, in one form or another, of Russian literature and literary questions. Many passages investigate the psychological process of poetic creation, offering serious documentation of the compulsive, trancelike state in which Godunov-Cherdyntsev, and no doubt other poets, create rhythms, gather and store rhymes, discover metaphors. And the problem of the perception and understanding of poetry, a central concern in all of Nabokov's work, is treated here in purely Russian terms as a debate between the radical nineteenth-century critic Chernyshevsky and a modern poet of symbolist provenience. Chernyshevsky believed that life was primary and art only secondary, capable of edifying and instructing only as it imitated and illuminated the former. Godunov-Cherdyntsev in *The Gift* fashions a fictional biography of Chernyshevsky which portrays the purveyor of such dull nonsense as a nearsighted, nephritic, and angular bore. That "biography"—by a modern Russian poet, who would have been silenced, imprisoned, or executed in the homeland—is a judgment upon those who would use literature as educational entertainment. That poet, the voice, certainly, of Nabokov, specialized not in obvious everyday reality, apperceived and manipulated for the good, say, of society, but in fantasy, infantile reasons and associations, reflections or shades of the real world ("the shadow of the waxwing slain, on the false azure of the window-pane"), and he conspicuously wastes the small change of familiar mental processes. That extraordinary novel, *The Gift*, is, among other things, a polemic with common-sense notions of poetry entertained by Russian radical critics of the nineteenth century and by their descendants, the smug pseudo-Marxist philistines of the Soviet Union—a polemic carried on by one of the great exiles.

*   *   *

A stunning example of Khodasevich's double exposure is Limonov's *This is Me, Eddie,* a book from which I have already drawn a few texts. That book is a powerful defamiliarization, not only of Russian life both in the homeland and in the emigration but also and especially of American life, presented in an astonishing variety of candid shots. And the narrator's angle of vision is abnormal, askew: he is a Soviet *émigré* but one not yet educated in the clichéd pieties of American life. He is estranged as a down-and-outer even among the *émigrés.* He hasn't made it in American life. Not only has he not landed a job as poet-in-residence anywhere, but the best job he could get was that of busboy, in a high-class hotel it is true. He speaks for the down-and-out but speaks with a Russian voice in Russian, and as he does he remembers how it was to be down and out and rejected in Moscow too. One hears in that book the authentic voice of those on the bottom who very seriously hate those who have made it, whether here in our own dear land, or at home in Russia. The mute, inert misery of skid-row alcoholics, hopeless dropouts, and low-grade crooks, the desperate hatred of these exiles for the clean world, Limonov articulates for us. From their point of view "there isn't a hell of a lot of difference between here and there."

Estrangement is a mutual experience of Eddie and the Americans among whom he lives. As he prepares his cabbage soup (*shchi*) on the balcony of his cheap hotel room in midtown Manhattan in full view of hundreds of high office windows, he looks up and reflects on how he hates all those clerks, secretaries and managers—not all of them but many of them, he corrects himself—hates them because they live boring lives, because they sell themselves in slavery to a job, because they wear vulgar checked trousers, because they make money and have never seen the world. But when he imagines them looking down at himself half naked cooking up *shchi* in a pot on his cheap balcony, he understands perfectly their own disorientation to him: "Of course they don't know what cabbage soup is. All they see is that every other day a man on the balcony cooks up, in a huge pot, some barbarous stuff that gives off a lot of smoke." The double-edged defamiliarization in that scene on the balcony in mid-Manhattan, and of many other scenes in the book that could be adduced, is a rare feat of what Bakhtin would no doubt call the "dialogic imagination."

And Limonov's range is astonishing, reaching from a filthy playground where he accommodates a black fag in a sandbox to the superrich elegance of a splendid Connecticut estate, where the millionaire owner has original Salvador Dalis hanging in his john. Limonov's double-exposed film has special piquancy also in that it includes sex-role double images. The narrator represents his desperate sexual pursuit of men and women, boys and girls—let us just note in passing that Humbert Humbert too had a severe sexual hangup—as a dedicated search for Love, for "juncture" with some other human being who really cares. His wanderings in search of love lead him full circle from the young and beautiful black thief Johnny in the alleyways of New York to aging penthouse gays with deteriorating but well cared for and highly polished bodies. What strange goings-on we do see, and of course the whole point of estrangement, according to Shklovsky, is that we *do see* something. The rich homosexual playboy "Raimon" tries to seduce the narrator but only disgusts him, and that priceless scene is caught in one double-exposed frame: "When he grabbed me we staggered around like two Japanese Sumi wrestlers."

Iosif Brodsky (b. 1940) is certainly one of the important poets of the twentieth century, and as such he became an exile and a wanderer almost by necessity. As I have noted, because he had no regular employment and worked only at the poet's trade, he was brought to trial in Leningrad in 1964 on the charge that he was a "parasite," one not engaged in in "useful labor," and he was sentenced to five years at hard labor, a sentence later commuted, probably in response to vigorous protest from both Russian and Western writers. The record of his trial, published in the West, is evidence of the dominance in the Soviet Union, at least at certain times and places, of vulgar and dull-minded philistines, characters held in check for the most part in democratic societies. Brodsky's claim that he was not a parasite, but actually a hardworking poet, met with the objection of the judge: "Who has determined that you are a poet? Who appointed you to the ranks of the poets?"

After his return from a year and a half at hard labor Brodsky continued to write poetry and do translations, but his poetry was published for the most part in the West. A selection of lyrics and long poems was published in New York in 1965, and another in 1970, while the poet was still in the Soviet Union.

Brodsky's poetry deals with the persistent unsolved questions of existence: time, origins, space, life and death, along with the psychological puzzles of dislocation, depression, and insanity. While it conveys a sense of ultimate bafflement with such problems, the total effect of his work is a kind of happy transcendence achieved by sheer exuberant virtuosity of imagery and language. Brodsky's poetry, even when it deals with melancholy and death, should have a positive therapeutic value: just as the reading of Mandelshtam's poetry was said to be "good for the lungs and a cure for tuberculosis," so Brodsky's lines might be useful in psychiatric practice. Even when he speaks of death Brodsky's poetry makes death its own, appropriates it totally, triumphantly realizes its utter blackness and emptiness. One of his best poems, on the blackness of a black horse, forces the language to yield up every image of blackness it has, to reveal all possible inflections of the words for black and dark. As the black horse approaches the lonely campfire,

> He was black, he felt no shadow.
> So black he couldn't be any blacker.
> As black he was as midnight pitch.
> As black as the forest before us.
> As black as the inside of a needle.
> As that place in the chest between the ribs.
> As the hole in the ground where a seed is planted.
> I think it must be black inside us.

And in the poem "Elegy for John Donne" we experience not loss but riches in the long, illimitable list of all the things that "sleep" now that the poet, John Donne, is dead:

> John Donne has gone to sleep, and everything is sleeping.
> The walls are asleep, the floor, the bed, the pictures,
> the table is asleep, the rugs, the locks, the hook,
> the whole wardrobe, the buffet, the candle, the curtains . . .

The long poem *"Gorbunov and Gorchakov"* is a dialogue in an insane asylum between two committed madmen, who discuss with a certain mad logic all the anguish of their lives in the hospital, their dreams, their hangups, their preferences, their philosophical and political beliefs, their opinions of one another. The dark passages and strange whorls of a madman's mind we explore with sympathy, stunned recognition, and, it would seem, enhanced understanding.

For Brodsky, God does exist, in some sense, but his attributes are a matter of poetic conjecture:

> God looks down. And men look up:
> But each has a peculiar interest of his own.

The Artificer may be too subtle for us, but his work we can know. The lyric "The Butterfly" is an intellectually and strophically intricate meditation on the short, literally fleeting life of a complex little miracle of pattern and color, the butterfly. The following is George Kline's translation of the third stanza:

> Should I say that, somehow,
>   you lack all being?
> What, then, are my hands feeling
>   that's so like you?
> Such colors can't be drawn
>   from non-existence.
> Tell me, at whose insistence
>   were yours laid on?
> Since I'm a mumbling heap
>   of words, not pigments,
> How could your hues be figments
>   of my conceit?

It is fascinating to read Brodsky's poems because, filled as they are with the inventory of light and life, they present the negative of those things, darkness and death, as matters for contemplation not totally immune to the power of human thought. As Milosz put it, "His larger enterprise is to fortify the place of man in a threatening world."

Brodsky is quintessentially the poet of exile, one who was prolific after leaving the homeland and who writes beautifully about the lands and the experiences of his exile, Florence, London, Ann Arbor, and Cape Cod. His work is still another example of the Sorrento photograph effect. A number of poems might be used to illustrate his subjective apprehension of those places: "Mexican Divertissement" (1975), "December in Florence" (1976), "Lithuanian Divertissement" (1971), but the best of these and one of his most characteristic and strongest poems is "Lullaby of Cape Cod," which masterfully develops the themes of exile and wandering, inexplicable survival, and space and time as mysteries in a lonely human life. Translation can only weakly reflect the original, and paraphrase must violate the structure of meter and rhyme, but a judicious mixture of the two can perhaps convey something of the poem's profundity and power. The setting is a seaside resort on Cape Cod on a stiflingly hot summer evening at the hour "between the dog and the wolf," when that part of the globe is immersing itself in night, when a steeple crowned by a cross "apathetically darkens and disappears, like a bottle forgotten on the table." Stifling heat and the disappearance of objects in the advancing dark are the chief sensual images of the poem. The opening line, "The eastern end of the empire sinks into night," locates the poet in one of the two empires where his life has been spent, and contains a reminder of the *other* empire where he was born. Some pages later he reflects on the impasse confronting a man who has encompassed both:

> I write from an empire whose edges
> sink deep beneath the sea. Having tasted
> two oceans and two continents, I feel
> almost like the great globe itself.
> I mean, there's nowhere else—no way out.
> Somewhere else is a scattering of stars,
> and they're burning.

And once again, he remarks on the insufficiency of a single globe for human purposes:

> Because when it's light there, here,
> in your hemisphere, it's dark. So to speak,
> one orb is not enough for two ordinary bodies.
> The globe was glued together God knows how.
> And there wasn't enough of it.

The paradox of survival, the presence of one's exiled self here or any-where, is the repeated motif of the poem, and it is realized through a rich set of variations on the image of sea creatures finding their way onto land. "Strange to think that you've survived, but it happened." The crab survived:

> Crawling onto an empty beach from the ocean's depth
> a crab digs into wet sand . . . and sleeps.

And a stranded fish survives:

> Man survives like a fish in the sand:
> crawls off into the bush, and getting up on crooked legs,
> walks away (his tracks like a line of writing)
> into the heart of the continent.

Adaptation and survival are built into the nature of things:

> As long as shoes exist
> there's somewhere to stand.
> A surface. Dry land. And its beaches
> will attend to the quiet song of the cod.

Euclidean space, which makes travel arduous, has been cancelled out for the wanderer by Lobachevsky (and Einstein), whose parallel lines do meet, making again for his survival. And a bird who has lost her nest will look for some place to put her eggs:

> Drops them in the hoop on an empty basketball court.

Space and time aid in adaptation:

Space backs off like a crab, letting time move forward.

There are a number of stanzas on the paradox of the point in space where a body is at a given moment:

> The place where I am is paradise.
> Because paradise is a place of helplessness.
> Because it's one of those planets where
> there's no perspective.
> The place where I am is a peak
> as of a mountain. Above there's only air, and old Chronos.
> Preserve these words; for paradise is a dead end.
> A cape stuck out into the sea. A cone.
> The prow of a steel ship
> and you can never cry out "Land ahead!"[3]

Those images of isolation and immobility at a single point in space—paradise—provide a counterpoint to the leitmotif of free exile, the exploration of time and space, that is the accepted lot of the poet, whose work is the summit and realization of life. The poem began with the free fish, the poet's figure, coming up onto land, caught in the net of houses, surviving somehow on the land, and journeying deep into the continent. It ends with another free fish, the cod, an exile from the sea, knocking at his door.

Iosif Brodsky along with Solzhenitsyn, Sinyavsky, Aksyonov, and in the earlier period Nabokov, Khodasevich, Tsvetaeva, and many others forms the exile stream of modern Russian literature, a gift lavished upon the world by a state that, like Shakespeare's base Indian, "threw a pearl away, richer than all his tribe." At the time it expelled Brodsky, and the others, that state clearly could not distinguish pearls from worthless baubles. And how could it? As Shklovsky put it, "When Christ was alive the state could not understand his Aramaic, and it has never understood simple human speech." The Soviet state could hardly be expected to understand Brodsky's strong and simple language.

"Young Prose" and What Became of It

At the high point of the thaw in the early sixties, the moment when Solzhenitsyn's *One Day* was published in *New World*, a number of young writers broke decisively with the traditional form and content of Soviet literature. Those writers dealt with the problems of Soviet young people primarily, and their principal though not exclusive outlet was the journal *Youth* (*Yunost*) under the editorship first of Valentin Katayev and after 1962 of Boris Polevoy. Founded by Katayev in 1955, *Youth* was from the beginning friendly to unconventional content, and also to experiment with form. In very loose affiliation with the journal *Youth* a number of writers, some of whom remained in the Soviet Union after others emigrated, attained wide readership and popularity, and not only among the "youth." The journal itself had a circulation of well over two million (in contrast to *New World*'s roughly 175,000), and everybody read it.

The new movement included Bitov, Kazakov, Iskander, and Nagibin in prose, and Yevtushenko, Vosnesensky, and Akhmadulina among the poets, writers who have already been mentioned; but the chief figures were Aksyonov, Gladilin, and Voinovich, all of whom are now in exile. The most daring of the young iconoclasts was Vasily Aksyonov (b. 1932). He is the son of Evgeniya Ginzburg, whose account of her eighteen-year exile in the Magadan area has been dealt with above (see chapter 13). He was seven when his mother was arrested and taken away, and he was a teenager when, her term at hard labor ended, she managed to bring him to Magadan where they built together a precarious home in the shadow of Kolyma, an experience which later served as the basis of part of his novel, *The Burn* (1980). Probably the most moving scene in Ginzburg's book is the account of her reunion with her son after eleven years in the camps, and their recognition of one another through a shared interest in Russian poetry. For Vasily Aksyonov a mother was "someone you can recite your favorite verses to, and if you stop she will go on from the time where you left off." When they met after eleven years, in the company of apelike and inebriate Soviet officers and camp officials, his injunction to his mother was simply, "Don't cry in front of *them!*" And Aksyonov himself has not cried or given ground much; he managed to maintain his integrity and individuality as a writer, until at last he was forced into the emigration and stripped of Soviet citizenship.

Since the appearance of his first novel *Colleagues* (1960), Aksyonov has been prolific and uncompromisingly original. In *Colleagues* Aksyonov, who was trained as a doctor and had worked in various health institutions, presented amusing and sometimes edifying episodes from the lives of his young medical colleagues, whose ethical problems are his central concern. The novel brought him fame and position as a writer. But probably the most brilliant product of the youth prose movement was Aksyonov's novel *A Starry Ticket* (*Zvezdnyi bilet*, 1961), which seems to have been read by almost everyone and was bitterly attacked and vigorously defended in the Sovet press of the sixties. The novel deals with adolescent characters who think and talk in an idiom that instinctively rejects established formulas. Critics immediately suspected in Aksyonov himself an ironic attitude toward high ideals and serious purpose, but his young Dimkas and Mityas are, rather, authentic instances of adolescence. They clip and cut the accepted grammatical and syntactic patterns of their elders, they mangle and misuse the sacred idioms of socialism. They are in love with jazz, sports, offbeat clothing, and, of course, with falling in love. The purposeful aimlessness of their existence is itself a kind of system . . . a deliberate method of searching for independence and self-expression. The seventeen-year-old Dimka answers his older brother's reproaches: "Your career was decided for you before you were born, but I'd rather be a tramp and suffer privation than spend my whole life like a little boy, doing only what other people want me to do." The teenagers run away to Estonia (not very far!) instead of "going to the university" and taking advantage of the opportunities and privileges offered them in the safe prestigious ruts of Soviet society. "Going away to Estonia," a safe Soviet republic, may be a premature metaphor for leaving the homeland of Soviet socialism; the rejection of cant and hypocrisy, of "living by the lie," in Solzhenitsyn's well-known phrase, is implicit in this Soviet adolescent rebellion. Dimka works and grows up, but there is no suggestion that he will ever fully accept the world of his elders.

Much has been written about the sources of Aksyonov's style in this early work, and the principal "influences" are said to have been Hemingway and Salinger—his *Catcher in the Rye*—both of whom were admired and widely read in translation in the Soviet Union. The influence of Hemingway, and to a lesser extent Salinger, on Soviet writers in the sixties has been argued so often that it would be well to consider the matter carefully, since the question of influence here is more than usually complex. Salinger was popular in the Soviet Union because the irreverent teen-age idiom of Holden Caulfield provided a vehicle for the expression of deep alienation from the clichéd rhetoric of official literature; in other words Aksyonov, and also, as we shall see, Voinovich, *chose* to be influenced by Salinger because Salinger gave them what they needed. No one has ever suggested that Salinger or Hemingway influenced the style of Solzhenitsyn's *One Day*, but when he elected to tell Ivan Denisovich's story in the obscene idiom of the prisoners, Solzhenitsyn was responding to exactly the same need for authenticity that moved Aksyonov. Similarly Kazakov narrowed his focus to the subjective experience of a single mind, and Bulat Okudzhava in *Good Luck, Boy!* rejected general statements about battle in favor of the fragmented perceptions of a frightened, naïve youngster. All of the best writers of the early sixties have in common the imperative need to reject the ringing affirmative rhetoric of official literature in favor of authentic human speech on concrete matters. The effect on the readers was like a breath of pure air after a lifetime spent in smog.

Hemingway was an "influence" chosen by certain writers, and Hemingway has obligingly provided us with a passage which defines precisely the special quality in his own writing that was needed at that time in the Soviet Union. In one of the great passages in *A Farewell to Arms* (written in 1929), the hero and Gino, who is a "patriot," are talking, and Gino says of the recent mighty battles: "What has been done this summer cannot have been done in vain." And in his own mind the hero answers Gino's brave words:

> I did not say anything. I was always embarrassed by the words sacred, glorious, and sacrifice and the expression in vain. We had heard them, sometimes standing in the rain almost out of earshot, so that only the shouted words came through, and had read them, on proclamations that were slapped up by billposters over other proclamations, now for a long time, and I had seen nothing sacred, and the things that were glorious had no glory and the sacrifices were like the stockyards at Chicago if nothing was done with the meat except to bury it. There were many words that you could not stand to hear and finally only the names of places had dignity. Certain numbers were the same way and certain dates and these with the names of the places were all you could say and have them mean anything. Abstract words such as glory, honor, courage, or hallow were obscene beside the concrete names of villages, the numbers of roads, the names of rivers, the numbers of regiments and the dates.

The weariness with stale abstractions and hunger for particular people and places were felt also by Russian writers of the sixties, and some of them listened to Hemingway as a writer who knew not only his own secrets but theirs too.

Among the young writers Aksyonov was probably the most resourceful in the use of language, no doubt the most fertile in stylistic innovation, and certainly the most original in his manipulation of plot and narrative viewpoint. He moved with each work farther away from realistic narrative in the direction of experimentation with the novel form. The latter is at times carried to surprising lengths: there are two distinct first person narrators, in addition to a third person narrator in close attendance on them, in *A Starry Ticket;* a number of viewpoints are given in *Oranges from Morocco* (1963), whose formal innovations were a source of consternation at the time. In *An Excess Stock of Barrels* (*Zatovareunaya bochkotara,* 1968) there are frequent shifts of narrative perspective, variations (to put it mildly) in spoken idiom, stylistic parodies, intrusion of slogans and songs, in fact an agglomeration of stylistic elements where critics have spotted influences from Hemingway through Gogol and Belyi to Pynchon and Robbe-Grillet. But what we have in the end is purely Aksyonov, his very own hand.

The concept of "carnivalization" as developed by Bakhtin in his book on Rabelais clearly applies to what Aksyonov is doing, carnivalization of language especially. In the course of a linguistic *bouleversement*, nonstandard language overwhelms the standard and proper language. "Unofficial elements of speech," as Bakhtin puts it, the unpublishable realm of language, is freed from prohibition and counterposed on the printed page to official norms. Thus Aksyonov's later experiments, though they seem far enough away from Hemingway, still carry out the same project of freeing the Russian literary language from the philistine banality of the Soviet printed page.

In 1976 Aksyonov published in *New World* a characteristic work based on his tenure as a Visiting Professor at UCLA and entitled *Open Twenty-four Hours a Day Non-Stop (Kruglie sutki non-stop,* 1976). Though written before Aksyonov emigrated and published in the Soviet Union, that piece is a magnificent example both of the double-exposure technique utilized in the work of Khodasevich and Nabokov and of carnivalization. Even the published text, which had to go through the Soviet censorship mill, is full of double exposures, but in this case I suspect a deliberate technique at work rather than the photographer's absentmindedness; in fact we may have here the carefully structured double talk known as Aesopian language. Los Angeles provided the material necessary to create a carnivalesque atmosphere, but the American scene as a whole seems—to the unpracticed eye of this visitor—to be infected by the freedom of California and to provide an implicit contrast to fond memories of home with its rigors of discipline and frozen streets. "LA" offers Hare Krishnas, swamis, hippies, radical kids, a Renaissance Fair that upsets all cultural identities, and the complete messing up of established hierarchies in dress: the narrator is impressed by the fact that it did not really matter whether he wore a tie to dinner or not. Some do; some don't. The whole crazy carnival is felt as a protest against the American middle-class culture that, from a quite different social viewpoint, repelled the effete aristocrat Humbert Humbert. In the macaronic mixture of American and Russian speech we sense a muffled protest also at the Soviet philistine. To an orthodox Soviet editor or reader all those scenes of Women's Liberation demonstrations and the Struggle for Homosexual Rights no doubt seem evidence of capitalist decay in an advanced stage, but with a slight shift of the viewing angle and superimposed on a photograph of Moscow the picture of "LA" is a kind of creative chaos, a superflux of freedom that makes all things possible and could lead anywhere, God knows where. What can a Soviet Russian say to a culture that even permits a well-behaved dog to accompany his master to class? As the Professor, Aksyonov, writes: "All through the lecture he lay down quietly on the floor at his master's feet, kept looking at me, said nothing, only two or three times he yawned politely."

Some of Aksyonov's works—they might be called novels for want of a better term—were published only abroad: *Our Golden Bit of Rail* (*Zolotaya nasha zhelezka,* 1980), *The Burn,* and *Crimea Island* (1980). In the first two, various characters in turn become the focus of narration, sometimes in their own style or in terms of their own special needs, prejudices, and literary or scientific preoccupations. Documents, letters, dreams, reports, and many other things variegate the language style. The result is a verbal texture in which a "pattern in the carpet" is not always easy to make out, but these novels do present an astonishing variety of characters, experiences, and linguistic idiosyncrasy. Aksyonov's language and that of his characters is as a rule an invented idiom, studded with what are known in Russia as "barbarisms," that is, foreign words, usually American, along with scientific terminology, racy colloquial dialogue, and parodies of orthodox narrative idiom. Svirsky has pointed out that Aksyonov's books are indispensable, moreover, to any linguist concerned with the rich vagaries of contemporary Soviet slang. His sentences are, to use Shklovsky's terminology once more, deliberately impeded, retarded, made palpable both as to vocabulary and sentence structure.

The Burn includes a number of characters who collectively represent Aksyonov's generation, and indeed Aksyonov himself. The many narrators, the common fatherhood of whom is evidenced by their shared patronymic Apollinarovich, include a writer, a jazz musician (saxophone), a sculptor, a doctor, and a scholar. The five have many attitudes in common, and all participated in the youth movement. Pantelei A. Pantelei, the writer, has experiences very like those of Aksyonov himself as a writer, including a public confrontation with Khrushchev. And Aksyonov's Magadan childhood is reflected in the experience of the young man Tolya Von Shteinbok. The images of Magadan and the attitude toward the apelike oppressors of those who "love poetry" link this book to his mother's memoirs, as does their shared hope for the humanization of the apes. The enemies and tormentors of his mother and of the future narrators, each of whom realizes one facet of Aksyonov, are the company of official brutes described by Evgeniya Ginzburg and here characterized by Aksyonov: "The lout of the communal life completed his ascent, attained the dream of his nightmares—a general's stars."

An ambivalent and fascinating character is Captain Cheptsov who seems at first to embody the low cruelty of the regime but later reveals a few struggling traits of humanity. Here one is reminded of those ambivalent, rapidly changing Russian faces that Aksyonov sometimes features: "The women suddenly smiled sweetly. There you have it! That ability of Russian women to turn in a twinkling from sullen, wary suspicion to heartfelt warmth: that's really a gift!" And the best source of hope is the new father that Aksyonov (Tolya) found in the inferno of Magadan, a character based on a real person, Evgeniya Ginzburg's second husband, whose solidity and faith offer more than a little human hope.

The novel *Crimea Island* has as its setting a Crimea which is no longer a peninsula—"a half-island"—but a full island separated from and independent of the Soviet Union, an island where a capitalist democracy flourishes in the sun. This novel is thematically linked to *Open Twenty-four Hours a Day, Non-Stop,* with the difference that in the earlier novel the contrast of sunny California with the grim Soviet Union was carried out by superimposition, whereas in the later novel the two are in close geographic juxtaposition. It's clear we are intended to understand that the island is indeed California: it has the same "freevays," the same crush of automobile traffic on "veekends," the same supercharged cars and elegant houses perched precariously and beautifully on sheer cliffs. It has "bitniks" and "viminslib," all such lexical items transposed but not translated into Russian. And should there still be any doubt about where we are we have a conversation about "earthquake country":

> "Aren't you disturbed that your amazing house is built in a seismologically dangerous area?"
> "But it would be crazy to live on Crimea Island if you're afraid of earthquakes."

The hero of the novel, Luchnikov, has rejected the program of the Crimea *émigrés* and aristocrats to reconquer the Soviet Union militarily and annex it (they'd heard of David and Goliath) in favor of a "convergence" theory of his own: Crimea Island should simply join the Soviet as a constituent republic, thus bringing about a union of democracy and socialism, even at some sacrifice of democracy. Some very important Soviet figures oppose this because they depend on Crimea Island for technology and consumer goods and do not want to lose it as a place to spend pleasant holidays away from brotherly but gloomy Moscow. In the end Luchnikov's plan fails, since the Soviet Union can only understand "reunification" as occupation by Soviet troops. *Crimea Island* is, in comparison with earlier novels, relatively subdued in structure, and, once the reader accepts the violation of geography which locates California in the Black Sea, almost realistic.

In addition to his major novels Aksyonov has written a number of distinguished short stories. One of these has usually been singled out as especially poignant, and is frequently anthologized. "Half-Way to the Moon" deals with a subject close to Aksyonov: humanization through love. The hero, Kirpichenko, is as rough as a bear, an ex-soldier and an ex-convict who had never lived in a proper home. He falls in love with a stewardess, Tanya, on a flight from Khabarovsk to Moscow. The sudden stirring produces a sea change in him. He buys a book by Chekhov and reads it, though he had never read anything before. He feels things, cries, notices the landscape: snow and trees. He spends his whole vacation and goes through all his money just flying back and forth from Khabarovsk to Moscow and from Moscow to Khabarovsk hoping to see Tanya again. And that is all he wanted—just to see her. He does see her, finally, in the airport at Khabarovsk. He does not even speak to her, but he knows he will remember that such a being could exist . . . *did* exist. And that is enough.

Aksyonov was obliged to leave the Soviet Union in 1979 largely because of his sponsorship of the illegal publication *Metropol*, and he was soon after deprived of his Soviet citizenship.

Vladimir Voinovich (b. 1932) is another of the writers who were young in the early sixties and who, however different he may be from the others, still shared with them an attitude and a style. Voinovich was not associated with the journal *Youth*, but published in the main in Tvardovsky's *New World*, where his first story, "We Live Here," was published in 1961. The story was warmly reviewed by Tendryakov and others and secured a place for Voinovich among the young writers who featured a new intonation. Indeed it is a minor masterpiece. The author's modest purpose is, as he puts it, "to write about Goshka and the other people" who live in the remote collective farm village of Popovka. He brings each of them to life in a few casual, humorous strokes. Goshka, a good fellow, is taking extension courses to finish his high-school education. He hates slackers and phonies and punches them when he can, but he has no general observations to offer on any subject. Liza and Sanka, both construction workers, are in love with him. In simple physical terms, he loves Sanka, but she goes off to Moscow to become a singer and broaden her horizons. He does think of life and death:

"Here today and gone tomorrow."
"Are you afraid of death?"
"Yes."
"Why? If you die there's nothing to worry about. No German to study."
"I don't know. Maybe I'm curious. I want to know what'll happen tomorrow."

Goshka is a good fellow by instinct, as are most of the characters in the story. Two characters are inspired by "perspectives and history," Ilya, who is in charge of the Cultural Club, and Vadim, a city poet who has come to Popovka in search of "practical experience." Ilya, who secretly writes poetry on agricultural themes, has managed to get an expensive grand piano for the Cultural Club. On this precious, shiny instrument he has placed a sign: "Do not touch!" Vadim, the lyrical "I" whose verse sings of toil and sweat "in the mines," loses the workers' attention when they learn that he was never actually employed there. The efforts of the village to acquire culture are pathetic or ridiculous and are never sentimentalized. Slogans, inspirational thoughts, socialist exploits are lightly satirized by Vadim's inept verses, and it is no doubt symbolic of the remoteness of literature from the masses that Vadim himself, disconsolate and unappreciated, leaves the village for his native habitat, Moscow.

Voinovich is a master of humorously creative dialogue. His characters tell their own story, not in their thoughts, for they have none to speak of, but in their innocent conversation. The main burden of narrative and characterization is borne, without the author's intervention, by the dialogue, which is reduced to the simplest elements of basic communication. Take, for example, the following conversation between the Farm Chairman and the spokesman for a work gang who has just asked one hundred rubles a day per man:

"Well, you won't pay it?"
"I won't," said the Chairman positively.
"You won't?"
"I won't."
"Give me a light . . . All right. For the last time, will you or not?"
"I will not,"said the Chairman.

Voinovich is evidently abreast of the literary culture of his day. The influence of Zoshchenko can be felt in his satire of perennially ridiculous humanity. His teen-age characters have a nihilistic naïveté that reminds one of Salinger, and his laconic dialogue suggests that he too has learned from Hemingway. But he has an individual style and a spring of optimistic fun that sets him off from all of these.

His story "I Want to Be Honest" (1963) was negatively reviewed in the Soviet press because it supposedly revealed serious flaws of attitude and ideology. Its central character, Samoikhin, offers a continuous first-person reflection concerning his work and his problems, most of them slight and seemingly unimportant. He simply chatters on, describing a life that has many things in it—everything but interest and enthusiasm. The story gradually develops in a very low key a distinct undertone of tragedy, a sense that something essential is missing from Samoikhin's life, that his very activity only serves to fill a kind of vacuum. The pseudophilosophical reflections of one of the characters—an *autodidact*—on the nonexistence of external objects and other people provide humorous interludes, but they also contain the leitmotif of the story, the persistent sense of unreality.

Voinovich's "Two Comrades" (1967) offers a frightening portrait of a future careerist, hypocrite, scoundrel, and "poet" in his first adolescent efforts at "making it." The sensitive young man who narrates the story is intelligent, genuinely interested in poetry, and not too selfish. His "comrade" is a vulgar hunter after flashy clothes, money, and girls. When they are both caught by a peculiarly vicious set of hooligans, this comrade beats his friend without mercy at the behest of the gang in order to escape a beating himself. In the end he turns to literature, because poetry "pays well." The comrade is an embodiment of those grubby and mean qualities that spoil life.

During the sixties Voinovich wrote a brilliantly humorous satirical treatment of the Soviet way of life which circulated widely in *samizdat* and at last appeared in the West in 1969. For that volume the regime and especially the security police never forgave him, since the latter appear in it as inept, clownish thugs. The first two parts appeared under the title *The Life and Remarkable Adventures of the Soldier Ivan Chonkin* (1975) and the remainder under the title *Pretender to the Throne* (1979).

The hero of this imposingly lengthy "novel" is a common soldier named Chonkin who is such an honest and good-hearted simpleton that he creates disasters that expose the idiocies of the regime itself. Chonkin has reminded almost all commentators of Hašek's *Good Soldier Shweik*, and the comparison is not without merit, since in both cases honest stupidity thwarts the best laid plans. The difference is that Shweik as a member of an oppressed nationality in the Austro-Hungarian empire harbors imbecilic attitudes organically hostile to the military regime. Chonkin on the other hand is fatuously loyal to Stalin, but knows no better than to ask a political instructor at a lecture "whether it was true that Stalin had two wives," a question that so violates the Stalin icon that the instructor reaches a state of near hysteria in berating Chonkin for asking it. And he never answered it.

Chonkin's opportunities for creative confusion are abundant. A Soviet airplane has crashed not far from the headquarters of a collective farm and he is assigned to guard it. He guards it, but the authorities forget he's there and he becomes part of the collective farm picture. He moves in with the collective farm postmistress, Nyura, and they are very helpful to one another, until he hears a rumor that she has slept with Borka, her pig, of whom she is indeed very fond, as she is of all animals. Chonkin believes the malicious gossip—there was so much circumstantial evidence—and he gives her a choice: either me or him. "Unless we slaughter the boar," says Chonkin, "there will be talk." But if he should kill him, then there would be talk, too. People are so nasty.

The collective farm offers a number of openings for weird misunderstanding. The Chairman, Golubyov, is a drunken incompetent whose reports of production are faked and who is so afraid of being caught at something that he is sure Chonkin is an inspector of some kind sent to spy on him. In a long hilarious interview he feels out Chonkin, whose imbecilic answers convince him that the man really is smart and a plant, good at pulling the wool over your eyes. Yet he reflects that it may not be so bad, life in prison will probably be better than on his collective farm. In one of the better scenes of really heroic drunkenness in modern literature Golubyov and Chonkin find themselves late at night unable to walk, or to find the way back to the collective farm headquarters. They are at last able to make some headway by crawling along the ground on their bellies, guided by the stars.

Then there is Gladyshev the self-taught Soviet Marxist, Michurinist agronomist, and follower of Lysenko who loves to explain at length his plan for crossing tomatoes with potatoes and getting a plant that will produce both, tomatoes above ground and potatoes under. This is to be one of the great achievements of socialist agriculture, and Chonkin is impressed. Gladyshev experiments with a great variety of manures— horse, cow, pig, chicken—which he keeps in his house, to the great discomfort of his wife, Aphrodite, who cannot stand the smell. Nor can anyone else for very long. If Voinovich had said simply that the absurd Gladyshev was to be associated with the popular word for fecal matter, the effect would have been strong, but nothing like the detailed, prolonged, realized metaphor with which he characterizes the Soviet fraud Lysenko and his followers.

The local NKVD, when it gets word that an unknown and suspicious character "posing as a soldier" is in the area, sends out an eight-man squad to take him in—the eight men a prime fictional instance of concealed unemployment in the Soviet Union. But Chonkin understands nothing, except that his duty is to guard the plane from these attackers, and with Nyura's help he captures the whole detachment and takes them prisoner. When the NKVD captain who sent them out, Milyaga, tries to find out what is wrong, Chonkin captures him too. Meanwhile the war has started and German invaders are expected, so when a regiment of Soviet troops sent out to deal with "Chonkin and his band" capture Milyaga, who has given Chonkin the slip, the captain thinks they are Germans, and in another superlative scene, tries to convince them of his command of German and his love for Hitler. The NKVD has probably never been visited with such contemptuous ridicule.

Voinovich has a magnificent gift of language, an ear for absurd dialogue, a sure control of the apparatus of humor. Bitter though his own experience of the Soviet Union has been he is one of the most successful Russian humorists, surely on a level with Zoshchenko, and worthy of comparison with Gogol. His narrative style is a *skaz* closely related to Gogol and his narrator is ridiculously self-conscious, and circumstantial about his characters and the funny things that happen to them. Assuming for himself the fool's mask, he sometimes speaks intimately and confidentially to the reader, as in the opening lines of the book:

> It is now impossible to say exactly whether it did happen or did not, because the incident with which the whole story began (and has continued almost to the present day) happened in the village of Krasnoye so long ago that almost no eyewitnesses from that time remain. Those who do remain tell it differently, and several do not remember it at all. But to be truthful, this is not after all the kind of story worth remembering for very long. As for me, I heaped together everything I heard about it and added a little of my own, added perhaps even more than I heard. Ultimately, this story seemed so amusing to me that I decided to put it down in writing; however, if it seems uninteresting, boring, or even stupid to you, then the hell with it, pretend I said nothing.

Voinovich has written some other things published only in exile. "By Mutual Correspondence" is the story of a vile character who corresponds with lonely women for amusement and with no intention of marriage, only to be caught and trapped for life by an older, and smarter, female who needed a man—*any* man. *The Ivankiad* (1976) is the account of the author's resistance to the efforts of a party boss to take a room away from him in an apartment building so that the boss might break through the wall and install in that room a new private toilet for himself. It is written in outrage, but with Voinovich's unfailing gift for humorous statement.

Another prominent representative of young prose who emigrated in the seventies was Anatoly Gladilin (b. 1935), whose stories dealing with the ethical and intellectual problems of his generation began appearing in *Youth* in 1956. Gladilin wrote a number of things during the period of the thaw that place him in the thematic and stylistic company of Aksyonov and Voinovich. His characters are young, iconoclastic, often outwardly flippant but really exploring the problems that face a male human being who is almost, but not quite, an adult. The problem of noncommunication between the young and the moribund old is sensitively handled in *The First Day of the New Year* (1963). Like Aksyonov, Gladilin experimented with narrative viewpoint and introduced semidocumentary materials into a fictional context: letters, diaries, newspaper stories.

His novel *Forecast for Tomorrow* was never published in the Soviet Union but appeared in the West in 1972. Its central problem is the one which agitated the young men of the early sixties, the place of an individual human being in society and his relationship to humanity as a whole. The hero in his debate with himself comes down firmly in favor of the concrete particulars of his life—his own family—as against considerations of the future and humanity in general. After leaving the Soviet Union Gladilin wrote an account of his experiences there as a young man with a heterodox pen. *The Making and Unmaking of a Soviet Writer* (1979) is a report on the several varieties and levels of censorship with which such a writer somehow coped. It is an important document, not only on the young prose of the sixties, but on the Soviet literary establishment itself.

Religious Quest: Maximov and Ternovsky

Vladimir Maximov is among the powerful writers of the twentieth century and all his power has been devoted to the production of what has been called "a kind of holy epic against an evil ideology." Soviet Communism figures in Maximov's world as a kind of anti-Christ. Like the anti-Christ it wore the mask of Christ himself, mimicking the virtues of pity for the weak and devotion to mankind and enlisting the support of good men, only to show them in the end its own diabolical features. The central character in *Seven Days of Creation* (*Sem dnei tvoreniya*, 1973), Pyotr Lashkov, was drawn to the movement as a young man and for most of his life had been a convinced Communist, but in his old age he has seen through the deception and now seeks a way out in personal salvation. The subtitle of the first section of the work, "A Journey to Find the Self," carries the essential lesson of Lashkov's agonizing search for a religious definition of himself and a spiritual counterweight to the bankrupt materialism of the state. The intervening five days of the search take us through the Soviet world at almost every level, and reveal an extensive gallery of characters in a variety of occupations and environments.

Maximov (b. 1932) is uniquely equipped to write this anti-Soviet epic. The Soviet Literary Encyclopedia tells us that he was reared in a "children's camp," but it does not tell us that his father was arrested in 1933, or that the camp in which he was reared harbored young criminals as well as the children of "enemies of the people." He lacked even a "middle" or high-school education, though later he finished a vocational school and was qualified as a stonemason. He travelled widely in the Soviet Union, working at a great variety of construction sites as well as on collective farms. He was twice confined in a mental hospital. Once he was a member of the editorial board of the Soviet journal *October*. The accidents of his biography brought him into close contact with the seemingly infinite variety of Soviet characters he portrays: workmen, peasants, criminals of every age and type, underground religious fanatics, party operatives—honest men as well as careerists and time-servers—prostitutes, war invalids, inmates of insane asylums in various stages of mental dissolution, and *many others.*

He began writing poetry for a provincial newspaper in the Kuban, and published in 1954 a volume of verse which received, to put it mildly, an unfriendly reception. His story *We're Taming the Earth* (*My obzhivaem zemlyu*, 1961) was published in Paustovsky's *Pages from Tarusa* along with other writers, the new wave of the sixties, Kazakov and Okudzhava, whose work in that volume has already been mentioned. That story deals with the members of an expedition in the far north beyond the Arctic Circle, where danger, privation, and the challenge of labor test each one. The short novel *A Human Still Lives* (*Zhiv chelovek,* 1962) features a runaway from a labor camp whose life as he remembers it is in some details not unlike that of Maximov himself. An early exile from Soviet society because of his father's arrest and imprisonment, the hero soon drifted into the criminal world, committed violent acts, became a professional thief and smuggler, then a soldier in the war, then a prisoner in the camps. The point of the title is that in spite of his lifelong experience of only vileness and brutality, a human soul still survived in this criminal—he could be reached, touched if you will, by unexpected kindness.

Seven Days of Creation, already mentioned, is one of the three novels which comprise a statement of Maximov's view of Soviet life and his conviction that the way out of the materialistic impasse is to be found in religion. A recurrent memory of Pyotr Lashkov stands as a symbol of the illusory nature of the material world. In the scene he repeatedly recalled he saw himself as a young boy during the Civil War, who spied a smoked ham in a burnt-out merchant's shop window and crawled under gun fire to reach that ham. The danger was great, but by a miracle he crossed the square and reached the broken window, stretched out his hand to grasp the ham, and felt, not the meat, but the rough surface of painted cardboard. The terrible struggles of the Soviet years have, he seems to say, been directed toward an illusory goal.

Pyotr has lived his life as a loyal Soviet workman, devoted to the cause in spite of growing doubts, a rigid disciplinarian toward himself and his children, who have drifted away from him. He has felt little warmth toward others all his life, but the stirrings of faith make a change, give him the sense of "beginning again." The seventh day of the novel, the "Day of Hope and Resurrection," is a single blank page left to be filled in.

The second novel, *Quarantine* (1973), brings together in enforced isolation from the outside world a trainload of people journeying from the south to Moscow, where a cholera epidemic has forced the train to halt just short of the city. The novelistic situation is similar to that contrived by Solzhenitsyn in *The Cancer Ward* and other things: an accidental assemblage of very different people thrown together in an abnormal situation and forced to come face to face with their own lives and with each other. In *Seven Days* the past of a character is given in rapid shifts of consciousness, a technique which is motivated in *Quarantine* by dreams and, at times, by alcohol-induced memories. There are also long narratives in the characteristic language of a given passenger, and occasional reminiscences. And Maximov is an absolute magician in the fashioning of dialogues. Frequent laconic interchanges between characters reproduce with an uncanny ear subtle motilities in relationships of intimacy or love. The result is a versatile mosaic of speech styles, characters, and situations, informed by a sense of Russian history as well as of the human need, as Maximov sees it, for mercy and forgiveness, in a word, for love.

A third novel, *Farewell from Nowhere* (*Proshchanie iz niotkuda*, 1973), continues the search, through a lifetime of suffering and frustration, for some kind of religious fulfillment, for a fourth dimension, the most important one, "God."

Maximov left the Soviet Union in 1974 to reside in Paris. He became the editor of the monthly émigré journal *Kontinent* and has been one of the centers of the polemical storms that disturb émigré life. Uncompromising in his hostility both to Soviet Communism and Western liberalism, between which he seemed to descry sinister links, Maximov was close to Solzhenitsyn ideologically. Their principal opponent among the émigrés was Sinyavsky, who in 1978 founded his own journal *Syntaksis*, in order, as he put it, to achieve independence from the religious and nationalist ideological line of *Kontinent.*

Another writer with a deeply religious view of the world and an obvious affinity with Dostoevsky is Evgenii Ternovsky (b. 1941), who left the Soviet Union in 1974 and settled in Paris, where he contributed to two émigré journals, *Russian Thought* and *Kontinent.* His novel *Strange Story* (1977) is uniquely interesting in that it gives a rich and varied account of Soviet everyday life and Soviet characters from the viewpoint, not of an intellectual or a dissident, but of a middle-level Soviet bureaucrat, the novel's central character. That bureaucrat is a slightly awry human being; he seems to his colleagues a bit touched and perhaps a candidate for commitment. He is quite off the bureaucratic pattern: unambitious, thoughtful of others, prone to reflection on death and the last things, and open to a religious quest. He is alienated from the philistine milieu and from his wife and daughter, who are part of it and for whom their husband and father is beyond comprehension, a source of embarrassment and grief.

The first-person narrator is a human being at the nervous edge of desperation and insanity, and so are many of the characters he describes. For example, an upper-level bureaucrat, who is remote from his subordinates and seemingly self-contained and coldly organized, is actually a miserable alcoholic seeking some kind of emotional support in affairs with women—or men—possibly in religion. Or there is the pure and good prostitute, who may be modelled on Dostoevsky's Sonya but is in every phrase and gesture a thin pathetic Moscow girl hooked on drugs and at the brutish disposal of a thug-pimp.

The narrator is a distraught citizen in search of *something* and not able to find it; the one thing he knows absolutely is that he must reject the materialism of the culture that nourished him. In search of the something he needs, the narrator becomes a literally homeless wanderer in Moscow, dependent on friends for a place to stay at night, spending many nights in railway stations or the police station or other strange abodes. His tragic experiences on the outer fringe involve him and the reader in many aspects of Soviet everyday life (*byt*) that have never been treated in any branch of Russian literature: taxicab whores and their driver pimps; users and peddlers of narcotics; the police stations and the shocking, inhuman faces of Russian thugs and criminals; the railroad stations at night, crawling, literally, with human beings who have nowhere else to go; hopeless, shambling alcoholics; the poor and the sick. What Ternovsky allows us to glimpse, in a journey motivated by his narrator's search for a faith, is the underside of that materialistic world, the smooth nap of which we saw in the novels of Trifonov.

Something like Maximov but perhaps lacking his range and versatility, Ternovsky is a sensitive recorder of Russian speech in various circles of the Soviet inferno. Near the summit we hear the voices of two distantly related upper-class wives discussing a valuable object:

> "What about the Arabian furniture? Will you really sell it?"
> "Of course. I'll let you have it cheap. Because we're relatives."

And near the bottom an old grandmother, "a heavy woman with a weary and pleasant face," waiting in the station with her grandson, who has one leg shorter than the other:

> "Where would you be from," I asked.
> "From Syzran. I taken my grandchild to Sergey."
> "What Sergey?" I asked. She seemed astonished at the question.
> "To the Holy Saint Sergey in the Great Monastery."
> "What monastery?"
> "Oh, you! Zagorsk, of course."
> "For him you went?" Meaning the boy.
> "For him." She sighed. "The poor thing is a cripple . . . I'm awful sorry for him. He's got nobody but me . . . But Christ has mercy, he's our only hope . . . So we heard mass and went to confession and communion . . . Then kissed the relic of the Holy Saint. I bought enough holy water to last the whole year, and after that, God willing, we'll come back."

That scene in the railway station is interesting also because the words of the ignorant old peasant woman touch the quick of the novel: pity and love for the unfortunates who have nowhere to turn and nowhere to go. And the narrator witnesses here also a case of religious comfort applied effectively to a hopeless situation. The drab old ladies at the cemetery gates who offer prayers in return for alms ("What name do you want us to mention in our prayers?") represent also a level of desperation that only faith can help, even if it cannot heal.

The narrator in his effort to find again the practicing Christian he has stumbled on (much as Pyotr in *Seven Days* fell in by accident with an underground Christian meeting) is frequently lost, quite literally, in a Moscow snowstorm and unable to locate the apartment where the Christian man lives. His inability to find the right building—all the enormous hulks look alike—is a realistic detail of Moscow life here raised to the level of symbol: he is lost in the world and cannot find his way to Christianity or to himself. Baldly stated the symbol sounds a bit obvious, but the realistic particulars of a heartbreaking search in Moscow in the snow are realized so vividly that the symbol—the "word," so to speak—takes on flesh.

Many things in the novel remind one of Dostoevsky, especially the sense of brain fever in the main character, his existence on the fringe of sanity, and his frantic wanderings hither and yon. The dependence on Dostoevsky is at times too mechanically clear, as in the last scene when the suicide of the young prostitute seems modelled on the ending of *The Gentle One*. Ternovsky has provided in this, as in his novel *Reception Room* (1979), a wonderful superfluity of scenes and characters—faces, language, flesh and clothing, the sense and smell of the people—but these riches are not yet fully structured in the novel form.

Truth through Obscenity: Yuz Aleshkovsky

The work of Aleshkovsky circulated in *samizdat* long before it began appearing in the West in 1980. Three of his songs about the labor camps appeared in the illegal collection *Metropol* in 1979, and shortly thereafter Aleshkovsky emigrated. Those songs dealt with the deeply taboo subject of sex, including Lesbian sex, in the camps. He is himself a graduate, so to speak, of the prison camp system. Aleshkovsky in the few things he has so far published proves himself master of the Russian spoken by criminals, prisoners, and policemen. It is in their milieu that the events of his stories transpire, and always from the idiosyncratic viewpoint of one of them. A story is typically given in a long *skaz* monologue by a criminal or by a secret policeman not far removed from the criminal world. Aleshkovsky himself points to the model of Joseph Conrad's narrator Marlow, of whom people said that "one man could not continue a tale so long, and others couldn't listen so long. That, people insisted, was improbable." But the polite and educated reader of Aleshkovsky listens with rapt fascination as his foulmouthed narrator runs on and on in a language so filthily obscure that it requires a glossary to follow it, telling of characters living beyond the pale of normal human feeling and regaling us with a superflux of anecdotes featuring beastly cruelty, corruption, horrifying lawlessness among the police, and criminals who seem to have fallen well below the human species in language, gestures, and even appearance. The narrator of these loathsome deeds feels no loathing whatever at them, just as in many of Babel's stories, the *skaz* narrator relates with rich circumstance horrors which do not horrify him at all.

Aleshkovsky's work, especially the novel *Nikolai Nikolaevich* (1980) and the long monologues *The Hand* (1980) and *Kangaroo* (1981), fills a considerable lacuna in the extensive underground literature of criminals, prisons, and police operations. That literature had heretofore given us the story almost exclusively from the viewpoint of prisoners, both male and female, and by preference those innocent of the crimes charged to them. Aleshkovsky gives us the viewpoint of the jailers, not the jailed, of the murderer, not his victim. And the world his narrator sees is so different from ours—I speak for the *polite* reader, in Russia or abroad—that we watch it with rapt fascination, and listen to its dialect as to a linguistic discovery. Aleshkovsky explains his consistent use of such language in the words of the KGB operator who is his narrator in *The Hand*, a passage which is clearly an authorial intrusion:

> I speak foully because foul language, the Russian kind, is a salvation to me personally in that malodorous hole our mighty, truthful, majestic—and so forth—Russian language has gotten into. They're driving it to death the poor thing, all of them, propagandists from the Central Committee, and the stinking journalists and the filthy writer types and nonwriter types, and the censors, and the self-satisfied technocrats . . . They're trying to knock the life out of it. But I have a feeling they won't succeed. They won't kill it!

Transcendence and Tragedy: Erofeev's Trip

Since the "poem" of Venedikt Erofeev (b. 1933), *Moscow to the End of the Line* (*Moskva-Petushki*, 1980), appeared in *samizdat* about 1968 it has circulated widely and rapidly and has had many devoted readers in the Soviet Union and outside. It was published in the Israeli journal *Ami* (no. 3, 1973). That "poem"—as the author calls it—is an astonishing—and magnificent—performance. Among other things it is a study of alcoholism by a man who must have suffered the disease himself. Moreover it deals in the most eloquent imagery with alcoholism as perhaps the most serious social problem in the Soviet Union, in fact a national catastrophe. The author tells us that the cable-laying crew of which he was foreman laid a bit of cable in the morning then drank themselves into a stupor for the rest of the day, then the next morning pulled out that cable and laid it again, only to repeat the alcoholic performance of the previous day. When he describes such a scene for us we may be inclined to chuckle at it as satiric hyperbole, but the author himself would probably insist that it is realism pure and simple. Indeed it is fitting and proper that the Soviet Union should have given birth to a book which not only poses the social problem but also reveals the inner world—the inner light, so to speak—of the alcoholic himself.

Erofeev's marvellous book is one for which the literary world was totally unprepared. Until it appeared the author was known only to a circle of Moscow friends among whom his sparse writings circulated. Some of the first readers of *Moscow to the End of the Line* even assumed that Erofeev must be a punning pseudonym, since that is the name of a brand of vodka. One who knew him cited Erofeev as proof of the essential health of Russian literature and the possibility of great books appearing in it as if by accident: "Here's a man who was drunk for twenty years, then he suddenly wakes up and gives us *Moscow to the End of the Line.*" Even though at the present writing Erofeev has not left the Soviet Union, he is properly placed among the exiles, since his best work cannot be published at home.

Erofeev called his book a *poema*, a term applied strictly to large-scale, frequently epic, verse productions such as the *Iliad* or *The Divine Comedy*, and also to historical or romantic epics of major dimension and serious statement. The authors of prose works have from time to time, by analogy, designated them as *poemy:* Gogol called his *Dead Souls* a *poema* because he planned to model it on the tripartite structure of *The Divine Comedy.* The word is also used loosely of such epic novels as *War and Peace.* Erofeev's use of the genre term suggests that his hero's alternately agonized and blissful search for escape from Moscow by way of the Kursk Station—terminus of the interurban line—to Petushki at the very end of the line, may be more than a fictional treatment of a social problem, it may indeed be an alcoholic metaphor of man's fate.

As the story opens the hero confides to his readers that he, a native of Moscow, has never seen the center and showpiece of Moscow, the Kremlin. Every time he set off to see it something bad happened. A few glasses of vodka for a start at Savelovsky Square, then another at Kolyaevsky and a couple of bottles of beer on the way; then he asks, how could you go down Chekhov Street without downing a couple of glasses of "hunter's" vodka. And then, "Of course I couldn't get across the Sadovy Ring without drinking something, could I? I couldn't. So, I drank a little more of something." So, it turned out that no matter which way he turned, he always ended up at the Kursk Station. His situation is like that of the folk-tale hero who has a choice of three roads to take, but each leads to his inevitable doom: "Just go, go in some direction. Doesn't matter which. Even if you go to the left you'll get to the Kursk Station; if you go straight, you'll still get to the Kursk Station; if you go to the right, still the Kursk Station. So go to the right, just to be sure of getting there."

The story contains a hymn to alcohol and the blissful state it causes. That hymn is of course offered ironically, but at the same time it is a deeply serious and tragic statement about the alcoholic's rejection of the real world. The world to a sober man is totally repulsive, a sight to be endured only under the influence of alcohol in any form. In the absence of the canonical distillate there are "cocktail" recipes, for instance: "Methylate Spirits, 100g., Velvet Beer, 200g. Refined Furniture Polish, 100g." And how hard it is to get through those early morning hours before the liquor stores open. The angels are on *his* side and sing to him, telling him of possible openings out of the miasma, a store, for instance, where they sell cool red wine even before the legal hour of 9:00 A.M. The sweet, unworldly innocence of the true alcoholic is celebrated here in, as Vera Dunham puts it, "the high registers of ornate, lofty, festive diction":

> Oh, if only the whole world, if everyone were like I am now, placid and timorous and never sure about anything, not sure of himself nor of the seriousness of his position under the heavens— oh, how good it could be. No enthusiasts, no feats of valor, nothing obsessive! Just universal chickenheartedness. I'd agree to live on the earth for an eternity if they'd show me first a corner where there's not always room for valor. "Universal chickenheartedness." Indeed, this is the panacea, this is the predicate to sublime perfection.

The benefits to the human enterprise are many and impressive: freedom from the philistine world of cant, competition, and great goals; achievement of gentleness—and poetry. The gestures of drinking from the bottle relate one to tragedians and artists, Othello giving his final speech, or a great pianist throwing his head back. A drunk is chaste, moreover, no danger to women. Faith in oneself and belief in life fluctuate between the high of intoxication and the low of an untreated hangover.

Time and space are measured out in terms of the number, nature, and manner of drinks taken in. The distance to Petushki, the end of the line and the goal of life, is likewise measured in units of alcohol consumed. Petushki is the place where the son who loves and admires him lives, where a woman waits for him, to whom he is bringing "cornflowers" and confections, where the sun shines and the birds always sing. After a blackout marked by surreal dreams of revolution over really important issues such as the opening time of liquor stores, the hero awakes in the train to find that it is dark outside. That is strange, because the train was due in Petushki at 11:15 A.M. Actually the Petushki of his dreams turns out to be a Moscow street on a dark night, where he is confronted by four vile beings with eyes that look like the "thick swirling dung water at the bottom of a toilet bowl." He tries to escape them and to find his Kursk Station again, but ends up instead at the Kremlin. At last he sees it, but they overtake him there and pursue him, and at last beat him to death. As he tells us: "Since that time I have never regained consciousness. And I never will."

The blessed state of inebriate innocence and Petushki itself were both illusory. Hard and fatal reality is at the center, the Kremlin, where death has an appointment with the hero.

Shklovsky or the early Jakobson might have said that the drunken train ride from Moscow to Petushki and back to Moscow again simply motivates an experimentation with untried narrative devices, and that is true as far as it goes. This poem about a horrible reality is delivered in exalted, transcendent language with many literary allusions both apposite and absurd, and the ugly, threatening reality is refracted through the alcoholic haze as a kind of cubistic displacement of recognizable images. Stylistically it is an achievement.

Some critics tell us that the book's message is that life in the Soviet Union can be endured only with the help of vodka. That is certainly true, but if that were all the book told us then it would not be worth reading. Erofeev's reach transcends the Soviet border. Like the folk tale about the hero with many roads to take but only one destiny, Erofeev's book is really telling us something dark and tragic about human life. The hero's hoped-for happy land "away from here," Petushki at the end of the line, was only a romantic illusion maintained by alcohol. And like the gentle Jesus this chaste and gentle alcoholic is in the end crucified by evil beings, uttering in his final agony some of the Last Words: "May this cup pass from me, O Lord! . . . Why has thou forsaken me?"

Poetry of the Daft: Sasha Sokolov

Russian literature in the sixties and seventies both at home and abroad was engaged in a search for new forms. Some of the results of that search appeared in *gosizdat*, but the major and most daring experiments could flourish only in *samizdat* or in exile: Aksyonov's mixture of fantasy and reality, Erofeev's alcoholic grotesques, and Aleshkovsky's illumination of Soviet life and even Soviet history through the mentality and in the language of criminals and policemen. Sasha Sokolov's *School for Fools* (1976) is a brilliant contribution to this exploration of new possibilities in narrative. Other writers have limited the narrative focus to the frame of a single mind, and sometimes offered the continuum of that mind's experience in terms of the unclassified trifles of immediate perception and the arbitrary associations they may occasion.

Sokolov has reminded many of James Joyce, whose stream of consciousness technique takes us through the hyperdeveloped literary and
philological apperceptive mass of Stephen Daedalus, then explores the
earthy contours of Molly Bloom's cerebrations. Sokolov has set himself
a subtler task: to follow the mental processes of a young man suffering
from schizophrenia, and this he does with deep imaginative empathy.
The patient who carries the narrative suffers from faulty memory and
random association, loss of the consciousness of time, as well as of a
sense of his own identity.

The random movement of any mind freely reacting to stimuli and
memory is here exaggerated to the point of—well, insanity. The normal
consciousness of an "other" in the mind's dialectic, to whom silent
thoughts are addressed, and who responds in a mental dialogue, here
assumes the literal shape of an alter ego split off from and at odds with
the central self. The narrator is thus riven in two, and narration is carried on in the second person rather than the first, with every thought
shaped in the expectation of a polemical response. The result is something like Dostoevsky's *Notes from Underground*, where the narrator debates with an imagined hostile reader, except that Dostoevsky's narrator is not cut off from reality and could indeed expect a hostile
reception. In *A School for Fools*, the character's thoughts move by tan-
gential and accidental associations from one person or place or word to
another, building a marvellous inventory of objects and images related
only in the narrator's mind. Here, in Carl Proffer's translation, is an example of a thought process developed out of an accidental verbal association:

> This is zone five, ticket price thirty-five kopecks, the train takes
> an hour and twenty northern branch, a branch of acacia, or, say,
> lilac blooms with white flowers, smells of creosote, the dust of
> connecting platforms, and smoke looms along the track bed, in the
> evening it returns to the garden on tiptoe and listens intently to the
> movement of the electric trains, trembles from the rustling noises,
> and then the flowers close and sleep, yielding to the importunities
> of the solicitous bird by the name of Nachtigall; the branch sleeps,
> but the trains, distributed symmetrically along the branch, rush fe-
> verishly through the dark like chains, hailing each flower by name,
> dooming to insomnia the following: bilious old station ladies, am-
> putees and war-blinded traincar accordion players, blue-gray line-
> men in sleeveless orange tops, sage professors and insane poets,
> dacha irregulars and failures—anglers for early and late fish, tan-
> gled in the spongy plexus of the limpid forest, and also middle-
> aged islander buoy-keepers whose faces, bobbing over the metal-
> lically humming black channel waters, alternately pale and scarlet.

The translation is excellent, but no translation could possibly register all of the purely verbal associations that motivate the movement of thought.

Such a mental procedure offers endless possibilities for the construction of private systems of meaning, and the narrator takes full advantage of them. The structural principle of this monologue is digressive, in the sense that any thread can lead anywhere, and the thread of consistent narration, temporal and logical, is never recovered. Sokolov's richly poetic verbal resources are employed here in a project which has important epistemological implications.

Critics have suggested that Sokolov's work is related to Faulkner (*The Sound and the Fury*), the surrealist Breton (automatic writing), and of course to Joyce and Butor. Sokolov is indeed in that company, though it would seem without full awareness of predecessors and relatives. His latest novel *Between the Dog and the Wolf* (1980) gives further evidence of Sokolov's importance in Russian literature. He reveals in it once again his virtuosity in the invention of poetic language and narrative structures. His works are, it has been said, "a serious event in the history of Russian prose."

Perversion of Logic as Ideology: Alexander Zinoviev

Zinoviev (b. 1922) was a professor at Moscow University and a logician with a world-wide reputation when his book *The Yawning Heights* (*Ziyayushchie vysoty*) appeared in the West in 1976. He became the object of systematic harassment until allowed to emigrate in 1978 to Germany, where he accepted an appointment as Visiting Professor of Philosophy at the University of Munich. The paradox which is the title of his book beautifully conveys its dismal thesis: that the "shining height" of socialism, the "radiant future which has recently dawned," is actually a bottomless abyss of human ugliness and banality, and that, in fact, it could not have been otherwise. The action is set in a country of uncertain geography, which "occupies almost the entire land surface and has frontiers with every country in the world," and whose name is Ibansk, a coinage which goes easily into English as Fuckupia. Of course all of its inhabitants are named Ibanov, the sense of which in English should now be obvious. They are distinguished from one another only by such appellations as Chatterer, Slanderer, Boss, Hog, Truthteller, Dauber, Sociologist, and many others, including one named Member (*chlen*). Some of the characters clearly represent actual people: the Boss is Stalin, Hog is Khrushchev, and Dauber, who figures as the creator of Hog's gravestone, is the artist Neizvestny. Truthteller is obviously

Solzhenitsyn, and Poet may be Yevtushenko or possibly another of the men of letters who serve as liberal fig leaf for the regime. Many of the Ibanskians have not yet been identified, but the important point is that they are all Ibanovs: Zinoviev's satirical weapon ranges widely and spares hardly any element in the society. There are a few exceptions, Neizvestny for instance, but even the intellectuals are futile: "The life of a thinking Ibansk intellectual is first and foremost conversation. And conversation is first and foremost a disorderly and sterile debate," and again, "The discussion followed all the rules of scientific debate—everybody shouted at the top of his voice and didn't listen to a word anybody else said."

Critics attuned to questions of genre may have moments of dismay if they try too hard to classify this work. The "novel" is made up of about a hundred brief conversations, many essays, a dissertation, notes for a book, a report on an experiment with rats, dialogues and disquisitions on set themes, and frequent defense of Ibanism from the mouths of citizens bent on fostering their careers. Each separate item is concerned with Ibansk history, Ibansk life, Ibansk values, and the Ism that orders things in Ibansk, and the whole is tied together by the thread of a lengthy "ballad," found on an outhouse wall in Ibansk, which provides at certain intervals scatological commentary on all the matters touched upon. There is nothing that could be called a plot, though things do develop from the days of the Boss, "when part of the Ibanskian people were in the camps, another part was set to guard them, and a third were preparing cadres for the other two," to the Time of Perplexity, in the throes of which the writing takes place, and almost into the final agony of the Age of Prosperity. Bakhtin's notion of the modern novel as the carnivalized miscellany of many voices certainly applies to this one.

Moreover there is a certain chaotic charm in the way one thing follows inconsequently upon another in clear defiance of a well-known law of the Ism according to which nothing ever happens "by accident." And the form does seem intended to mirror everyday life in Ibansk, where one thing does follow another for no particular reason, where the disappointments of the latrine may be followed by a session in the cooler, after which outrage converses with itself in the Beer Bar, and then the refusal of a travel document ("he's sick and he has family problems") leads to a disquisition on the makeup of scientific delegations, then friends gather somewhere to hold forth on the informer as a social institution, or to savor the latest anecdotes, after which Wife "goes shopping," that is to say she stands in lines all morning and returns home with much less, which in turns leads to thoughts about the

Special Stores and the Marxist maxim "to each according to his needs" in its Ibanskian transformation, "to each according to his social position." Reading the novel is like an experience of the aimless, bitter frustration of Ibansk life itself, viewed of course from an aesthetic distance.

And like that life it goes on, and on, and on, for 829 pages. A principle of the book's structure is endless iteration. Pelion is laboriously piled on Ossa, and then, that having been done, the whole process is repeated many times in a way that, in spite of obvious differences recalls Solzhenitsyn's *The Gulag Archipelago* in its overwhelming accumulation of evidence. A point is made, then repeated from a different perspective, then reduplicated in new language, then reaffirmed in another narrative, then recapitulated in a literary reference, or once more clinched in the cogent terms of mathematical logic. Yet the reader wants to read on, is ever eager to experience new variations on the old, established themes. To understand the reason for such rapt fascination is to understand the nature of Zinoviev's wonderful book. Very much in the manner of Swift, he exposes moral absurdity by repeatedly explaining and defending it in its own shoddy terms and with its own poor arguments. He manages to convey a sense of high intellectual power and seemingly unlimited verbal resource at grips with the tongue-tied banality of evil and, even though overwhelmed by it, still scornful and contemptuous.

Here are just a few examples, given in no particular order. "Anyone can make an honest error" is a frequent defense of murderous incompetence. Things happen in Ibansk "for one reason or another and usually for another." But nothing happens in Ibansk by accident: "That's a deviation from the rule, but it's no accident." The indefensible is easily explained: "You were excluded from the delegation because you're untalented. I tell you that as a friend." And there are leading scientists who do not work at science but "have gone on to more responsible posts." Prisons are "part of the superstructure." And on crime: "The Bosses aren't concerned with the discovery of crime but with creating the impression that crimes will not remain undiscovered if they are committed." Ibansk is able to send the biggest delegation to a scientific convention, "a clear proof of the advantages of our system." An Ibanov returns from abroad with dirty pictures of women "of all nationalities except our own." There are many people in Ibansk who "speak first and don't think afterward." The art regime rejects Dauber because "in technique his paintings did not fit our ideology and in content they were on a low level of achievement." One's quality as an artist is determined by "the social position of the arse he licks." And of Thinker, a flourishing careerist: "Insofar as everyone who didn't have a job as good as his was more stupid than he was, he thought his position perfectly justified. But insofar as all those who had jobs superior to his were also more stupid than he was, he felt himself unjustly passed over." Of course there is a caste system, corruption, careerism and indifference, but those are just "isolated facts . . . Taking a broad view nothing of the kind exists at all . . . simply slander." "Civilization . . . progress . . . to a higher level." One citizen went to an exhibition of abstract art "where each picture put him in mind of women because he never thought of anything else." The Leader disliked Dauber's etching: "Our people feel no need for this kind of thing," he said, "because our people need something quite different." The discussion of painting between Hog (Khrushchev) and Dauber (Neizvestny) "followed the classic Ibanskian formula: 'You're a fool.' 'You're another.' " The Ibanskian approach to problems is upbeat and positive: "We are often asked if God exists," wrote Secretary. "We answer this question affirmatively: Yes, God does not exist." Ibanskians like to be mistaken for foreigners because foreigners are treated well, but also, and chiefly, because other Ibanskians might look at them and say, "Look, there goes another foreigner, the swine!" and in our life, "Everything obsolete and outmoded must be strangled in embryo."

What we have seen is only a tiny sample of the kinds of linguistic behavior satirized in the book, whose chief target is a system of clichés that screens reality and hobbles thought. Intimately related targets are the tendency of all Ibanskian life to mediocrity, the brutish inefficiency of all organs, including the police, the corruption of supposedly liberal enterprises, the Taganka theater, for instance. The norms of the society ("Be like everyone else" is the fundamental norm) are treated exhaustively in a dissertation authored by Schizophrenic (who may be the author), and a scientific experiment with rat society provides interesting analogues to collective behavior in Ibansk. As for the prospect of change, Chatterer (who may also be the author) reads from the report of that experiment: "And yet the rat paradise (as we called the experimental ratorium [*krysarii*]) ceased to exist at a moment when we least expected it: Somehow or other lice got into the ratorium, multiplied at amazing speed, and created their own society on the model of the rats. And then . . ." And of the future: "Our life is so ordered that we can't avoid seeing the future down to the last detail. It's appalling."

The kinship of Zinoviev with the great satirists of Western Europe has been suggested by many commentators, and no doubt his closest relative and probably an intimate confidant is Jonathan Swift. The author of *Gulliver*, though he differs from Zinoviev in his preference for clearly plotted action, provided a model for exploring a labyrinthine social system and exposing its Lilliputian pomposity and vacuity. And Swift is at least as pessimistic as Zinoviev: remember that it is us, the Yahoos, who are a threat to the decent life of the good Houyhnhnms. But Swift died at an advanced age in Dublin, the city where he was born, while Zinoviev was expelled from the Soviet Union and stripped of his citizenship for "circulating materials harmful to the state." Such is the reality of Ibansk.

Zinoviev's *The Radiant Future* (1978) continues the satirical project of his first book, but in shorter compass and with more than a semblance of plot. But the best things in it read like a superflux shaken from the heavily laden *Yawning Heights:* essays on socialist realism, on the rhetoric of Stalinism, on purges, on toilet paper, and many other things.

A Gathering of Writers

The Russian writers now living in exile are indeed an impressive gathering, and the task of choosing among them those worthy of critical mention has not been easy. Yury Maltsev's excellent book on *samizdat* and exile literature, entitled *Free Russian Literature* (*Volnaya russkaya literatura*, 1976), lists a score or more of fascinating writers who might be treated at length and some of whom must be mentioned. Among the most interesting of the later exiles is Sergey Dovlatov (b. 1941), whose experiences as a journalist and at other occupations has afforded material for a number of stories and sketches. Dovlatov stands apart from some of his immediate contemporaries in that his style is simple and lucid, and his satire mixes humor with sharpness. In fact Dovlatov has succeeded in raising the pointed anecdote to the level of art. His *Invisible Book* (*Nevidimaya kniga*, 1978) is the "creative biography" of a writer who "never made it" in the Soviet Union, an account of the response of higher-ups to his manuscripts, and what became of them. The sketches of people and situations are brilliant, the documents included are very revealing, and the book is peppered with witty asides: the story of an "unhappy love affair that ended in marriage"; the response of an editor: "Your stories are remarkable. Lousy, but remarkable." There are bits of absurd dialogue that remind one of Zoshchenko: " 'Do you know Yuri Kamponeets?' 'Yes, sounds familiar. The name Yuri I've heard. Kamponeets I'm hearing for the first time.' " "What a beautiful wife you have! I've never seen anything like her, not even in the subway!"

"We like your stories. We're returning them." And at last, "If I gave my stories to Brezhnev, he'd say 'I like them, but what will the higher-ups say?'" Several of Dovlatov's short stories were published in the *New Yorker* magazine, "Jubilee Boy" (1980), "Somebody's Death" (1981), and "Straight Ahead" (1982). Based on his experience as a journalist in the Soviet Union, those stories are remarkable for their brief sketches of official characters and everyday situations as well as for dialogue that sparkles with absurdity and sustained *non sequitur*.

Yury Mamleyev (b. 1931), we are told, was once the center of a circle of young writers who regarded him as their teacher. He has been fairly prolific of short stories, and has written two novels and some essays. He has not been published in the Soviet Union but his writing circulates in *samizdat* and recordings on tape, or *magnitizdat*. Some of his things are strangely moving, but he is not for the squeamish. Shock and disgust are the feelings he seems to aim at provoking. Sex is a frequent theme, but the principals are likely to be scabrous and repulsive, or psychotic and unpredictable. Morose sodomy or odious oral incest is often an outcome of the sexual drive. Unashamed bestiality is another. Hacking, coughing, spitting, fellatio, and filth occur in these stories apparently with no motivation except to turn sensitive stomachs. One of his most monstrous (I use the word advisedly) stories, "Relations Between the Sexes," describes a simple-minded young man and a stupid girl he picks up and takes to his room. She is more than ready to give in, but he thinks he has to rape her, which he does brutally and bloodily. Mamleyev's stories lack, on the whole, components of satire, humor, or even social commentary. It has been said that he is creating a phantasmagoric rather than an obscene world. Whatever he's doing, he does it powerfully and compellingly.

Vladimir Maramzin (b. 1934) fell afoul of authorities in 1974 when he participated in the *samizdat* publication of a five-volume collection of Brodsky's poetry. Sentenced to a long term for this anti-Soviet activity, he left the Soviet Union in 1975 and settled in Paris. His stories and sketches already had wide circulation in *samizdat* and his novella *The Story of Ivan Petrovich's Marriage* (*Istoriya zhenitby Ivana Petrovicha*, 1964–74) appeared in the West in 1974. Maramzin's prose owes something to Zoshchenko, and, most readers agree, even more to Platonov, especially in his deliberate roughening of the narrative style, and in the tendency of his characters to extravagant statement. He adds original touches of his own. His characteristic stance is that of a narrator struck—struck dumb, almost—with sheer amazement at the unlikely events he unfolds. In the story "Pushpull," for instance, the narrator remains throughout bemused and unbelieving at the announced program of a KGB colonel charged with responsibility for literature to solicit dissident manuscripts, pay for them and publish them, as a means of feeling the pulse, so to speak, of the society. Maramzin's stories have considerable documentary value, also, in that they deal with obscure corners of Soviet life to which few have had access: from the inside of a KGB headquarters, for instance, to a shabby worker's dormitory. An element of the grotesque in them only enhances their documentary value.

An important figure in the emigration is Victor Nekrasov (b. 1911), author of the famous novel *In the Trenches of Stalingrad* (1946), which presented the great battle in sober, unheroic scenes. During the sixties he published some powerful short things: "The Second Night" (1960) focused on the experiences in battle of a sensitive young man who has just killed a German soldier in a night raid, and "Kira Georgievna" (1961), an exploration of emotional indifference in a woman whose feelings have been wounded too many times. His accounts of travel in the west are original and beautifully honest. His contribution since emigrating in 1974 has been considerable, both as an editor and as a contributor to *Kontinent*, the émigré periodical.

Among the exiles there are a number of poets, and some of them have a secure place in the history of Russian literature. Dimitry Bobishchev (b. 1937) is one whose verse tends to serious philosophical statement, to the contemplation, as Frost put it, of "the secret that sits in the middle and knows." His poetry on the whole ignores the news of the day. Natalya Gorbanevskaya (b. 1936) is a fascinating poet with a long history of courageous dissident activity. She participated in the struggle for human rights in the Soviet Union and was one of a handful of demonstrators on Red Square against the invasion of Czechoslovakia in 1968. She was one of the editors of the *Chronicle of Current Events*, a clandestine paper which publicized violations of human rights in the Soviet Union. For this activity she has twice been confined by the KGB in mental hospitals. She is not lacking a civic sense, though the events of her own life are beautifully transmuted into poetic image. For instance:

He made a wry face
And for an answer announced
That the sun is for summer
And that winter's for frost,

And I know that already,
Know myself,
That through the long winters
You won't lose your mind
If you don't lose your mind.[4]

Conclusion

In Ivan Bunin's fine novel *The Village* (1910) a disillusioned country poet, Kuzma Ilych, reflects on the barbarism of the Russian nation, revealed in their treatment of literary geniuses. One possible answer to the poet is that not the nation itself but the Czarist regime persecuted those writers; but an even more devastating indictment could be brought against the people and the regime in the twentieth century by many a disconsolate Kuzma Ilych: "What a savage nation! Poets they drive to suicide: Mayakovsky, Yesenin, Tsvetaeva; their best writers of prose they sent to prison or into exile: Pilnyak, Babel, Zamyatin, Solzhenitsyn; sensitive critics they hounded to death: Voronsky, Lezhnev; satirists they treated as traitors: Bulkagov, Zinoviev; theater directors with an original touch, they deprived of liberty: Meyerhold." The list could be expanded for several pages. Barbarism in the waste of literary talent has characterized the nation in modern times, too.

Yet Kuzma Ilych is omitting something. What he neglects to say is that the reason writers have been treated so abominably in Russia is that in Russia they are important. This paradox conceals the key to the Russian literary riddle. Literature in the nineteenth century was a source of knowledge and a well of hope. Russian writers satisfied a demand not only for aesthetic experience but for ideas. In the great majority they accepted the role of educator and uplifter. Gogol sought to improve morals, Turgenev to instill respect for the enserfed folk, writers of the so-called Natural School to expose social injustice, Dostoevsky and Tolstoy to find and preach a firm faith. Because their work and their message was taken seriously by the people the attention of the autocratic government was frequently drawn to these writers. Sometimes they suffered from this. The literary history of Western Europe in the nineteenth century offers no clear parallels.

In Soviet times, too, literature has been important—in fact a matter of life and death. Consider the literary disputes and the interest in them of highly placed personages. Lenin himself took a hand in the discussion of the Proletcult. Probably the most stimulating comments on Mayakovsky and Pilnyak came from the pen of Trotsky. Bukharin had a sophisticated understanding of modern poetry. Lunacharsky was a man of broad culture and tolerant taste who took an active part in literary work. To read and to argue about literature was an important part of the work of government leaders. Their successors of the Stalin era shared the conviction that literature is important, though they knew little or nothing about it. The distance from Bukharin to Zhdanov is polar: Bukharin knew literature, whereas Zhdanov did not; Bukharin did not represent himself as an authority, Zhdanov did; Bukharin's intervention tended to increase variety in literature, Zhdanov's intervention narrowed the range. But somehow Zhdanov knew that literature is important, and therefore he periodically scrutinized and purged the ranks of its producers.

There was one important difference between Zhdanov and his successor, Khrushchev. The latter was also ignorant of literature, but he seemed to be cheerfully aware of his ignorance and reluctant to make authoritative judgments. His important speech to the Union of Writers in 1959 was crudely jocose and casual. "You cannot control the unknown," said Shklovsky in 1920; and the ironic realization of that idea in contemporary Russian life was Khrushchev's frank expression of interested ignorance. He modified this eminently sane viewpoint in 1963 when he spoke out scornfully on modernism. And yet, after Khrushchev's fall, no clearly appointed lawgiver appeared. This may be the result of profound changes in the cultural level of those masses of whom the state must take some account. The unstilled voice of liberalism in the sixties and the miracle of *samizdat* in the seventies is evidence that education may be having its effect on the Party itself, and a return to the simple precepts of Stalinism would be difficult.

But literature is still regarded as important and as vitally bound to life. The crowds that gathered in Moscow to hear the poet Yevtushenko are evidence that the tradition of literature as social commentary continues in Russia, and that the writer will not be without honor. The whole tendency of the recent period has been toward recognizing that the literary artist, though his work be firmly anchored in the soil of a particular social group, must fashion for himself his own view of reality and find his own means for expressing it. This is the meaning of the quiet exploration of individual experience in so much contemporary writing. Writers tend to reject formulaic statement in favor of simple, tentative thought processes. After nearly a generation of clearly stated socialist tendency in literature, the new men of the sixties and seventies, in the words of a character in a proletarian novel of 1929, refuse to "reduce this magnificent tongue-tied life to the terms of a poor Marxist dialect."

That the demand for freedom from censorship so cogently expressed in Solzhenitsyn's letter to the Union of Writers has widespread support was made evident in the appearance during the summer of 1968 of an essay written by the leading Soviet nuclear physicist, Professor A. D. Sakharov. In this unpublished but widely circulated essay he said that "the salvation of mankind requires intellectual freedom, freedom to obtain and distribute information, and freedom from intimidation by officialdom." Censorship, he said, has killed the "living soul" of Soviet literature. Sakharov's intelligent and courageous statement offered strong support to Solzhenitsyn and others who opposed ignorant and wasteful official policies. In spite of official harassment, including his forced removal from Moscow, Sakharov continued through the seventies his campaign for radical reform of the Soviet system.

There is one other matter that both Bunin's Kuzma Ilych and any modern counterpart omit, and it is the most important thing. That "barbarous nation," Russia, produced in both the nineteenth and twentieth centuries one of the world's great literatures. In spite of Czarist censorship, Russian literature gave us Pushkin, Gogol, Turgenev, Tolstoy, Dostoevsky, Chekhov, Bely, and many others not widely known who shared the same space. Among European literatures of the nineteenth century, Russian literature was perhaps the greatest. And in the twentieth century, since the revolution of 1917, Russian literature under Lenin, Stalin, and their successors, stretched on the rack as it was, persecuted and tormented far more cruelly than in Czarist times, is still one of the bright lights of civilization. To survive and prosper in so unfriendly an environment required a high level of vitality; and great human fortitude entered into the process. As we have seen, some of the finest products of contemporary Russian literature circulated first in *samizdat*: Pasternak's unpublished poems and his novel *Doctor Zhivago*, Solzhenitsyn's novels and his account of the Soviet camp system, *The Gulag Archipelago*, the poetry of Osip Mandelshtam and Joseph Brodsky, and many other things. And this magnificent literary activity persisted, even though the organs of state security defined it as "anti-Soviet agitation," and punished it severely. Manuscripts circulating as *samizdat* almost inevitably found their way abroad, where they were actually published in *tamizdat*, then brought back into the Soviet Union by various travellers, a form of purely literary commerce that taxed the resources of the security organs, whose iron curtain behaved more like an iron sieve. Books that moved in this weird commerce were, as we know, among the greatest of the century.

Even more striking than *samizdat* literature was the persistence of literary values in *gosizdat*, where writers were obliged to take account of the tasteless bigotry of official tutors and guardians. And yet it is a fact that Trifonov's *An Old Man* and Rasputin's *Farewell to Matyora*, works of high art that throw a burning light on the destiny of human beings in the twentieth century, were published in *gosizdat*. That, too, along with *samizdat*, *tamizdat*, and the work of exiles, is evidence of persisting life in the divided body of Russian literature.

Notes

2. Mayakovsky and the Left Front of Art

1. L. Kassil, *Mayakovskii sam* (Moscow, 1960), p. 146.

2. The full text of the note, together with a photographic reproduction, is given in *Literaturnoye nasledstvo* (Moscow), 65 (1958): 199.

3. Ilya Ehrenburg, *Liudi, gody, zhizn* (Moscow, 1961), p. 399.

4. Vladimir Mayakovskii, *Polnoye sobraniye sochinenii* (Moscow, 1955–1958), I, 19.

5. Ibid., p. 21.

6. Ibid., p. 27.

7. Lawrence Stahlberger in *The Symbolic System of Mayakovsky* (The Hague, 1964) sees in the central character of this poem the archetypal image of the poet as scapegoat, who must suffer for all.

8. V. Katanyan, *Mayakovskii, literaturnaya khronika* (Moscow, 1961), p. 77.

9. Ibid., p. 495.

10. Mayakovskii, *Polnoye sobraniye sochinenii*, II, 506.

11. Quoted in I. Mashbitz-Verov, *Poemy Mayakovskogo* (Kuibyshev, 1960), p. 106.

12. L. Trotsky, *Literatura i revolyutsiya* (Moscow, 1924), p. 73.

13. Mayakovskii, *Polnoye sobraniye sochinenii*, I, 26.

14. Ibid., XIII, 204.

15. Katanyan, *Mayakovskii*, p. 365.

16. See R. Jakobson, "O pokolenii, rastrativshem svoikh poetov," *Smert Vladimira Mayakovskogo* (Berlin, 1931); and his "Unpublished Verses by Vladimir Mayakovsky," *Russkii literaturny arkhiv* (New York, 1956). See also the in-

troduction by Patricia Blake to Mayakovsky's *The Bedbug and Selected Poetry* (New York, 1960); and Edward J. Brown, *Mayakovsky: A Poet in the Revolution* (Princeton, 1973).

17. One of the best recent works on Blok is A. Jakobson, *Konets tragedii* (New York, 1973). An excellent general study is Avril Pyman, *The Life of Alexander Blok*, especially for this period vol. II, *The Release of Harmony* (London, 1980). On Mandelshtam, see Clarence Brown, *Mandelstam* (Cambridge, Eng., 1973); and Steven Broyde, *Osip Mandelshtam and His Age* (Cambridge, Mass., 1975). There is a translated collection of his prose: Jane Gary Harris, ed., *Mandelstam: The Complete Prose and Letters* (Ann Arbor, 1979). For Zabolotsky, see Robin Milner-Gulland, "Zabolotsky and the Reader, Problems of Approach," *Russian Literature Triquarterly*, 8 (1974). A thorough, sensitive, and scholarly study of Tsvetaeva is Simon Karlinsky, *Marina Cvetaeva: Her Life and Art* (Berkeley, 1966).

3. Prophets of a Brave New World

1. For an overall treatment of Zamyatin see Edward J. Brown, *"Brave New World," "1984," and "We"* (Ann Arbor, 1976). An original and stimulating analysis of *We* is Richard Gregg, "Two Adams and Eve in the Crystal Palace: Dostoevsky, the Bible, and *We*," *Slavic Review*, 24, no. 4 (December 1965). Translations from *We* are from Gregory Zilboorg, trans., *We* (New York: Dutton, 1924). All translations have been checked for accuracy.

2. There is an excellent translation into English of Olesha's autobiography: Judson Rosengrant, trans., *Not a Day without a Line* (Ann Arbor, 1978). Probably the best study of Olesha is Nils Ake Nilsson, "Through the Wrong End of the Binoculars," in Edward J. Brown, ed., *Major Soviet Writers* (New York, 1973). Also very important is Elizabeth Klosty Beaujour, *The Invisible Land* (New York, 1970). Translations from *Envy* are from A. R. MacAndrew, trans., *Envy and Other Works* (New York: 1967). Translations have been checked for accuracy.

4. The Intellectuals, I

1. The contribution of Gorky, a writer of an older generation, in preserving literary life during the years of hunger and oppression should not be forgotten. Both Fedin in *Gorky Among Us* (Moscow, 1943), and Zamyatin in his essay on Gorky in the collection *Litsa* (New York, 1955), attest to his influence and authority in their movement.

2. The best short study of the Serapions in English is William Edgerton, "The Serapion Brothers, an Early Soviet Controversy," *American Slavic and East European Review*, 8, no. 1 (1948). A later and more detailed account is Hongor Oulanoff, *The Serapion Brothers* (The Hague, 1966).

3. Yurii Libedinskii, *Sovremenniki* (Moscow, 1958), p. 165.

4. For a treatment of Shklovsky and the Formalists, see Victor Erlich, *Russian Formalism—History, Doctrine*, 2nd ed. (The Hague, 1965).

5. The best work on both Pilnyak and Ivanov is Robert Maguire, "The Pioneers, Pilnyak and Ivanov," originally published in his *Red Virgin Soil* (Princeton, 1968); reprinted in Edward J. Brown, ed., *Major Soviet Writers*.

6. See note 5 above.

7. For a detailed account of these events see Max Hayward, "Pilnyak and Zamyatin," *Survey*, 37 (April-June 1961).

8. Evidence for this comes from the testimony of generally reliable participants in the salon.

5. The Intellectuals, II

1. Quoted in I. Babel, *Detstvo i drugie rasskazy* (Tel Aviv, 1977), p. 362.

2. Babel's work has attracted the attention of some of the most acute critics, both in Russia and elsewhere. Shklovsky's article in *Lef*, no. 5 (1924), "Isaac Babel: A Critical Romance," ironic and impressionistic in style, stresses the anecdotal form of Babel's tales. Lionel Trilling in the introduction to Babel's *Collected Stories* (New York, 1955) has a number of interesting insights; and Renato Poggioli, "Isaac Babel in Retrospect" in his *The Phoenix and the Spider* (Cambridge, Mass., 1957) contains both information and ideas. Marc Slonim, *Portrety sovetskikh pisatelei* (Berlin, 1933) contains stimulating commentary on Babel and others. Very important also are Maurice Friedberg, "Yiddish Folklore Motifs in Isaak Babel's *Konarmia*," in *American Contributions to the Eighth Congress of Slavicists* (Columbus, 1979); and S. Markish, "The Example of Isaac Babel," *Commentary*, 64 (November 1977). For a comprehensive account of Babel's work see Patricia Carden, *The Art of Isaac Babel* (Ithaca, 1972); and James Falen, *Isaac Babel: Russian Master of the Short Story* (Knoxville, Tenn., 1974). Of special interest is Gregory Freidin, "Fat Tuesday in Odessa: Isaac Babel's 'Di Grasso' as Testament and Manifesto," *Russian Review*, 40, no. 2 (April 1981). Quotations from Paustovsky, "Reminiscences of Babel" are from Blake and Hayward, *Dissonant Voices in Soviet Literature* (New York: Pantheon, 1961).

3. Ernest J. Simmons in *Russian Fiction and Soviet Ideology* (New York, 1958) has contributed a detailed and perceptive study of Fedin's work.

6. The Proletarians, I

1. A full account of this and other proletarian movements is to be found in Edward J. Brown, *The Proletarian Episode in Russian Literature* (New York, 1953; reprinted 1971).

7. The Proletarians, II

1. See Edward J. Brown, *The Proletarian Episode in Russian Literature* (New York, 1953; reprinted 1971), p. 78.

2. A fascinating and well-documented account of this process is Maurice Friedberg, "New Editions of Soviet Belles-Lettres: A Study in Politics and Palimpsests," *American Slavic and East European Review*, 13 (1954): 72–88.

3. Some interesting ideas on Sholokhov are to be found in Helen Muchnic, *From Gorky to Pasternak: Six Writers in Soviet Russia* (New York, 1961). A penetrating study of the role of the hero in certain proletarian novels is provided by Rufus Mathewson, *The Positive Hero in Russian Literature*, 2nd ed. (Stanford, 1975). Also important is D. H. Stewart, *Mikhail Sholokhov, a Critical Introduction* (Ann Arbor, 1967). On the controversy over the authorship of *The Silent Don* see R. A. Medvedev, *Problems in the Literary Biography of Mikhail Sholokhov* (Cambridge, Eng., 1977). The charge of plagiarism has been answered effectively by Herman Ermolaev in a review article which appeared in the *Slavic and East European Journal*, 18 (1974).

8. The Critic Voronsky and the Pereval Group

1. V. Ivanov, in *Znamya*, nos. 5 and 6 (1958).

2. The facts concerning Voronsky are contained in the Ivanov article cited in note 1 above, as well as in G. Glinka, *Na perevale, sbornik proizvedenii pisatelei gruppy Pereval* (New York, 1954).

3. Voronsky's views were presented in a series of articles in the magazine *Krasnaya nov*, most of which were later published in book form. The following volumes are most important: *Iskusstvo i zhizn; sbornik statei* (Moscow, 1924); *Na styke, sbornik statei* (Moscow, 1923); *Literaturnye zapiski* (Moscow, 1926); *Literaturnye tipi* (Moscow, 1927); *Iskusstvo videt mir* (Moscow, 1927).

4. Raissa Messer, "Estetika Bergsona i shkola Voronskogo," *Literatura i iskusstvo*, no. 1 (January 1930).

5. Ivan Katayev, *Izbrannoye; povesti i rasskazy, ocherki* (Moscow, 1957).

6. N. L. Brodsky, *Literaturnye manifesty ot simvolistov k oktyabryu* (Moscow, 1929), p. 272.

7. A. K. Voronsky, "Po povodu odnoi vstrechi," *Iskusstvo i shizn*, p. 219.

8. Sborniki, *Pereval*, nos. 1–6 (Moscow, 1922–1928); *Rovesniki*, no. 7 (Moscow, 1930); *Rovesniki*, no. 8 (Moscow, 1932).

9. As quoted in G. Glinka, *Na perevale*, p. 26.

10. *Na literaturnom postu*, no. 9 (May 1930): 103.

11. *Literaturnaya gazeta*, May 19, 1930.

12. A part of this chapter was first published in *Survey*, 37 (July–August, 1961).

9. The Levers of Control under Stalin

1. The period of the First Five-Year Plan is treated in detail in Edward J. Brown, *The Proletarian Episode in Russian Literature* (New York, 1953; reprinted 1971).

2. A. Afinogenov, *Dnevniki i zapisnye knizhki* (Moscow, 1960).

3. Three articles published in 1956 in the collection *Literary Moscow* (II) revealed much about the system of administration in literature: A. Kron, "Zametki pisatelya"; M. Shcheglov, "Realizm sovremennoi dramy"; and L. Chukovskaya, "Rabochii razgovor." Writers who emigrated in the sixties and sev-

enties have written in harrowing detail about the various levels of censorship. The best work on the actual conditions in which literature is produced is Alexander Solzhenitsyn, *The Oak and the Calf* (New York, 1980), which will be discussed later. Another is Anatoly Gladilin, *The Making and Unmaking of a Soviet Writer* (Ann Arbor, 1979).

4. As quoted in Alexander Werth, *Musical Uproar in Moscow* (London, 1949).

11. After Stalin: The First Two Thaws

1. The period under discussion is treated in detail in George Gibian, *The Interval of Freedom* (Minneapolis, 1960). A selection of translated articles and literary works characteristic of the period, introduced by an excellent brief survey, is in Hugh McLean and Walter Vickery, eds., *The Year of Protest: 1956* (New York, 1961). This work points out clearly that there were two distinct periods of "thawing out" after Stalin's death. The excerpt on "the Drozdovs" is quoted from this collection.

12. Into the Underground

1. Andreii Sinyavskii, "Literaturnyi protsess v Rossii," *Kontinent*, no. 1 (1974).

2. Max Hayward, ed., *On Trial: The Soviet State Versus "Abram Tertz" and "Nikolai Arzhak"* (New York, 1966). See Rufus Mathewson, *The Positive Hero in Russian Literature* (Stanford, 1975), for an excellent statement on Sinyavsky; see also Deming Brown, "The Art of Andrei Sinyavsky," *Slavic Review*, no. 4 (1970), for another interesting viewpoint and analysis.

13. Solzhenitsyn and the Epic of the Camps

1. The Nobel lecture is published in John Dunlop, ed., *Alexander Solzhenitsyn: Critical Essays and Documentary Materials* (New York, 1975).

2. In his "On Solzhenitsyn's Symbolism," in Kathryn Feuer, ed., *Solzhenitsyn; a Collection of Critical Essays* (Englewood Cliffs, New Jersey, 1976).

3. See Vladimir Lakshin, *Solzhenitsyn, Tvardovsky, and Novji Mir* (Cambridge, Mass., 1980), for a defense of the editors of *New World.*

4. Roy Medvedev, "Solzhenitsyn and Tvardovsky," in *Political Essays*, European Socialist Thought Series, no. 8 (Nottingham, England, 1976), pp. 110–119.

5. The letter has been translated into Italian and published in *l'Unita*, June 27, 1978.

6. Translations of Shalamov are from John Glad, trans., *Kolyma Tales* (New York: Norton, 1980).

7. Translations of Eugenia Ginzburg are from Ian Boland, trans., *Within the Whirlwind*, introduction by Heinrich Böll (New York: Harcourt Brace Jovanovich, 1981).

14. The Surface Channel, I

1. Andreii Sinyavskii, "Dve literatury ili odna," *Novyi amerikanets*, June 14 and 20, 1981.

2. Donald Fanger, "The Peasant in Literature," in Wayne S. Vucinich, ed., *The Peasant in Nineteenth-Century Russia* (Stanford, 1968).

3. See, for instance, John Dunlop, "Reclaiming the Russian Past," *Times Literary Supplement*, November 19, 1976.

4. See Solzhenitsyn, *The Oak and the Calf*, Harry Willetts, trans. (New York, 1980), p. 521.

5. An interesting treatment of Belov, Rasputin, Shukshin and others is to be found in Geoffrey Hosking, *Beyond Socialist Realism: Soviet Fiction since Ivan Denisovich* (New York, 1980).

6. The essay appeared in *New World*, no. 8 (1966).

15. The Surface Channel, II

1. In her *The Soviet Novel: History as Ritual* (Chicago, 1981).

2. The remarks were made in an interview with the Associated Press and *Le Monde*, republished in *The Oak and the Calf* (New York, 1980), p. 521.

16. Exiles, Early and Late

1. See his "Problemy izucheniya literatury russkoi emigratsii pervoi treti XX veka," *Slavica Hierosolymitana*, 3 (1978).

3. Translated by Edward J. Brown from Joseph Brodsky, *Chast' rechi* (Ann Arbor, 1977).

4. Translated by Edward J. Brown from Natalya Gorbanevskaya, *Poberezh'e* (Ann Arbor, 1973).

Grateful acknowledgment is made to Farrar, Straus & Giroux, publisher of Joseph Brodsky, *A Part of Speech* (1980), for permission to quote from translations published in that volume. The poem "Lullaby of Cape Cod," portions of which appear on pp. 356–357, has been translated from the Russian by Edward J. Brown and published here by the kind permission of Farrar, Straus & Giroux, who hold exclusive English language translation rights for the poem. All applications for permission to quote from or to publish "Lullaby of Cape Cod" should be addressed to Farrar, Straus & Giroux.

Selected Bibliography

Aragon, Louis. *Littératures soviétiques.* Paris: Donoël, 1955.

Blake, Patricia, and Max Hayward, eds. "Dissonant Voices in Soviet Literature," *Partisan Review,* nos. 3–4 (1961).

———— eds. *Halfway to the Moon: New Writing from Russia.* New York: Holt, Rinehart & Winston, 1965.

Brown, Deming. *Soviet Russian Literature since Stalin.* New York: Cambridge University Press, 1978.

Brown, Edward J. *Mayakovsky: A Poet in the Revolution.* Princeton: Princeton University Press, 1973.

———— *The Proletarian Episode in Russian Literature, 1928–1932.* New York: Columbia University Press, 1953. Reprint, New York: Octagon Books, 1971.

———— ed. *Major Soviet Writers: Essays in Criticism.* New York: Oxford University Press, 1973.

Clark, Katerina. *The Soviet Novel: History as Ritual.* Chicago: University of Chicago Press, 1981.

Crowley, Edward L., and Max Hayward, eds. *Soviet Literature in the 1960's.* New York: Praeger, 1964.

Dunham, Vera S. *In Stalin's Time: Middle-Class Values in Soviet Fiction.* Cambridge: Cambridge University Press, 1976.

Dunlop, John B., Richard Haugh, Alexis Klimoff, eds. *Alexander Solzhenitsyn: Critical Essays and Documentary Materials.* New York: Macmillan, 1975.

Eastman, Max. *Artists in Uniform: A Study of Literature and Bureaucratism.* New York: Alfred A. Knopf, 1934.

Eng-Liedmeier, A. *Soviet Literary Characters: An Investigation into the Portrayal of Soviet Men in Russian Prose, 1917–1953.* The Hague: Mouton, 1959.

Erlich, Victor. *Russian Formalism; History—Doctrine,* 2nd ed. The Hague: Mouton, 1965.

Ermolaev, Herman. *Soviet Literary Theories, 1917–1934. The Genesis of Socialist Realism.* Berkeley: University of California Press, 1963.

Etkind, Efim. *Notes of a Non-Conspirator.* London: Oxford University Press, 1978.

Forgues, Pierre. *Ecrivains soviétiques d'aujourd'hui.* Les lettres nouvelles, no. 25. Paris: Juillard, 1962.

Friedberg, Maurice. *A Decade of Euphoria: Western Literature in Post-Stalin Russia, 1954–1964.* Bloomington: Indiana University Press, 1977.

———. *Russian Classics in Soviet Jackets.* New York: Columbia University Press, 1962.

Gerschenkron, A. *Economic Backwardness in Historical Perspective: A Book of Essays.* Cambridge, Mass.: Harvard University Press, 1962.

Gibian, George. *Interval of Freedom: Soviet Literature during the Thaw, 1954–1957.* Minneapolis: University of Minnesota Press, 1960.

Hayward, Max, ed. and trans. *On Trial: The Soviet State Versus "Abram Tertz" and "Nikolai Arzhak."* New York: Harper & Row, 1966.

——— and Leopold Labedz, eds. *Literature and Revolution in Soviet Russia, 1917–1962.* London: Oxford University Press, 1976.

Holthusen, Johannes. *Russische Gegenwartsliteratur,* 2 vols. Bern and Munich: Francka, 1963, 1969. Translated as *Twentieth-Century Russian Literature: A Critical Study.* New York: Ungar, 1972.

Hosking, Geoffrey. *Beyond Socialist Realism: Soviet Fiction since Ivan Denisovich.* New York: Holmes and Meier, 1980.

Ielita-Wilczkowski, Cyril. *Ecrivains soviétiques.* Paris: Revue des Jeunes, 1949.

James, C. Vaughan. *Soviet Socialist Realism: Origins and Theory.* London: Macmillan, 1973.

Karlinsky, Simon, and Alfred Appel, eds. *The Bitter Air of Exile: Russian Writers in the West, 1922–1972.* Berkeley: University of California Press, 1977.

Kasack, Wolfgang. *Lexikon der russischen Literatur ab 1917.* Stuttgart: Kroner Verlag, 1976.

Kaun, Alexander. *Soviet Poets and Poetry.* Berkeley: University of California Press, 1943.

Kratkaya literaturnaya entsiklopediya, 9 vols. Moscow: Sovetskaya entsiklopediya, 1962–1978.

Lo Gatto, Ettore, *Storia della letteratura russa contemporanea.* Milan: Nuova Accademia, 1958.

Lukacz, Gyorgy. *Der russische Realismus in der Weltliteratur.* Berlin: Aufbau-Verlag, 1949.

Maguire, Robert A. *Red Virgin Soil: Soviet Literature in the 1920's.* Princeton: Princeton University Press, 1968.

Maltsev, Yu. *Volnaya russkaya literatura, 1955–1975.* Frankfurt/Main: Possev, 1976.

Mathewson, Rufus W. *The Positive Hero in Russian Literature,* 2nd ed. Stanford: Stanford University Press, 1975.

McLean, Hugh, and W. N. Vickery, eds. and trans. *The Year of Protest: 1956.* New York: Random House, 1961.

Milner-Gulland, Robin, et al., eds. *Russian and Slavic Literature.* Cambridge, Mass.: Slavica Publishers 1978.

Mirsky, D. S. *Contemporary Russian Literature, 1881–1925.* New York: Alfred A. Knopf, 1926.

Muchnic, Helen. *From Gorky to Pasternak.* New York: Random House, 1961.

Oulanoff, Hongor. *The Serapion Brothers: Theory and Practice.* The Hague: Mouton, 1966.

Poggioli, Renato. *The Phoenix and the Spider.* Cambridge, Mass.: Harvard University Press, 1957.

———— *The Poets of Russia, 1890–1930.* Cambridge, Mass.: Harvard University Press, 1960.

Pozner, Vladimir. *Panorama de la littérature russe contemporaine.* Paris: Kra, 1929.

Ruhle, Jurgen. *Literatur und Revolution.* Cologne, 1960.

Shneidman, N. N. *Soviet Literature in the 1970's: Artistic Diversity and Ideological Conformity.* Toronto: University of Toronto Press, 1979.

Simmons, Ernest J. *Russian Fiction and Soviet Ideology: Introduction to Fedin, Leonov, and Sholokhov.* New York: Columbia University Press, 1958.

———— ed. *Continuity and Change in Russian and Soviet Thought.* Cambridge, Mass.: Harvard University Press, 1955.

———— ed. *Through the Glass of Soviet Literature: Views of Russian Society.* New York: Columbia University Press, 1953.

Slonim, Marc. *Soviet Russian Literature: Writers and Problems, 1917–1977.* New York: Oxford University Press, 1977.

Stahlberger, Lawrence L. *The Symbolic System of Mayakovsky.* The Hague: Mouton, 1964.

Struve, Gleb. *Russian Literature under Lenin and Stalin, 1917–1953.* Norman: University of Oklahoma Press, 1971.

Svirskii, Grigorii. *Na lobnom meste: literatura nravstvennogo soprotivleniya (1946–1976).* London: Overseas Publications Interchange, 1979.

Swayze, Harold. *Political Control of Literature in the USSR, 1946–1959.* Cambridge Mass.: Harvard University Press, 1962.

Tertz, Abram [Andrey Sinyavsky]. *On Socialist Realism.* New York: Pantheon, 1960.

Trotsky, Leon. *Literature and Revolution.* New York: Russell & Russell, 1957.

Vickery, Walter N. *The Cult of Optimism.* Bloomington: Indiana University Press, 1963.

Yarmolinsky, Avrahm. *Literature under Communism.* Bloomington: Indiana University Russian and East European Institute, 1960.

Zavalishin, Viacheslav. *Early Soviet Writers.* New York: Praeger, 1958.

Index

Mikhail Sholokhov "the Silent Don"
Remizov
Bely, Chekov, Bunin, Gorky, Gogol
"the Calf and the Oak" Solzhenitsyn
"The First Circle"
Rasputin (1937)
Puskin

Osip Mandelshtamm (poet)
Joseph Brodsky (poet)

'An old man' Trifonov